D1426420

Soldier in the Sand

Soldier in the Sand

A Personal History of the Modern Middle East

Simon Mayall

Pen & Sword
MILITARY

First published in Great Britain in 2020 by
Pen & Sword Military
An imprint of
Pen & Sword Books Ltd
Yorkshire – Philadelphia

ISBN 978 1 52677 773 7

Printed and bound in the UK by TJ International Ltd, Padstow, Cornwall.

Pen & Sword Books Limited incorporates the imprints of Atlas, Archaeology,
Aviation, Discovery, Family History, Fiction, History, Maritime, Military,
Military Classics, Politics, Select, Transport, True Crime, Air World,
Frontline Publishing, Leo Cooper, Remember When, Seaforth Publishing,
The Praetorian Press, Wharncliffe Local History, Wharncliffe Transport,
Wharncliffe True Crime and White Owl.

For a complete list of Pen & Sword titles please contact

PEN & SWORD BOOKS LIMITED
47 Church Street, Barnsley, South Yorkshire, S70 2AS, England
E-mail: enquiries@pen-and-sword.co.uk
Website: www.pen-and-sword.co.uk

Or
PEN AND SWORD BOOKS
1950 Lawrence Rd, Havertown, PA 19083, USA
E-mail: Uspen-and-sword@casematepublishers.com
Website: www.penandswordbooks.com

This book is dedicated to my father,
Paul Vincent Mayall

Contents

Acknowledgements

I find writing a rather solitary occupation, and I am easily distracted. I have therefore been most grateful to those friends who have tempted me away from London, and then locked me in a room, ignoring my pleas for diversion, or those who have entrusted me with their empty houses, where my failure not to use the time wisely would be a double failure. These include Tanya, Ken and Pam, David and Curly, Shannan and Hannah, Art and Mindy, Martin and Julia, Tresham and Tessa.

I would also like to thank Henry Wilson, and Pen & Sword, for having the confidence to publish *Soldier in the Sand*, and George Chamier for his rigorous and elegant editing. While I believe the facts in the book to be correct, the opinions regarding events and personalities are mine alone, as are any mistakes.

Maps

Map 1 – The modern Middle East

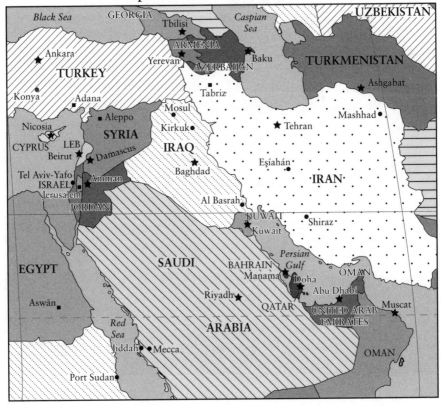

Map 2 – Topography of the Middle East

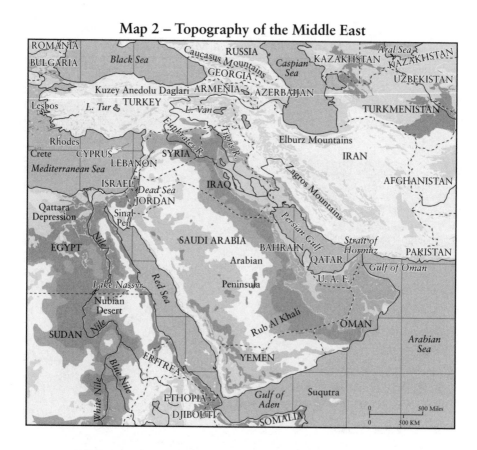

Map 3 – The Sunni/Shia split in the Middle East

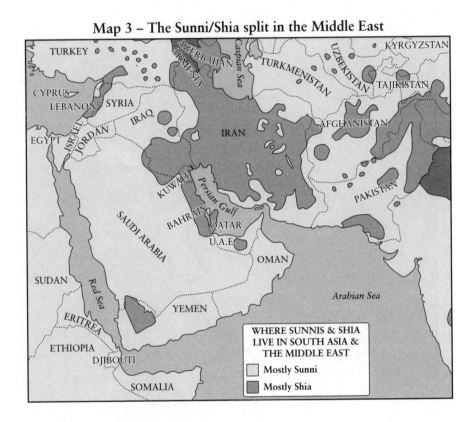

WHERE SUNNIS & SHIA
LIVE IN SOUTH ASIA &
THE MIDDLE EAST

☐ Mostly Sunni

■ Mostly Shia

Map 4 – The expansion of Islam under the Arabs 622–900 AD

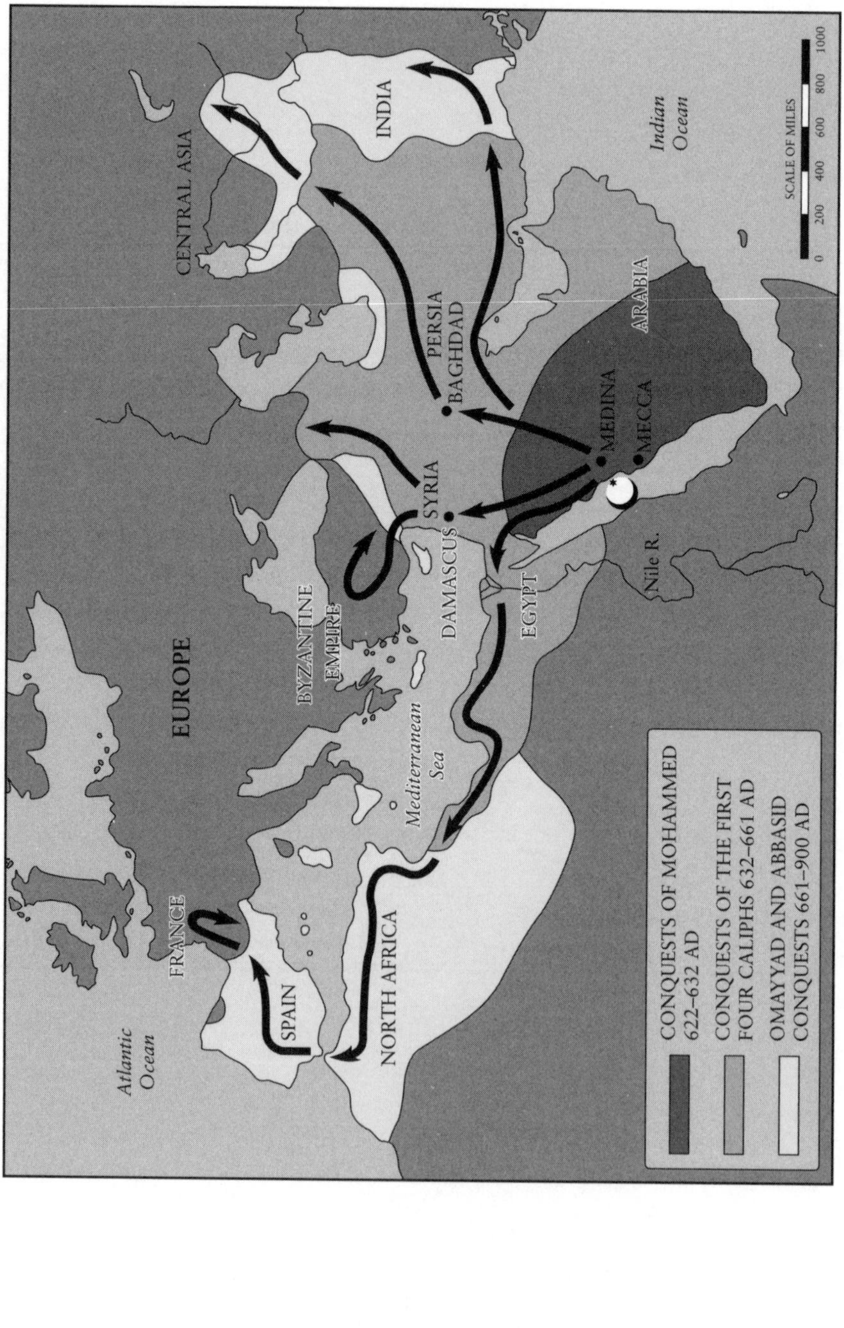

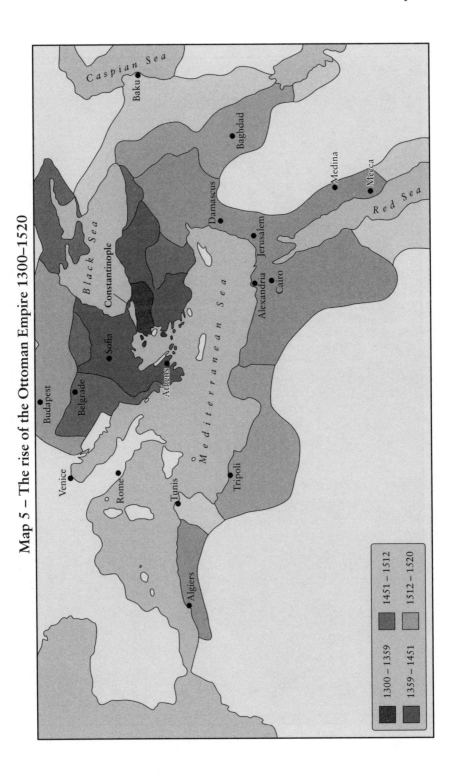

Map 5 – The rise of the Ottoman Empire 1300–1520

Caspian Sea

Baku

Baghdad

Medina

Mecca

Damascus

Red Sea

Black Sea

Jerusalem

Constantinople

Alexandria

Cairo

Mediterranean Sea

Sofia

Athens

Budapest

Belgrade

Venice

Rome

Tunis

Tripoli

Algiers

1451 – 1512

1512 – 1520

1300 – 1359

1359 – 1451

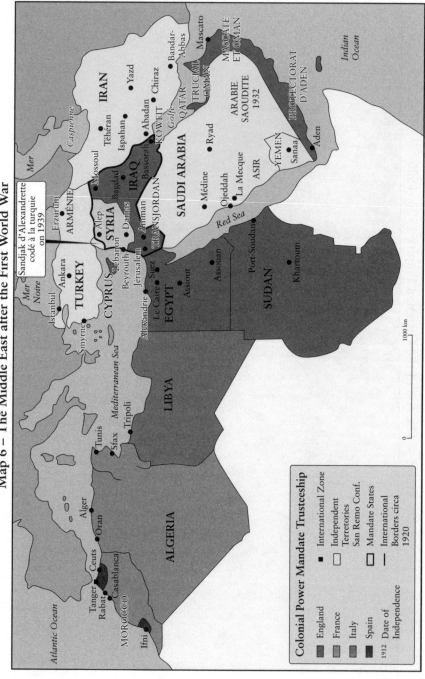

Map 6 – The Middle East after the First World War

Map 7 – Energy in the Gulf

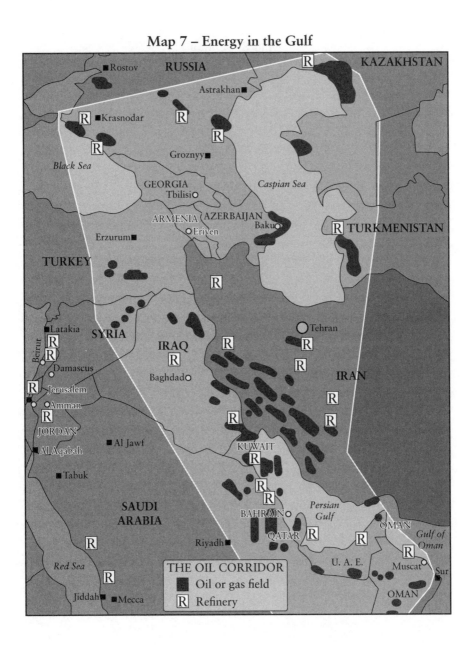

Map 8 – Oman

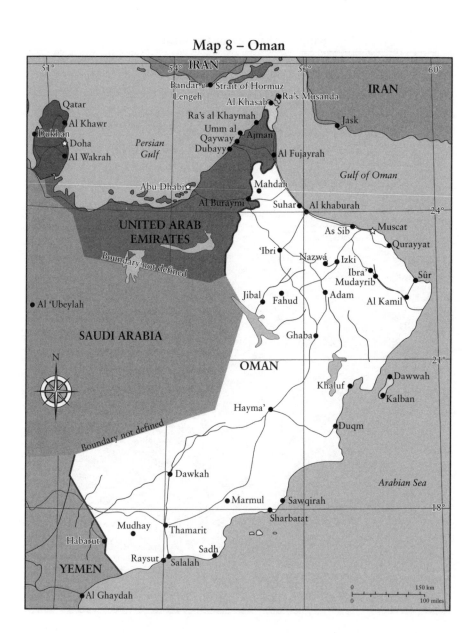

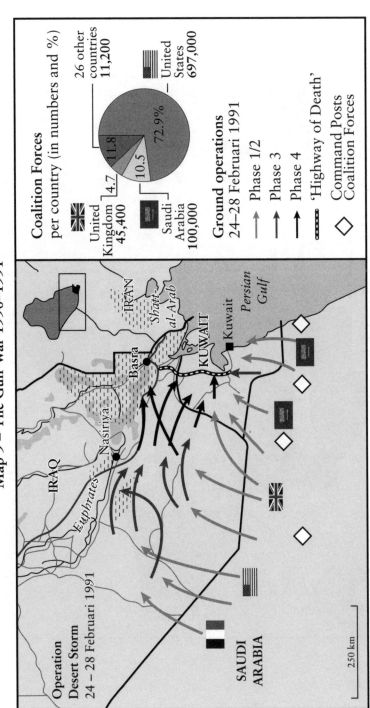

Map 9 – The Gulf War 1990–1991

Operation
Desert Storm
24 – 28 Februari 1991

IRAQ

Nasiriya

Euphrates

Basra

IRAN

Shatt-
al-Arab

KUWAIT

Kuwait

Persian
Gulf

SAUDI
ARABIA

250 km

Coalition Forces
per country (in numbers and %)

26 other
countries
11,200

United
States
697,000

72.9%

11.8

4.7

10.5

United
Kingdom
45,400

Saudi
Arabia
100,000

Ground operations
24–28 Februari 1991

Phase 1/2

Phase 3

Phase 4

'Highway of Death'

Command Posts
Coalition Forces

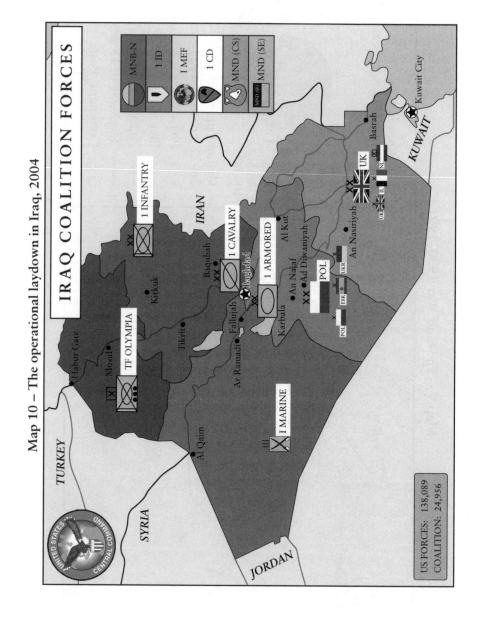

Map 10 – The operational laydown in Iraq, 2004

Map 11 – The fight against Islamic State 2015–19.
How the area under IS control has shrunk

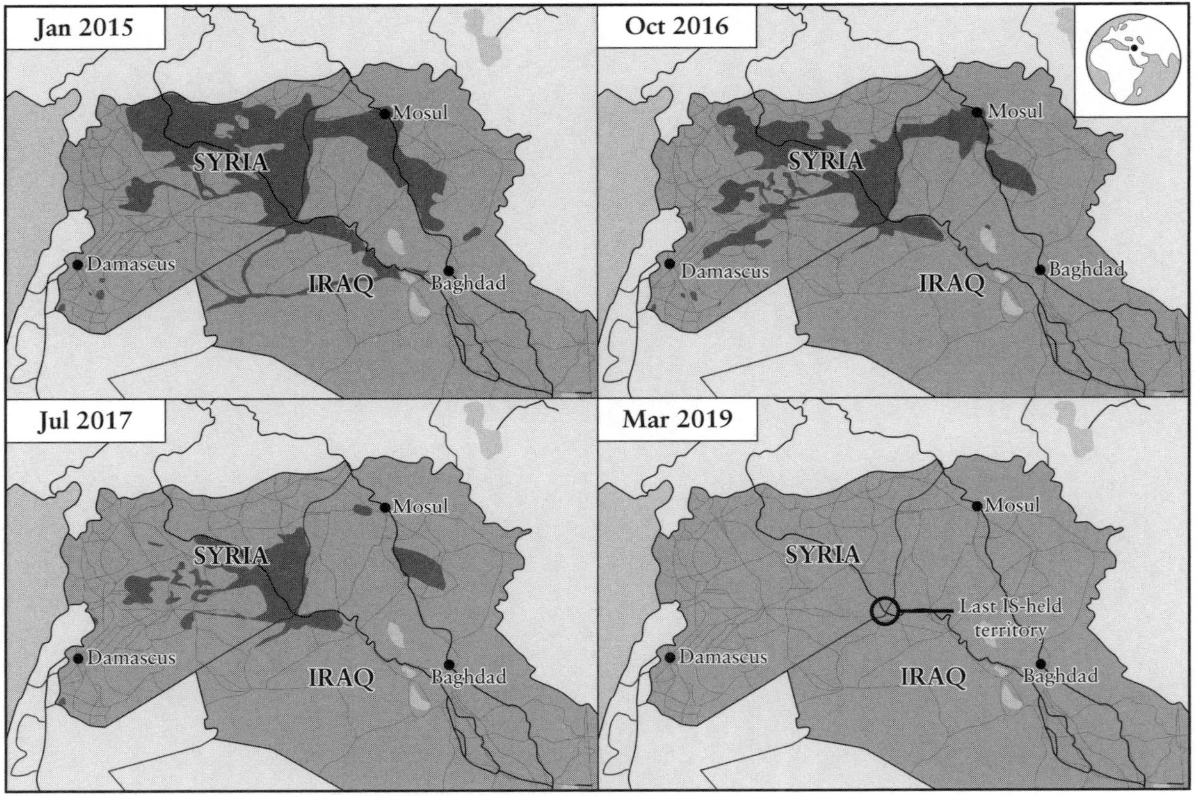

Glossary

Abbasids –The third major Sunni caliphate after Mohammed's death, based on a dynasty descended from Mohammed's uncle. Overthrew the Umayyad caliphate in 750 AD, and largely ruled from Baghdad until the Mongol sack of the city in 1258. Existed as 'shadow caliphs' in Cairo until the overthrow of the Egyptian Mamluk dynasty by the Ottomans in 1517.

Adoo – Enemy. Generic name for insurgents in the Oman Dhofar War.

Ashura – The tenth day of *Muharram*, the first month of the Muslim calendar. The date Hussein bin Ali was killed at the Battle of Karbala (680 AD).

Ayatollah – honorific title for high-ranking Shia clergy, mostly in Iran. Literally, Eye or Reflection of God.

Basij – Persian word for 'movement'. Young, irregular paramilitary forces within the Iranian Revolutionary Guard Corps (IRGC).

Caliph – Chief Muslim civil and religious ruler, regarded as the successor to the Prophet Mohammed.

Dar al Islam – House of Islam, sometimes called *Dar as Salaam*, the House of Peace.

Dar al Harb – House of War. Broadly, the non-Islamic world.

Eid al Adha – The Feast of the Sacrifice. This holy day honours the willingness of Abraham to sacrifice his son as an act of obedience to God.

Eid al Fitr – Festival of Breaking the Fast. This holy day marks the end of the month-long fasting of Ramadan.

Fatwa - An important but non-binding legal opinion on a point of Islamic law, given by a qualified Islamic jurist.

Fiqh – Islamic jurisprudence. Described as the human understanding of divine law, as revealed in the Koran. The basis for Islamic religious consensus.

Firqat – Local militia, loyal to the Sultan of Oman, raised during the Dhofar War.

Hadith – Record of the traditions or sayings of the Prophet Mohammed. They offer guidance on morals and religious law second only to the Koran.

Hajj – The annual Islamic pilgrimage to Mecca. This pilgrimage is one of the five pillars of Islam and is a mandatory religious duty for all Muslims, at least once in a lifetime.

Haram – Forbidden. If something is considered *haram*, according to the Koran, or *fiqh*, it remains prohibited, because harmful, whatever the intention.

Hijra – Departure. This is the migration, or journey, of the Prophet Mohammed and his followers from Mecca to Medina in 622 AD, after the warning of a threat to assassinate him. The *hijra* is the start of the Islamic calendar.

Iftar – Breaking of the fast. The evening meal with which Muslims end their daily Ramadan fast at sundown. Normally a family or community event.

Ikhwan – The Brethren. The first army of the House of the Al Saud tribe. In due course they became the Saudi Arabian National Guard (SANG).

Islam – Submission, or return to God. An Abrahamic, monotheistic religion, teaching that there is only one God (Allah), and that Mohammed is the messenger (*Al Rasool*) of God.

Jaish – generic Arabic word for army. Also in popular usage for armed groups e.g *Jaish al Mahdi* (Army of the Mahdi), a Shia paramilitary group active in Iraq after the invasion and occupation of 2003.

Jihad – Struggle. Mohammed drew a distinction between the Greater Jihad, the spiritual struggle within oneself against sin, and the Lesser Jihad, the struggle or fight against external and internal enemies of Islam.

Kafir – Infidel. The term is applied to anyone who rejects or disbelieves in the God of Islam, or the tenets of Islam. In *takfiri* ideology (see below) it can be applied equally to infidels, heretics or apostates.

Kharajite – 'Those who leave'. An early Islamic breakaway group, who rejected the authority of Caliph Ali when he sought arbitration with his enemy, Muawiyah, rather than trust to God's judgement in battle. Their single-mindedness and refusal to compromise remain a source of inspiration to many Muslims in the modern era.

Koran (or *Quran*) – The Recitation. The central religious text of Islam, believed to be a revelation from God to the final prophet, Mohammed, through the Archangel Gabriel. While the Bible is seen as 'divinely-inspired', the Koran is seen as the 'literal word of God'.

Madrassa – Any type of school, although it can often refer to a specifically Islamic institution that focuses on the teaching of the Koran.

Majlis – A Council, or meeting to discuss a variety of issues. It can also refer to a legislative assembly, and a public or private reception room.

Muslim – A follower of Islam, 'one' who submits. Muslims (Sunni, Shia and other denominations) represent about 90 per cent of the population of the Middle East and North Africa, and around 24 per cent of the global population.

Nakba – Catastrophe. In widespread use across the Middle East and Muslim world to refer to the events of the 1948 Palestine war that led to the uprooting of around 700,000 Palestinians.

Ottomans – A Turkic state and Empire that ruled much of south-east Europe, the Middle East and North Africa between the fourteenth century and the collapse of their Empire at the end of the First World War. Conquered Constantinople in 1453, and defeated the Egyptian Mamluks in 1517. The fourth major Sunni caliphate.

Peshmerga – 'Those who face death'. The military forces of the Kurdish Regional Government (KRG) of Iraq, and also of the autonomous Kurdish regions of Syria.

Qods – The Holy One, the Arabic name for Jerusalem.

Qods Force – A branch of the IRGC specialising in unconventional warfare and military intelligence operations outside Iran. It was commanded by Qassim Suleimani until his killing by a US drone strike in January 2020.

Ramadan – Ninth month of the Islamic calendar, and a commemoration of the Prophet Mohammed's first revelation. The month of Ramadan is marked with fasting from dawn to dusk, prayer, reflection and community. Observance of Ramadan is one of the five pillars of Islam.

Rashideen – 'The Rightly Guided'. A term used in Sunni Islam to refer to the 30-year reign of the first four caliphs, after the death of Mohammed. This includes Ali (the fourth caliph), whose followers broke away after his death, and the death of his sons, Hasan and Hussein, to coalesce around the Shia branch of Islam.

Salafists - Adherents of an Islamic school of thought that advocates a return to the traditions of the first three generations of Muslims (broadly the period of the Prophet Mohammed and the Rashideen), which were regarded as an unadulterated, pure form of Islam.

Salat – Prayer. As one of the five pillars of Islam, Muslims have obligatory, standardized prayers five times a day.

Shahada – Testimony. One of the five pillars of Islam, *Shahada* is the Islamic creed, declaring belief in the 'oneness' of God, and the acceptance of Mohammed as God's messenger.

Sharia – God's immutable divine law, derived from the religious precepts of Islam, particularly the Koran and the *hadith*. The manner of its application is a major source of friction between Muslim fundamentalists and modernizers.

Shia – 'Follower'. A contraction of *Shia'at al Ali*, 'Followers of Ali', who believed that Mohammed had nominated Ali ibn Abu Talib as his successor. A minority mainstream branch of Islam (c.10–15 per cent). The majority sect in Iran, Iraq and Bahrain, with significant minorities in Syria, Lebanon, and Yemen.

Sunni – From the Arabic for 'tradition' or 'habit'. Majority branch of Islam (c.85–90 per cent). Named for those who believed Mohammed's successor as the first Caliph, Abu Bakr, was selected according to the prevailing customs.

Takfiri – Derived from *kafir*, 'an infidel', a *takfiri* is a Muslim who accuses another Muslim of apostasy heresy or deviation from Koranic teaching or *Sharia* law. Used as a term of abuse by Shia against Sunni fundamentalists such as Salafists and Wahhabis, who believe the Shia are heretics. A *takfiri* ideology and mindset underpins many of the more violent Sunni extremist groups like Al Qa'eda and Islamic State.

Ulema – 'The learned ones'. The *ulema* are Muslim scholars who are recognized as having specialized knowledge of Islamic law and theology, and have an important role in guarding, transmitting and interpreting religious knowledge.

Umayyads – The second major Sunni caliphate. Established, with a capital in Damascus, after the Muslim civil wars between Caliph Ali and his sons, and Muawiyah. The dynasty was overthrown in 750 AD by a rebellion led by the Abassids

Umma – Community. Commonly used to mean the collective community of Islamic people, a Commonwealth of Believers, subject to sharia and the five pillars of Islam.

Zakat – Alms-giving, from the Arabic for 'that which purifies'. A religious obligation or tax (traditionally around 2.5 per cent of wealth), and one of the five pillars of Islam.

Introduction

Even by the standards of the Middle East, the first year of the new decade got off to an eventful and unsettling start. On the morning of 4 January 2020, General Qassim Suleimani, commander of the Quds (Jerusalem) Force, the international 'arm' of the Iranian Republican Guard Corps (IRGC), was killed in a US drone strike just outside Baghdad's International Airport. Along with him died Abu Mahdi al Muhandis, the commander of the Iraqi Shia Popular Mobilisation Forces. The killings put the Iraqi government, already reeling from months of anti-establishment, and anti-Iranian, protests and demonstrations in a very difficult position regarding the US military presence in their country. The brilliant and sinister Qassim Suleimani, the 'Rommel' of the IRGC, had been in the vanguard of the Islamic Republic's network of Shia militias, proxies, allies and supporters across the region, which had done much to contribute to the violence and chaos of the previous two decades. He had helped to mastermind Shia opposition to the Coalition in Iraq, his forces had helped ensure President Bashir al Assad's continuing hold on power in Syria, and his militias had fought 'alongside' the Americans in the destruction of Islamic State (IS) and its 'caliphate'. It had been an impressive record of operational service, and the huge outpouring of grief at his death, evidenced in Tehran, Baghdad, and other Shia centres across the Middle East, gave some indication of the esteem he had been held in by his followers. It was also why Iran felt compelled to respond despite the risks of provoking a wider conflict. In the event they launched a series of missile strikes on US bases but, whether by luck, judgement, or good targeting, inflicted no casualties. Subsequent statements and actions demonstrated just how quickly the political temperature had risen, how volatile and dangerous the whole situation had become, and how devastating the consequences of further escalation might be. Having impressively seized the moral high ground in this latest episode in the forty-year confrontation between the United States and the Ayatollahs of Tehran, Iran then proceeded to abandon it by shooting down a Ukrainian airliner, killing all 176 people on board, many of them Iranians. Demonstrations of national solidarity in the wake of Suleimani's death rapidly turned to protests against the political and economic ineptitude of the Iranian government.

On 10 January the passing of the highly-respected, but ailing Sultan Qaboos bin Said al Said of Oman was announced, marking the end of a fifty-year reign significant for its measured development and impressive political judgement. On 28 January President Trump unveiled his long-awaited Middle East Peace Plan, designed to offer a 'realistic and achievable' solution to the Arab-Israeli conflict that had dogged the politics of the region from the establishment of the State of Israel in 1948. Although it appeared to diverge markedly from the UN-endorsed 'Two-State' solution of the 1993 Oslo Accords, and was rejected by the Palestinians and the Arab League, it was a sign of the times, and the changed 'facts on the ground', that the most vociferous external critic of the Plan was Shia Iran, while the majority of Sunni Arab governments and regimes were considerably more guarded. However, this alignment of Israel and the Sunni Arab world in order to confront Shia Iran was soon threatened by Israeli ambitions regarding the status of Jerusalem and proposals unilaterally to 'annex' large areas of the West Bank.

The last months of the previous decade had been similarly 'action-packed'. In late October 2019, President Trump announced that US Special Forces had killed Abu Bakr al Baghdadi, the self-styled Caliph Ibrahim of Islamic State, in a complex, daring and dangerous raid into Northern Syria. The success of the operation had required the cooperation of Iraq, Turkey and Russia but, in a sign of the fractured nature of American politics, President Trump had not sought to inform his Democrat rivals. This was five and a half years after Abu Bakr had declared the advent of the new caliphate from the *minbar* of the Grand Mosque in Mosul, and only several days after Trump had announced the withdrawal of US troops from Northern Syria and, with it, the 'desertion' of their Kurdish Coalition allies. The combination of these events proved the continuing military prowess of the US military, but it also marked a further dilution of the American reputation and credibility as a reliable and consistent partner in the region. Meanwhile in Syria the tragic and brutal nine-year insurgency and civil war entered its 'end game' in the frozen hills and fields of Idlib province, although even this may be simply the introduction to a further round of regional conflict.

Some months earlier, British Royal Marines had boarded an Iranian tanker off Gibraltar, assumed to be shipping oil to Syria in breach of

European sanctions against the regime of President Bashar al Assad. The action also served to support the American policy of 'maximum pressure' on the government of the Islamic Republic of Iran. This had been growing since President Trump, in May 2018, had withdrawn America from the Joint Comprehensive Plan of Action (JCPOA), a multilateral agreement concluded in 2015 to put a verifiable halt to Iran's potential ability to develop nuclear weapons. In retaliation, the IRGC, 'shock troops' of the Iranian regime, had seized the British-registered tanker *Stena Impero* in the Straits of Hormuz, that 22-mile-wide stretch of water between the Arabian peninsula and Iran through which pass, every day, around twenty tankers carrying 21 million barrels of oil, approximately 20 per cent of global oil consumption. The US had already deployed a carrier 'battle group' and B52 bombers to the region as part of its increasingly hardening stand-off with Iran, and the US and UK now again began providing military maritime escorts to commercial vessels, tactics not seen in the Gulf since the 'Tanker Wars' of the 1980s. Along with swingeing economic sanctions, much of the US strategy for confronting Iran had rested on building up a regional alliance of those states that shared a desire to curtail Iranian activities, beyond just their nuclear ambitions. The Kingdom of Saudi Arabia, with its ambitious new Crown Prince, Mohammed bin Salman al Saud (MBS), had been seen as a key element of this plan. However, in the nature of Middle Eastern politics, this coalition-building operation had hit a snag.

In a bizarre episode, during a period of encouraging social, economic and cultural reform in Saudi Arabia, in October 2018 a Saudi Arabian journalist, Jamal Khashoggi, had visited his country's consulate in Istanbul to obtain the certificate of divorce that would permit him to marry his Turkish fiancée. He was not seen alive again. Khashoggi had been regarded as a Saudi 'insider', but somewhere along the line he had become a critic of the House of Saud, a tendency that had become more apparent with the rapid elevation to prominence of the young MBS, who he accused of driving the Kingdom to bankruptcy with his grandiose development schemes. In a period when the old ethnic, confessional and ideological rifts of the region had been starkly re-energized by the Coalition intervention in Iraq, the 'Arab Spring' and the ambitions of Shia Iran, Jamal Khashoggi's close association with Turkey, Qatar, the Muslim Brotherhood and the anti-Trump media of the United States put him on a collision course with the Sunni Arab power-brokers of Riyadh. He was lured into the Saudi consulate in Istanbul and despatched, violently, by a team of operatives well-known to be close associates of the Crown Prince. Moral objections aside, and even accepting the claim that this was 'a rogue operation', the incident was a severe blow to the reputation of Saudi Arabia.

The high hopes raised internationally by the Crown Prince and his 'Vision 2030' were already fraying under the combined pressures of: a failing military campaign in Yemen, now the scene of a major humanitarian crisis and complex, tribal internecine warfare; thwarted ambition in Syria; an ill-thought-through confrontation with Qatar; and the public humiliation of many senior Saudi royals, who had been incarcerated in the Riyadh Ritz Carlton Hotel and subjected to a financial 'shakedown'. Saudi Arabia remained an absolutely vital part of the global energy equation and was seen as a key partner in trying to bring the long-running Israeli-Palestinian issue to a conclusion, as well as a strategic ally in facing down Iranian ambitions in the region. At a stroke, a bungled political assassination undermined the capacity of the Kingdom to play this keystone role. As Talleyrand said, when informed that Napoleon Bonaparte had abducted and executed the Duc d'Enghien, a notorious royalist critic, 'This is far worse than a crime; it is a mistake.' On 15 September 2019, a series of drone and cruise missile attacks took place on the Saudi Aramco facilities in the Eastern Provinces. Assumed to have been launched by Iran, probably via her proxies in the region, the incident had already given a very stark indication of the potentially catastrophic consequences for the global economy were the current series of confrontations in the Middle East to tip over into outright conflict.

Pliny the Elder, writing in the first century AD, declared, '*Ex Africa semper aliquid novi*'. The same might be said of the modern Middle East, where hardly a day goes by without some remarkable headline being generated by the longstanding historical and religious antagonisms of the region or by the follies and atrocities of some malignly motivated individual or group. By the time of Khashoggi's death, an unlikely 'grand coalition', all with their own conflicting or competing objectives, had smashed IS pretensions to leadership of the Islamic world through a revived caliphate. However, the destruction of IS's trappings of 'statehood', and in due course the killing of its leader, by no means destroyed or defeated the poisonous extremist ideology that had fuelled its rise. Meanwhile, the government of President Sisi in Egypt, established in the wake of the chaos following the Arab Spring of 2011, continued its campaigns against Islamist terrorism and the Muslim Brotherhood. In Turkey, the increasingly muscular 'neo-Ottoman' ambitions of President Erdogan were seen in the violent confrontations with Kurds and with Assad regime forces in northern Iraq, and in the north-east Syrian province of Idlib, while Turkish intervention in Libya, on behalf of the Islamist-leaning 'official' government in Tripoli, had helped repel the challenge of the Benghazi-based Field Marshal Hafter, and his Saudi, Emirati and Egyptian backers. Russia, having intervened decisively on President Assad's side in Syria, had tentatively embarked on a similar course of action in Libya, utilising 'mercenaries', courtesy of the Wagner Group private security firm, although with less success. In both theatres of conflict the Russians had sought to take advantage of confused, and confusing, American strategic objectives, and messaging. The Trump administration, meanwhile, had further destabilized the dynamics of the Israeli-Palestinian relationship and any hope of achieving the longstanding 'Two-State Solution', by moving the American Embassy to Jerusalem and giving a 'green light' to further Israeli settlement activity in the West Bank. The US were also escalating the confrontation with Iran, which had taken advantage of the turmoil in the region, not least the removal of Saddam Hussein's broadly secular Sunni Arab regime, to extend its 'reach' through Iraq, Syria, Lebanon and Yemen, via its proxies, partners and Shia co-religionists.

As 2020 unfolded none of these issues, tensions or conflicts became any closer to resolution, or any less complex, complicated or violent. However, international attention was significantly distracted by the challenges of Coronavirus, as was the capacity of international institutions to make any useful or helpful interventions. Indeed, the medical and health crisis itself threatened further to exacerbate the already serious political, social, economic and employment situation across the region. This was not how the twenty-first century was supposed to unfold

In 1990, in the wake of the fall of the Berlin Wall, Francis Fukuyama published his seminal work, *The End of History and the Last Man*. In this he posited that, with the apparent triumph of 'liberal democracy', the 'West' had won all the major ideological, political and economic arguments. Tribal, feudal, national, religious, imperial and ideological conflicts had had their day, and a broad set of universal principles now applied globally. The subsequent decade seemed to vindicate Fukuyama's more optimistic predictions, and many observers and policy-makers willingly bought into this narrative and its positive assumptions.

At around about the same time, Samuel Huntington published his equally influential but altogether gloomier thesis, *The Clash of Civilizations and the Re-making of the World Order*. This work had at its heart the possibility of renewed competition, confrontation and even conflict between 'civilizations'; defined as comprising peoples who shared a strong sense of ethnic, religious, cultural and historical affinity, as deep as or arguably deeper than any attachment to the Western model of the 'nation state'. Huntington counselled against failing to heed the warnings of history or believing that the West's predictions for the future were a settled matter. He wrote that 'the West had conquered the world, not by the superiority of its ideas or values, or religion, but rather by its superiority in applying organized violence. Westerners often forget this fact, non-Westerners never do.' He identified a trend that would become much more pronounced as the world advanced into the twenty-first century: that there would be a growing series of direct challenges to the post-Cold War 'settlement' and the 'rules-based liberal world order' by 'civilizations' other than the 'West'. These would have their own pronounced senses of 'historical entitlement' and would increasingly possess the means to pursue them. Such a sense of 'entitlement' would often be based on very selective, but nevertheless strongly felt, historical grievance and inspiration.

Huntington identified an 'Orthodox Christian civilization' based on Russia, with allies in the Balkans and the Eastern Mediterranean, and a 'Sino civilization' largely grouped around the Han Chinese people. Shorn of their Marxist-Leninist and Maoist ideologies, both Russia and China would again become traditional power-players, with no real pretensions to 'universalism', although both with regional, indeed wider, ambitions. Controversially, but with justification given the evidence, he also drew attention to the pretensions and presumptions of an 'Islamic civilization'. Acknowledging the claims of many of its followers that Islam is a 'religion of peace', he noted, however, the violent modern reality of the interfaces between the Muslim world and those of Christianity, Hinduism, Buddhism and Judaism, as well as the ethnic and confessional divisions within the Islamic world, and he commented starkly that 'Islam has bloody borders . . . and bloody innards.' In the early decades of the twenty-first century it would become increasingly difficult not to agree with important elements of his proposition, however gloomy they were. Huntington would just as confidently apply the same commentary to Western Europe in its trajectory from 'Christendom', through the era of the religious wars of the Reformation, to the World Wars and the horrors of Nazism and Stalinism.

The 'Middle East' is an 'elastic' concept. Indeed, many US policy-makers refer to the region as 'West Asia' (see Map 1). Its traditional geographical definition encompasses the transcontinental region centred on Mesopotamia and the Levant and flanked by Egypt, Turkey, Iran and the Arab Gulf States. It is the birthplace of civilizations, empires and religions, and a passageway for marching armies and migrating peoples. Its geography has determined its history, its history most certainly drives its politics, and its demography, in both variety and size, will have a decided impact on its destiny. There are mountain ranges, river valleys and deltas, vast sand seas, cities as ancient as time and conurbations barely a generation old. It contains those 'cradles of civilization', Egypt and Mesopotamia, the font of the three great monotheistic religions of Judaism, Christianity and Islam, the great cities of Jerusalem, Mecca and Medina, Damascus and Baghdad, and eighteen countries, including old, populous and poor republics, like Egypt, and some new, relatively small and strikingly rich monarchies, like Qatar. There are around 400 million people in the Middle East, a figure predicted to rise to 650 million by the middle of this century, sixty languages and some of the most intractable ethnic, tribal and religious conflicts and confrontations in the world. It is an area of huge diversity, striking disparities, breathtaking sights, evocative sounds and smells, and countless anomalies.

The Middle East is also understood as a geo-political entity. But which Middle East are we speaking of? The Middle East of Egypt with its mix of Pharaonic glories, Pashas, popularism and population; the Middle East of Turkey, the Ottomans, Ataturk and Erdogan; the Middle East of the strife-ridden states in Mesopotamia and the Levant, and the epicentre of the Arab-Israeli conflict; the Middle East of Imperial and Islamic Revolutionary Iran; or the Middle East of the Arabian Peninsula, with the Holy Cities, the city-states of the Gulf, and with its significant concentration of global energy reserves? The answer is, of course, all of the above, and each of them feel and exhibit a keen sense of historical ownership and entitlement. The Middle East is also understood to be largely synonymous with a Muslim identity, and the glories and achievements of Islam are everywhere to be seen across the region. However, not only does the area contain confessional splits and schisms, religious minorities and the State of Israel, but many of the most iconic monuments that we associate with the region long pre-date Islam: the Pyramids, Palmyra, Petra, Persepolis, Babylon and Nineveh, the Wailing Wall of Temple Mount, Hagia Sophia and the great Theodosian Walls of Constantinople.

Some generalizations about the Middle East are easy, but not necessarily helpful while other generalizations may be difficult and contentious, but contain important nuggets of truth. The majority of the population is Muslim, but there are large and significant minority communities of other religions. Within Islam itself there is a multitude of schools of thought and of religious traditions, from the *takfiris* of Islamic State to the mystical Sufis and the 'whirling dervishes' of Turkey. Most people speak Arabic, but many who do are not Arabs or Muslims; while Iranians and Turks are Muslim they are most certainly not Arab. The bulk of the Muslim world is Sunni, but the Shia are in the majority in Iran, Iraq and Bahrain, and form important minorities in Syria, Lebanon, Saudi Arabia, Kuwait and Yemen. These confessional bonds, often stronger than the ties of ethnic solidarity, are what have given the Iranians such an advantage in the period of modern Sunni fractiousness. Across the whole region the population is young, and it is growing. On average, 70 per cent are under the age of thirty, and 30 per cent are under the age of fifteen. Almost half the population of Saudi Arabia was born after 9/11. This has huge implications for the political, economic and social development of the region. Religion and tribe are highly important elements of the cultural identity of individuals and communities, and loyalty to the nation can often come a distant third, while the absence or the stunted growth of 'impersonal institutions' within many, relatively new, nations, makes loyalty to the state a very transactional affair.

Despite the broad geographical limits of the term 'Middle East', the unifying power of Islamic history, the Muslim religion and the Arabic language means that, at different times and for different purposes, the idea of a 'wider Middle East' can also include the Maghreb and North Africa to the west, and Afghanistan and Pakistan to the east. It was in Central Asia that the combination of Cold War competition, Islamist extremism and Gulf petro-dollars set the conditions for 9/11 and all that followed. Some of this book will also cover events in the Balkans, where the ebbing of the Ottoman tide left raw and unsettled Christian and Muslim blood-feuds and enmities that persist to this day.

Huntington perceived the challenge from Islam as stemming from its powerful sense of 'universalism' and its claims to be the last and most complete form of guidance and direction from God. Therefore, to its most committed adherents, the Islamic code was applicable to, indeed enforceable on, all Muslims in all Muslim countries, but additionally, from the twentieth century, also increasingly on Muslims in non-Muslim countries. All were deemed to be part of the *umma*, the worldwide community of Islam. In addition, as the recipients of God's 'final word', Muslims, especially Arabs, had a responsibility to convert the rest of the world, although in the glory days of its early expansion Islam did make some allowance for the sincere, if misguided, adherents of Christianity and Judaism, other 'peoples of the book'. Huntington also drew attention to a high degree of 'particularism' in the Middle East, because it was so riven by confessional and ethnic divisions. Arabs, Egyptians, Turks, Persians, Kurds, Jews, Christians, Sunni and Shia Muslims: all embraced their own strong sense of ethnic and/or religious identity, based on the historical experience of triumph and disaster, dominance, subservience and repression, and on multiple competing religious certainties.

When examining historical experience, it is fair to say that 'geography is history'. Where a people live, whether on the coast, in the mountains on fertile river plains, in tropical, desert, temperate or icy climates, determines what they do and can do, and what can be done to them. Some regions of the world are the natural focus for ambition, competition and conquest. Mesopotamia, the 'land between the rivers' of the Tigris and the Euphrates, the 'Fertile Crescent', is one of these. Attractive to successive waves of nomadic predators, who in turn became settled imperial powers themselves, this area is bounded to the north by the Anatolian plateau of modern Turkey, to the east by the Zagros Mountains and the central plateau of Iran, to the south by the deserts of the Arabs and to the west by the Nile and its Delta (see Map 2). It is the 'cockpit' of the Middle East, and Arabs, Turks and Iranians have always looked to this rich region, not simply for its wealth, but for the 'strategic depth' it offers them. That contest for control of Mesopotamia and the Levant continues to be played out today, and the Iranians are winning it.

If 'geography is history', then 'history is politics', in that a people's sense of themselves and of their historical and cultural reference points continues to have modern relevance. The region between the Zagros mountains and the Mediterranean has been dominated, in its time, by the Pharaohs of Egypt, the Achaemenid, Sassanian and Safavid Empires of Persia, the Umayyad and Abbasid caliphates of the Arabs, the Egyptian Mamluks, the Turkish Ottomans and the imperial powers of France and Britain. More recently, Cold War confrontation, energy politics and regional conflicts have drawn the superpowers, America, the Soviet Union and, more recently, Russia, into a see-sawing competition for influence and advantage. The 'Holy Lands' of Palestine and the Levant, including the city of Jerusalem, are sacred to Jews, Christians and Muslims alike. The Arabs retain a marked sense of superiority as the original recipients of God's word given to them by His Prophet Mohammed, their 'custodianship' of the Two Holy Cities', exercised on Islam's behalf by the House of Saud, and through the continuing dominance of the Arabic language across the Islamic world. They also nurse a sense of grievance and humiliation with regard to the Turks, whose Ottoman empire usurped Arab leadership of the Sunni Muslim world in the sixteenth century. However, beyond the ethnic rivalry between Sunni Turks and Arabs, there is a further virulent split within the Arab Sunni world, whose more extreme Islamic fundamentalists espouse the *takfiri* ideology. This rejects the 'nation state' as an illegitimate division of the *umma*, and *takfiris* reserve for themselves the right to define as 'heretical', and therefore subject to reprisals any religious, political or cultural activity that they deem to be 'un-Islamic'.

The Turks themselves also harbour a marked sense of superiority, based on the glories of the Ottoman Empire and a similar sense of grievance that the great days of Ottoman power and hegemony have long vanished. The Egyptians, the most populous Arab-speaking nation in the region, can never quite forget their pre-Islamic greatness under the Pharaohs, while harbouring jealousy of the wealth and status of the monarchs of Saudi Arabia, resulting from oil and their 'custodianship' of the Holy Cities of Mecca and Medina. Sunni Arabs, Turks and Egyptians together hate and fear their Iranian neighbours, the regional threat they have always represented and their championship of the 'heresy' of Shi'ism, adopted in the early sixteenth century by Shah Ismael, the first Safavid ruler. In their turn, the Persians, conscious of a pre-Islamic greatness similar to that of the Egyptians, resent having received the blessings of Islam from the 'backward' Arabs, while they view the Turks as parvenus. Adding to the complexity of all these four-way, great-power considerations is the presence of many other strong and distinct minority ethnic or religious groups: Kurds, Jews, Christians, Druze, Maronites, Zaidis, Yazidis, Turkmens and Alawites, among others. Volatility, violence and vehemence in the region should come as no surprise, but understanding what lies at the heart of it requires a degree of patient study, curiosity and empathy.

Like most Britons, I love my own country, its history and traditions, but I am also drawn to the wilder regions of the world, seduced by their history, their stories, their romanticism and exoticism. The Middle East is one such region. In expressing such sentiments I might be accused by Edward Said and others of 'Orientalism', of 'representing the Middle East in a stereotyped way that is regarded as embodying a colonialist attitude'. That is most certainly not my intention but, like everyone, I am the product of my upbringing, my own culture and history, and of my experience. *Soldier in the Sand* is, at heart, the story of the modern Middle East as seen through the life and experiences of a senior British Army officer, his parents and grandparents. The book is a mixture of history, religion, ideology, culture and personal anecdote, told through three overlapping prisms. The first is that of the politics, history and religion of the region, and the inspirations, triumphs, frustrations and humiliations that still exert a powerful influence on contemporary attitudes and behaviour. The second is that of British policy, engagement and ambition in the Middle East, from the imperial era to the fight against Islamic State and the current efforts to constrain Iranian ambition. The third prism, personal and anecdotal, is that of a professional soldier who, by family background, intellectual choice and professional necessity, found his life, academic interests and career path focussed, from an early stage, on this fascinating, fractured and frustrating area of the world.

My personal and professional engagement with the region has been longstanding and extensive. Apart from Iran, I have visited every country in the 'wider Middle East'. My maternal grandparents and then my parents lived and worked 'East of Suez', and at an early age I was brought up in Aden. Raised on the tales of Sultan Haroun al Rashid and the *One Thousand and One Nights* of Scheherazade, I have smoked *narghile* pipes in the shade of the Umayyad Mosque of Damascus, climbed the steps to the Citadel of Aleppo and signed the visitors' book in the historic Baron Hotel. I have shopped and haggled in the Khan Khalili market of Cairo and the Grand Bazaar of Istanbul. I have seen moonlight on the Nile, the Bosporus and the Tigris, and swum in the Red Sea, the Indian Ocean and the Persian Gulf. I have stood on the battlements of a score of Crusader castles, flown across the great sites of Nineveh and Babylon and wandered alone among the ruins of Palmyra. In uniform, and in civilian clothes, I have sat in the palaces, *majlises*, offices and camps of kings, crown princes, presidents, generals, ambassadors, sheikhs, tribal chiefs and militia leaders. I have commanded British soldiers, Omanis, Iraqis and Kurds. I have protected Muslims from Catholic and Orthodox Christians, Arabs from other Arabs, Sunni Muslims from Shia, Shia Muslims from Sunni, and both Sunnis and Shia from the ideological extremists of their own religion. I have been overwhelmed by the kindness and generosity of so many people; I have laughed and smiled a lot; I have been humbled by the fortitude and strength of those who have suffered loss and bereavement; I have been saddened, sometimes horrified, by the visceral levels of violence I have encountered. I have received a professional and personal reward, or lesson, in every encounter.

One could read books about the Middle East and Islam for a lifetime and still not get to the end of them. The objective of *Soldier in the Sand* is to educate, illuminate and, where appropriate, amuse the reader. I once gave a series of lectures, 'History and the Crisis of ISIS', about the Middle East, on a Cunard liner. I took my listeners all the way back to the birth of the Prophet Mohammed and the foundation of Islam and then brought them forward through 1,500 years of history, religion and culture to the modern day. At the conclusion of the last presentation, a delightful gentleman in the audience came up to me.

'General', he said enthusiastically, 'we have really enjoyed your talks. We are still a bit confused but, thanks to you, now at a very much higher level.'

He stopped, and looked a little flustered. I laughed. I like to think that I knew exactly what he meant.

'This is the Middle East', I said. 'That might be the best you can hope for.'

This is not an academic book, and the opinions expressed are my own, but I trust that the history the book relates has a respectable academic integrity. It most certainly does not claim to be a comprehensive history of this highly complex region, although it does aim to encompass many of the major events and trends in the Middle East over the last century. For the observer of Middle East politics, and for the interested 'lay' reader, I hope that the book will help to explain the origin of many of the contemporary political problems that confront the region, while confirming the longstanding and enduring importance of history, religion and ethnicity. I also hope that the general reader will enjoy the portrayal of one officer's career in the British Army over the last forty years as much as I have enjoyed living it.

Chapter 1

Inspiring Past and Dark Future

N o one studying the modern Middle East can fully understand it
without reference to the heavy hand of history and religion on its
collective and individual shoulders. The jihadi videos on social
media – it can take a strong stomach to watch them – contain constant
references to the Prophet Mohammed, to the caliphate, to jihad, to Jews,
Zionists, Western 'crusaders' and the 'corrupting influence' of the USA.
These are carefully chosen reference points of inspiration and grievance
which all Muslims can recognize. There is also a second set of targets in
the shape of the internal enemies of Islam, of Sunnism and of the Arabs:
the heretic Shia and their Persian backers, the liberals and secularists
who 'pose' as Muslims, the compromisers and those who ignore the literal
interpretation of the Koran, the 'illegitimate' military and monarchical
rulers who suppress the 'true' adherents of Islam, and who help sustain
the shameful division of the *umma*. Islam, and the Muslim world, has been
plagued from the outset by schisms, but a primary rift, from which so much
else has flowed, was the issue of succession to the Prophet Mohammed.
However, as in the other great monotheistic religions, successive generations
have also found much to fall out over in the interpretation of the sayings
and writings of their founders. It is therefore worth setting out, in a little
detail the origins of Islam and the circumstances of the great ideological
splits that have affected the religion and its adherents almost since the
death of Mohammed.

The Prophet was born around 570 AD in the pagan and idolatrous desert
city of Mecca. He was orphaned early and brought up by his uncle, Abu
Talib. Both were from the small Al Hashem clan, known to history and
the present day as the Hashemites, who were, in turn, part of the large
and influential Al Quraishi tribe. This tribe would provide the caliphs, the
successors to Mohammed, and spiritual leadership of the Islamic world for
the next 900 years. Mecca itself lies about 70 kilometres inland from the
Red Sea port of Jeddah. Despite its inland position, it was a major trading
centre, polytheistic and with a diverse population, and had traditionally

been a 'pilgrim' site since the prophet Abraham's time. However, in the sixth century it was a place of little significance. The major geopolitical fact of the world into which Mohammed was born was the centuries-old, titanic confrontation between the Byzantine Roman and Sassanian Persian empires, whose armies, like immense glacial movements, periodically flowed to the east and west of the great Euphrates and Tigris rivers of Mesopotamia. In 313 the Roman Emperor Constantine had declared that Christianity, for three centuries a despised, persecuted and humble religious sect, would now become 'the most favoured recipient of the near-limitless resources of imperial favour'. Constantine had subsequently moved the capital of the Roman Empire to a new site, Constantinople, in recognition of the administrative, economic and manpower demands of incessant war in the east. In 395, the Emperor Theodosius, whose gigantic landward fortifications would protect Constantinople until its final fall in 1453, made Christianity the official state religion of the Empire. By Mohammed's time, although riven by its own theological frictions, *all* the lands surrounding the Mediterranean, including Spain, North Africa and the Holy Land, including Jerusalem, were Christian and had been so for nearly three centuries.

In the Byzantine-Persian struggle both empires had traditionally recruited large numbers of Arabs as auxiliaries and mercenaries, using them in a range of military tasks, not least in dominating and contesting the large desert expanses south of the great rivers. In the middle of the sixth century a plague catalysed by a volcanic eruption in the Pacific and comparable in scale and virulence to the Black Death of the fourteenth century swept across Central Asia, Mesopotamia and the Near East. Populations were wiped out, cities and towns were depopulated, crops failed, security evaporated and trade routes collapsed. Tax returns diminished, and with them the capacity to pay for the upkeep of the armies which sustained the imperial frontiers and fought the imperial wars. In such an environment the bonds of loyalty and duty frayed and broke, not least among the Arab levies who served primarily for money and status. The facade of imperial omnipotence was fractured on both sides of the great rivers of Mesopotamia. The Arab tribes were primed to respond to any new and compelling call on their loyalty and ambition.

Around 610, while the empires were wrestling with these convulsions, the Archangel Gabriel first appeared to Mohammed. From unpromising beginnings, Mohammed had followed a merchant's life, accompanying his uncle to Syria where, according to Islamic tradition, a Christian monk or hermit had predicted his later life as a prophet of God. Mohammed had routinely prayed to a deity, often for weeks at a time, in the Cave of Hira on the Mountain of Light, about two kilometres outside Mecca. Tradition holds that it was during one of these visits that Gabriel first appeared to him, on behalf of the 'true God', and commanded him to recite the verses that would, in time, and over many years, constitute the Koran, 'the recitation'. For several years after this visitation Mohammed struggled with the implications of these first revelations, until he could convince himself that he was both able and worthy to be a messenger for God. The Koran is different from the Christian Bible, since it is believed to be the direct Word of God, merely recited by Mohammed, and therefore divine. It also goes beyond the Biblical remit of merely the moral and ethical, by setting out a set of laws, akin to the Jewish Torah, which govern most aspects of life, including issues of political authority. While Christ instructed his followers to 'render unto Caesar what is Caesar's, and to God what is God's', implying a capacity to adapt in the face of political, social and cultural change, the Koran is deemed not to be liable to subsequent human interpretation. In many ways, the *hadith*, those sayings and actions of the Prophet which jurists feel have sufficient authentic provenance, are closer to the Bible.

Mohammed increasingly attracted enemies in Mecca as the divine revelations led him to preach against the polytheism of the local tribes. In 620, according to tradition, he travelled with the Angel Gabriel, on the winged steed Buraq, to Jerusalem and the site of what would become the 'furthest mosque', the Masjid al Aqsa. From here he was transported to heaven, leaving his footprint on a stone. In 622, fearing for their lives, Mohammed and other Muslims, those who submit to God's word, migrated to seek the protection of Medina, a city that better understood monotheism through its long engagement with Judaism. This was the fabled *hijra*, from which the Islamic calendar is dated. From here Mohammed proclaimed a greater religious community, the *umma*, in which he intended to include all 'peoples of the book', the Torah, the Bible and now the Koran.

However, the concept of the *umma* increasingly applied only to those who adopted Islam, and in time it came to imply the universal community of all in the Islamic faith. In the crucial last decade of his life, 622–632, as Mohammed moved between the cities of Mecca and Medina, the five basic pillars of Islam were established. These were: the *shahada* or 'creed', the most basic foundation of Islam which opens with the statement, 'I testify that there is no God but God, and Mohammed is the messenger of God';

salat, 'daily prayers', normally said five times a day; *zakat*, 'almsgiving', traditionally supposed to equate to 2.5 per cent of a person's wealth; Ramadan, 'fasting' during the ninth month of the Islamic calendar; and *hajj*, the pilgrimage to Mecca, to be undertaken at least once in a Muslim's lifetime.

In this time Mohammed spoke and acted like a religious prophet, but, unlike Jesus Christ, he was much more than that. He was a political leader, an administrator and a military commander. These multiple responsibilities meant that he encompassed within himself both spiritual and temporal leadership, something which was to have long-lasting implications for his successors, the caliphs. Mohammed also drew attention to the Islamic requirement to conduct jihad ('struggle'), although drawing a fine distinction between the 'greater jihad', the inner struggle to lead a good Muslim life, and the 'lesser jihad', the martial defence of the religion against infidels, heretics and apostates.

Thus, although there are many close associations between Christianity and Islam, they mask profound differences. While Islam experienced dramatic early military success and political expansion, Christians had initially suffered over 300 years of being treated as a despised minority sect. Although Christianity did finally establish itself as the official state religion of the Roman Empire, it would experience a mortal challenge from this new religion, Islam, with its pretensions to be the 'last word' of God. Muslims accepted Jesus's importance as a prophet but rejected his status as 'the son of God'. When they seized Jerusalem and completed the construction of the Dome of the Rock mosque in 692 they added Koranic verses to denounce Christian error: 'Praise be God, who begets no son, and has no partner' and 'He is God, one, eternal. He does not beget, He is not begotten, and He has no peer.'

There early developed a deeply divisive issue within Islam over what constituted the legitimate line of succession to the Prophet. Who had the moral and spiritual authority to be the *caliph*, or to give the full title, '*Khalifat Rasul Allah*', the 'righteous successor of the messenger of God'? Islam had taken root in the culture and tradition of seventh century Arabia, and this profoundly affected the Koranic guidance on a whole range of attitudes and strictures regarding diet, dress and relations between the sexes, let alone politics and war. This body of legal instruction was aggregated into *sharia*, those issues subject to the immutable, divine word of God, and *fiqh*, issues of legal consensus determined by Islamic jurists. In terms of succession, the tradition, the *sunna*, from which the designation of the majority Muslim grouping, Sunni, derives, determined that the successor should be chosen from those best qualified to lead. However, given the pre-eminence of Mohammed as the last, and therefore the greatest, of God's Prophets, others felt that the succession should come through a bloodline descendant of Mohammed. Having no surviving sons from his several marriages, Mohammed's closest male relative was his cousin, Ali ibn Abu Talib, a son of his own protective uncle and Mohammed's son-in-law by marriage to his daughter, Fatima.

Ali ibn Abu Talib was clearly a remarkable boy, and man. He was with Mohammed when the Prophet began to receive the divine words that would form the Koran. Ali was the first to accept God's message from God's Prophet and, at twelve, was the first young male to embrace Islam and become a *Muslim*. With Fatima he had four children, including two significant sons, Hassan and Hussein, and until Mohammed's death in 632 Ali was a trusted confidant and lieutenant. By then many assumed that Mohammed had chosen Ali as his successor. However, even while Ali and others were preparing Mohammed's body for burial, another significant group of followers chose Abu Bakr, the father of Mohammed's youngest wife, Aisha, to be the first Caliph. Despite the outrage of his supporters, Ali accepted the judgment, for the sake of Muslim unity, but this issue of succession would have seismic implications for the history of Islam, and for the region. Abu Bakr died only 27 months later, but in his short time as Caliph he launched the new Islamic faith on a spectacular trajectory of expansion and conquest, defeating tribal and religious opponents throughout the Arabian peninsula and then initiating a series of confrontations with the mighty Byzantine and Sassanian Empires.

Abu Bakr died in 634 and was followed as Caliph by his close friend, and political and military adviser, Omar. Omar's own 10-year tenure encompassed one of the most dramatic periods of history, as he consolidated the gains of Mohammed and Abu Bakr in Arabia, continued the aggregation of collected writings into the Koran and established the concept of Islamic scholarly jurisprudence, that became enshrined in *sharia*. Sweeping up those Arab tribes across Mesopotamia who had previously served as imperial auxiliaries, Omar completed the destruction of the Persian Empire, while dealing a body-blow to the Byzantines at the decisive Battle of Yarmouk, and conquering the Holy Land and Syria. By the time of his assassination in 644, the caliphate stretched from the eastern border of modern Libya, through most of the Near East, across Mesopotamia and Persia and on into the Caucasus.

To Ali's dismay, the mantle of Caliph now fell on the shoulders of Uthman bin Affan of the important Umayyad clan, once again from the dominant

Al Quraishi tribe of Mecca. Under his caliphate, Muslims contested the Byzantine dominance of the Eastern Mediterranean, while others pushed west along the North African coast and crossed into Spain via Gibraltar (*Jebel Tariq*). However, in 656, amid accusations of nepotism and corruption, Uthman was besieged in his house in Mecca and assassinated.

This was Ali's moment, and he became the fourth Caliph at the age of fifty-six. He moved his capital to Kufa in Iraq, now joined with the city of Najaf and a major site of pilgrimage in modern Iraq. Despite the Prophet Mohammed's exhortations about Muslim unity, Ali was confronted by members of the Umayyad clan, who militarily contested his right to be Caliph. The Umayyads in Damascus and Ali in Kufa both inherited old tribal animosities and the deep-rooted political and cultural differences between Syria and Iraq which had been formed through centuries of contrasting styles of earlier rule by Romans and Persians.

After a violent but inconclusive clash in 657 at the Battle of Siffan, Ali sought to sustain the unity of the *umma* by offering a 'ceasefire' and a chance for arbitration. The lengthy, inconclusive and unsatisfactory nature of this arbitration weakened Ali's position, even among his own supporters. Under the slogan 'arbitration belongs to God', a vociferous minority broke away who came to be known as the *Kharijites*, 'those who leave', claiming that only God could determine the legitimate Caliph through battle, not man-made negotiation. They demonstrated their opposition to almost everyone in a series of violent attacks on their former allies in Ali's forces, and on those other Muslims they deemed to have compromised with Koranic direction, declaring them to be *Kafir* (heretics and infidels). Inspired by their example, this *takfiri* ideology grew within Islam, nurturing a violent hatred of perceived heresy in all its forms. In the successive cycles of historical renewal and decline in the Muslim world, Al Qa'eda and Islamic State are merely among the most virulent and violent modern manifestations of this tendency to demonize nonconformists. It was around this time of heightened religious and political tension that Ali's supporters chose to designate themselves as *Shia'at al Ali*, the 'followers of Ali', more recognizable today as the Shia (see Map 3). Given the geographical power-centres of the competing factions, Shi'ism became most deeply entrenched in the areas east of the River Tigris, in Eastern Iraq and, crucially, in Persia. There were also strong opponents of the Sunni Umayyads in what are now the coastal areas of Syria and South Lebanon. These developed, in time, into the Alawite branch of Shi'ism, the modern power base of the Syrian Assad family, and more recently they formed the core adherents of Hezbollah, the Lebanese Shia 'Party of God'.

In 661, Ali was attacked in the Grand Mosque of Kufa, by a *Kharajite* wielding a poison-coated sword, and died a few days later. With Ali's death ended the thirty-year period that had contained within it the consolidation of the Prophet's teachings and the springboard for the extraordinary success and early expansion of Islam. Although Ali's son, Hassan, was acclaimed as the fifth Caliph, the Umayyad leader, Muawiyah, gradually eroded his support through bribery and intimidation, until Hassan offered to yield the Islamic leadership to him, on the single condition that Muawiyah would not name a successor during his caliphate, and would allow the *umma* to choose a successor on his death. Hassan died in 669, possibly poisoned by his wife on the instigation of Muawiyah, and his younger brother, Hussein, succeeded him as sixth Caliph. However, in 680 Muawiyah named his son Yazid as a competing Caliph, and so began the Umayyad dynasty with its capital in Damascus, which would last until 750. Hussein, by now living in Medina, refused to give allegiance to Yazid and moved to Mecca. Here letters reached him from Kufa, the Shia 'capital', asking for help. Hussein marched north but near the city of Karbala on the Euphrates he was ambushed by Yazid's soldiers. The story of his final struggle, killing and beheading are the stuff of Shia mythology, and the anniversary of his death is marked every year by Shias with very public displays of grief, on the day of *Ashura*, a key event in the Shia calendar. The murder of Ali, and the subsequent 'martyrdom' of his sons Hassan and Hussein, institutionalized the confessional division within Islam and brought with it lasting confrontation and conflict.

This split between Sunni and Shia would be accompanied by an almost equally virulent conflict within the Sunni world itself, as the struggle for leadership over the centuries moved between rival interpretations, competing families and ethnic groups, compounded by the violent opposition of the *takfiri* ideologues of the *Kharijite*s, who rejected all the imperial pretensions and the trappings of power of successive Sunni caliphs. In classical Islamic thought, with its emphasis on the integrity of the universal *umma*, the existence of competing Muslim states, let alone conflicts between them, should have been a theological impossibility, and should have made the application of the concept of jihad to competition between Muslims equally impossible. However, from the death of Mohammed, Muslims almost immediately entered a period of internecine warfare that not only split Islam between Sunni and Shia, but would provide a body of precedent and theological interpretation to justify war against a range of enemies. In this Islam was akin to Christianity. The enemies of Islam were not just the obvious Christian 'infidel' but, increasingly over time, the Muslim 'heretic', those whose beliefs were at variance with Islamic orthodoxy, the 'apostate', who might explicitly renounce Islam, the 'blasphemer', who made impious remarks about Islam and the 'compromiser', who was corrupted by 'false' political models and seduced by alien cultural mores. All could, indeed must, be confronted in a generalized 'defence of Islam'. Until Islam triumphed universally, Muslim theology theoretically divided the world in two: the *dar al-Salam*, the House of Peace, where Muslims ruled but other 'peoples of the book' were permitted to exist; and the *dar al-Harb*, the House of War, the rest of the world. A 'truce' was, however, possible for those Muslims unfortunate enough to live in 'infidel' lands, as long as Islamic worship and custom were protected by law. This fine distinction would be challenged as Muslim communities grew in Western countries from the nineteenth century as the Ottoman Empire, Turkish successor to the earlier Arab leadership of Islam, collapsed and as social media magnified the siren voices of Islamist extremism.

In the cycles of decline and renewal that marked the later Ottoman caliphate, the attempts by the Islamic world to square the circle between adopting the perceived mechanisms of Western success while sustaining Islamic 'integrity' continue to resonate today. 'Reformers' advance the case that sharia has been interpreted too rigidly and Islamists are therefore 'failing God' by allowing the *umma* to be put in a position of inferiority. Islamists argue that Islam has been 'corrupted' and that the *umma* is being punished by God for not strictly applying sharia. While Westerners often fail to grasp the coincidence of religion with every other aspect of life in Islam, political and social, Muslims find it difficult to accept that elements of Western dominance in the last centuries have been bound up with the successful struggle, from a liberal, democratic perspective, to relegate religion to the personal sphere and to embrace individual and collective 'choice'. These failures of understanding have set the stage for uncomprehending confrontations between the West and the Islamic world, and for increasingly bloody conflict within the Islamic world. The latter phenomenon was to be particularly poorly understood in the policy-making of the era following the collapse of the Soviet Union, 9/11, the invasion of Iraq and the 'Arab Spring'.

Islam is much more than a religion. It is, is perceived as, and was propagated as, a complete socio-political system. This has made it an extremely difficult standard to adhere to, given the pressures, temptations and day-to-day compromises required by daily life in both the political and personal spheres. The principal function of any Islamic 'government' was assumed to be to enable the individual Muslim to lead a 'good Muslim life'. In other words, to live a life in accordance with Koranic instruction and teaching. This 'good Muslim life' depended on strict adherence to sharia law and, since this 'law' was based on divine revelation, it was not, theoretically, open or subject to change or human interpretation. However, sharia produced no body of general laws, unlike Christianity, and developed no structure or hierarchy comparable to that of the Christian Church, and therefore, despite the caliphs, no one had the unquestioned power or authority to generate an 'orthodoxy' that believers could coalesce around or that people could be compelled to believe in, or at least subscribe to. Additionally, in the 'real world' in which the rulers of Muslim polities had to operate, in which they had to lay down practical laws in order to exercise their responsibilities, to facilitate day-to-day government, to collect taxes, to raise armies and to wage wars, there were only precepts and admonitions in the Koran. Therefore, in Islam such laws, those things a Christian 'Caesar' could demand, had no independent legitimacy in the eyes of those compelled to obey them. There was then, and is now, for modern Muslim fundamentalists, no de jure authority for rulers, only de facto power. In times of upheaval, man-made laws can be rejected as arbitrary impositions. Hence, in Islam, there has not been scope for the evolutionary development of political or secular institutions, something increasingly recognized in the West as 'legitimate reform'. While not alone in this phenomenon, when change came in the Islamic world, it almost always took the form of a crisis, as power was challenged from below, in the name of God above.

Chapter 2

Expansion and Decline

Superimposed on the story of the religious foundations of Islam was the stunning political and military success of Islam's initial expansion (see Map 4). Into the vacuum created by the debilitation of the Byzantine and Sassanian Empires swept bands of Arabs from the Hejaz and from Yemen, small in number but inspired by their new religion. They swept up their ethnic brethren from both empires into their army, converting them to Islam and shaking the foundations of both the Byzantine and Persian civilizations. Within a hundred years Arab Muslims had stormed through North Africa and across the Pyrenees into France, while also occupying Syria and the Holy Land and hammering on the doors of the Caucasus and the Hindu Kush. The Umayyad dynasty, those opponents of Ali, oversaw this first dramatic upheaval, and it seemed to be 'divinely inspired', so dramatic was its scale and speed. Despite this, the Umayyads were not without rivals and internal division. Arabs descended from one of Mohammed's younger uncles, Abbas ibn Abd al-Muttalib, attacked the moral character and administration of the Umayyads. From their base in Khorasan in Persia they raised a revolt. In a series of battles, these Abbasids, campaigning under the sign of the Black Standard, defeated the Umayyads and in 750 eliminated the whole family, save one male member. This Black Standard would be raised repeatedly in Sunni Islamic history, notably and most recently by Islamic State, and it flew in sharp contrast to the white flags of Shi'ism. In 762 the capital of the new Sunni Abbasid caliphate was moved from Damascus to the newly established city of Baghdad on the Tigris, close to Persia and the heartlands of Shiism.

The sole remaining heir of the Umayyads, Abd al-Rahman, fled to Spain, where he sustained the Umayyad claims, refusing to recognize the new caliphate, and where his successors extended their realm across much of the peninsula. From here they also proclaimed themselves to be Caliphs, in competition with the Abbasids of Baghdad. In one guise or another, the Muslims would remain in Spain, in times of golden expansion and bickering decay, until their expulsion by King Ferdinand and Queen Isabella in 1492. Spain would remain the only major part of the Sunni Arab world that was lost to the 'infidels', and it thereby retained a unique place in the literature and iconography of Islam, and particularly in the grievances of Islamist extremists and fundamentalists. It was no coincidence that Madrid railway station was bombed in 2004 by Al Qa'eda, in retaliation for Spanish support of the Coalition invasion of Iraq.

Although successful, the Abbasids always struggled to contain the ethnic and tribal divisions within their vast and sprawling caliphate. Their attempts to reward their Persian supporters were deeply resented by many Arabs, and their attempts to assuage local Shia resentments irritated their Sunni core supporters. Under great and powerful caliphs such as Haroun al-Rashid of 'Scheherazade and the Thousand Nights' fame, the Abbasids fought the Byzantines, Persian uprisings and Shia rebellions. At a certain point in the late eighth century, Haroun al-Rashid took his capital to Raqqa on the Euphrates, the future 'capital' of the IS caliphate. However, under 'unworthy' successors the empire began to fragment. In the 920s, the Fatimids, a Shia group in North Africa tracing their roots back to Mohammed's daughter, established a capital, and with it a further rival caliphate, near Cairo. This Shia caliphate would last until the late twelfth century, when it was overthrown by Salah ad-Din Yusuf bin Ayyub, better known to history as Saladin. The Abbasid caliphate waxed and waned across the centuries, but its scientific and cultural achievements encompassed much of what is now seen as the 'Golden Age of Islam', when the Muslim world outstripped the West in science, medicine and astronomy, not to mention hygiene. The later weakness of the Abbasid caliphate forced them, however, to compromise with exterior forces, most notably Seljuk Turkish mercenaries from Central Asia, who progressively relegated the Abbasids to mere titular leadership of the *umma*.

This period of increasing weakness in the eleventh and twelfth centuries coincided with that of the Crusades. Often characterized as a Christian 'offensive' against the Muslim world, crusading was very firmly seen by Christian contemporaries as a 'counter-offensive', given the aggressive nature of Islamic expansion since the seventh century. Despite appeals to the solidarity of the *umma*, the Muslim world was fatally split at this juncture. Cairo, Damascus, Aleppo, Mosul, and Baghdad, the great cities of Islam, were centres of rival powers and competing confessional creeds, and such fissures would consistently thwart a concerted Muslim attempt to counter the crusading presence in the Near East. On 15 July 1099, the

Crusaders' efforts were crowned with success when they took Jerusalem and established a kingdom across the Levant. However, in the late twelfth century, the Abbasids, through the agency of Saladin, a Kurd, united Sunni Islam long enough to overthrow the 'heretical' Fatimids of Cairo. In 1187, Saladin went on to defeat the Crusader army commanded by the hapless King Guy de Lusignan at the battle of the Horns of Hattin, and retook Jerusalem.

The Crusader kingdom would limp on until 1291, when its new capital at Acre fell to the Egyptian Mamluk dynasty. However, this continuing but declining Crusader presence was seen by contemporary Muslims as merely an irritation compared to the mortal threat posed by the devastating invasion of the Mongols. In 1255, Hulagu, a grandson of the Mongol chief Genghis Khan, was sent to destroy the Muslim states of the Middle East, including the Abbasids, the Mamluk Sultanate of Cairo and the Shia sect of the Assassins, named for their use of hashish to inspire suicidal acts of political violence. He was to 'treat kindly those who submitted, and utterly destroy those who did not'. The Assassins read the writing on the wall and handed over their mountain fortress of Alamut after a brief siege, largely disappearing from history. The Abbasids in Baghdad did not. The Caliph, Al Mutasim, confronted the Mongol horde and then tried to negotiate. He was refused. In February 1258 the Mongols swept through Baghdad, and the Tigris was said to have run black with the ink of the countless books thrown into it from the Grand Library of the city. At least 100,000 people were killed, possibly as many as quarter of a million. Baghdad's glorious architectural and cultural heritage was razed to the ground. Believing that spilling the blood of the Caliph would unleash heavenly retribution, the Mongols wrapped Al Mutasim in a large carpet and trampled him to death under the hooves of their horses. Surrounded by massive and macabre pyramids of rotting skulls, Baghdad was left to lie desolate and deserted for several centuries, while the remaining Abbasids departed for Cairo, to be sustained as Caliphs in an increasingly fictitious construct under the slave-warrior dynasty of the Mamluks, eventually to become known as the 'shadow Caliphs'. On the brink of possibly extinguishing Islam, Hulagu was recalled back to Mongolia, and in 1260 the Mamluks defeated a Mongol army at Ain Jalut in a battle of lasting significance for Muslims.

Meanwhile, the usurping Seljuk Turks were taking up and continuing the Islamic struggle with the Byzantines. In the early fourteenth century, under their leader Osman, a Turkish corruption of the Arab name Uthman, a branch of the Seljuks established a small state in Bithynia, in north-east Anatolia. They became known to history as the Ottomans. With a combination of good leadership, the nurturing of the *ghazi* spirit that inspired and rewarded aggressive raiding, and an appeal to the Muslim concept of jihad, their success was instant. They moved their capital to Bursa in 1326 and crossed the Dardanelles in 1346, becoming embroiled in the civil wars that wracked Byzantium at the time. The Ottoman victory in 1389 on the Field of Blackbirds in Kosovo effectively ended Christian Serbian power in the region. Both Sultan Murad and the Serbian leader, Prince Lazar, were killed, and both armies were decimated. The Ottomans recovered, the Serbs did not; neither did the Byzantines. In 1453, Mehmet al Fatih, 'the Conqueror', battered down the walls of Constantinople, hurling down the cross from the top of the dome of Hagia Sophia and bringing the Byzantine Empire to an end.

The Ottoman Empire now entered a phase of rapid expansion that almost rivalled that of the Umayyads (see Map 5). For both Christendom and Islam, this period was momentous. For many centuries Islam and Christianity had confronted each other in three main arenas. In Spain, the *Reconquista*, the Christian re-conquest, was coming to a victorious conclusion. In the Mediterranean, growing Ottoman maritime power was beginning to match that of the Christians, and a profitable partnership had grown with the Muslims corsairs of the Barbary Coast of North Africa. In the East, the Christian battle-lines had retreated inexorably back from the Levant, through the Balkans, to the borders of the Holy Roman Empire. In 1492, the last Muslim ruler of Granada left Spain, and with him went many Jews who would find a more congenial home under the Ottomans. In the same year Christopher Columbus sailed west to try and reach China and India, thereby hoping to outflank the Mongol and Muslim dominance of the 'Silk Routes'. In 1498, Vasco da Gama sailed east into the Indian Ocean, beginning the European rivalry for control of trade routes that, in time, developed into the great clashes of the European and Asian Empires. Money and wealth soon began to flow back into Europe in huge quantities from the New World. It could have been used to fund the confrontation with the 'Great Turk', but much of it was squandered in dynastic clashes between the Habsburgs of Spain and Austria and the Valois of France and, in due course, between the forces of Catholicism and the Protestant Reformation states, including England. Islam was most certainly not alone in its internal power struggles and its divisions along ethnic and religious lines.

In the late fifteenth century, while the Ottoman Turks were taking over the banner of Sunni Muslim expansion from the Abbasid Arabs, there grew to prominence in the politically shattered landscape of Persia a group of 'Turkicized' Iranians, the Safavids. This family claimed a political legitimacy based on their descent from the male heirs of Ali and therefore a championship of Shi'ism. In 1501, Ismail, a local leader of Azeri, Kurdish and Greek descent, captured Tabriz, declared himself Shah and proclaimed Shi'ism as the official religion of his 'empire'. This represented a major political and religious challenge to the Ottomans and the Mamluks of Egypt, who were both ethnically and culturally different from the Persians and who, as Sunnis, viewed Shi'ism as heresy. In due course many Muslims would come to see Protestantism in the Christian world as some equivalent of Shi'ism. The challenge could not go unanswered, and in 1514, Sultan Selim I, known to history as Selim the Grim, invaded Persia, defeating Ismail and taking his capital. The occupation of Tabriz did not last long, but the ensuing Battle of Chaldirin, another historically decisive encounter hardly known in the West, marked the start of 300 years of frequent and harsh warfare between the Turkish and Iranian power-blocs. In the fight for Mosul in 2017, Islamic State fighters would taunt the Iraqi Shia militia as 'Safavis', castigating their 'heresy' and implying their subservience to the Shia Ayatollahs of Tehran. The allusions were not lost on either side, although they may well have passed by most Western observers.

A key aspect of legitimacy for successive caliphates was control of the Holy Cities of Islam, Medina and Mecca. In 1516, freed from threats in the Balkans and Persia, Selim the Grim moved to complete the Ottoman conquest of the Middle East, defeating the Mamluks outside Aleppo and quickly seizing all of Syria. In January 1517 he entered Cairo, taking back to Istanbul with him the cloak and sword of Mohammed and the last of the 'shadow caliphs'. With them went Arab control of the Holy Cities until the twentieth century. It was a defining moment in Islamic history. Despite the fights, the frictions, the fictions and the factions, leadership of the Sunni Islamic world, nominal or otherwise, had been in the hands of one Arab tribe for nearly 900 years. The third and last great monotheistic religion had risen in the deserts of Arabia, where God had given his direction, in Arabic, to an Arab, who had been charged with proselytizing the faith throughout humanity. That era was now over and, however ragged the reality may have been by the end, the sense of loss and betrayal was palpable and long-lasting. The Arabs were now almost wholly subordinate to the Turks, a nomadic people from the east, and, despite Egyptian efforts in the nineteenth century, they would not really re-emerge as independent 'players' in the region for another 400 years.

Under Selim's successor, Suleyman the Magnificent, the Ottoman Empire continued its irresistible expansion. Suleyman took Belgrade in 1521 and destroyed the Hungarians at Mohacs in 1526. He laid siege to Vienna in 1529 and again in 1532, while consolidating his rule across the Balkans. He took Baghdad from the Persians, along with most of Mesopotamia, down to Basra on the Arabian Gulf. In 1543, when the last Abbasid 'shadow-caliph' died, he took the title, ruling as both Sultan of the Ottoman Empire and Caliph of Islam. He established a de facto alliance with France against the Habsburg Empire, and his fleet wintered in Toulon in 1543, with Toulon Cathedral temporarily transformed into a mosque, to the outrage of many Christians. However, his ambitions were blunted in 1565 by the Knights of St John, in Malta, just before his death. Not long after that, in a rare display of Catholic unity, the battle fleet of the Holy League destroyed Ottoman naval power at the Battle of Lepanto in 1571, before Europe once again descended into internecine warfare, with dynastic and confessional conflicts which reached their apogee during the Thirty Years War. That war culminated in the Treaty of Westphalia, seen as a key building-block in the growth of the Western idea of the nation state. This religious blood-letting in Europe was to be succeeded by wars of nations, empires and ideologies as the millennium progressed. However, European wars of religion appeared so distant by the twentieth, let alone the twenty-first century, that it seemed to come as a surprise to many Western policy-makers and commentators that these issues still commanded such strength of feeling in the Middle East. As a result, they repeatedly underestimated the strength and virulence of old ethnic and religious rivalries and the powerful influence of religious extremists, or misinterpreted the motivations of those who opposed invasion, occupation or rule.

The breaking of the last Turkish siege of Vienna in 1683 is often seen as the 'high-water mark' of Ottoman and therefore Islamic expansion, although its retreat was not so readily apparent at the time, and indeed the Ottomans only departed the historical stage some 230 years later. In the eighteenth and nineteenth centuries, European power continued to increase and Ottoman power declined. Military technology and organization developed, and the Ottomans found themselves confronted, on several fronts, by forces that coveted their possessions and sensed their growing weakness. As with the Romans and the Byzantines before them, wars with Persia drained the imperial coffers, while a new and aggressive

Russian Empire challenged the Ottomans in the Balkans, the Caucasus and Central Asia. Napoleon's invasion of Egypt in 1798 opened up all manner of possibility for Western powers in the Middle East, and his defeat there by the British drew Britain firmly into the politics of the Eastern Mediterranean, culminating in a British 'hostile takeover' of Egypt in 1882. Western European powers had routinely sought to thwart Russian expansion by supporting the old Ottoman enemy, notably in the Crimean War of the 1850s, but the price of their support was a debilitating and humiliating Ottoman economic servitude. Internally, the Sultans became increasingly weak figures, trying to sustain their imperial possessions and their putative leadership of the Islamic world, while unable or unwilling to implement the reforms that their Empire needed. In the wake of the French Revolution and the Napoleonic Wars, the siren voices of 'nationality' and 'self-determination' sparked revolts in Greece and unrest in other Balkan countries. In Egypt, always conscious of its great Islamic and pre-Islamic historical legacy, there was increasingly independent thinking, and action.

For a time, the Islamic identity of the Ottomans and the moral authority of their Sultan-Caliph largely held together the Muslim heartlands of Anatolia, North Africa, Mesopotamia and the Arabian Peninsula. However, the 'subject peoples', Jews, Orthodox and Catholic Christians, Armenians, all covered by the Ottoman *milliyet* system of self-regulation in return for taxes, began to chafe. By the early twentieth century, Western imperial powers had come to be dominant in Morocco, Algeria, Libya and Egypt. There was also a strong British presence in the Gulf, and Russian sponsorship was loosening the Turkish hold on the Balkans, and in Central Asia. Several bloody wars in South-East Europe led to a mass migration of Muslims back to the Ottoman heartlands, although large Muslim communities remained in many newly constituted Balkan states. The Turkish Committee for Union and Progress, better known to history as the 'Young Turk' movement, held the real power in the Empire at this point. Wrestling with competing reformist movements at home, militarily challenged on several fronts, feeling betrayed and abandoned by former subjects and allies, and economically bankrupt, the Ottomans opted to join the Germans and the Austro-Hungarians in the First World War. They were supremely ill-prepared for the demands of large-scale industrial warfare. It was a fatal decision for the Ottoman Empire, the Middle East, indeed the whole world.

Early in the war, some western observers saw in the weakness of the Ottomans the opportunity of an easy victory, which might compensate for the losses being endured on the Western Front and help take the pressure off a beleaguered Russia. The Kaiser had persuaded the Ottoman Sultan to declare jihad, in the hope of getting the Muslim subjects of the British Empire to rise in revolt, a scenario captured vividly in John Buchan's *Greenmantle*. Despite British fears, particularly regarding Muslim soldiers of the Indian Army, this call to arms had had only very limited impact. Conversely, the British early on identified a chance to play on historical Arab-Turkish antipathy and to split the Ottoman Empire on ethnic lines, despite both parties being Sunni. Allied focus came to rest on the Dardanelles, an imaginative operational move that might have achieved important strategic goals, but which would fail on the back of poor planning, lack of resources and faltering leadership. It was not long after these setbacks that my grandmother and her sister had arrived as military doctors in Malta.

Meanwhile, a young officer, an Arabist and archaeologist called Thomas Edward Lawrence, had arrived in Cairo, assigned to the Arab Bureau. He arrived at a complex and interesting time. A number of Arab officers in the Ottoman Army were in contact with Sherif Hussein, the Emir of Mecca, and a member of the original Al Hashem clan of Mohammed. These officers foresaw a new Arab renaissance, freed from the shackles of Ottoman control. On their behalf, Sherif Hussein was in contact with the British High Commissioner in Egypt, Henry McMahon, offering to lead an Arab uprising against the Ottomans. In return he wanted a British guarantee of an independent Arab state including the Hejaz deserts of Arabia, Syria and the lands of Mesopotamia. The McMahon-Hussein correspondence took place fitfully over several months, but in October 1915 events reached a climax with Hussein demanding a firm Allied commitment, at the same time as the Gallipoli campaign was struggling. Under pressure, McMahon made a broad-brush commitment, with some reservations, that was agreeable to Hussein. However, unbeknownst to McMahon, an Anglo-French accord, known to history by the names of its co-authors as the Sykes-Picot Agreement, was being negotiated in London. In this, a large proportion of Syria, including modern Lebanon, was to be awarded to France, and a goodly part of modern Iraq to Britain. Unaware of this deal, Lawrence had been sent to the Hejaz as the Arab Revolt was breaking out, where he identified Prince Feisal as the best potential leader. The story of Lawrence of Arabia and the Arab Revolt is well known, and has been well told, repeatedly. While Lawrence has had his detractors, what he recorded in his monumental book, *The Seven Pillars of Wisdom*, largely stands up to scrutiny. His writings on the Arabs themselves would have important contemporary resonance and relevance, and would become required reading for Coalition officers during the gruelling occupation of Iraq nearly a century later. He described compellingly Arab strengths and weaknesses as soldiers, their mercurial nature, their loyalties, their values, their generosity and their ability to bear a grudge and nurse a vendetta. While pursuing his military objectives, Lawrence did what he could to influence and shape British policy in the region, and to mitigate, where possible, the consequences of Britain's increasingly conflicting objectives.

The Arabs took the Ottoman-held town of Aqaba in summer 1917, using Lawrence's plan for a surprise landward assault. This convinced the Allies there might be merit in resourcing and supporting an Arab revolt. While not decisive in itself, Lawrence's strategy of irregular warfare increasingly tied down large numbers of Turks, not least in Medina, and the guarding of the supply railway became a major and demanding task. On 11 December 1917, General Allenby, having largely defeated the Ottoman forces in Palestine, entered Jerusalem on foot, in marked contrast to the mounted entry of the German Kaiser in 1898. Despite pressure from the British and French Ministries of Information, Allenby also avoided any use of the terms 'crusade' and 'crusader', insisting he was engaged in a fight against the Ottomans, not Islam. It was only shortly before this historic event that another one, with consequences to the present day, took place: the signing and announcement of the 'Balfour Declaration'. This was a concordat between the British Government and some Jewish 'leaders' that seemed to fly in the face of provisions in both the McMahon-Hussein correspondence and the Sykes-Picot Agreement of the previous year. While perhaps understandable in the context of the titanic struggle the British were involved in, it contained much ambiguity and lack of forethought in committing the British Government to 'look favourably on the establishment in Palestine of a national home for the Jewish people . . . it being understood that nothing shall be done which may prejudice the civil and religious rights of existing non-Jewish communities in Palestine'. It was a commitment made on behalf of a large number of Jewish people worldwide, but in 1917, despite their historical claims to Jerusalem and the Holy Lands, Jews only constituted about three per cent of the population of Palestine. Championing their new status would prove extraordinarily difficult and divisive, and those who knew the region well, notably Lawrence and Gertrude Bell, were deeply sceptical and prescient in their anticipation of trouble to come. Bell wrote, 'It's like a nightmare in which you foresee all the horrible things which are going to happen and cannot stretch out your hand to prevent them.'

Allenby's onward march was delayed by the continuing demands of the Western Front, while Lawrence, now well aware of the provisions of the Sykes-Picot agreement, urged the Arabs to try and seize the major Syrian cities. In October 1918, after the Allied advance had re-started, the British and Arabs almost simultaneously reached Damascus. Battered, beaten and betrayed, the Ottoman Empire capitulated on 30 October, some eleven days before the guns fell silent in Flanders.

The fallout from the collapse, defeat and dismemberment of the Ottoman Empire, a cataclysmic historical event, lives with us today, as do the consequences of the rise of the modern Republic of Turkey and its influence on surrounding nations. France, Britain, Italy and Greece had been secretly planning the partition of the Ottoman Empire since the Gallipoli campaign of 1915, and the Treaty of Sèvres, signed with the rump Ottoman government on 10 August 1920, was even harsher than the Treaty of Versailles had been on Germany. It effectively pushed the Ottomans back to the areas the Seljuks held in the fourteenth century (see Map 6). The Ottoman army was capped at 50,000, the navy at seven sloops, and no airforce was permitted. Those responsible for the Armenian 'genocide', in which hundreds of thousands of Armenians had died, either through maladministration or by government policy, were to be tried. The latter provision was an accusation that continues to incite violent reaction in Turkey to the present day. France, already embedded in Morocco and Algeria, was to get Syria as a League of Nations Mandate Territory, and parts of the Turkish Mediterranean coast. France also looked to ally with local Christian communities, breaking the historical integrity of Syria by constructing a Christian-dominated country of Great Lebanon on the coastal side of the Syrian highlands extending from Tripoli to Palestine. They also formed a 'statelet' for the Druze and one for the Alawites, the Shia minority in Syria who soon became the chief agents of French occupation. The French were a little ahead of themselves, for Feisal, leader of the Arab Revolt, had been crowned King of Syria after the seizure of Damascus by the Arabs. In July 1920, before Sèvres was even signed, the French advanced on Damascus with an armoured column and, in the Battle of Maysalun, another battle known throughout the Arab world and almost totally unknown in the West, overwhelmed the Syrians, forcing King Feisal to seek the protection of the British. The French General Gourard reportedly went to the tomb of Saladin, in the Umayyad Mosque in Damascus, and kicked it, saying, 'Awake Saladin. We have returned. My presence here consecrates the victory of the Cross over the Crescent.'

Maysalun became synonymous, in the Muslim world, with heroism against overwhelming odds, as well as treachery and betrayal by the West.

The Greeks were given control of Smyrna, modern Izmir, and retook control of Thrace, the last Ottoman Muslim holding in mainland Europe. Italy was confirmed in its possession of the Dodecanese Islands, seized at about the same time Italy had taken the Ottoman provinces of Tripolitania and Cyrenaica, from which they had constructed modern Libya. A Zone of the Straits was planned for the Dardanelles, the Sea of Marmara and the Bosphorus. Russian sensitivities, in a country now wracked by war and revolution, were not considered. Most of the major Ottoman ports were to be declared of 'international interest' and turned into 'Free Zones'. Armenia was recognized as a separate state, and the Kurds, populous across both the Ottoman and Persian Empires but traditionally ever-divided amongst themselves, would get a homeland, although opinion was divided over which areas it would include. The British got an important League of Nations Mandate for Iraq, including the oil-rich regions around Mosul and Kirkuk. They also got one for Palestine, where they would soon feel the heat of trying to mediate between the conflicting claims of the local Muslim majority and their regional co-religionists, and the local Jews, the Jewish diaspora and their Western backers. Britain also held on to her Protectorate status in Egypt and the Sudan and further carved out an odd 'keystone'-shaped state called Trans-Jordan, the consequence of French actions in Syria. Hoping to fulfil the spirit, if not the letter of their agreements with the Arabs during the war, Feisal was now offered the throne of Iraq, while his brother Abdullah became King of Trans-Jordan, an area that was both 'inside' and 'outside' the British Mandate territories of Palestine and Iraq. It looked and was messy, but it proved to be remarkably resilient, largely due to the calibre of its monarchs and to sustained British support. Meanwhile, the Hashemite heartland of the Holy Cities was attacked by a new and aggressive Arab competitor, the House of the Al Saud, with its religiously inspired Wahhabist brethren, the *Ikhwan*.

This set of Allied ambitions did not last long. General Mustapha Kemal Pasha, an Ottoman hero of the Dardanelles, buoyed by the support of Turkish nationalists, set up a Grand National Assembly in Ankara, in the centre of Anatolia, the core Turkish heartland, to oppose the Treaty. In just two years his armies threw the Greeks out of Turkey, retook Istanbul and control of the Straits, overturned almost all the Allied proposals for the division of Anatolia and thwarted the Kurdish drive for a homeland.

In the 1923 Treaty of Lausanne he secured the independence of a territory similar to that of present-day Turkey. Across the whole of the Middle East, the new Republic of Turkey thus became the only Muslim state genuinely independent from foreign direct or indirect control. The Sultan, whose position and title, like that of the Japanese Emperor in 1945, had been preserved by the treaty of Sèvres, was now forced to abdicate. The Sultanate was abolished in November 1922, and Mehmed VI went into exile on board a Royal Navy destroyer. In March 1924, Mustapha Kemal, who in 1934 would became known as Ataturk, 'Father of the Turks', broke the last formal links with the Ottoman Empire by abolishing the caliphate and, with it, any Turkish claims to universalism. No one took up the baton again, despite much discussion, until Abu Bakr al Baghdadi, the Caliph of IS, in 2014.

In short order, the Syrians rose up against French rule in Damascus, the Turks around Mosul attacked the British, while the Arabs took up arms against them in Baghdad. In addition, there was renewed unrest in Egypt, and new tension in Palestine. Oil was by now pulling new players into a region already roiled by conflict. The Middle East, perennially subject to perennial conflict and confrontation between Arabs, Turks and Persians, and to Sunni and Shia factionalism, now experienced the presence of resurgent infidel powers and new political constructs which challenged traditional ideas of identity and loyalty. Any belief in the integrity of the *umma* was shattered, and there was a new sense of humiliation and betrayal.

Chapter 3

Child of Empire – An Imperial Heritage

In 2015, as my 40-year career in the British Army was coming to an end, my family had been engaged with Britain's policies, presence and aspirations to the east of Suez in one capacity or another for almost exactly a century. Both my parents were only children, and the paths that brought a Royal Air Force officer and West End actress together, in an unlikely meeting at a bus-stop in Lower Regent Street in 1950, were in stark contrast. The imperial genes ran most strongly through my mother's family. My maternal grandfather was a Milne, born in Aberdeen in 1891. His own grandfather had been a farm labourer, but through hard work and a good Scottish education, Alexander George Milne became a civil engineer with Sir Bruce White, Wolfe Barry and Partners, a company that specialized in port and maritime engineering. Like so many of his own generation, and of those before and after him, he took his Scottish expertise to a wider world through the agency of the British Empire. Celtic talent, drive and ambition were always magnified on the global stage through the prism of England's power, wealth and population size,

Alec Milne's diligence, intelligence and skill as an engineer were recognized early on. As a result, and to his disappointment, on the outbreak of the Great War, he received a letter declaring that he was in a 'reserved occupation' and not eligible either to volunteer for the armed forces or be conscripted. Instead, he spent the war years at Rosyth, pioneering the development of concrete boats as part of the drive to address a critical national steel shortage. It would be this technology that was used in the 'Mulberry Harbours' of D-Day. In 1924, when the cataclysmic consequences of war were still resounding throughout the world, he took a ship to India. As the SS *Empress of India* turned south into the Bay of Biscay, the 33-year-old Aberdonian passed the shoreline of a Europe utterly transformed from the certainties of his youth. In the bloodbath of 20 million dead and countless wounded and dispossessed, the Russian, Austro-Hungarian and Ottoman Empires had collapsed. Germany still stood, but shorn of its imperial possessions, its Grand Fleet scuppered and lying at the bottom of Scapa Flow, and bent double under the 'War Guilt' clauses of the Versailles Treaty and the crippling reparations imposed by the victors. In Russia the Bolsheviks had won the brutal civil war which followed the toppling and execution of the Tsar. Already the shape of the next conflict was discernible, between the aggressive pretensions of Bolshevism, harnessed to the remarkable capacity for suffering of the Russian people, and the nationalist appeal of Fascism, allied to a visceral sense of grievance and the extraordinary capacity for focused national endeavour of the Germans.

The victors themselves had little enough to cheer about. My grandfather was now part of an Empire that was at its historically widest extent, but victory had come at huge financial and human cost. The imperial edifice was under pressure, and the additional lands and responsibilities that fell to the United Kingdom, including the new Mandate Territories of Palestine, Trans-Jordan and Iraq, may have looked attractive on ever-pinker world maps, but were of little or no benefit to a country trying to recover from the ravages of five years of war. The French had secured the recovery of Alsace and Lorraine, but they, too, had been bled white. With the withdrawal of the United States, no longer 'guarantor of last resort' for the nascent League of Nations, to its continental fastness, an anaemic France and a weary and over-stretched Britain were left as the painfully inadequate torch-bearers of democracy and liberalism.

In due course the SS *Empress of India* docked at that great natural bastion, the Rock of Gibraltar, the original Muslim gateway to Spain. Ceded formally to Britain in 1713, this strategic outpost had long been a source of contention between the British and Spanish governments, but in 1924 the strength of the Royal Navy, and the British commitment to its status as a 'Crown possession', made any Spanish objections irrelevant. The ship then entered the Mediterranean, which in 1924 was fundamentally a 'British lake'. For 1,200 years the northern shore of this 'lake' had been held by Christian powers, while the southern shores were in the hands of successive Islamic caliphates and their allies. In the early twentieth century, the southern shores may have remained Muslim in character, but from the Atlantic to the Suez Canal the countries along them were all controlled by European powers.

From Gibraltar my grandfather sailed to Malta. This island, important to anyone attempting to control the central Mediterranean, had been crucial in the struggle between the Ottomans and the European Christian powers. In 1798 Malta was seized from the Knights of St John, heroes of the 1565 siege, by Napoleon on his way to Egypt and was subsequently taken by

Britain in 1809. In Malta's Grand Harbour were the headquarters, home base and workshops of the British Empire's mighty Mediterranean Fleet. Here, too, was the main military hospital in the Mediterranean, where my grandmother had served as a doctor in 1916.

From Malta my grandfather pulled briefly into Cyprus, another Mediterranean island of great historical significance, taken from the Ottomans by the British as part of the settlement at the Congress of Berlin in 1878. While of great strategic importance to the British Empire, it brought with it complex and periodically violent confrontations between its Turkish and Greek communities. Then there was a stop in Haifa, where the British were already finding their new Mandate for the Holy Land to be a veritable nest of hornets. How could it be otherwise, given the historical and religious significance of this territory for the adherents of three major faiths? At last, after two weeks, the ship entered Port Said and the entrance to the Suez Canal. The Canal was then, and remains, one of the great waterways of the world and a vital element in global maritime commerce. Thirty thousand ships pass through it each year, generating important income for the Egyptians, who have run it since the Suez Crisis of 1956. In 1875, debt had forced the Egyptian king to sell his Canal shares to the British, and in 1882, after the bombardment of Alexandria and victory at the battle of Tel el Kebir, the British had established a 'Protectorate' in Egypt, gaining a dominant position in Egypt and Sudan and, with that, full control of the Canal. It was to prove a vital piece in the British imperial jigsaw, cutting the journey between India and the North Atlantic by over 7,000 kilometres and by several weeks.

From Port Said, my grandfather sailed south to the Bitter Lakes, passing the great garrison of Ismailia, which had helped repel the German-Ottoman attacks of 1915 and now guaranteed the security of Britain's vital waterway. Here the *Empress of India* and the other ships in the convoy would have marked time to allow the northbound convoy to pass. The Canal's traffic was primarily commercial and international, but among the ships would have been transports taking British Crown servants to and from their imperial postings, wives and children joining husbands and fathers, families off to populate the Dominions, and those battalions and regiments of the British Army who were rotating through the imperial military bases. There would also have been the occasional brooding hull of one of His Majesty's Royal Navy warships, charged with defence of the King Emperor's overseas dominions and colonies and with guaranteeing the freedom of the seas. These ships themselves were dependent on unrestricted access to the oil of the Middle East, much of it now lying under British 'protection' in Iraq and the Arabian Gulf. Steaming into the Red Sea itself, my grandfather would have had the desert lands of Egypt on the starboard side, stretching west to the Nile and the wonders of the ancient Pharaonic world. On the port side, in the Arabian deserts, Abdul Aziz al Saud had established himself as Sultan of Nejd, and in the same year that my grandfather sailed, had seized the Holy Cities of Mecca and Medina from the Hashemites in a violent campaign led by the Wahhabist 'brethren'. In 1932 the Kingdom of Saudi Arabia would be founded. Passing the Arabian ports of Yenbo, Jeddah, Mocha, and Hodeidah, famous for their trade in pilgrims, slaves, frankincense and coffee, the *Empress* passed through the Bab al Mandab, the 'Gate of Tears', that narrow stretch of water between Yemen and Somalia, and entered the southern Arabian port of Aden. This would be our own family home some thirty-five years later. Aden was another of the 'pearls' in the 'necklace' of imperial bases that allowed the Royal Navy to sustain its dominance of the global sea routes and Britain to hold onto its vast imperial possessions East of Suez.

Four weeks after departing from Liverpool, my grandfather disembarked at the monumental Gateway of India in Bombay, as Senior Assistant Engineer of the Bombay Port Trust. It was a professional commitment that would hold him in India for twenty-four years, and would probably have lasted longer without the Second World War and the unstoppable momentum for Independence. In 1926, immersed in his supervision of the construction of Bombay's new commercial port, he met Dr Mary Agnes Murphy, newly transferred from the Lady Hardinge Hospital for Women and Children in New Delhi, to the Bombay General Hospital. A single, highly-qualified female medical professional, driving her own Eric Campbell motorcar looked after by the same *syce* who tended to her Arabian mare, she was an extremely unusual individual in Bombay's rigid social hierarchy.

My grandmother would have been a remarkable woman in any age, but the combination of a very forward-looking father, Patrick Murphy, and the circumstances of the early twentieth century conspired to create opportunities that could never have arisen in earlier generations. Murphy consistently told his daughters that they were 'not to wait on their brothers' and that they were to look to 'get on in the world', irrespective of matrimonial prospects. He coached them in biology, Greek, Latin and mathematics, at which my grandmother excelled. Indeed, she would go on to win an all-Ireland prize for mathematics in 1904. Three of the daughters and one of the sons went to medical college to train as doctors. This was ground-breaking by the standards of the time, and my grandmother, the eldest daughter, was the trail-blazer. She went from the Loreto Convent, via Queen's College Cork, to University College Dublin, where she was the only woman in her medical class, as were her sisters, Lil and Evelyn in their turn – they were excluded from the prestigious Trinity College because they were Catholic. Agnes qualified as a doctor in 1912, having also achieved a diploma in Tropical Diseases. From Dublin, my grandmother went to her first practice in Edinburgh, and shortly afterwards to Bradford, as an adviser in the Municipal Public Health Department, an area of specialization all her professional life. She was twenty-eight years old when war broke out.

In 1916, when the 1914 cries of 'It will all be over by Christmas' had long faded, Dr Murphy answered the call for female volunteer medical staff, along with her sister Lil. By that stage of the conflict the butcher's bill had reached such a level that male military doctors could not be turned out in sufficient numbers. Agnes and her sister were among sixty female doctors who took advantage of a new dispensation allowing them into front-line medicine. In the British Army all doctors were officers, and there were no female officers in the Army. However, this was no time for the tidy-mindedness of military bureaucracy. My grandmother and great aunt wore the cap badge of the Royal Army Medical Corps, but no badges of rank, and they sailed to take up medical appointments in Malta, known since the Crimean War as 'the Nurse of the Mediterranean'.

The sisters arrived on a troopship full of medical staff, along with reinforcements and battle casualty replacements for the ongoing campaign in the Eastern Mediterranean, which was now switching from the Dardanelles to Salonika.

Despite the circumstances of her deployment, it is clear that my grandmother's life on Malta was not all work. Despite being largely tone-deaf she had a box at the Valletta Opera House and she rode regularly. Sometime in late 1916 she was thrown from a horse and was badly enough injured to be evacuated to England and spend six months in hospital. Britain was still reverberating from the shock of the casualties on the Somme, where British forces suffered 20,000 killed, and a further 40,000 wounded, on the first day of the offensive alone. It was at about this time that my great aunt Lil was sent to Salonika, where a dismal attempt was being made to try and knock Bulgaria out of the war. The records show that her first two attempts to leave Malta were thwarted by German submarines sinking the Royal Navy escort vessels.

Having recovered from her fall, my grandmother went back to college in 1917 to study pathology, another male-dominated specialization. In early 1918 she volunteered again for front-line service and found herself at Etaples, in Northern France, just before the great German offensive of March 1918. There is little record of my grandmother's work during those days, but it must have been horrendous, with the medical staff receiving a seemingly endless stream of shattered and mutilated bodies.

My grandmother was 'demobbed' in early 1919 and took a pathology appointment in the Curragh, returning to an Ireland that was seething with discontent and revolutionary spirit. In 1916, even as thousands of gallant Irishmen were 'going over the top' and dying on the Somme, Dublin was just recovering from the Easter Rising. Many of the British civil and military leaders who would have to wrestle with the demands of managing new political entities in the Middle East would have been depressingly familiar with the religious and political complexities of Ireland, the competing demands on loyalties, and the propensity for such sectarian tensions to spill over into communal violence.

For my grandmother, and for so many other Irish people trying to find some form of peaceful equilibrium within which to get on with their personal and professional lives, it was a disturbing and troubling time. In 1924, she decided to sail to India to join the Women's Indian Medical Service. Great aunt Lil also went east, in her case to Malaya. There she met and married George Bentinck, a gallant officer with a Mention in Dispatches and a Military Cross from his service with the Royal Scots at the Somme. He was by all accounts a good-looking man, with a dashing reputation among the tin-mining community of Ipoh. Many of the louche and mildly disreputable stories he and Lil imparted over dinner to Somerset Maugham would appear, to their embarrassment, in Maugham's books, most notably *The Casuarina Tree* and *Ah King*.

War and Irish politics had provided a tough education for my mother's family. Sectarianism was something the British encountered all across their Empire. It was a constant source of friction and violence, but it could also be used by Imperial administrators, who often favoured employing minorities in the bureaucracy and security forces in the face of opposition from the local majority population. This was the model in French Syria and British Iraq. Many years later, the experience of the malign influence of sectarianism in Northern Ireland would continue to have a powerful and lasting effect on many senior British officers. We would have been well advised to have remembered its pernicious influence, and to have urged our political masters to heed it, when we were confronted with the myriad ethnic and religious divisions which plagued our interventions in Afghanistan and Iraq and thwarted our ambitions, post-9/11.

Chapter 4

The Jewel in the Crown

The India that both my maternal grandparents went to in 1924 must have seemed indescribably exotic. When they met they were both mature adults, already with successful careers. My grandfather was thirty-five and my grandmother nearly forty. The sub-continent was well on the way to some form of self-government or Dominion status, although it would take the catalyst of the Second World War to accelerate the strident calls for the full independence that India and Pakistan would both achieve in 1947. Both my grandparents were very conscious that a significantly important element of their appointments was to train their Indian subordinates, Hindus, Muslims and Sikhs alike, to assume their professional responsibilities when the British, eventually, began transferring power.

India, that extraordinary edifice which the British Government inherited from the East India Company in 1858, had been a fundamental building block of the British Empire, and a source of huge, if often neglectful, pride to the British. The Indian Civil Service was a highly professional body, and the very best of British civil servants eventually strove to join it. Never much larger than a cohort of 1,300, these mandarins became admiringly known as 'the heaven born' for their sheer intellectual calibre. In defence and foreign policy, India had responsibilities from Siam to Egypt, and in the First World War, Indian Army troops, all volunteers, served in France, in East Africa, at Gallipoli and in the wider Middle East, including Iraq. The Indian Army retained a mix of British and Indian regiments, among which the artillery remained very firmly in British hands. In view of the ethnic and religious diversity of India, and as a way of managing sectarianism, the infantry battalions adopted an imaginative and successful model of having Hindu, Sikh and Muslim companies. The Muslims among them proved largely indifferent or impervious to the Ottoman Sultan's declaration of jihad in 1914. In all, more than a million Indians, of all religious persuasions, served the British Imperial war effort.

My grandparents were married in October 1927 at St John's Cathedral in Bombay, and I have the silver cigarette box given to my grandfather by his colleagues in the Bombay Port Trust. Their wedding night was spent in the Bombay Taj Hotel, the scene of a bloody terrorist attack by the Pakistan Muslim group, Lashkar e-Taiba, in 2008, and they spent their honeymoon on a cruise to Malaya, staying at the Runnymede hotel in Penang, and then with Aunt Lil and George in Ipoh. Not long after their wedding, my grandfather was appointed Chief Engineer of the Cochin Port Trust, in the province of Kerala, and they took the train south, accompanied by my grandmother's Eric Campbell motorcar, her horse and her *syce*. Sadly, the pairing of two intelligent and successful people does not guarantee a harmonious marriage, and my grandparents were temperamentally very ill-matched. Despite this, they settled into the Chief Engineer's house in Cochin, and my grandfather began his work on dredging the harbour and constructing Willingdon Island from the spoil. They entertained regularly, and in turn were entertained themselves, not least by the Sultans of Cochin and Mysore. We have several invitation cards from that period, including one bidding my grandparents to a dinner in honour of Admiral Dönitz, who was briefly to be Führer on the death of Hitler. My mother was conceived in Cochin, but my grandmother, conscious of the dangers of a first confinement at forty-three, even without the challenges of the Indian climate, opted to sail back to England. My mother, Alexis Leonora Milne, was born on 30 June 1929.

Although mother and daughter returned to India, my grandparents' marriage was failing, and in late 1935 my grandmother and mother returned to Britain. My mother's gilded childhood of servants, pith helmets, elephant rides and summers in the Nilgris Hills and at Ootacamund was over. Separated, although they never formally divorced, the onset of war in 1939 ensured that my grandmother hardly saw my grandfather again for the best part of a decade. My grandfather was Chairman of the Cochin Port Trust throughout the war, when Cochin was one of the busiest ports in the world, and only Independence severed his longstanding links with India. In 1946 he was awarded the Companion of the Indian Empire for his contribution to the Imperial war effort and received letters of congratulation, which we still have, from the Viceroy, Lord Wavell, the Commander-in-Chief, Field Marshal Auchinleck, and Mountbatten, the incoming Viceroy. By this date, the worsening political situation in the sub-continent had convinced Clement Attlee's Labour Government of the need to hasten the end of the British Raj in India. Gandhi told Lord Mountbatten that he realized the departure of the British would lead to enormous bloodshed, particularly since the hopes of sustaining a unitary state had been dashed on the twin sectarian rocks of Hindu nationalism and Muslim separatism. The only way bloodshed could be avoided, Gandhi said, was for the British to remain, but this, he made clear, was neither possible nor desirable. My grandfather was invited to stay and work with the new Indian government, but he chose to hand over to his Indian deputy, who he had long been preparing for his new role.

In the meantime, my grandmother and mother had been in Germany in late August 1939, staying at Düren, on the Rhine, with a relative, Rellie Taffs, who had been wounded and taken prisoner in the First World War and had subsequently married his nurse, Ilsa. My mother could recall the sight of German troops moving across the Rhine, in order to secure the frontier with France, just prior to the invasion of Poland. On the evening of 30 August a telegram arrived telling them, 'Uncle Cecil is extremely ill, please return to England without delay.' My great-aunt Evelyn had read the warning signs correctly, and my mother and grandmother reached Dover on the last ferry out of Antwerp. A day or two later, and they would have been interned for the duration of the war.

My grandmother had her own very vivid memories of the carnage of the First World War, and as an Irishwoman she now chose to 'sit this one out', by returning to the Irish Republic and putting my 10-year-old mother into the Loreto Convent in Bray. Eamon de Valera had decreed Gaelic as the national language after the foundation of the Free State of Ireland, so my mother was effectively barred from taking any exams. My grandmother decided, however, that she should instead take elocution lessons. My mother cannot recall what 'speech defect' this was designed to correct, but it soon took her into the rich theatrical world of Dublin and to the Gate Theatre, the brainchild of Hilton Edwards and Micheal Mac Liammoir, where she became, successively, juvenile and adolescent lead actress. In the bitter winter of 1947 she was in *Ill Met by Moonlight*, which transferred from Dublin to London's Vaudeville Theatre but closed after three weeks because the weather was so foul. At roughly the same time, my grandfather said his final farewell to Cochin, and my grandparents chose to try and resurrect their marriage by setting up house together in Wimbledon. It was not a success, and my mother decamped to 'digs' in Porchester Place. With several theatre, film and television credits already to her name, she was understudying Geraldine McEwan in *Who Goes There*, with Nigel Patrick, at the Duke of York's Theatre in St Martin's Lane. On the evening of Saturday, 19 September 1950, she was waiting at the bus-stop in Lower Regent Street for a No 16 to transport her back to her lodgings. Also at the bus-stop was a tall, good-looking man with aquiline features and dark hair. When, after a lengthy wait, the bus failed to appear, he offered to share a taxi. My mother politely declined but she did accept his offer to walk her home from Piccadilly to the Edgware Road. My father asked to see her again, and they agreed to meet for lunch the next day, although she warned him that she might be late due to an audition. She was – by about three hours. My father was still waiting.

My father's family background had none of the glamour or imperial resonances of my mother's. Not for him the almost routine passage to and from India; the dark skins; the searing heat and the monsoon rains; the chatter of foreign tongues; the kaleidoscope of colour and noise that characterized the ports, railway stations and bazaars of the exotic East. That would come. Paul Vincent Mayall was born in Brecon on 18 April 1931, the child of another poorly matched union: that of Vincent Harry Mayall, a watchmaker and proprietor of several jewellery shops, and Irene 'Rennie' Powell. Often lodged with his grandparents, whose residence in Abergavenny is now the Red Dragon Tattoo Parlour, my father was, like my mother, an only child. His was an austere, but not necessarily an unhappy upbringing. At the outbreak of the Second World War he had travelled no further than to France, on a cross-Channel ferry. My paternal grandfather had been too young for the Great War, and now his skill as a watchmaker also put him into a 'reserved occupation'. The family moved to North London, where he was employed designing and manufacturing increasingly sophisticated bomb-sights, at a time when the RAF's bombing campaign was almost the only way to take the fight back to the Germans. After Dunkirk, my father and his parents, like so many British people, crouched around the wireless hearing Churchill confirm that the Battle for France was over and that the Battle of Britain was about to begin. Almost every night, through the summer, autumn and winter of 1940, my father slept under an upturned sofa, listening to the sounds of the Blitz, feeling the percussion of German bombs, watching the glare of fires and hearing the thump-thump-thump of the anti-aircraft guns positioned on the viaduct at the end of his road. Every day, he would run out with his friends to gather shrapnel, and occasionally brass cases, from the duels of the night before. He attended Haberdashers' Aske's School in Cricklewood, coming out during breaks and after class to watch the Royal Air Force and Luftwaffe dog-fight their way across the London skies, chasing each other in mortal combat, their progress, tragedy and triumph marked by white contrails against the azure sky of that summer of high drama. His dream of becoming a Royal Air Force pilot was born.

My father eschewed university, and in 1948 went before the RAF selection board. He impressed them with his intelligence, enthusiasm and commitment, but they decided that his talents and personality would make him a first-class officer in the RAF Regiment. This was akin to a 'private army' for the 'junior service' and was designed to provide ground protection for Britain's global network of airbases. By 1948 the 'Regiment' was 66,000 strong. Reluctantly steered in this direction, my father was posted to the Royal Military Academy Sandhurst for his initial officer training, rather than to RAF Cranwell. Sandhurst and the RAF Regiment had not been 'Plan A' for my father, but he excelled in this environment, and it gave him a 'khaki backbone' and a close affinity to the British Army. After two years of training and education, he graduated as a Pilot Officer in August 1950. He was based in Catterick, awaiting his first posting to the Canal Zone in Egypt, and visiting his parents in Cricklewood, when he had met my mother.

Chapter 5

First Exposure – Suez and Beyond

I have no recollection of having conducted the battalion band of the Gordon Highlanders on the troop ship to Aden in 1959, but I do have the grainy 16mm colour film to prove that I did. There is a rather taller, uniformed figure in the picture who appears to be doing something similar, and it is quite clear from the looks on their faces that the bandsmen are taking his direction more seriously than mine. However, there we were, on the aft deck of the SS *Oxfordshire*, being serenaded by military musicians as yet another group of soldiers, families and dependants were deployed East of Suez to man, defend, or to prepare for withdrawal from, Britain's remaining imperial possessions and 'protectorates'. In the late 1950s these remained extensive. Despite Indian independence, there were still Gibraltar, Malta, Cyprus, Aden, the Gulf Trucial States, Ceylon, Malaya, Singapore, Borneo, Hong Kong and many smaller entities not to mention extensive, residual colonial possessions across Africa. There was still a British military presence in South Korea, as part of the UN Forces monitoring the unsatisfactory armistice with North Korea, and Britain was involved in fighting a series of complex insurgencies by nationalists, communists or a potent mix of both.

We had set sail from Southampton in early January 1959, six weeks after my brother Mark's birth. My father was already in Aden, having deployed some months earlier to join 84 Squadron RAF, flying Blackburn Beverleys. He had managed to hitch a lift back to England for Mark's birth, but now he was waiting for us as the SS *Oxfordshire* docked in Aden, prior to departing for all ports east to Hong Kong. I can only imagine the sense of expectation and anticipation as my parents caught sight of each other across the railings of the promenade deck.

My parents' unlikely first meeting had soon blossomed into an intense and loving relationship. My mother's thespian career continued to thrive, but my father, newly commissioned, was now on his way to the Suez Canal Zone. Britain had been struggling since the end of the war to repay the huge debts incurred in the course of that titanic struggle. Her problems came 'not in single spies, but in legions and battalions'. Churchill's wartime ambitions for the British Empire were being challenged by the anti-imperial sentiments of the United States, the realities of a ravaged Europe, a predatory Soviet Union with a keen sense of entitlement based on the scale of her sacrifice, a global drive by peoples for self-determination and Britain's own economic weakness. The Tory party, and with it Winston Churchill, had been rejected by the electorate in the May 1945 election. Many of those voting Labour were among the hundreds of thousands of servicemen still overseas. Years later, having joined the British Army, I heard the standing joke that the only battle honour of the Royal Army Education Corps was 'General Election 1945'. Since that time, Attlee's Labour government had been trying to deal with the existential issue of Britain's place in the world, while introducing a far-reaching programme of social and economic reform, including the launch of the National Health Service.

Whilst committed to giving independence to India, even a Labour government could not easily give up on the idea of 'Empire', but they had neither the resources nor the will to sustain it with confidence or credibility. Another decision with long-term consequences had been the declaration of intention to relinquish the Mandate for Palestine. The full consequences of a commitment to the establishment of a Jewish 'homeland', without prejudice to the existing population and communities, had only become more and more clear during the decades of friction and internecine fighting that had characterized the fractious Mandate period. The pressures of large-scale Jewish immigration to Palestine during the 1930s, magnified through the prism of Nazi persecution, provoked an Arab and Muslim reaction. After the war, when the Nazi crimes against the Jewish people had been so dramatically exposed, and with increasing American support for the transformation of the Jewish 'homeland' into a 'state', both Jewish immigration pressure and Arab Muslim resistance grew. British civilian and military officials found themselves in an increasingly uncomfortable and politically ambiguous position, as did the soldiers and local police. Increasing Jewish attacks on British facilities and personnel had culminated in the blowing up of the King David Hotel in Jerusalem in 1946 with many casualties. The outrage had convinced Britain of the need to relinquish this increasingly volatile and violent commitment. France had already given up on her unequal struggle in Syria and Lebanon, ending her own mandate in those territories in 1946. At the same time, Britain still needed to sustain a position in the Eastern Mediterranean that guaranteed the security of the Suez Canal and secured her vital links to the East and, with them, the increasingly important flow of oil from the Gulf. She settled on a plan to increase her presence along the Canal itself, in the long-standing garrison cantonment of Ismailia.

In 1948 the British formally relinquished responsibility for Palestine, and President Truman committed American support to the new 'state' of Israel. This move initiated a new and decisive phase in Middle East politics and it provoked an instant attempt by the neighbouring Arab states of Egypt, Syria and Jordan to crush the Israeli state at birth. The attempt failed, and the subsequent dispossessions and expulsions of around 700,000 Arabs from their historic lands, characterized as the *nakba* ('catastrophe'), would have a traumatic and lasting impact. These people would soon become designated as 'Palestinians', and their refugee status, their demands to return to their lands and properties and the adoption of their cause by their fellow Arabs and the wider Muslim world would add further complexity to an already volatile region. So began a fresh and destructive new phase of Middle Eastern politics which would see three more major Arab-Israeli conflicts in the next twenty-five years, and thereafter numerous episodes of violence, assault and counter-attack, terrorism and repression. The Arab defeat of 1948 contributed to an already deep sense of humiliation and grievance. Largely written out of history for 400 years under the Ottomans, their striking efforts in the First World War had restored an element of self-confidence to the original Arab champions of Islam, although the new political entities, under League of Nations 'Mandates', had smacked of a new form of colonialism. Now, Israeli political and military success, seemingly supported by the old imperial powers, confirmed all their old prejudices. It would get worse.

Egypt's role in the Second World War had been both important and ambivalent. The British had established a 'protectorate' over the country in 1882, but a revolt in 1919 led to the British Government issuing a unilateral declaration of Egypt's 'independence' in 1922, and to the Egyptian sultan becoming a king. In due course this led to the 1936 Anglo-Egyptian Accord, which guaranteed a British presence in the country for another twenty years. It was also the year King Farouk ascended the throne. The Accord did not materially alter the reality of British influence and involvement in this proud and ancient country. Indeed, in the 1930s the headquarters of the British Mediterranean Fleet was moved from Malta to Alexandria. This unequal relationship became patently clear when in February 1942 the British requirement to secure Egypt and defend the Suez Canal led to Sir Miles Lampson, the British ambassador, surrounding the King's

Abdeen Palace and threatening him with exile if he did not dismiss his pro-German government. King Farouk capitulated, but neither he nor many other Egyptians would forget this new humiliation. Egypt had been vital in the defeat of the Italians, and then the Germans, in North Africa. It had also been from Egypt that the Allied campaigns against the Vichy French forces in Lebanon and Syria had been launched, the short-lived Iraqi revolt of 1941 suppressed and the forced abdication of the Persian Shah orchestrated. Despite its pivotal role in British operations across the Middle East, Egypt itself only formally declared war on Germany in 1945. This was long after any fighting in the Western Desert had ended, but it did seal for Egypt a place in the new United Nations organization.

The huge military base at Ismailia, to which my father was posted, housed around 80,000 personnel. Today, Ismailia is known in Egypt as 'The City of Beauty and Enchantment', but it was not viewed quite like that by the succession of British soldiers and airmen who spent long months of their time in uniform guarding its lengthy perimeter. It had been a military base since 1882, and it was here that in 1928 Hassan Banna had founded the politically significant Muslim Brotherhood, and where his own anti-colonial attitudes were honed. The Brotherhood would become a highly influential trans-national Sunni Islamist organization, combining political activism with wide-ranging Islamic charity work. The Brotherhood's stated goal was to make the Koran 'the sole reference point for ordering the life of the Muslim family, individual, community and state'. In this, it acknowledged the political reality of the Islamic world after the First World War, in which new nations and states had, at least temporarily in their hopes, replaced a caliphate with pretensions to speak for all Muslims of the *umma*. Hassan Banna, in a theme that would be routinely taken up by Islamists, declared not only that Muslims were politically dominated by the West, but that Islam had lost its social dominance because Muslims had been corrupted by Western influences. Muslim Brotherhood beliefs and activities were marked by a strong degree of social conservatism, particularly with regard to women, and its most frequently used slogan was 'Islam is the solution'. While their language would become more 'inclusive' and accommodating in later years, their record in power would confirm the reality of their ambition. This was in stark contrast to those reformers whose slogan was 'modernization is the solution'. The two schools of thought would remain in confrontation and conflict up to the modern era.

From an early following of around eight hundred, by 1948 the Brotherhood had grown, in Egypt, to a membership of over two million, displaying in its political programme a strong anti-British sentiment. The Brotherhood would always have an ambivalent relationship with the Egyptian state, particularly after the fall of the Egyptian monarchy in 1952. Supported in its early days by Saudi Arabia, the Brotherhood would in time come to be a major opponent of the Gulf monarchies. Hassan Banna himself was assassinated in 1949, and periodically large numbers of the Brotherhood would be imprisoned, while many also fled abroad. Although the Brotherhood was a transnational organization, its strength remained in Egypt, and it would become a major political player during the 'Arab Spring', albeit with strong backing from Turkey and President Erdogan, who subscribed to the same philosophy, and from the Gulf State of Qatar, through the medium of the Al Jazeera television network. Differing attitudes towards the Brotherhood in different Muslim states, throughout the events of the Arab Spring and its aftermath, would further contribute to existing major faultlines in the region.

My father's passage to the Canal Zone had been eventful in itself. The Hastings aircraft in which he was travelling crash-landed in Malta, killing two passengers. Shaken but otherwise unhurt, the remainder flew on two days later. At their next stop, in Cyprus, the talk was all of the trial of two soldiers of a Scottish infantry battalion who had rolled grenades into their Sergeants' Mess, killing three people. So far, their only substantive plea of mitigation was that they had supposed it to be the Officers' Mess. In early August 1951 my father took command of a newly formed detachment of 35 Light Anti-Aircraft Squadron RAF, equipped with 40mm Bofors guns and allocated to the air defence of the vital aerodromes of the Canal Zone. This was heady stuff for a young man who had not, until then, ventured further abroad than Boulogne. His year in Egypt was one of great political drama, played out in Cairo and London, as the Egyptians chafed ever more stridently against the British presence. My father was very conscious of this rising resentment and well aware of the sporadic violence aimed at British personnel, installations and interests. With the end of the War, and with imperialism in retreat, the Egyptians were restless. In October 1951, not long after my father's arrival, King Farouk's government, frustrated in their negotiations with the British for full independence, unilaterally abrogated the Anglo-Egyptian Treaty of 1936. Britain felt the size of its presence could allow it to ignore this provocative move, but there was a steady escalation in hostility and violence which the Egyptian authorities did little to counter. In January 1952 a confrontation with Egyptian police lead to the deaths of forty-one Egyptians and, in the subsequent rioting in Cairo eleven British citizens were killed, among a number of other Europeans. There was also heavy damage to property, including the burning down of that iconic imperial edifice, Shepheard's Hotel. In that July the nationalist 'Free Officers' movement, led by General Naguib but including a bright, ambitious and articulate young colonel called Gamal Abdul Nasser, forced King Farouk to abdicate. His baby son was placed on the throne, but by June 1953 the 'Free Officers' had abolished the monarchy and established the Egyptian Republic. In a replay of history, King Farouk, like the last Ottoman Sultan thirty years earlier, was taken into exile on board the royal yacht *Mahroussa.*

My father, junior officer though he was, was at the epicentre of a highly complex geopolitical equation. In the 1950s the Middle East was dominated by six distinct but interlinked struggles: the first was the Cold War battle for influence between America and the Soviet Union. This struggle, which would be largely won by the US in the 1970s after the 1973 Yom Kippur War, would be re-ignited in the wake of Arab Spring of 2011, when American ambitions in the region, already suffering from the sad and costly experience of the 2003 invasion and occupation of Iraq, were again challenged by a resurgent Russia; the second was the anti-colonial struggle of Arab nationalists against the remaining centres of British imperial power in Egypt, and that of the French in Algeria and Morocco; the third was the Arab-Israeli dispute, inflamed by the triumph of the newly-founded Israeli state over an Arab coalition in 1948, and the growing problem of the long-term future of the Palestinians; the fourth was the competition between Egypt, with its keen sense of historical significance, and the newly independent states of Iraq and Syria, for leadership of the Arab world. The latter two states, both established from the post-Great War settlement of the Middle East, each contained capital cities from the 'glory days' of Arab Sunni leadership: Damascus and Baghdad.

A fifth struggle was that of the Egyptians and other Arabs to try and keep a developing Turkey out of their affairs, thereby checking any attempt at neo-Ottomanism, while also attempting to stop an historical urge by Iran for influence across the region, manifested in both their military power and their leadership role in the Shia areas of Muslim world. A sixth struggle was the confrontation between those Sunni Arabs who had embraced nationalism, secularism and economic socialism, and those of the fundamentalist persuasion, including the *takfiris,* who all looked back for their inspiration to the origins of Islam and were prepared to advocate various levels of violence and resistance to help recreate it. Into this mix had also been thrown those who embraced that new manifestation of political Islam, the Muslim Brotherhood of Hassan Banna and his later adherent Sayyid Qutb. The Muslim Brotherhood's charitable endeavours contrasted with the corruption and capriciousness of state officialdom, and in time they became skilled at using the language of 'fairness', 'democracy' and 'liberalism' to disguise their aim of implementing an austere sharia-compliant political and social programme. This usefully confused Western observers, who heard what they wanted to hear. The British, albeit having washed their hands of Palestine, continued to occupy Suez and therefore to sit rather uncomfortably within this complicated and fractious geopolitical Venn diagram.

Nasser was a Muslim, but he was also a secularist, a modernist and a nationalist. Daily confronted by the glorious monuments to past Pharaonic greatness, he saw it as Egypt's, and his, destiny to unify and lead the Arab world. Drawing on the example of fascist and communist propaganda successes in the 1930s, he harnessed the power of radio to reach out to those poor, disenfranchised millions across North Africa, the Levant and the Arabian Peninsula who hankered for a 'leader' and a 'cause'. Historical antipathy to Western Christian powers, resistance to colonialism and imperialism and an enduring sense of humiliation had driven much of the Arab world to support or sympathise with Nazi Germany and Japan during the Second World War. It would also underwrite their inclination towards the Soviet Union and Communist China in its aftermath. The influence of *Sawt al Arab* ('Voice of the Arabs'), with its daily diatribes against imperialism, colonialism, Western corruption and British perfidy, cannot be underestimated, as it fed another period of Arab 'heroic optimism' in the Middle East. Although they spoke Arabic, the Egyptians, ever-conscious of their millennia-old history, long pre-dating Islam, had never really considered themselves to be Arabs like those desert nomads who had exploded from the Hejaz in the seventh century. However, the new circumstances of the 1950s now made Nasser actively identify the Egyptians with the wider Arab and Muslim cause. His first move, after the removal of King Farouk, was to negotiate a new political settlement with the British. This he did in October 1954, whereby the British and Egyptians concluded an agreement on the phased evacuation of the Canal over the following twenty months, with a British 'right-of-return' during the seven years after that. The Suez Crisis of 1956 and the failure of Anglo-French 'brinkmanship' would blow a hole in that plan, with further profound consequences for the region and for the Western powers involved.

Meanwhile, Britain's Middle East Command headquarters would move from Suez to Aden.

Against this complex political backdrop, of which he was only vaguely aware from mess gossip and infrequent briefings by the military 'chain of command', my father trained up his platoon, exercised in the desert, made infrequent forays into Cairo, and combated flies, heat and boredom by riding his motorbike up and down the length of the Suez Canal. Ismailia was the only occasion in his 37-year career when my father drew his weapon 'in anger'. Pilfering and theft were constant problems on the base, which was home or workplace to thousands of indigenous workers. One evening, as the 'orderly officer', he was confronted by the sight of a local Egyptian making off with an impressively long section of copper piping. Given the political and security situation, there were standing orders to shoot 'looters', but only after three warnings. To my father's considerable relief, by the time he had issued the third iteration of 'Stop, or I shoot!' the culprit had rounded the corner and was well on his way home.

The RAF now wanted him to return to Catterick to attend an advanced course for the RAF Regiment. My father, who had been in correspondence with my mother on a daily basis since his arrival in Egypt, saw this as a chance to pursue this relationship at much closer range, and he also spotted the opportunity to move across to the General Duties Flying Branch. His superiors wisely saw that this was a longstanding and strongly-held vocation that should be respected. Too tall for fighters, he would find himself committed to the RAF's rapidly expanding Air Transport Command. In early 1953 my father landed back in an England still in mourning for the death of King George VI. A month later, he was at Moreton-in-the-Marsh to start his pilot training. Two months after that, he was engaged to my mother, and they were married at Brompton Oratory on 19 December 1953.

By this time the Cold War was in full swing, with a nuclear stand-off in the important Central European arena and hotter manifestations on the fault-lines of imperial withdrawal and nationalist aspiration. The Communists had triumphed in the bloody Chinese civil war that had followed a barbaric decade of Japanese occupation. The Korean War, which had opened so badly for the United States and the UN, had drawn to a bloody stalemate, and an uneasy armistice existed on the 38th Parallel. The French, in their attempt to hold on to their possessions in Indo-China, were getting closer to their Calvary of Dien Bien Phu, and the Americans were about to begin their own long march to defeat in Vietnam.

By contrast, in the same arena, the British, certainly as seen in the context of the time, were having considerably better fortune conducting their own counter-insurgency campaign in Malaya, although not without their own operational controversies. In the febrile atmosphere of the Cold War, Western policy-makers viewed the struggles as ideologically motivated, which they often were, and inspired and supported by the Communist powers, which was often the case too. However, in confronting both violent and non-violent opposition they routinely failed to factor in strong elements of nationalism, the desire for self-determination, a keen sense of historical humiliation and an equally keen sense of disgust at the blatant corruption of so many local leaders.

In the Middle East, the various proxy-Cold War regional and local confrontations continued to play out. In Egypt, the volatile situation which would soon develop into the Suez Crisis had moved rapidly forward since my father's departure in early 1953. Notwithstanding the Anglo-Egyptian Agreement of 1954, Nasser had become increasingly aggressive across the region: supporting the attacks by *fedayeen* irregulars into Israel; intervening in North Yemen to try and overthrow the King as part of his ongoing competition with the Saudis; and giving aid to those elements in Algeria who were attempting to expel the French. He was particularly irritated by the formation of the Baghdad Pact in early 1955, comprising Pakistan, imperial Iran, Iraq, whose pro-British Prime Minister, Nuri al Said, was seen as a competitor for leadership in the Middle East, Turkey, which was still wedded to the Western-orientation of Ataturk, and Britain, the long-time 'oppressor'. He had also noted the British complicity in the overthrow of the Iranian Prime Minister, Mohammad Mossadegh, in 1953. Despite political differences, in late 1955 the US and UK had offered to help Nasser build the Aswan High Dam, in order to draw him away from the USSR and Communist China. But in early 1956 Nasser announced a huge arms deal with Czechoslovakia, then in the Warsaw Pact, and also engineered the removal of General Sir John Glubb, the famous 'Glubb Pasha', from his command of King Hussein's Jordanian Arab Legion, along with all other British officers. Anthony Eden, who had succeeded Winston Churchill as Prime Minister in April 1955, was incandescent, although how much of his rage and obsession was due to geopolitical angst, and how much to the amphetamines he took to mitigate the pain of a botched medical operation, is difficult to judge. In any case, he now saw Nasser as Britain's 'Enemy Number One' in the Middle East. In all this he therefore probably failed to notice in the 'Hatch, Match and Despatch' columns of the *Daily Telegraph*, a week later, the arrival of one Simon Vincent Mayall, on 7 March, delivered at the Royal Free Hospital, Islington and weighing 9lb 4oz.

The year 1956 was to prove a watershed, for the Suez Crisis had global and regional consequences which continue to resonate today. From every perspective it was a disaster for Britain, but it was little better for the United States, whose failure to support their great natural ally would bring them scant benefit. Blood and treasure were spilt and spent, intelligence was misused and mistrusted, domestic politics suffered tremendous upheaval and political loyalties were tested to destruction. An issue of national interest, which properly planned, explained and prosecuted, might have had a strikingly different outcome, was the cause of demonstrations and civil disobedience on a scale not seen again until the invasion of Iraq in 2003. In international affairs it catalysed further resistance to the colonial powers, allowed opponents to coalesce and split allies, leaving lasting legacies of mistrust and bitterness.

In early 1956 the US had also secretly engaged with Nasser to try and achieve a lasting settlement between Egypt and Israel. Nasser, however, did not believe his bid for leadership of the Arab world would be well served by peace with Israel and alignment with America. The result of the failure of this initiative, and disquiet with the Egyptian arms deal led, in June, to the Western powers withdrawing their support for the Aswan Dam. On 26 July, in response to this 'slap in the face', Nasser gave a speech in which he used the name of Ferdinand de Lesseps, the builder of the Suez Canal. It was the codeword for the Egyptian military to seize the Canal and implement a policy of nationalization. Elements in both the British and French political establishments saw this as a serious challenge to 'world' order and to their national interest and reputation. Geopolitical connections were made between oil supplies, gold reserves, balances of payment and the ability to sustain armed forces to counter Soviet aggression. The ambivalent attitude of the US, which soon turned to outright hostility, led the British into concluding an ill-judged secret pact with the French and Israelis, with the primary aim of regaining control of the Canal, but also to deal Nasser and his regional leadership pretensions a major blow. The latter was of particular significance for the French, who rightly suspected Nasser of giving support to the Algerians in their independence struggle.

My parents watched these developments with the same interest and worry as people all around the world. It was an area they both knew well. As the proverbial 'war clouds' gathered, my father watched as his Army friends from Sandhurst, and his RAF colleagues, began to prepare for the coming conflict. At that time he was flying Avro Ansons on the diplomatic run to Europe, including to the far side of the Iron Curtain. At one stage he had flown Winston Churchill to Bonn, where he was to receive the Charlemagne Peace Prize from Konrad Adenauer; my father was rewarded for his efforts with a visit to the cockpit by the great man himself and the presentation of a signed photograph, a cigar and a cigar box, all of which are still in the family.

The military phases of the Suez campaign were supposed to include: an Israeli invasion of the Sinai; an Anglo–French ultimatum to both Israel and Egypt to withdraw from the Canal Zone; an Anglo–French operation (Operation Revise, within which the British part was called Operation Musketeer) to seize the Canal; the defeat of the Egyptian army; the restoration of Western control of the Canal. By this stage, the planning and the diplomatic to-ing and fro-ing had taken the 'conspirators' into October, and international and domestic calculations and opinions were changing. As the Anglo–French force readied itself, the people of Hungary rose up against their Soviet-backed government. The brevity of the 'Hungarian Rising' almost mirrored that of the Suez adventure, but the world's focus on Egypt allowed the Soviets to conduct their brutal suppression with very little international outcry. The US, who did not wish to be associated with the Anglo–French–Israeli plans, applied huge political and economic pressure on Britain.Although the combined attacks took place on 29 October, by 7 November pressure from all sides had forced a ceasefire before any useful objectives had been taken that could be used in armistice negotiations. During this period, Nasser had ordered all forty ships that had the misfortune to be in the Suez Canal at the time to be sunk. Shipping would not move again until later the next year.

Much of the national pride my parents had experienced in 1945 was dissipated by the outcome of this dismal affair. Like many British people, in fact many people the world over, they saw Britain's reputation diminished and her power and influence further eroded. The US did not come out of it well, either, having to all intents and purposes backed Nasser, even at the expense of good relations with Britain, France and Israel. Although it was American diplomatic and economic pressure that had been important in forcing an armistice, the Egyptians gave the public credit to the Soviet Union. At the same time, the US had been muted in their criticism of the Soviet actions in Hungary, which gave the Germans concern about the reliability of US security guarantees. In short, Britain and the US lost influence in the Middle East, while the Soviets gained it. The British now chose to follow a foreign policy based on the assumption that Britain would never again wish to find itself on the 'wrong side' of a major foreign policy issue from the Americans. Meanwhile, the French made a diametrically opposed assessment, never wishing again to be in the position of having to depend on the US for diplomatic or military support. The limitations of both positions would be exposed over time, and they would re-emerge most dramatically in the contrasting positions Britain and France took regarding the US rationale for the invasion and occupation of Iraq in 2003. In January 1957 Eden resigned, a broken man, and his successor, Harold Macmillan, began the process of re-building relationships with the US, while accelerating the process of full British de-colonization.

Nasser's next move, in the wake of his blinding success over Suez, was to actively engage with the other newly independent states of Syria and Iraq, which he did with mixed success, given their own ambitions in the Middle East. Iraq would collapse into chaos in 1958, accompanied by the assassination of the Hashemite King Feisal II and the whole royal family. Hashemite Jordan would almost go the same way. In that same year, Egypt, Syria and, slightly improbably, Yemen, joined politically to form the brief and unsuccessful United Arab Republic. Both Syria and Iraq would experience the rise of the Ba'athist ('Renaissance') Party, which manifested a potent combination of secularism, Arab nationalism and economic socialism. In Damascus, the Ba'ath Party would eventually come to be dominated by the Assad family from the minority Alawite community, while in Baghdad it would be led by Saddam Hussein from the minority Sunni population. The third strand of Nasser's grand plan for the region was to challenge the leadership pretensions of the monarchies of the Arabian Gulf, in particular those of the Kingdom of Saudi Arabia.

Chapter 6

An Aden Childhood

Yemen is an extraordinarily complex political and social entity which has proved difficult to fit into the modern concepts and structures of 'nation' or 'state'. It has a coastline on both the Red Sea and the Indian Ocean, a demanding, mountainous interior in the north and west and great shale and sand deserts in the east, along with the vast and impressive *wadis* of the Hadramawt. It has always had strong cultural and trading links with Ethiopia, Eritrea and Somalia. Despite a strong Jewish and Christian heritage, the Yemenis were early converts to Islam and crucial in the early expansion of the religion, including its transmission to the Far East. A good deal of wealth accompanied Yemenis back from Malaya and Java over many centuries. Mohammed sent Ali to the main city of Sana'a in 630, and Yemenis took a significant part in the early Muslim victories in Arabia and Syria. Over the years the Zaidis, a liberal and moderate sect within Shi'ism, taking their name from one of Ali's great-grandsons, came to dominate the highland north of Yemen. The southern coastal Yemenis remained as adherents of Sunnism. Governing the country has always been notoriously difficult. Several dynasties exercised a loose control over the various fiercely independent tribes, and endlessly shifting alliances took or held power at various stages of Yemen's history, while generational blood-feuds thwarted any hope of sustained peace or economic development in many areas. Despite this, the port of Aden had become prosperous and prominent at an early stage. Its position at the head of the Red Sea, commanding the entrance and exit through the Bab al Mandab, had always guaranteed its interest to seafarers and traders.

The Ottomans exercised a distant and awkward rule over Yemen for a hundred years after their overthrow of the Mamluks in the sixteenth century, seeking to protect pilgrim routes to the Holy Cities and the spice trade to the East Indies. However, Ottoman rule was largely replaced by local dominance under the Zaidi imams of northern Yemen, from their capital in the wonderful city of Sana'a, a UNESCO World Heritage site since 1986, and sadly battered in the current, multi-dimensional conflict in that country. Confrontation with the Turks continued over decades. Like the tribes of the Persian Gulf, the Yemenis of the coast were great traders, but also often skilled and predatory pirates, and sooner or later their activities were going to rub up against the British as they expanded their imperial and commercial reach to the East. In 1838, two years after the Yemenis were accused of maltreating British survivors of a shipwreck, their leader ceded 194 square miles of his country to Britain, including the magnificent port of Aden, dominated by the crater of an extinct volcano. In 1839, in the face of local resistance, Captain Stafford Haines of the Indian Navy landed with 700 Royal Marines and annexed Aden to the Bombay Presidency of the East India Company. Aden's strategic importance was hugely enhanced when the Suez Canal opened in 1869. In 1905 the British and Ottomans came to an agreement that effectively divided Yemen into two spheres of influence and, in effect, two countries. The Zaidis continued to hold Sana'a and the two ports of Mocha and Hodeidah, while the British held Aden and increasingly extended their influence along the Arabian Sea coastline as far east as the Dhofar region of neighbouring Oman. Here, British influence became contiguous with their longstanding arrangements with the rulers of the Arab states of the Gulf.

The Aden Protectorate, as it became known after the conclusion of several dozen local agreements with local Sunni tribal leaders, backed up by the judicious use of RAF bombing *pour encourager les autres*, formed a curious strip of pink on the school-maps of Empire. It was policed by the 'Aden Troop', largely drawn from the Scinde Horse and Poona Horse of the Indian Army and utilizing local Arab levies to act as scouts. Aden rapidly became important as a watering and coaling stop for ships, and grew in significance as oil became the dominant fuel for the Royal Navy. In 1937 it became a Crown Colony, the only such British possession in the Middle East. Control of the Suez Canal and the entrance to the Red Sea was vital throughout both World Wars for the free movement of British, Imperial and Dominion troops and had been another factor in the robust but doomed British response to the Suez Crisis. The original 1952 deal with Nasser, which had seen Ismailia ceded to Egypt, already argued for an expansion of the Aden base, and while my father was kicking his heels in Ismailia, my maternal grandfather had once again sailed east, this time to supervise a major land reclamation project and the subsequent construction of the Mu'alla Straits. This became a new district of Aden where many of the increasing numbers of servicemen and their families lived, shopped and dined out. Some years later, his company had installed in my parents' flat the only air conditioner in a junior officer's accommodation.

The Suez debacle seemed to make the case for Aden as an imperial base even stronger, while at the same time the very public humiliation of Britain, the source of endless comment on *Sawt al Arab*, encouraged some local Yemenis to agitate for the end of colonial rule. This agitation would only truly hit its stride when Nasser actively intervened in 1962 to try and overthrow the royal rulers of Sana'a in North Yemen, involving his ill-prepared and ill-equipped armed forces in a vicious insurgency campaign and, in doing so, provoking a Saudi response. This produced the interesting sight of a secular, nationalist Sunni republic seeking to topple a Shia monarchy, which in turn was being defended by an autocratic, religious Sunni kingdom. The conflict, which at its height absorbed over 70,000 Egyptian troops in a debilitating and failing campaign, was in large part responsible for Egypt's dire showing in the Six Day War of 1967. Yemen was always seen as a domestic security issue for the House of Al Saud, and from 2015 Saudi Arabia would embark on an equally difficult campaign in that country as they tried to destroy the political pretensions of the Zaidi Houthi tribe, who this time were being supported by fellow Shia from the 'revolutionary' Islamic Republic of Iran.

The Mayall family posting to Aden, from 1959 to 1961, fell in a happy time between the angst of Suez and the downward spiral of violence, across all Yemen, provoked by Nasser's interference in the country. My parents always spoke of that time in Aden as one of the highlights of their service life. My father had been promoted to Flight Lieutenant and now, having passed the magic age of twenty-five, was entitled to a pay rise, marriage allowance and a married quarter. We lived within 'Crater' itself, accessed by an aperture cut through the volcanic rock where Abel, or both Cain and Abel, were reputed to be buried. We occupied a first-floor flat opposite the Aden Armed Police Barracks, the site of a major mutiny in 1967. Every morning, we were serenaded by an Arab pipe band playing 'Scotland the Brave'. It is always difficult to differentiate between genuine memories, imagined memories that are the product of film or photographs and those from family folklore. I do believe that I can remember flashes from that golden period because the setting was so dramatic and romantic that it seared itself into my young memory-banks. The glorious sunshine; the heat; the swimming; the exotic trips to beaches and clubs; the souks; the sound of Arabic voices; the friendly attention paid by the locals to two small blond-haired boys. My father and mother seemed impossibly glamorous in that environment. The black and white photographs and the grainy 16mm colour film of the period testify to a spectacularly happy time, with my parents, young and sun-tanned, frequently appearing in dinner jacket, ball-gown and mess kit as they took part in all that the small but active social life of Aden could offer. My mother had a naturally sociable nature, honed by her time in the theatre. My father, while hugely affectionate and amusing within the family, always displayed an impressive reserve in public. He was well liked and respected, but he did not encourage the casual intimacy that often characterizes service life. Always highly regarded by his superiors and subordinates, he had few really close familiars among his peer group. His height and bearing made him a natural commander of those 'honour guards' that were put together routinely to greet the multitude of visitors who passed through the new Headquarters of Middle East Command, including Lord Louis Mountbatten.

Each weekday, my father would appear in his immaculately pressed khaki drill uniform or his equally well-ironed flying overalls. Taking advantage of our single air conditioner, during the summer months we all slept in the same room and rose early to catch the brief cool of the morning. Mohammed, our houseboy, would have prepared breakfast, and my parents would sit with cups of tea on the veranda, listening to the Scottish 'airs' from the Police Barracks. My father was always a highly affectionate family man, and Mark and I would have our usual tussle with him, one small boy in his arms and another wrapped around his leg, as we all laughed and he tried to kiss my mother farewell. His evident pride in his sons was almost Mark's undoing when he balanced him on his hand and nearly put his head into a languidly rotating ceiling fan. In due course he would drive off to Khormaksar airbase in our beige Volkswagen Beetle. With my father's departure we would either get ready to go shopping with my mother or go to one of the two beach clubs: Tarshine for the officers, Gold Mohur for the smart civilian set. The latter was the favoured destination, with a lively bar over which was hung an impressive stuffed swordfish. The beach itself had a diving platform some hundred yards offshore, and shark-nets down both sides. Sometime in the early afternoon, when the military day was over, husbands and fathers would appear from offices, barracks and the airbase to join their wives and children for lunch

Aden was also my first taste of school. I had developed a strong sense of exclusion when I saw the marginally older offspring of our neighbours don school uniform, heft their school satchels on their shoulders and embark on the school bus. I demanded to be allowed to join this 'band of brothers' and sisters. The local school was run by nuns and, after incessant pestering, my mother managed to convince the Mother Superior that I was 'a fair bet' for a classroom place, despite my age. On the appointed day I joined the queue at the bus-stop and, slipping my hand from that of my mother, I joined the ranks of the academic toiling masses. I have little recollection of that day, only of my mother's oft-told anecdote that, on returning from my first brush with formal education, she advised me to leave my brand-new, shiny satchel by the door.

'For school tomorrow', she said.

'But I have been to school', I replied.

An early exposure to the old saw, 'Be careful what you wish for, it might come true.' In fact, I thoroughly enjoyed school then, and always did. I absorbed information quickly and I learnt to read and to write early. This was thanks, in no small part, to the efforts of my grandmother, Agnes Milne, who had embarked on a troopship to come and visit us in Aden, and who stayed with us for an extended period. A love of reading has stayed with me all my life.

My father's duties often took him away for extended periods. Aden was a vital and busy hub between the 'mother country', the Far East, the Gulf States and East Africa. As a key element of Headquarters Middle East Command, Khormaksar airbase was a scene of constant comings and goings of RAF aircraft and civilian carriers, plying their trade along the imperial web of air routes. In my parents' time, Hunter fighter jets, Canberra bombers and photo-reconnaissance aircraft, Beverley and Valletta transport aircraft, Belvedere helicopters and units of my father's old branch, the RAF Regiment, were based there. There was also a major naval port and dockyard and a large Army contingent, in Aden itself, in bases across the tribal areas and on rotational deployments up and down the Gulf. These included HMS *Juffair* in Bahrain, which would be closed in 1971 as part of the 'withdrawal from East of Suez' and re-opened in 2018, a signal of renewed, albeit overdue, British ambition in the region. Everywhere that my father flew was a Royal Air Force base: RAF Nairobi; RAF Mombasa: RAF Khartoum; RAF Masirah in Oman, RAF Sharjah; RAF Habbaniya in Iraq; RAF Karachi in Pakistan; RAF Colombo in Ceylon; RAF Changi in Singapore. In addition, the RAF routinely supported the Army in their various 'up-country fire-bases', notably in the Radfan and at Beihan. Here there were sporadic policing operations against pan-Arab and communist-inspired tribal unrest, and against more traditional banditry. It is almost unbelievable today to consider the continued global military reach of Britain in the late 1950s and early 1960s, and how, in a mere generation, Britain chose to withdraw from swathes of the world where our presence was not merely tolerated, but routinely warmly welcomed. My father often said it seemed to him that 'every time I took off, another British base closed underneath me'.

Occasionally, my mother, brother and I would join him on one of his trips, under a scheme known as 'indulgence flights', whereby family members could hitch a lift on an aircraft if there was no dangerous cargo on board or no higher-priority passengers. On several occasions we flew to Mombasa, staying at the Nyali Beach Hotel. We still have the cine-footage of our hire car being ferried across the Kilifi Creek by chanting locals hauling on fixed ropes, and I can still recall, with disgust, stepping on a large millipede, thankfully with sandals on. Mine, not his. Two of my parents' close friends in Aden were Guy and Sylvia Watkins. He was then a young captain in the Royal Horse Artillery who would go on to be a general and, in time, Chief Executive of the Hong Kong Jockey Club. In Aden, Guy was routinely based with his gun troop in Makerios, an artillery 'fire-base' covering the Dhala Road. Rather than be separated from his family, he had arranged for Sylvia and their young son Michael to be accommodated with him in his rather spartan stone billet. My father's aircraft was a Blackburn Beverley, a large transport plane known by the Arabs as *Abu Batn*, Father of the Fat Belly. He regularly used to 'drop in', to provide 105mm ammunition, replacement gun crews and powdered milk for Michael. His landing, at the perilously short airstrip, required professionalism and nerve, but the take-off, in which the aircraft simply dropped over a precipice before the engines caught enough lift from the thin, hot air to counteract gravity, felt like an act of God. The outstanding wildlife painter David Shepherd visited Aden at this time and captured my father's Beverley aircraft making a dramatic desert landing, among camels and oil drums, in a painting called 'Reverse Thrust at Beihan'. The picture now hangs in the RAF Club in Piccadilly. Many years later, I managed to get my father a signed copy of this work for his seventieth birthday. David Shepherd's son-in-law, Graeme Lamb, would become a noted British general, and he and I would serve together, many years later, in Baghdad.

With an Air Officer Commanding commendation under his belt, and having won the Lord Trophy, awarded to the best tactical air transport crew in the RAF, my father was posted back to UK to take up a place at the RAF Staff College in Bracknell. It was with a marked degree of reluctance that we boarded the SS *Nevasa* in January 1961 to sail back to Southampton. Today, staff training for all three services is conducted in a 'joint services' environment, reflecting the demands of modern operations, although there are 'single-service modules' within the overall course. In my father's day, and mine, each service had its own staff college. His entry to Bracknell coincided with the birth of my second brother, Justin.

Each staff college brought together about 100–150 officers from all branches of each service, at about the same ages and stages of their careers, for an intensive programme of lectures, seminar discussions, staff exercises and command tasks, designed to expand professional knowledge and identify talent. Many of those attending would have been contemporaries in initial officer training, while others would have met on later career postings. Staff College also included many officers from allied and partner nations, particularly from those countries whose history was closely linked to that of the UK. These were traditionally from the former colonies and protectorates in Africa and the Middle East, but attendance was increasingly extended to allies within NATO, as the UK's foreign policy focus changed through the 1960s. Attendance by overseas 'friends' at Staff College was seen as an important aspect of so-called 'soft power', aiming to reinforce the natural inclination of countries to sustain close relationships with Britain. It did this through the use of courses to foster or develop a British military culture in other armies, to encourage good personal relationships and to impart a useful shared doctrinal approach. Over time, some of this partnership activity might be translated into important diplomatic support during critical times or significant defence sales, a major contributor to Britain's prosperity. These, in their turn, would help reinforce deeper and closer international cooperation. All through my career I would be a passionate advocate of this 'defence engagement', particularly in the Middle East, where relationships between the British royal family and the Gulf rulers, and between our militaries, provided strong bonds of association.

At a certain stage of their respective year-long courses, the officers of all three staff colleges used to come together for a 'joint phase', designed to deepen the exposure of the services to each other. Even within a single-service staff course there are 'peer groups' based on specialization and experience, and it often takes time to break down those barriers. The Army was, by far, the worst culprit, with its multitude of single-cap-badge regiments. The British Army continued to reflect the political philosopher Edmund Burke's observation on the British attachment to 'the small platoons' of life: 'To be attached to the sub-division, to love the little platoon we belong to in society, is the first principle of public affections. It is the first link in the series by which we proceed towards a love of our country and mankind.' All my career, and in all my politically-aware life, I have applauded the wisdom and humanity of Burke's observations.

One of my father's cavalry contemporaries, Shane Hackett, who would go on to be a 'four-star' general and Commander-in-Chief of NATO's Northern Army Group, always said, only half in jest, 'I never joined the British Army, I joined my father's Regiment.' While some of the young officers across the three establishments might have met in the great imperial bases or on the operations that accompanied withdrawal from Empire, the professional knowledge that the three services had of each other was often limited. Albeit crowned with success, unlike Suez, the later experience of the Falklands War exposed once more the ad hoc approach with which we had continued to conduct tri-service operations, and it galvanized the momentum to construct a better model of force generation and command and control.

One of my father's lasting memories of Staff College was of a bearded gentleman from the Foreign Office who, coming to brief on the Middle East, fell off the stage in mid-address. Not all speakers at staff colleges, however intelligent or talented, have the ability to command an audience. This can be particularly so if there has been a course Dinner Night the evening before. This gentleman was clearly '30-love down' within ten minutes. He had chosen to adopt the high-risk strategy of forsaking the podium and getting up on the stage, pacing to-and-fro across it while setting out the principles of Britain's security policy towards foreigners. The young cynics in the audience, which was most of them, were shaken from their slumbers as the Whitehall mandarin lost his footing and almost fell at the Commandant's feet. He gamely got back up and carried on. By this stage he had the full attention of those members of the course who, having been asleep, had missed the spectacle and were hoping the gentleman might be courteous enough to repeat it. At the end of his allotted forty-five minutes, the Commandant passed the ball to the students for questions. The combination of slumber, and subsequent concentration more on his foot-fall than the content of his talk, meant that any knowledge of what the speaker had actually said was in short supply. The students could feel the eyes of the Directing Staff, the senior instructors, boring into the backs of their heads, willing them to open the batting with something incisive. There was an extended and embarrassing silence until, to almost audible relief, a tall and languid officer from a Guards battalion unwound himself from his seat and stood up. In a tone that oozed concern and kindness he said, 'I am sure the course would be interested to know if you hurt yourself when you fell off the stage.' To very barely stifled laughter from the auditorium, the Commandant leapt up. Fixing the still standing 'Guardee' with a piercing glare, he suggested an early break for lunch.

While the words of the Foreign Office official may have been lost between his beard and the floor of the Staff College auditorium, he would have had a lot to say. In 1961 Harold Macmillan was Prime Minister. In 1913 he had gone up to Balliol College, Oxford to read Modern History. He never took a degree. Only he and one other, of the thirty-eight students who went up to Balliol in his year, survived the First World War, and he did not feel he could go back. 'I was sent down by the Kaiser', I heard him say at a College dinner when I was at Balliol myself some years later. Macmillan knew the world well. In addition to his distinguished war record in the Guards, he had had a glittering public career, opposing appeasement alongside Churchill and Eden and then serving in the politically-charged environment of North Africa in the Second World War. Here he had espoused the idea that Britain's post-War role would be to 'play Greece to America's Rome', acknowledging the reality of the United States' new assumption of 'Great Power' status. Despite his share of responsibility for failing to predict the negative American reaction to Suez, it was his close relationship with President Eisenhower, dating from 1942 in Algeria, which allowed relations to be repaired so quickly. In 1958, in the wake of the assassination of the royal family in Iraq, the subsequent collapse of the Baghdad Pact and the increasing influence of the Soviet Union, he had moved decisively to restore the confidence of Britain's Middle East allies. In 1957 he had already used the RAF and SAS to defeat a Saudi- and Egyptian-backed revolt against the Sultan of Oman, and in 1958 he had deployed airborne battalions from 16 Airborne Brigade in Cyprus to stabilize King Hussein's Jordan against Egyptian-backed subversion, an operation in which my father had been involved. In July 1961 he deterred a threatened Iraqi invasion of Kuwait by putting ashore a Royal Marine brigade group in that small and newly 'independent' country. It would not be the last time the UK would come to the assistance of Kuwait, or other Gulf States. However, despite these significant and decisive interventions, Britain would soon lose the confidence and will to sustain her national position East of Suez, constituting a significant blow to her reputation and credibility as a major power.

At the conclusion of Staff College, most students depart for their first formal staff appointment, often in a policy branch or an operational headquarters. However, my father was posted to RAF Abingdon in Oxfordshire, on promotion to Squadron Leader, to resume his flying career in Air Transport Command. He was given a largely 'independent' role, commanding what was known, prosaically, as Transport Support Element (TSE); although he rarely spoke about it, it was clearly some sort of Cold War 'cloak and dagger' organization. My mother seems to have known little about TSE, although she does recall periodic visits by a gentleman wearing a slightly theatrical cloak who would go into a private 'huddle' with my father in the dining room of our small married quarter. Meanwhile, the rest of the family were able to take up our 'indulgence' opportunities again, with excursions back out to Aden, thereby avoiding the horrendous winter of 1962, and occasional 'hops' to RAF Luqa in Malta. Not long after our arrival in Abingdon, the long and bloody French attempt to cling onto Algeria came to its denouement, and General de Gaulle, to great national angst, had to announce France's withdrawal. It was another bitter blow to French national pride.

In 1964, my father, with great regret, accepted the temporary suspension of his flying and took up a staff appointment in the Air Force Department of the newly formed Ministry of Defence (MoD), while moving the family to our first proper home, in Camberley. The new institution was the product of the drive and influence of the first genuine Chief of Defence Staff, Lord Mountbatten, royal and political favourite, national hero, architect of the handover of India and inspecting officer of my father's honour guard in Aden. Our next overseas posting would now take us all well to the east of Aden.

Chapter 7

Retreat from East of Suez

On a hot and humid March morning in 1967, the overnight train from Singapore to Kuala Lumpur pulled into the ornate Central Station. Out stepped 'Acting' Wing Commander Paul Mayall, now on secondment to the Royal Malaysian Air Force, a slightly frazzled wife and three over-excited children. My brothers would enjoy a delightful tropical childhood for the next two years, while I would spend them 'commuting' between Kuala Lumpur and St George's College, Weybridge.

By the time we arrived in Malaysia, the British position East of Suez was becoming ever less credible and convincing, the product of a combination of growing political demands for the British to depart, by no means always reflecting genuine local sentiment, and, more importantly, a declining British will and determination to remain. Since we had left Aden in early 1961 the situation there had deteriorated dramatically, and it was already heading towards eventual withdrawal. In 1962, the British Government had sought to consolidate their position by forming the Federation of South Yemen from fifteen small 'protected states' stretching along the Yemeni coastline which had benefitted from British intervention in their interminable blood-feuds. In 1963 they had merged this new Federation with the existing Crown Colony of Aden. However, despite these positive moves, the British were up against strong headwinds in the region. Local, tribal resistance to the British presence had been exacerbated by the intervention in Yemen of Nasser's Egypt under the banner of pan-Arabism, aided by both the Soviet Union and the People's Republic of China, whose Communist 'godlessness' was offset, in many Muslim Arab eyes, by their sponsorship of nationalist movements and their hostility to imperialism and colonialism. In addition, the British, despite long association with Yemen, mistakenly assumed that the power and influence of the local sultans was similar to that of the Indian Maharajahs, and failed to fully factor in the tribal and religious sufferance that the sultans operated under. In addition, the combination of a weak economy, the growing costs of the welfare state and the sapping demands of sustaining

British imperial presence East of Suez, undermined the confidence of British foreign policy-makers. In Dean Acheson's memorable phase, Britain had 'lost an Empire, but had not yet found a role'. These issues haunted policy-makers throughout the 1960s, and in 1968, in part driven by the trials of sustaining the British presence in Aden, the decision was announced of an intention to withdraw fully from East of Suez.

By 1963, in contrast to the relatively benign conditions under which we had lived in Aden, anti-British guerrilla groups with varying political objectives began to coalesce into two larger, rival organizations: the Egyptian-supported National Liberation Front (NLF) and the communist-backed Front for the Liberation of Occupied South Yemen (FLOSY). In the traditional style of all revolutionary movements, particularly in a society as riven with tribalism and sectarianism as Yemen, these groups were as active in attacking each other as they were in taking on the British. Hostilities had begun in earnest on 14 October 1963 with an NLF grenade attack on British High Commissioner Sir Kennedy Trevaskis as he arrived at Khormaksar Airport to catch a London-bound flight. The grenade killed a woman and injured fifty other people. On that day a state of emergency was declared. Among further such attacks, a grenade killed a teenager and wounded four others at a birthday party on the RAF base. Much of the guerrilla activity focused on assassinating off-duty British soldiers and policemen, and much of the violence took place in Crater, where we had lived and which housed the old Arab Quarter, a rabbit warren of habitation. British forces attempted to intercept weapons being smuggled into Crater along the Dhala Road, but their efforts met with mixed success. Despite the toll on British forces, the attrition among the rebels was far higher, largely due to inter-factional fighting, an example of the revolutionary fratricide which was to be a feature of so many conflicts in the Middle East. On one level there was a Monty Pythonesque element to this 'alphabetti-spaghetti' of competing groups; on another it was a tragic reflection of the fissured nature of a society in which British concepts of justice, administration, governance and economic development had not found a very fertile soil. Despite the British deaths, the real losers were, and tragically continued to be, the poor inhabitants of that starkly beautiful country.

On 20 January 1967, the NLF provoked large-scale street riots in Crater and the Mu'alla Straits. After the Aden Police lost control, the British High Commissioner deployed British troops to suppress the riots. As soon as the NLF riots were crushed, pro-FLOSY rioters took to the streets, and the fighting between British forces and pro-guerrilla rioters lasted into February. Among the violent incidents of the time was the destruction of an Aden Airways Douglas DC-3 by a bomb in mid-air, killing all on board, a ghastly precursor of what was to become an all too frequent terrorist tactic.

Not long after our arrival in the Far East, the Aden Emergency was further exacerbated by the Six Day War of June 1967, pictures of which we watched with our parents on our black-and-white television. Nasser claimed, falsely, but with some credibility given the Suez Crisis, that the British had helped Israel, and on 20 June this incited a mutiny by hundreds of soldiers in the South Arabian Federation Army which also spread to the Aden Armed Police, whose barracks had been opposite our flat. The mutineers killed twenty-five British soldiers, in three separate ambushes, and shot down a helicopter. As a result, much of Crater was now occupied by rebel forces. The repatriation of families had already been speeded up, and the Gold Mohur and Tarshine Beach Clubs had closed. The shopping malls of the Mu'alla Straits, my grandfather's contribution to the 'golden age' of Aden, when British visionaries could still nurse ideas of a 'Singapore of the Red Sea', were bereft of European shoppers, with shopkeepers driven out of business by lack of trade or threats of violence. Order was partially restored in July 1967, when the Argyll and Sutherland Highlanders entered Crater under the command of Lieutenant Colonel Colin Campbell Mitchell, of 'Mad Mitch' fame, who managed to occupy the entire district in a single night, with no casualties.

Nevertheless, repeated guerrilla attacks by the NLF against British forces soon resumed, causing Britain to bring forward plans for a complete evacuation of Aden by the end of November 1967, several months earlier than had been originally planned by Prime Minister Harold Wilson, and without a proper agreement on the succeeding governance arrangements. 1st The Queen's Dragoon Guards, the Regiment that I would command some thirty years later, was the last armoured-car force of the British occupation. As Tony Blair would later promise to the Afghans, Wilson had committed Britain to supporting the local South Yemeni rulers 'in perpetuity'. The hollowness of that commitment was soon exposed when, following the British departure, the NLF seized power from the rival FLOSY, established the Marxist People's Democratic Republic of Yemen and killed many of those tribal chiefs previously committed to accommodation with the British. It was one of those disappointed chiefs who would later comment that it was better to be an enemy of the British because they would possibly try to buy you, whereas as a friend they would definitely sell you. The NLF soon turned their sights on fomenting revolution in neighboring Oman and across the wider Gulf. The four- or five-year political cycles of the Western democracies had proved, and would continue to prove, a poor foundation for long-term foreign policy promises.

The Suez Canal had already been shut by Nasser on the eve of the Six Day War, and it remained closed in the wake of that war because it served as the demarcation line between the Egyptians and the Israeli–occupied Sinai desert. Much of the international traffic that had flowed through the Red Sea ceased, and shipping was again forced to go around the Cape of Good Hope. The same would happen after the Yom Kippur War of October 1973. The British naval base at Aden had also closed in 1967. The combination of these factors would deprive the new, oil-poor nation of South Yemen of valuable revenue and precipitate severely disruptive economic conditions, political turmoil and tribal conflict, all of which would continue to plague Yemen to the present day. With a young and fertile citizenry, the population of Yemen would rise from 6 million in 1967 to 27 million in 2018. Civil war followed in North Yemen, followed by war between the North and South, unification into the single state of the Republic of Yemen, then a fresh, although short-lived, civil war in the new political entity. A growing population, the confessional divide between the Sunnis and the Zaidi Shia, the historical and geographical division between north and south and resultant cultural differences, would all help to make Yemen a battleground for the modern proxy war between Sunni Arabs and Shia Persians. The resulting dislocation and chaos would also provide a fertile ground for one of the most virulent and effective franchises of modern *takfiri* ideology, Al Qa'eda in the Arabian Peninsula (AQAP) and, subsequently, Islamic State.

Malaysia, in contrast, was deemed to have been an altogether more politically successful episode in the retreat from Empire, and in confronting a communist-backed insurgency. It also had a far more beneficial outcome for the indigenous peoples. Although, as in Indo-China, there was a very strong and brutal leavening of communist ideology in the opposition to the colonial presence, the British had identified a genuine nationalist element in the independence movement in Malaya, particularly among the Muslim Malays, and responded to it. This perhaps contrasted with the French and American experiences in Indo-China, where there was a failure fully to comprehend all the factors contributing to the resistance struggle, and where maybe too much attention was paid to ideological issues in the context of the Cold War. The geography of the Malay Peninsula was undoubtedly an important factor, but by addressing the political demands of the nationalist agenda the British went a long way to undermine the ideological appeal of the communists. The British, who could then largely depend on the Malays, sought to separate those elements of the Chinese community who looked for peace, stability and racial equality, from others susceptible to Chinese-inspired communism. Despite the religious element of opposition to Britain in many theatres, there was little evidence of Islamism influencing the resistance movements in Malaya, largely because Britain had addressed the more important issues of nationalism and independence head-on. We would be late to identify a similar political strategy in Iraq in the next century, although when we did, our military efforts had much greater effect.

Much had changed in Britain by the time we returned at Easter 1969. Much was also about to change in the Middle East. The government of Harold Wilson was clearly running out of steam. The prospects of a new British industrial revolution, forged in the 'white heat of technology', had dissipated in the face of weak economic growth, currency crises and trade union militancy. The repair work with America, achieved by Macmillan in the wake of Suez, was partly undermined by Wilson's refusal, rightly or wrongly, to send even 'a single bagpiper from the Black Watch' to join the US efforts in Vietnam. It is easy to forget, in today's partisan US politics, how divisive and politically charged the issue of the Vietnam War was in America during this period. The Labour Party also had a traditional disquiet with empire and anything that smacked of colonialism. In addition, there was a longstanding commitment to the welfare state, and many Labour MPs gave defence issues, not least the demands of overseas commitments, a low priority. The 1964 Budget had set a defence spending cap of £35 billion (2016 values), and this had forced a reappraisal of strategic priorities. For nearly twenty years Britain had tried to balance a triad of commitments based on its nuclear deterrent, its status as a founding member of NATO and its historical position East of Suez. The attempt to sustain this tripod within the budget cap led to serious political tension, not just between parties, but also within the Labour government. In 1968, Wilson claimed that economic weakness had now forced the UK to prioritize NATO and the nuclear capability over Britain's overseas presence. This was disingenuous, given that the Labour government would increase overall public spending by nearly a third between 1964 and 1970, primarily in order to expand the welfare state, albeit by significant borrowing.

The 1966 Defence Review had at least attempted to preserve a limited role East of Suez, and Dennis Healey had declared that 'the theatre we should leave is the Far East', making military planners, much of the British public and our allies, particularly in the Middle East, assume that, at least, the British commitment to the Gulf could be sustained. In 1967 there was a final attempt to sustain a credible military presence within the budget cap. It failed, and a complete withdrawal was announced in 1968, to be effected by 1971. The announcement provoked dismay and disappointment. Despite seriously 'unhelpful' US ambivalence over Suez, the Americans valued the British presence overseas as helping them to shoulder the increasingly heavy burden of 'Free World leadership'. Coming on top of the failure to join US efforts in Vietnam, President Johnson expressed his 'deep dismay' to Wilson. The US Secretary of State, Dean Rusk, was even less emollient and confronted Foreign Secretary George Brown with the undiplomatic but telling words, 'For God's sake, act like Britain.'

While the withdrawal from the great Far East naval and air bases in Singapore seemed a sad but natural extension of the consequences of Indian independence and the gradual handover of power in Malaysia, the decision also to withdraw from the Gulf came as a great shock to the rulers and people of those small but increasingly important tribal 'states'. Already rattled by the erosion, and then desertion, of the British position in Yemen and Aden, and the subsequent growing threat to the Dhofar region of Oman, the various sultans, emirs and sheikhs viewed British disengagement very dimly.

The British locus in the Gulf was, and often continues to be, misunderstood or misrepresented. On the one hand are those who caricature Britain's role in the region as yet another example of 'colonial oppression', from whose 'yoke' the locals must have been overjoyed to have been liberated. On the other hand are those who believe that Britain's continuing relationship with these modern states, formed in the wake of our withdrawal, is a compromise of our values, because their culture does not conform to liberal assumptions about what constitutes 'proper modern behaviour'. Both opinions demonstrate a wilful failure to understand the different models of control and influence exercised by Britain in its imperial past, or the nature of Arab society, which includes a large degree of 'conservatism by consent' and where social constraints are often 'organically' set by a powerful mix of religious direction and cultural assumption. It is therefore worth setting out the origins and development of the symbiotic relationship between the British and the Gulf states and their rulers in a little detail.

Prior to the British presence in the Gulf and the development of a 'Pax Britannica', the preoccupation of the Gulf rulers had largely been that of protection against each other. Faced with external threats, they had little option but to seek the protection of a regional power. Over the decades this had been the Ottomans, the Safavids of Persia, the Al Saud tribe, the 'pirate' powers of the Qawasim tribes of Sharjah and Ras al Khaimah, and the Omanis. In return for protection, some form of subservience or relinquishment of independence was expected. Without overstating it, personal honour was also central to the politics of regional political relations. Where a power took another 'state' under protection, they undertook an obligation to exercise that responsibility fairly and diligently. This was both a religious and a cultural assumption, and the British would adopt it.

From 1600 to 1858, the period of the East India Company, Britain's relationships with the Gulf rulers were conducted by diplomats of the British Presidency of Bombay. From 1858 until Indian Independence in 1947 they were conducted by the India Office, and from 1947 by the Foreign Office, subsequently the Foreign and Commonwealth Office (FCO). The important security and protection element of the relationships was, and remains, reflected in the strong military ties between Britain and the region, and occasionally colours the differences in approach between the FCO and the MoD, and between diplomats and senior officers. This can lead to such accusations as 'the gung-ho military' or 'that hotbed of cold feet'. Such natural friction is, inevitably, further shaded by the political 'hue' of the British government of the day.

Before the nineteenth century, British interests in the Gulf were limited broadly to three areas: the shipping lanes between Bombay and Basra, at the northern end of the Persian Gulf, which connected India with Britain, via Aleppo; the East India Company's trade with Iraq, Iran and Oman; and the protection of British ships and subjects in the region. Britain had little interest in the bulk of the interior of the Arabian Peninsula. However, in 1797, at the height of the war against Revolutionary France, the Qawasim tribes began to threaten British shipping, as part of a wider campaign of maritime raiding. The scale and frequency of attacks increased, and by this stage Napoleon's ambition to destroy the British position in the East had become apparent. Britain sent several naval expeditions against the Qawasim, blockaded their ports and, victorious over Napoleon, in 1820 imposed the 'General Treaty' that drew a line under the piratical activities of the Sharjah sheikhs. In 1822 they established the post of Political Agent for the Lower Persian Gulf in Bushire, on the south-western Persian coast, with responsibility for conducting relations with local rulers and protecting British interests. In due course, this position was upgraded to Political

Resident, with a network of subordinate agents in all key sheikhdoms. There was a second network of agents throughout southern Iran. Sir Rupert Hay described an agent-ruler relationship that would be instantly recognizable to those who continue to conduct political, diplomatic, military or commercial business in the region today:

> The close personal relationship between the Political Agents and the Rulers is an outstanding feature of the British position in the Persian Gulf. They meet each other frequently, and more often socially than for political talks. Possibly the social meetings are more important than the official ones, as a hint, dropped here and there in the course of a casual conversation, is often more effective than formal advice, and the Rulers, being Arabs, are quick to resent any attempt to teach them their business. Usually, the relations between a Ruler and his Political Agent are, outwardly in any case, those of personal friends.

Despite this encouraging relationship, and high levels of mutual interest and cooperation, the British also established a Persian Gulf Squadron of five to seven 'men-of-war' in the age of sail, and two to four gunboats in the age of steam. It was commanded by the 'Senior Naval Officer in the Persian Gulf' (SNOPG), better known as 'Snowpeg'. From the 1930s until the British withdrawal from the Gulf in 1971, SNOPG was based in HMS *Juffair* in Bahrain.

The British naval presence was not resented. Far from it. Much to British surprise, the Political Resident was approached by rulers on numerous occasions to use the ships of the Squadron to protect them from each other, particularly during the six-month pearl-diving season. Far from a symbol of oppression, the Royal Navy was seen as ensuring 'fair play' between the competing sheikhdoms. The British were at first reluctant to cooperate, not fully understanding these requests and concerned about the consequences of taking up such responsibilities. In 1835 the first 'Maritime Truce' was signed to cover the pearling season. The signatories were from families very recognizable today: the Qasamis of Sharjah, the Al Nayans of Abu Dhabi, the Maktoums of Dubai, the Nuaimis of Ajman, among many others. Despite these well-documented events, there is still a popular perception that the Maritime Truce was imposed by the British, rather than being the result of self-interest on the part of local rulers. It was a mark of the precarious nature of security in the region that Hennell, the British Resident at the time, reported how, days after the signing of the Truce, 'News came in from all quarters of the joy and satisfaction diffused amongst the inhabitants of the whole line of the Arabian coast of the Gulf on the intelligence reaching them of the establishment of the Truce.'

So successful was the new 'Trucial System', and so evident the economic and security advantages of peace, that in 1843 the British agreed to underwrite a 'Ten-Year Maritime Truce', noting that 'The rulers are now quite as much interested in its maintenance as ourselves.' In 1853, going even further, the Resident invited the rulers to sign a 'Perpetual Maritime Truce', which they all readily agreed to, with the consequence that from then onwards those sheikhdoms were referred to as the 'Trucial States' and their coastline as the 'Trucial Coast'. This was the model that the British attempted to employ in South Yemen in the twentieth century, aiming to convince warring tribes that submission to a British-enforced set of truces would transform the security and economy of the whole region. While running counter to the vendetta and blood-feud culture of the area, it did prove remarkably successful until the 1960s.

After joining in the Perpetual Maritime Truce, the Gulf rulers also signed 'Exclusive Agreements' binding them to cede control of their external affairs to the British Crown. With the signing of the Exclusive Agreements, the international legal status of the Gulf sheikhdoms became that of 'British-protected states'. They were never colonies. The Gulf was of great strategic importance to Britain, particularly after the opening of the Suez Canal. It was also an area in which pressure could be exerted on the Persians, when the Shahs of the Qajar imperial dynasty threatened Britain's position in India during the period of the 'Great Game', that Anglo-Russian competition for power and influence across the sub-continent. It became even more important with the transition of the Royal Navy from coal to oil and the discovery of substantial oil reserves in the region, including in the Gulf itself, from the 1930s onwards. British policy was well summarized by one Political Resident as:

To maintain the independence of the Arab sheikhdoms, so long as they preserve law and order, and to maintain a system of administration that will satisfy, or at any rate be tolerated by their subjects, to avoid any greater degree of interference in their internal affairs than is forced upon us, but at the same time to prevent any other foreign power from dominating them or obtaining any special privileges in the Gulf.

Much of this assessment of the region could usefully have been heeded by the Wilson administration, and indeed by many subsequent British governments. A position based on mutual self-interest, and a high degree of mutual regard was to be squandered in a manner that helped neither British interests, nor those of the states and inhabitants of the Persian Gulf, nor the wider region.

With the discovery of oil in Iran (1908), Bahrain (1932), Kuwait (1938), Qatar (1940), Abu Dhabi (1958) and Oman (1964), and Britain's increasing reliance on this fuel, British policy became concerned with protecting her oil supplies from the Gulf and with increasing her share of the lucrative energy concessions (see Map 7). The Kingdom of Saudi Arabia had discovered oil in 1938, near Dhahran, but had a jealously guarded relationship with the Americans, from which sprung the energy colossus Saudi Aramco. The security of these precious resources led Britain to expand its military commitment in the region to include air and land forces, as well as the long-standing naval presence. In 1913 a relationship began between the British Army and what would become the Sultan of Oman's armed forces. In the 1930s, Kuwait had British forces stationed in the emirate, and this was extended to Qatar in 1935. In 1951 the Trucial Oman Scouts were formed, and in 1956 the British Army established a two-company garrison in Bahrain, expanded to nearly 2,000 servicemen after the attempted invasion of Kuwait by Iraq in 1961.

The relationship between Resident and local ruler was not uniformly serene. In Bahrain, the Resident was forced to intervene more directly than in any other sheikhdom. Three rulers were deposed and one governor exiled, five demonstrations of firepower were undertaken, including the destruction of the ruler's fort, five further threats of bombardment were issued, two public floggings of Bahrainis were administered and five blockades were imposed. None of this seemed to diminish Bahraini affection for Britain, and during the Second World War, when Bahrain was the only state in the Gulf to be bombed, by the Italians, who missed every target of any significance, they raised money by public subscription to buy ten Spitfires for the Royal Air Force. However, the fact of British protection did raise the issue of what has been described, in all imperial relationships, as 'the Chief's dilemma'. In other words, Gulf rulers could find themselves trapped between the competing interests of their own people and those of the British. This became even more pronounced during the period of withdrawal from Empire, the Arab-Israeli wars and the interventions of Nasser with his pan-Arab ideology and rhetoric. If rulers sided with the British to deal with demonstrations or violence they undermined their legitimacy in the eyes of their people. If they sided with the people, they risked British intervention. Better models of partnership could have been explored and developed to address this conundrum; 'cutting and running' over the issue of cost was about the worst option.

Oil, empire and aircraft had driven increasing post-war interest in the Gulf. The use of aviation to connect the Empire more quickly, and protect it more cheaply, became a British government priority. We had travelled to and from Aden on a troopship in the late 1950s, but in the late 1960s we would go to Malaysia and back by air. My father's early diversion to be a pilot in Transport Command was part of this increased emphasis on air routes. To globally-minded British strategists, who still wrestled to preserve Britain's worldwide presence, the regional airfields of Habbaniya, near Baghdad, and Al Shaibah, by Basra, along with Masirah, Sharjah, and Gwadar in the Omani possessions in Pakistan, were almost as vital as the Suez Canal and the Royal Navy bases at Aden and Bahrain.

Many of the new facilities, airports, bridges, municipal buildings and the like in the Gulf were designed and built by British architects and engineers, in the great imperial tradition. As Gulf wealth increased with the production of oil, and later gas, the Gulf cities began to develop from the mud-brick, pearl-fishing ports of pre-1971 photos, into the sophisticated metropolises that modern visitors to the Gulf know so well today. Given the very small indigenous Arab populations, the bulk of the manual labour came from the Indian sub-continent, a trend that has continued to this day. A parallel growth in primary and secondary education led to a huge demand for teachers, which was met from Egypt, Palestine and Sudan. This was a double-edged sword. Along with their educational qualifications, they brought with them the pan-Arab teachings of Nasser, as well as the ideology of the Egyptian-based Muslim Brotherhood, with its quasi-republican and Islamist teachings that ran counter to the traditional sheikh-based politics of the Gulf. The sudden profusion of inexpensive transistor radios enabled many Arabs to listen daily to the anti-colonial rhetoric of Nasser on *Sawt al Arab*. Whatever the British standing with the rulers and many of their people was, a report in 1957, post-Suez, noted:

Britain has been jockeyed into the position of appearing to oppose Arab nationalism . . . We have come to stand for concepts like 'colonialism' and 'imperialism', concepts that have ceased to have any definable meaning, but which can still arouse blind and irrational hatred among some audiences: you cannot argue with blind hatred.

It was a useful insight, because it drew attention to an important distinction between the regional 'ruling classes', who engaged on a regular basis with the British, and what has been described as 'the Arab Street', the poor and ill-educated public, who were prone to politically-charged emotions and reactions. A routine element of the traditional Arab greeting is '*shoo al akbar*' (What is the news?) reflecting the historic reality of the lonely isolation of nomadic peoples. This hunger for news, and a delight in stories, is part of the lure of 'conspiracy theories' in the region, often the wilder the better. The Americans would routinely find themselves in similarly uncomfortable situations as a result of many of their policies in the Middle East, not least those towards the state of Israel.

Throughout the 1950s and 1960s, local movements, inspired by a combination of Arab nationalism and socialist and communist ideology, sought to overthrow pro-British monarchies and establish Arab republics, often with the covert assistance of the Soviet Union or China. This was a powerful combination, and the direct threat it constituted, combined with relentless propaganda, periodic unrest on the 'Arab Street' and now the abrogation of security responsibility implied by the British declaration of withdrawal from East of Suez, was deeply unsettling for the Gulf rulers. Although ambivalent about the competing claims of nationalism, and a British presence that broadly guaranteed their survival, this sense of 'betrayal' was communicated down through the generations, and continued to be apparent in my dealings in the region several decades later. They were not the only ones who were dismayed. The news of the British Government's decision also met with a grim feeling of 'end of Empire' among those public servants scattered across British possessions and protectorates from Gibraltar to Hong Kong. There was a weary acceptance that the age of imperialism was over, but it was mixed with frustration that many elements in the British government actively willed this so, and the knowledge that it would not necessarily be to the benefit of those local populations we were abandoning to Communist-inspired demagogues. My father could recall from 1968 the angry exchanges in the officers' messes of the Far East, while also observing the Americans getting drawn further and further into the quagmire of Vietnam and, in the same year, watching the 'Prague Spring' in Czechoslovakia being snuffed out by yet another Soviet intervention.

Kuwait had actually pre-empted the British decision to withdraw by several years. Local pressure for 'statehood' had been strong, and Kuwait had already amassed significant oil wealth. This permitted it to contribute to its own protection but, although the Ruler now wanted autonomy in foreign affairs he also wished Kuwait to continue to look to Britain for defence guarantees. A new 'Treaty of Friendship', replacing that of 1899, was therefore signed in June 1961. Within days, the new republican rulers of Iraq resurrected an old Ottoman claim to Kuwait and announced their intention to annex it. A timely British intervention stabilized a dangerous situation, and an Arab League peacekeeping force replaced British troops in October of the same year. It had been a salutary lesson in vulnerability for the other Gulf States. Almost all had disputed borders with their neighbours, and potential quarrels with the two regional powers, Sunni Saudi Arabia and Shia Iran. It was at this stage that the British sought to put a genuinely militarily credible presence in the Gulf, with the establishment of a Persian Gulf Joint Task Force. It would be these same land, air and maritime force levels that would be claimed as impossible to sustain under the Wilson Government's budget cap of 1964.

However, the British government's stated economic rationale for withdrawal was both false and disingenuous. Costs, even with expanded force levels, were only £12 million a year, and oil exports alone from the Gulf were worth £2 billion a year. In addition, the rulers of Bahrain, Abu Dhabi, Dubai and Qatar had publicly stated that they were willing to pay for a continuing British presence in the region. Such offers were repeated to me on numerous occasions during my time visiting the Gulf, by the descendants of those rulers. Several days after these extraordinarily generous public offers were made, Denis Healey said to the BBC, 'Well, I don't very much like the idea of being a sort of white slaver for the Arab sheikhs . . . And I think it would be a very great mistake if we allowed ourselves to become mercenaries for people who would just like to have a few British troops around.' The very next day, Healey had to send a formal apology to the rulers whose generosity he had insulted, expressing 'regret for any offence he may have unintentionally given by the way in which he had phrased certain remarks' and his appreciation for the 'spirit' in which the rulers had made their offer. Sadly, given the broadly positive attitude to the British in the region, the damage was already done. Not only were the remarks offensive and insensitive, revealing a flagrant disregard and contempt for the work and relationship-building of many decades, they were ill-informed. The practice of foreign governments contributing to the maintenance of a

British military presence was well established, and it included West Germany paying a proportion of the costs of our commitment to the continent, via NATO. In addition, such arrangements covered the hundreds of British servicemen, of all three services, who served on 'secondment' and on 'loan service'. Some years later, I was to be one of those. However, the die had now been cast and insult added to injury.

We were back in UK by the time of the 1970 general election, and Edward Heath, acknowledging many of the arguments and opinions above, declared that he would reverse the 'withdrawal' decision if he won. When he did win, he found preparations for withdrawal, and local expectations of independence, already too far advanced to be reversed. So began a series of attempts, over many years, to put in place ad hoc arrangements to offer security reassurance to our Gulf friends. None of them ever looked altogether convincing, and all of them were constantly challenged back home by: pressures on the defence budget and competing priorities within it; the reluctance, indeed aversion, of many Whitehall officials to pursue further foreign commitments; and a wider failure, at the national level, to recognize the contribution that our defence presence in important parts of the globe, not least the Gulf, could make to our own security and prosperity

Bahrain became independent in August 1971, fifteen months after the Shah of Iran had relinquished the longstanding Iranian claim to that island following a UN-monitored referendum. Britain had argued long and hard with the Shah to drop this claim, and the quid pro quo was an increased level of UK military cooperation with Iran throughout the decade, until the Shah's fall in 1979. The demography of Bahrain was to be a constant source of friction in the decades that followed. The ruling Khalifa family was Sunni, and beholden in many ways to Saudi Arabia, while the majority of the population was Shia, looking to Iran for support and spiritual guidance. These tensions came to the fore again during the Arab Spring, complicating British support for the rulers. Qatar followed in September 1971, and the United Arab Emirates, formed from seven sheikhdoms of the Trucial States, in December. An aspiration that all nine 'states' might have formed a single political entity was, probably wisely, dropped.

On 30 November 1971, the day before the British relinquished their 'formal' defence obligations in the Gulf, the Iranians seized the three islands of Abu Musa and the Greater and Lesser Tunb from Sharjah and Ras al Khaimah. Arab condemnation of Britain was swift and strong, for Arab Sunni lands had been taken by Persian Shia 'heretics'. In Libya,

Colonel Gaddafi, now the head of state, nationalized the holdings of British Petroleum. He also evicted the British Army from their extensive all-arms training bases in the east of the country near Benghazi, forcing them to relocate to Canada, seen, probably rightly, as less politically volatile. The loss of the islands soured the last act of a long and mutually beneficial association. The US took over the British naval base in Bahrain, and permanently stationed their Fifth Fleet there in 1995, in the wake of the first Gulf War. The British position in Oman remained a special case and was not subject to any formal withdrawal. In 1970, the growing confrontation in Dhofar with the PFLOAG (Popular Front for the Liberation of Oman and the Arabian Gulf) and dissident supporters from the region provoked Sultan Qaboos bin Said bin Timur al Said to seek the British government's agreement to overthrow his father, the Sultan, the better to prosecute the war in the south. At a time of domestic tensions in Britain and rising violence in Northern Ireland, few noticed, among the headlines about withdrawal from 'East of Suez', that the British military were getting drawn into a complex, undeclared, but ultimately successful war in Oman.

Withdrawal from East of Suez was a disastrous political decision by the Wilson government that, sadly, the Heath government was unable or lacked the will to reverse. Despite the 'withdrawal', the reality was that the British presence remained strong, varied and widespread, although, in true British style, it did not demonstrate much policy coherence in coordinating the multiple remnants of a 150-year formal association. Fortunately, despite the best efforts of some elements of British officialdom to thwart them, the active engagement of many people who know and love the region and its people continued to keep the Union Jack flying in the Middle East, both physically and metaphorically.

Chapter 8

Oil, Arms and Iran

In 1971, after two years at staff establishments on our return from Malaysia, and shortly before the last Royal Navy ship passed through the Straits of Hormuz carrying away the last soldiers of our longstanding Gulf presence, my father was selected to join the personal staff of the Chief of Defence Staff (CDS), Admiral of the Fleet Sir Peter Hill-Norton. Coordinating the work of a ferociously busy outer-office, and dealing with the myriad of issues that arose on a daily basis, one of my father's most significant overseas trips in this appointment was for senior-level staff talks in Iran, a country then undergoing a programme of major transition under Shah Mohammed Reza Pahlavi. It was a fascinating yet unsettling trip, because despite a warm welcome and generous hospitality, the tensions at the heart of modern Iran were always discernible.

Iran has always been a very significant regional power. Iranians have a markedly strong sense of historical pride and entitlement which motivates them as much under the Ayatollahs as it did under the Shah and all previous imperial dynasties. Iran also shoulders a huge sense of national grievance. While some imperial histories continue to resonate down the ages, such as those of the Greeks, the Romans, the Byzantines, the Ottomans and the British, the Persian empires – Achaemenids, Sassanians and Safavids – seem to the Iranians to occupy an infuriating form of historical 'black hole'. Alexander the Great destroyed the immense empire of Xerxes, Darius and Cyrus, and then the Arab Muslims swept all before them in the seventh century, imposing the Islamic religion on the 3,000-year-old culture of Persian Zoroastrianism, fire-worship. This sense of grievance and exceptionalism constituted a major reason why Shah Ismael, first ruler of the Safavid dynasty, adopted Shi'ism as the state religion in the early 1500s. He was taking up the championship of the followers of Ali, in the heartlands of his original power base, but he was also trying to further distinguish the Persians from the upstart Sunni Arabs and Turks. Shah Ismael thereby exacerbated a centuries-old ethnic dislike with an additional confessional one. The history of the twentieth and twenty-first centuries has not done much to dispel this sense of historical entitlement and its accompanying grievances.

Iran's modern history has been bloody and disruptive. From the great Persian plateau, the Safavid dynasty confronted the Ottomans and the Russians, while constantly fending off yet more migrations from the Asian steppes. They invaded India in the 1730s, reaching Delhi and removing the Peacock Throne, and did such an effective job of undermining the Muslim Mughal emperors that the British East India Company was knocking at a much weakened door by the time of Robert Clive. Although by the mid-eighteenth century Persia had reached its greatest territorial extent since the Sassanians, a millennium earlier, the devastating Russo-Persian wars of the nineteenth century led to large and irrevocable losses of land in the Caucasus. Nationwide protests against the Qajar dynasty, who had replaced the Safavids, led to a constitutional struggle, during which the radical 1906 Constitution was drawn up. Among its many other provisions, it gave 'official recognition' to Persia's three minority religions, Christianity, Judaism, and Zoroastrianism. This has remained a building block of all subsequent legislation to this day.

In 1911, the Russians used Persian unrest as a pretext to occupy the north of the country, and during the First World War the British occupied much of western Persia, a continuing a pattern of interference that would contribute, by the time of the Shah's downfall in 1979, to Britain taking second place only to the Americans in the pantheon of Iranian 'villains'. The British only fully withdrew in 1921, but not before they had aided a military coup against the Qajars by General Reza Pahlavi, former commander of the Cossack Brigade. He became prime minister and was eventually declared monarch in 1925, becoming known as Reza Shah. In 1935 he reinstated the old name of Iran. During the Second World War, the threat of German invasion in the wake of the early successes of Operation Barbarossa led to another Anglo–Russian 'invasion', during which Reza Shah was forced to abdicate in favour of his son, Mohammed Reza Pahlavi, and Iran became a major conduit of Allied aid to the Soviet Union.

In 1951, Mohammed Mossadegh, a great advocate of both Iranian nationalism and democracy, was elected prime minister. Enormously popular after he nationalized Iran's British-dominated petroleum industry, he was deposed in a coup d'état in 1953, in a covert Anglo-American operation that confirmed many Iranians in their suspicion of the West and was certainly noted by Nasser in Egypt. After this coup, the returning Shah, who had temporarily fled the country, became increasingly autocratic, and Iran entered a long period of controversially close relations with the US.

Like the Ottomans before him, the Shah sought to buy or copy those aspects of society, culture and technology that he perceived to have given the West their superiority, while suppressing all forms of political opposition in an increasingly arbitrary and brutal manner.

The customary tensions between the modernist, secular ambitions of many Middle East regimes and the social conservatism of the bulk of the people, allied to conservative elements in the religious establishment, became increasingly apparent as the years went by. It posed a dilemma for the US and for other Western governments which persists to this day. How do the Western powers ensure regional stability, useful to their own interests but often based on repression, while also advocating human rights and freedom of expression, which Western policy-makers suspect will shake that same stability upon which their foreign policy objectives depend? These challenges would appear time and again through the late twentieth and early twenty-first centuries, and the conundrum they posed would be at the heart of Western reaction to the so-called 'Arab Spring'. My father's visit to Iran took place just before the spike in oil prices provoked by the Middle East energy embargo which followed the Yom Kippur War of 1973. The flood of money into Iran that accompanied the quadrupling of oil prices fuelled inflation and an arms race with the Saudis, as both sides looked to dominate the Gulf after the British exit. The majority of the senior Iranian staff officers, and their wives, who had hosted CDS, were subsequently arrested and executed after the fall of the Shah seven years later.

The year 1973 was a seminal one in both Britain and in the Middle East. President Nasser of Egypt had died in 1970. Humiliated in the Six Day War, his aggressive anti-monarchical, anti-colonial pan-Arabism had brought a great deal of turmoil to the region, and his command-led, autarkic socialism had largely led to Egypt's economic stagnation. He was succeeded by Anwar Sadat, who had the twin responsibilities of re-establishing Egypt's reputation in the region, and initiating major economic reform in order to stave off public unrest. He also had to deal with the threat from the Muslim Brotherhood, whose leader, Sayyid Qutb, Nasser had had hanged in 1966. Despite an ongoing peace initiative with Israel, Sadat, and Hafez Assad of Syria, were determined to reverse the outcome of the 1967 war by seizing back the Sinai and retaking the strategic Golan Heights. In October 1973, after much highly secretive preparation, including many 'exercises' to confuse Israeli intelligence as to their real intent, the Egyptians and Syrians struck, supported by a motley collection of contingents from across the

Arab and Muslim world and including a contribution from North Korea. On 6 October, the Jewish feast of Yom Kippur, the Day of Atonement, which coincided that year with the Muslim month of Ramadan, the Egyptian Army blasted its way across the Suez Canal, using huge high-pressure hoses to breach the massive sandbanks. An impressive armoured force, supported by a screen of anti-tank guided weapons and operating, initially, under a formidable air-defence missile 'umbrella', pushed forward into the Sinai. The battle ebbed and flowed on both fronts, with the Israelis slowly recovering from the shock of the Arab offensive and gaining the upper hand. At the same time, the two superpowers poured in military supplies to bolster their respective allies, coming perilously close to a nuclear stand-off in the process.

The situation was complicated by the psychological and political incapacitation of President Richard Nixon, now embroiled in the Watergate scandal and impeachment proceedings. Although they had faced defeat in the early stages of the war, the superior weaponry, tactics and leadership of the Israelis now enabled them to cross the Suez Canal themselves and advance on Ismailia, cutting the Cairo-Suez road and trapping the Egyptian Third Army on the east bank. The Suez Canal, blocked during the Suez Crisis and closed again after the 1967 Six Day War, was shut once more, and would not now reopen until 1975. On the Golan, the Israelis pushed back the Syrians and advanced within shelling distance of Damascus. Frantic diplomatic efforts produced UN Resolutions calling for the implementation of a ceasefire, and on 25 October the fourth Arab-Israeli war ended. Henry Kissinger, the US Secretary of State, fresh from the diplomatic 'triumphs' of ending, for a time, the Vietnam War and implementing a radically new strategic relationship with China, succinctly summarized the key issue at the centre of the Arab-Israeli conflict:

> The conditions that produced this war were clearly intolerable to the Arab nations and, in the process of negotiations, it will be necessary to make substantial concessions. The problem will be to relate the Arab concern for sovereignty over territories to the Israeli concern for secure boundaries.

Despite the peace treaty signed between Anwar Sadat and Menachem Begin at Camp David in late 1978, overseen by President Jimmy Carter, that core tension continues to lie at the heart of Arab-Israeli relations, in addition to the myriad of other concerns regarding the Palestinians and the status of Jerusalem. The war significantly changed the status quo in the region, giving the Israelis a new-found respect for the Egyptian armed forces, and the Egyptians some relief from the shame of 1967. For his troubles, Sadat was assassinated in 1981, at a military parade in Cairo, by outraged members of the Muslim Brotherhood who regarded him as a 'traitor' for signing a peace deal with Israel. Sitting next to Sadat at the time, and untouched by the attack, was General of the Egyptian Air Force, Hosni Mubarak, the man who would replace him until his own overthrow, thirty years later, during the Egyptian manifestation of the Arab Spring.

Oil and gas, two energy sources that drive the majority of activities in the modern global economy, have long dominated the politics of the Middle East, and they will continue to do so well into the twenty-first century. The oil-rich states, including Iraq and Iran, that cluster around the Persian Gulf, to give it its correct title, although it is wiser to simply refer to it as 'the Gulf' in Arab countries, comprise about 3.5 per cent of the earth's land mass, but contain about 50 per cent of the world's oil reserves and 40 per cent of its natural gas. In 1960, conscious of the lessons of the Iran and Suez crises, the Organization of Petroleum Exporting Countries (OPEC) was established. It comprised twelve countries: Iran, the seven Arab states of Iraq, Kuwait, Libya, Qatar, Saudi Arabia, Algeria and the UAE, Venezuela, Indonesia, Nigeria and Ecuador. Its objective was to resist pressure to reduce oil prices from the so-called 'Seven Sisters', the seven largest Western oil companies. Initially, OPEC confined its activities to gaining a larger share of the profits generated by the oil companies and greater control over their own production levels. However, by the early 1970s it had coalesced into a formidable unified exporter bloc and began to exert greater economic and political influence over energy companies and importing nations.

Shortly after the outbreak of the Yom Kippur War, OPEC had struck in response to US support of Israel. As Nixon authorized Operation Nickel Grass, the increased supply of military equipment to Israel, the oil cartel raised the price of oil by 70 per cent, to over $5 a barrel, and also agreed to initiate monthly oil output cuts of 5 per cent. President Sadat and King Faisal of Saudi Arabia had already met, and the Arab members of OPEC declared the US a 'principal hostile country'. The Shah of Iran, supposedly a close ally of the US, said in an interview:

> Of course the price of oil is going to rise. Certainly! And how! You
> buy our crude oil and sell it back to us, refined as petrochemicals,

at a hundred times the price you paid us. It is only fair that, from
now on, you should pay more for oil. Let us say ten times more.

A combination of measures soon drove the oil price to $12 a barrel, and
thereby provoked what has been described as 'the largest transfer of wealth
in history', from the rich industrialized West to the oil-producing states of
the Gulf. The consequences were dramatic. Some of this new oil wealth
would be spent on a vast range of ambitious and extraordinary infrastructure
projects and much would be spent on social development. Some of it would
be dispensed in the form of aid to underdeveloped countries, in line with
Islamic rulings on charity. Much of it would go on massive arms purchases,
exacerbating regional political tensions, not least between Sunni Saudi
Arabia, Shia Iran and Ba'athist Iraq. Although these tensions would be
managed through the 1970s, they would contribute to the fall of the Shah
in 1979 and fuel a re-energized set of conflicts as the new Iranian Islamic
Republic launched its ambitious bid for leadership of the Muslim world,
and the Sunni Arab nations responded. Saudi Arabia would also begin to
spend billions of dollars in the ensuing decades, helping spread the austere
and fundamentalist Wahhabi religious ideology throughout the world.
Some of this money, particularly during the period of the mujahideen
opposition to the Soviet Union's occupation of Afghanistan, would be
channelled through ostensibly bona fide religious charities such as the Al
Haramain Foundation. This organization, while supporting respectable
charity initiatives, also funded violent Sunni extremist groups, including
Al Qa'eda in Afghanistan. Other monies would find their way to religious
charities in Western Europe whose agendas were often similarly dubious
and disruptive.

   The embargo, or 'oil weapon' as it came to be known, had a substantive
impact across the global economy, depending on a country's level of
reliance on Middle East energy supplies. In the US this was only 12 per
cent, but it constituted 80 per cent in most European countries and over
90 per cent in Japan. China was yet to enter the market. It catalysed an
American drive to amass a significant 'strategic energy reserve', explore
additional potential oil and gas sites on the American continent, seek out
new fuel sources, and to invest in those technologies that would lead to the
'fracking revolution'. It also caused a revolution in vehicle design. Rationing,
speed restrictions and gas queues fuelled an uneasy sense of national
vulnerability. By late 1973, the US was so concerned by rising oil prices,

and the threat to their interests that these OPEC measures represented, that they contemplated military action to seize the eastern provinces of Saudi Arabia. The Prime Minister, Edward Heath, commissioned an intelligence estimate which concluded that America 'might consider it could not tolerate a situation in which the US and its allies were at the mercy of a small group of unreasonable countries', and that they would prefer a rapid operation to seize oilfields in Saudi Arabia and Kuwait, and possibly UAE, if military action was decided upon. Although it was assessed that the response of the Soviet Union would not involve force, the report warned that 'the American occupation would need to last 10 years, as the West developed alternative energy sources, and it would result in the "total alienation" of the Arabs and much of the Third World.' The US did not, in the event, feel the need to embark upon such drastic measures, but a sense that they just might did much to persuade the Gulf rulers that, despite the flood of petro-dollars that now poured into their coffers, they would be well advised not to push their luck.

Prime Minister Heath, meanwhile, had his own problems. While the US remained staunchly pro-Israel through this period, European countries developed a more nuanced diplomatic approach to the politics of the region. In 1967 Harold Wilson had supported Israel in the Six Day War, but in 1973, Heath, still smarting from having to accept his predecessor's ill-founded decision to withdraw from East of Suez, felt little reason to pander to an Israeli government, given the problematic history of British-Israeli relations. He therefore refused to allow the US to use British bases or the RAF airfield at Akrotiri in Cyprus. While Britain could have handled an oil embargo on its own, over the winter of 1973–4 there was also a stock market crash and a series of major strikes by coal miners and railway workers. It was this combination that led to a rolling programme of national power cuts, Ted Heath losing the 1974 election, and to my having to conduct my A-level revision by candlelight.

Oil and the issue of energy supplies and their security would continue to dominate the politics of the Middle East and the defence, security and economic policies of those countries who continued to depend on the unrestricted flow of 'reasonably-priced' energy. The hubris of OPEC was most notably demonstrated in 1980, when Saudi Arabia, through her oil minister Sheikh Ahmed Yamani, nationalized the Arab American Oil Company, the mighty Aramco. I can recall Sheikh Yamani appearing almost nightly on television, a genuinely global 'player' from a part of the world that, prior to the discovery of oil, was known almost solely as the birthplace of the Prophet Mohammed and the wartime playground of Lawrence of Arabia. At school, wags used to confront each other, jangling a handful or pocketful of loose change and demanding, 'Who am I?' To which the answer was 'Sheikh Yamani'! He was the author of the oft-quoted and highly perceptive remark, given what we now know of the scale of global energy reserves: 'The Stone Age did not end because we ran out of stones, and the Oil Age will not end because we run out of oil.'

Chapter 9

Scholar to Soldier

E ldest sons often fall into one of two categories: those who wish to emulate their fathers' careers, and those who have absolutely no intention of doing so. I was once told of a military officer's teenage son who had had printed a pre-emptive Christmas party T-shirt which read, 'Yes, haven't I grown. No, I am not going into the Army'! Not too welcoming, but it saved on small talk. I fell into the former category, and I not only wanted to join the military, I wanted to go into the Royal Air Force as a pilot. This ambition was inspired by the example of my father's career, by my early exposure to travel and exotic regions of the world and by a developing love of history and with it, in due course, politics. From a young age I felt that I wanted to take part in great events of national and historical significance. 'War is . . . the continuation of politics by other means', as the military philosopher Carl von Clausewitz famously put it, and the profession of arms appealed to me for precisely that reason. In summer 1973, with my father's encouragement and blessing, I presented myself at RAF Biggin Hill, the legendary Fighter Command base of the Battle of Britain, where the Air Force conducted their aircrew selection and assessment tests.

Over the next three days I was subjected to a series of medical tests, interviews and command tasks, then confronted with a series of mechanical aptitude tests, using devices that could determine whether you had the 'hand-eye' coordination and the reflexes to propel tens of millions of poundsworth of aerial hardware through the firmament. I categorically did not. The writing really had already been on the wall. I had displayed little real aptitude or interest in technology or science. My best grades were in History, Military History and English, and my worst were in Maths, Physics and Chemistry. My father was disappointed, but sanguine. 'What about trying the Army?' he said.

Some months after this crushing blow, I was walking down the corridor at St George's College, where I was confronted by the Headmaster. We greeted each other, and after a short pause he said, in that slightly nasal manner that lent itself so easily to schoolboy imitation, 'You are going to Balliol,

Mayall. History.' For several years I had anticipated the near future as being 'Sciences; Cambridge; the Royal Air Force'. Now, in the space of just a few weeks, it had become 'Humanities; Oxford; the Army'.

Over the following months I jumped through a series of hoops that would eventually take me into the next stages of my life: the three-day Army selection process at the Regular Commissions Board in Westbury, similar to Biggin Hill but with less emphasis on hand-eye coordination; three A-levels; an Oxford exam; a series of penetrating and demanding interviews at Balliol; three weeks at Sandhurst; and a short attachment in the Army to confirm that I was convinced about my choice of career. In the meantime, my father was selected to be Station Commander of RAF Northolt, another former Battle of Britain fighter base, usefully situated, for me, midway between the dreaming spires of Oxford and the nightclubs of London.

In 1975, in the short period between this first encounter with the Army and going up to Oxford, I visited Israel. It was not yet two years since the Yom Kippur War, and the reverberations were still being felt across the region, and wider. I landed in Tel Aviv and took a bus to Jerusalem, intending to walk the Via Dolorosa, visit the key Christian sites of the City and see Bethlehem and the Sea of Galilee. I was staying at the Casa Nova hostel, and I arrived with a rather one-dimensional view of Israel. The shadow of the Holocaust, and the circumstances of the Cold War, in which the ideological threat from the Soviet Union went hand-in-glove with Arab Muslim anti-colonialism, had cast Israel in the role of plucky outpost of the West and champion of democratic values. Clearly, the situation was considerably more complex than that, as quickly became apparent. Just some cursory reading, let alone speaking to the city's inhabitants, quickly revealed the deep emotions that Jerusalem excited in Jews, Christians and Muslims alike. Its place in the history and culture of all three religions was profound, real and highly divisive. The Torah and the Bible contain countless references to its significance, and Muslims had quickly taken up Jerusalem as the third most holy place in their own iconography. It had been the centre of the Jewish world from the time of King David, and of his son Solomon, who built the great Holy Temple on Temple Mount as a repository for the Ark of the Covenant.

In the late first century Roman retaliation for a major Jewish uprising led to the whole metropolis being destroyed. Jews were banned from the rebuilt city, which in due course benefited from Emperor Constantine's adoption of Christianity as the state religion of Rome in the fourth century. He raised the first Church of the Holy Sepulchre in 335 AD, over the site of Christ's crucifixion and entombment. In 1635 the predecessors of the Royal Scots Regiment were serving alongside the French Picardy Regiment during the Thirty Years War. The latter claimed to have been descended from the Roman legion that had guarded Christ's tomb. The Scots casually dismissed this proud claim with the remark that if they had been guarding the tomb the Holy Body 'would not have got away', earning for themselves the sobriquet 'Pontius Pilate's Bodyguards'.

The ban on Jews living in Jerusalem remained in place until the seventh century, when the Muslims under the third Caliph, Umar, seized the city The original Temple Mount became known as Al Haram al Sharif, the Noble Sanctuary, and the Umayyads in due course built the Dome of the Rock on it, with its uncompromising declaration of the nature of their God. From the outset the proximity to each other of the Temple Mount, the Dome of the Rock and the Church of the Holy Sepulchre would guarantee friction and conflict, although Umar, recognizing the importance of the Holy Sepulchre to Christians, refused to pray in the Church, in order that his Muslim supporters could not request its conversion to a mosque. Umar's own mosque remains, to this day, opposite the Church of the Holy Sepulchre.

Over the next 400 years, Jerusalem's prominence declined as Arab Muslim powers and dynasties, Sunni and Shia, competed for power. Christian rule had been re-established in 1099, when the Western knights of the First Crusade breached the city walls. However, Saladin retook the city for Islam in 1187, and it broadly remained in Muslim hands until the end of the First World War, although control passed from the Arabs to the Mamluks of Egypt, and in the sixteenth century from the Mamluks to the Ottomans. While the city was restored under Suleyman the Magnificent, and remained of great religious significance to three religions, it did not thrive during these centuries, being neither a great commercial centre nor a trading hub. A census of the population in 1845 recorded only 16,400 inhabitants, with 7,000 Jews, 5,000 Muslims, 3,500 Christians, 800 Turkish soldiers, and 100 Europeans. When Britain relinquished the Mandate of Palestine in 1948, the population of Jerusalem had risen to 165,000, but now two thirds of them were Jews, most of whom had arrived immediately before and after the Second World War.

As the British Mandate was expiring, the UN recommended the creation of a 'special international regime' in Jerusalem, separate from any Jewish or Palestinian state. However, this plan was not implemented, and when war broke out as the British withdrew, the Israelis seized what would become known as West Jerusalem, while the Jordanians took control of East Jerusalem, and with it the Old City and all the holy sites. Jordan also took the territory of the 'West Bank'. In the Six Day War of 1967 the Israelis pleaded with Jordan to remain neutral. When Jordan failed to heed that request, and attacked Israel, the Israelis captured East Jerusalem and occupied all the West Bank. Jewish and Christian access to the holy places was restored, but Muslim access was controlled and continues to be a source of violent contention. The final status of Jerusalem has consistently been one of the most important areas of discord between Israeli and Palestinian peace negotiators.

In my time in Israel I encountered great kindness from the Jews I met, but I also sensed an aggressive prickliness and an arrogant defensiveness. This should have come as no surprise. The state of Israel had been a remarkable creation, but by 1975 the elation of victory in the Six Day War had been replaced by the vulnerability experienced in the early stages of the Yom Kippur War, only six years later. The early settlers who came to Palestine in the years after the First World War were European, largely Ashkenazi, Jews. Some were fleeing persecution and pogroms in the East, often bringing with them pronounced Marxist ideas and ambitions, while others, from Western Europe, were trying to escape the cultural dilution of their Jewish identity. The assumption was that many more European Jews would in due course join them, but the murderous reality of the Holocaust thwarted that ambition. The Israel of the 1950s had been built on a ferociously independent spirit, forged by wartime horrors, the end of the British Mandate, socialist experimentation and the consequences of the large-scale expulsion of the Arab population. Victory in the Six Day War was a triumph for the State of Israel and the Israelis, and a source of great pride to Jews worldwide, but it came at a price. Very many Jews had lived in communities all across the Muslim world during the period of the Ottoman Empire, and then in the successor states, although many had deserted Baghdad for Israel after the violent fall of the Hashemites in 1958. Now, many thousands more of these 'oriental' Sephardi Jews were violently hounded out of lands and properties they had occupied for centuries, or chose to move, leading to a huge influx of Jews from a distinctly different cultural heritage into Israel. The Jewish refugee numbers significantly exceeded those of the displaced Palestinians. At about the same time, and never openly declared, Israel, aided by important technical support from France, became the only 'nuclear power' in the region, further adding to Arab and Muslim humiliation and resentment.

The shock of the 1973 Yom Kippur War changed Israel fundamentally. Hubris and a powerful sense of shared solidarity and success were now trumped by insecurity, mistrust and discord. Israel became more diverse, individualistic and economically advanced, but in the process, it also institutionalized divisions between a new breed of 'settler' in East Jerusalem and the West Bank, with their vision of 'Greater Israel', and those concerned about Palestinian, and a wider Muslim Arab revanchism. There were further schisms between ultra-Orthodox Jews and secular Israelis, between 'Occidental' and 'Oriental' Jews, and between Palestinian Israelis and Jewish nationalists. I sensed the echoes of this multi-faceted discord during my brief visit in 1975. In the 1990s, the mass Russian-Jewish immigration that followed swiftly in the wake of the collapse of the Soviet Union would add to the political and social complexity of Israel. The Russian Jews would bring with them great economic and intellectual energy, but they would be reluctant to shed their distinctive Russian values and culture. These internal tensions were magnified by the reality of being a Jewish state surrounded by concentric circles of antipathetic or actively hostile Palestinians, Arabs and Muslims.

I love institutions. I like the loyalties, the codes, the 'exclusiveness' and the historical 'back-stories' of these establishments. I enjoyed 'houses' at school, colleges at Oxford, regiments in the Army and clubs in London. Edmund Burke once again captured the essence of this appeal when he claimed that society and institutions were 'a partnership not only between those who are living, but between those who are living, those who are dead, and those who are yet unborn'. In 2018, the RAF powerfully captured that idea during their hundredth anniversary, with their memorable slogan: 'Commemorate – Celebrate – Inspire'. Balliol College had all the above, and while it was not as 'pretty' as some other colleges – indeed, some wag once said of it, 'C'est magnifique, mais ce n'est pas la gare' – it had a reputation for relentless academic success, and a long list of luminaries had attended it, including several prime ministers. The tutorial system, that 'jewel in the crown' of university education, had been largely founded by Benjamin Jowett, who had become Master of Balliol in 1870. In due course, while seminars and lectures remained important vehicles for learning and discourse, 'one-on-one' tutoring, in fact usually 'one-on-two', became the norm. So it was that, twice a week for the next three years, I would find myself sat in front of dons, in rooms that were almost caricatures of what a don's room should be, reading out an essay and having it gently critiqued.

Although we had to undertake a series of set courses for our History degree, we also had the opportunity to choose a 'Further Subject' in our third and last year. Spurred on by my visit to the Holy Land, and because I had so enjoyed studying the medieval history syllabus with a marvellous Balliol tutor, Maurice Keen, brother-in-law of the noted military historian, Sir John Keegan, I opted to study the Crusades. Maurice would, in due course, write the definitive book on chivalry. In an early tutorial on Henry I's administrative reforms, I had made a 'time mis-appreciation' and had resorted to copying out a large chunk of a work by R. C. Davies, whose contention was that by the end of Henry's reign no one again seriously questioned the concept of England as a unified state. I should have chosen a more obscure historian of the period. As I ploughed through my essay, with a justifiably uneasy conscience, Maurice reached behind him.

'Don't stop Simon', he said, 'I'll follow you in the book.'

At the end of my recitation he said, 'I always think that Davies slightly overstates his case, don't you?'

Elegant, clever and kind.

Like many students of the time, much of what I knew of the Crusades came through the pages of Walter Scott's books, *Ivanhoe* and *The Talisman*. King Richard the Lionheart had gone on crusade, he had fought Saladin, been taken prisoner by Leopold of Austria and tracked down in Durnstein castle by the troubadour Blondel. In retrospect, that was about it. There were also 'bad King John' and some Templar and Hospitaller knights in the mix somewhere. The Crusades were rather out of fashion in the 1970s, and they had been for some time. Edward Gibbon in his *Decline and Fall of the Roman Empire* had been pretty scathing about these great and consequential 'military pilgrimages' although, to be fair, he had had it in for the whole Catholic Church, not just its military offshoots. Even Sir Stephen Runciman, who described the Crusades so well in a magisterial, three-volume account, could not really disguise his dislike of the whole enterprise. In the shadow of the World Wars, de-colonization and retreat from empire, the Non-Aligned Movement and relentless Communist propaganda, the simplistic image of 'arrogant' Western knights inspired by a corrupt Church and attacking civilized, sophisticated Muslim Arabs, for no apparently good reason, had gained ground.

This image, too, seemed unhelpfully one-dimensional, because life for many in eleventh century Western Europe really had been 'nasty, poor, brutish and short', in Thomas Hobbes' memorable phrase. Death was ever present, through the agencies of those 'Four Horsemen of the Apocalypse', death, famine, pestilence and war. Allied to that, heaven and hell, salvation and damnation, were all too real to most people. Issues of orthodoxy and heterodoxy were fiercely contested, and 'infidels' and 'heretics' were seen as mortal enemies by most Christians. Christianity was the binding glue of the West, and even after the 'barbarian' invasions and the collapse of the Latin Roman Empire, it had continued to gain new converts, and the Mediterranean had remained a 'Christian lake'. That reality had been shattered in the middle of the seventh century, when the armies of Islam had taken the Holy Land, including Jerusalem, and swept through North Africa and Iberia. By the eleventh century, Christendom had been on the defensive for nearly four centuries, and the Church looked to harness the martial prowess of the knightly classes in its defence.

It is against this backdrop that the Crusades should be assessed. This is no place for a comprehensive history of the crusading period, but its influence still resonates today, and references to it appear repeatedly in the language of Al Qa'eda and IS. In 2010, in an AQ-inspired bomb plot, the 'package' sent from Yemen to the States was addressed to Reginald de Chatillon, a notorious Muslim bête noire of this period, beheaded by Saladin himself at the conclusion of the battle of the Horns of Hattin. A picture of a French aircraft taking part in the campaign against IS in 2016 revealed the words *'de Reginald de Chatillon'* chalked on the side of a 500lb bomb. Even the current Islamist president of Turkey, Recep Tayyip Erdogan, will speak of modern Western initiatives as 'Crusader-inspired interference'. Many Arabs and Muslims continue to draw a direct comparison between the Christian Kingdom of Jerusalem and the Jewish State of Israel, and hope the latter will meet the same fate.

In November 1967, in the aftermath of the Six Day War, the UN had passed Security Resolution 242. Until President Trump's Middle East peace plan of January 2020, this was the internationally-endorsed basis for a sustainable solution to the Arab-Israeli issue. Acknowledging the deep-rooted historical and religious complexities of the region, at its heart was a 'peace for land' deal, including a return to pre-1967 borders, and proposals for self-governing Palestinian entities. This would become 'the Two-State Solution', with the proposal that Jerusalem become a 'shared capital'. Suddenly, in 1977, in my second year at Balliol, after very little progress in the intervening ten years, not least because the Yom Kippur War had further hardened attitudes, we were all astonished to hear President Sadat of Egypt declare his willingness to go to Jerusalem to address the Israeli Knesset. While he did have some wider regional objectives, linked to Nasser's earlier ambition for Egypt to lead the Arabic-speaking world, he also had some very Egypt-focused aims, namely to recover the Sinai and pivot his country away from the Soviet Union and towards the United States. In this he was pursuing a bilateral path with the Israelis, while seeking American support. His initiative was outside the UN-backed Geneva process, ignored the Palestinian Liberation Organization (PLO) and was not sanctioned by the Arab League.

In summer 1978, over the course of six mentally demanding days, I sat my twelve Modern History papers. As I fell out of the University Schools onto Oxford's High Street, amateur photography of the time records an attractive blonde friend, a bottle of champagne and a haircut that was not going to survive five minutes at Sandhurst. Three years of wonderful and rewarding tertiary education were now over. In October that year, after two months travelling in America, the gates of the Royal Military Academy closed behind me. My parents and my brothers had recently departed for Canada, where my father was to be Defence Adviser at the British High Commission in Ottawa for the next four years. During his time there, in a stark example of the long-lasting bitterness of Middle East affairs, his Turkish diplomatic colleague was assassinated on his way to work by an Armenian terrorist group.

Meanwhile, in the United States, the gates of Camp David had been opened to President Sadat and the new Israeli Prime Minister, the former Irgun 'terrorist' and scourge of the British Mandate powers in Palestine, Menachem Begin. For thirteen days in September 1978 President Carter conducted personal 'shuttle diplomacy' at the Presidential retreat, resulting in the Camp David Accords that, to the astonishment of the world, and to cries of 'betrayal' from the Palestinians and their many Arab and Muslim backers and sympathizers, led to the Egyptian–Israeli peace treaty of March 1979. It was a stunning development, with huge regional implications. While Sadat and Begin would receive a joint Nobel Peace Prize, Egypt would be expelled from the Arab League for a decade, and Sadat himself would be assassinated by the Muslim Brotherhood.

Chapter 10

'New World Order' – Part I (1979)

The late 1970s were years of turbulence in the Western world, and in the Middle East. In 1974 President Richard Nixon had resigned in the face of almost certain impeachment following the Watergate scandal. He was replaced by his Vice President, Gerald Ford. The next year, South Vietnam, where 58,000 US servicemen had died trying to sustain the Saigon government in the face of a Communist-backed insurgency, fell to North Vietnam and its Viet Cong allies. In 1976, the Democratic Party's nominee, Jimmy Carter, became US President. Communist parties were active and successful in Western European elections, including in key NATO countries like Italy. In Britain, the Labour government had struggled on since 1974 with a three-seat majority, but in 1976 Harold Wilson resigned, to be succeeded by Jim Callaghan. This was a time of political tension, of continuing trade union militancy and of strikes. It was also the time when Margaret Thatcher unexpectedly defeated Edward Heath for leadership of the Tory Party.

In the Middle East and Central Asia, events were also beginning to unfold in a manner that was to compound the problems of Western policy-makers, reflecting the febrile nature of global politics with its clashes of competing ideologies and the realities of a region where political and economic development ambitions routinely confronted social, religious and cultural conservatism. Many of these threads would come together in a set of remarkable geopolitical events in 1979.

In Iran, after the 1953 coup against Prime Minister Mossadegh, the Shah had returned from 'exile' determined to drive forward a programme of modernization that would to return Iran to the position of regional dominance that he saw as Persia's historic birthright. In 1963, threatened by both Communists and the clergy, he had initiated the 'White Revolution', a series of reforms designed to further legitimize the Pahlavi dynasty by creating new support bases, while weakening those classes, particularly landowners and the religious establishment, who supported traditional approaches to the many pressing social and economic issues in Iran. The White Revolution consisted of several elements, including: land reform; the sale of state-owned enterprises; the enfranchisement of women; nationalization of the forests; a drive for greater literacy; and profit-sharing schemes in industry. These policies, unfortunately, had almost the opposite effect of that desired by the Shah, since they led to a huge increase in those classes traditionally most opposed to the monarchy: the middle-class intelligentsia and the urban working class. Land reform created large numbers of independent farmers, whose traditional loyalty was thereby weakened, while their attachment to the powerful and conservative Shia clergy, already critical of the Shah's reforms, remained constant and even increased. One commentator remarked, 'The White Revolution had been designed to pre-empt a Red Revolution. Instead, it paved the way for an Islamic Revolution.'

These were to be the longer-term consequences. Almost immediately on the initiation of the Revolution, a prominent Shia clergyman, Ayatollah Ruhollah Khomeini, led a protest movement declaring the Shah to be 'a wretched, miserable man' who had 'embarked on a path towards the destruction of Islam in Iran'. Riots followed and, in a 'battle of the narratives' that characterizes all revolutionary movements, the opposition claimed 15,000 dead from police fire, while anti-revolutionary sources asserted that only thirty-two had been killed. Khomeini was arrested, released, re-arrested and, in 1964, sent into exile, most of which he spent in Najaf, the Shia religious heart of Iraq, under the 'protection' of Saddam Hussein.

From 1973 onwards, the Shah had taken advantage of the huge increase in national wealth brought about by the rise in oil prices to drive forward ever more aggressively with his reform programme, fuelling, in doing so, the very forces who opposed it. In 1971, the year before my father's staff-visit to Tehran, the Shah had staged the 2,500th anniversary of the founding of the pre-Islamic Persian Empire at Persepolis. By all contemporary accounts it was a staggering display of conspicuous consumption which could have been deliberately designed to alienate, and then unite, the diverse coalition of conservative traditionalists and young liberals who opposed him. Similar opposition 'coalitions' would continue to manifest themselves across the Muslim Middle East, not least during the Arab Spring, routinely leading Western commentators and politicians to make over-simplistic assessments and to formulate policies based on ill-informed and naïve assumptions. Five years later, his hubris now inflated by ever vaster oil revenues, the Shah further angered pious Muslims by changing the first year of the Iranian solar calendar from the date of the Prophet Mohammed's journey from Mecca to Medina to that of the accession of the Achaemenid ruler, Cyrus the Great. While the Western world basked in the scorching summer of 1976 Anno Domini, and the Muslim world marked the year 1355, the Iranians now celebrated the Persian Imperial year of 2535.

The oil boom exaggerated the gaps between rich and poor and city and country, while with the restraining influence of the British gone, the Sunni Arab Kingdom of Saudi Arabia continued to confront the Shia empire of Iran across the Gulf. Both countries now had the wherewithal to conduct an impressive arms race, into which America and other Western countries threw themselves wholeheartedly, to compensate for their own economic weakness and to help their clients recycle their vast holdings of 'petro-dollars'. The Shah and his family were huge beneficiaries of this trend, as were the tens of thousands of foreign skilled workers who flooded into Iran to help deliver on the Shah's ambitions. High inflation, and then austerity, compounded the suffering of the poor and unskilled, particularly those uprooted from the land who made their way, in their hundreds of thousands, to the cities. Culturally conservative and religiously pious, many of them went on to form the core of the Islamic Revolution's demonstrators and 'martyrs'.

Alexis de Tocqueville had presciently noted in *The Ancien Régime and the Revolution* (1856) that 'an authoritarian regime is never more vulnerable than when it is attempting to liberalize itself'. The Shah of Iran's would prove to be no exception. Modernization, liberalism, secularism, greed and corruption, mass media, rising expectations and dashed hopes, seething jealousy, offended morals – all contributed to a volatile social and political churn. This, in its turn, was often concealed due to the brutal repression of SAVAK, the secret police, a very careful control of the regime's messaging and a wilful desire, particularly on the part of many Westerners, not to acknowledge the deep rifts in Iranian society and their potential for violence and revolution. Politicians, diplomats, businessmen, visitors, all spoke to people who looked or talked like them and who told them what they wanted to hear: that Iran was modernizing and reforming; that the economy was growing; that the opposition was fragmented and weak; that the influence of the clergy was moribund and declining. Few observers went to the rural areas or the urban slums, and fewer, even if they understood Farsi, listened to the sermons at Friday prayers that told of disenfranchisement, anger and religious disquiet. It was not to be the last time.

In January 1978, as I was contemplating the significance of Eleanor of Aquitaine's dalliance with her uncle, Raymond of Poitiers, and its influence on the outcome of the Second Crusade, the demonstrations against the Shah, which had begun in earnest in October 1977, intensified. In clashes in the city of Qom, a traditionally important Iranian religious centre, an unknown number of demonstrators were killed. Although in all Muslim cultures bodies are traditionally buried the day after death, the Shia custom is to hold memorial services for the dead forty days after their passing. Encouraged by Khomeini, who declared that 'the blood of martyrs must water the tree of Islam', new demonstrations broke out across the country on the forty-day anniversary. Government and 'Western' institutions and symbols were attacked, and the inevitable additional 'martyrs' were generated. Forty days later, another set of demonstrations took place, and again forty days after that. On each occasion, the paralysis and ineptitude of the government, and of the Shah, were revealed. Struggling to implement competing policies of leniency and repression, the security forces were ill-equipped, not least in training and equipment, to deal with these multiple challenges to Imperial authority. Despite this, a CIA analysis in June 1978 concluded that 'Iran is not in a revolutionary or even a pre-revolutionary situation'. On 19 August, when I was free-wheeling across the United States, arsonists barricaded the doors of the Rex Cinema in Abadan, burning to death the 422 people inside, the most costly modern terrorist attack, in human terms, prior to 9/11. Stirred up by clerics and agitators, the public blamed the Shah. Even when a subsequent investigation, held after the Shah's fall, revealed that the perpetrators were Islamist militants, the sole surviving arsonist was still executed for 'acting on the Shah's orders'.

Compounding the Shah's manifold problems was the attitude of the West. President Carter had publicly reprimanded him for human rights abuses and stopped the sale of even non-lethal defence equipment, which left the poor and conflicted army conscripts with the unenviable alternatives of using lethal force or ceding the streets to opponents of the regime. France had recently given asylum to Ayatollah Khomeini, who had been expelled from Najaf in a 'thank you' from Saddam Hussein to the Shah for a tip-off about a Soviet-backed coup. Inevitably, with asylum in France came the oxygen of publicity and much greater public exposure. Meanwhile, in his attempts to appease the opposition, the Shah threw some of his supporters to the wolves. The enemies of the regime scented blood, and in December, which coincided with the annual Ashura anniversary of the 680 AD martyrdom of Hussein, they mobilized nationwide protests of somewhere between six and nine million people. As would occur again during the Arab Spring, young people, women, secularists, reformers and socialists found themselves protesting alongside hard-line ayatollahs, clerics and social conservatives, who like their leader Khomeini were actively opposed to the liberal or reformist policies many of the fellow protesters were advocating. Western leaders were suitably confused: who should they be supporting, and what would the likely consequences be? Their vacillation further demoralized the Shah and his supporters.

At last, on 16 January 1979, mere weeks before I passed out of Sandhurst, the Shah capitulated and left Iran, never to return. His exile and subsequent death had elements of tragedy and farce, as he moved first to Egypt, then to Morocco, the Bahamas and Mexico. In November, much against President Carter's wishes, he arrived in the US for cancer treatment. From there it was on to Panama, then back to Egypt, where he died in early 1980. So passed the second, and last, of the rulers of the Pahlavi dynasty. His tomb is in Cairo's Al Rifa'i Mosque, where his father was buried and close to that of King Farouk, his former brother-in-law. The whole saga was deeply unedifying and gave little confidence, across the whole region, to those allies of the US who sought consistency in Western foreign policy.

Meanwhile, in February 1979 millions of Iranians had turned out to welcome Ayatollah Khomeini, who arrived at Tehran airport in an Air France plane. Already he had achieved an almost 'semi-divine' status, and almost every mark of the former monarchy had been torn down. Before his departure, the Shah had appointed a reformist prime minister, Shahpour Bakhtiar, but Khomeini now appointed one of his own, Mehdi Barzagan, commanding all Iranians to obey his nominee as a religious duty:

> Through the guardianship that I have from the Prophet, I hereby pronounce Barzagan as the ruler, and since I have appointed him, he must be obeyed. This is not an ordinary government. It is a government based on sharia. Opposing this government means opposing the sharia of Islam. Revolt against God's government is a revolt against God. Revolt against God is blasphemy.

In the clash between these rival premiers there could only be one winner. Bakhtiar fled to France, where he was assassinated in 1991. With institutions destroyed or dismantled, and security forces whose leadership was paralysed and whose rank-and-file were demoralized or had already deserted, Khomeini seized power and instituted the 'Islamic Revolution', which would have such consequences for the region, for Islam and for the wider world. Almost his first act was to denounce the Egyptian-Israeli Peace Agreement. From 1979 until 1983 Iran was in 'revolutionary crisis mode', akin to that of the

French Jacobins or the Russian Bolsheviks. Against the background of the American 'hostage crisis' and the eight-year war with Iraq, Khomeini and his loyalists implemented the '*wilayat al faqih*' or 'guardianship of the Islamic jurist'. This posited that Muslims, both Shia and Sunni, required Islamic 'guardianship' in the form of supervision by the leading Muslim jurists. Such rule was vital to protect Islam from deviation from traditional sharia law, and in doing so would eliminate poverty and injustice, stop the 'plundering' of Muslim lands by foreign 'non-believers', and stem the corrupting influences of 'the West'. To support this, Khomeini instituted the Revolutionary Council, the Revolutionary Guards with their vanguard, the Quds Force, Revolutionary Tribunals and Committees and the Islamic Republican Party. The combination was overwhelming for those who had championed the moderate, reformist elements of opposition to the Shah. Thousands were executed for 'political deviance', as so often in revolutionary periods, tens of thousands emigrated and subsequently hundreds of thousands would be sacrificed on the altar of 'defence of the revolution' in the war with Iraq.

Events that today would fill our television screens every minute, dominate the headlines and demand comment and assessment by an endless stream of pundits and 'experts', seemed, in 1979, far away and 'exotic', which in many ways, prior to mass travel, the internet and social media, they were. I was entering Sandhurst just as the Shah's problems were spinning out of his control, but our understanding of his fate was sporadic and disjointed. Our attention was taken up with parade-ground drill, the firing-range, weapon-cleaning, platoon attacks and trench-digging. We had lectures on Current Affairs, but our attention was far more on the Soviet Union and Northern Ireland than on the Middle East. After a final cold and wet exercise in Wales, a hundred or so officer cadets, including me, 'Passed Out' from Sandhurst and, via some specialized training, depending on which part of the Army we had chosen to join, were dispatched to our various regiments and battalions. I was fortunate to have been offered a commission in 15th/19th The King's Royal Hussars, an armoured reconnaissance regiment based in West Germany and charged with deterring Soviet aggression or, if we failed, dying bravely in resisting it. We were part of the British military contribution to NATO which Prime Minister Wilson had chosen to prioritize over British presence in the East. NATO's original role was succinctly summed up as being 'to keep the Russians out, the Americans in, and the Germans down'. It had been a highly successful construct. The lockdown of the Cold War confrontation in Europe meant that ideological competition had been 'exported' to other areas of the world. As a result, over the years the Cold War had gone 'hot' in Korea, Indo-China, Malaya, Central America and many other areas where decolonization created conditions for destabilization or state takeover by communist-backed forces. The Middle East and North Africa continued to offer a range of opportunities for Soviet ambition, and the 'godless' nature of communism could often usefully be forgotten by Arab states intent on opposing former colonial powers and forging new identities and political models in the region.

Largely unnoticed among this cacophony of geopolitical noise, Ali Bhutto, President of Pakistan, who had been deposed in a military coup in 1977, was executed in April 1979, and Saddam Hussein became President of Iraq in July of the same year. In November, as we were finishing our last regimental exercises and gunnery camps for the year, events in revolutionary Iran took another turn for the worse. Ostensibly in reaction to America allowing the Shah into the country for medical treatment, Iranian 'students' demonstrated outside the United States embassy in Tehran. Undoubtedly acting with Iranian government complicity, the 'students'then stormed the compound and took hostage fifty-two American diplomats and citizens. The crisis would turn into a 444-day stand-off, and it would colour American-Iranian relations to the present day. President Carter called the hostages 'victims of terrorism and anarchy', but the Iranians, certainly those supporting the Islamic Republic, saw it as vengeance for longstanding American interference in Iranian affairs. The whole issue became even more toxic in April 1980, some months after the Shah's death, with the failure of Operation Eagle's Claw. This over-complex plan to rescue the hostages, flawed from the outset by inter-service rivalry, tangled chains-of-command and equipment limitations, literally crashed and burned in the Iranian desert. The combination of the hostage crisis and a failed military operation undoubtedly contributed to Jimmy Carter comprehensively losing the presidential election later that year to Ronald Reagan. Many of America's present-day attitudes to Iran were forged in the course of these events and, with little understanding of or regard for Iranian pride in her long, glorious, pre- and post-Islamic imperial past, they continue to colour US policies towards the modern Islamic Republic

In a year of geopolitical surprises, the siege of the Grand Mosque in Mecca in November and December 1979 also failed to receive the coverage it deserved, although its consequences were again profound and long-lasting. In Islamic tradition, the turn of a century brings a *mujaddid*, a person who appears in order to help Islam cleanse itself of errors and corruption and restores it to its earlier purity. The first day of the Islamic year 1400 fell on 20 November 1979. Juhayman al-Otaibi was from one of the foremost families of Saudi Arabia, and his grandfather had ridden with Abdul Aziz al Saud and the *Ikhwan* in the early decades of the century. He now proclaimed that he was the *mujaddid* and that the House of Saud was illegitimate because it was corrupt, ostentatious and destroying Saudi culture through a policy of 'Westernization'. His group of 400–500 followers was well-motivated and well-trained, and many of them had been members of the Saudi Arabian National Guard, an organization distinct and separate from the conventional armed forces and supposedly bound by tradition, faith and family to the Al Sauds. King Khalid was on the throne in 1979, although he was out of the country at the time, and the Crown Prince was Fahd, who would be King at the time of the First Gulf War in 1990–1. He would be the sovereign who invited the 'infidel' Western Coalition Forces on to the soil of the 'land of the Two Holy Cities', exciting the dismay and hatred of the *takfiris*, including Osama bin Laden, and many other Muslims. The National Guard commander was Prince Abdullah, who would succeed Fahd as King in 2005. Abdullah, in turn, would be succeeded by his younger brother, Salman, in 2015. It was King Salman's son, Mohammed bin Salman (MBS), who would become the visionary, aggressive and somewhat reckless social and economic reformer of the present day.

After the insurgents had taken control of the Grand Mosque complex, the authorities had to get the *ulema* to issue a fatwa that permitted the use of force to evict them. With religious approval granted, the Saudi forces, assisted by counter-terrorism experts from Pakistan and France, the latter having supposedly undergone 'temporary conversion' to Islam, launched several assaults. On 4 December the Mosque was finally secured and the last insurgents were seized. Casualties were high, certainly much higher than reported, and the damage was widespread. The Grand Mosque was highly significant to Sunnis and Shia alike, and Ayatollah Khomeini lost no time in blaming the House of Saud, while attributing responsibility to the Americans and 'Zionists'. Across the Islamic world there were violent demonstrations, resulting in the burning of the US embassies in Pakistan and Libya. Al Otaibi and sixty-seven of his fellow rebels who survived the siege were beheaded for their crimes, their executions taking place in the squares of eight different Saudi cities.

Despite the insurrection being led by Islamists and Salafists, King Khalid, and his successor, King Fahd, chose to try and outflank them 'on the right' by giving the *ulema* and the conservatives even greater power and influence, in both foreign and domestic policy, over the next decade. The House of Saud seemed to believe that the solution to religious upheaval was simple: more religion. Pictures of women in newspapers were banned, then the female form was removed from television. Cinemas and music shops were closed down, and the school curriculum was adjusted to include more religious instruction, eliminating the study of any non-Islamic history. Gender segregation became stricter, and the religious police more aggressive. This shattering event had taken place not long after the triumph of the Islamic Revolution in Iran and Ayatollah Khomeini's declaration of an aspiration to speak for all Muslims in the *umma*. Saudi Arabia now needed something dramatic to re-establish its status in the Muslim world; it was seeking a national focus for its ever-increasing oil wealth and also now looking for a mighty cause to espouse. Such a cause was not long in coming.

On Christmas Eve 1979, as if all this had not already been enough for a single year, the news broke that the Soviet Union had intervened, in strength, in Afghanistan. It was a strategic move that took most Western intelligence agencies by surprise and confirmed, once again, the capacity of the Soviet Union to steal a march on the West when its attention was focused elsewhere. NATO had very robust warning and reporting systems in place in Europe in order to identify any Warsaw Pact attempt at invasion, but it was less responsive to similar actions in the Middle East or Central Asia. So began a series of events that would contribute to the collapse of the Soviet Union itself, lead to the formation of Al Qa'eda and the events of 9/11 and, in many ways, catalyse the Western interventions in the Middle East with whose consequences we are still wrestling today.

Modern Afghanistan is a landlocked country of some 33 million people. It is bordered by Iran to the west, Pakistan to the south and east, and China, and a collection of Muslim Central Asian republics, to the north. In 1979 its population was only 13 million. Ethnically split between Pashtuns, Tajiks and Uzbeks, it is a majority Sunni Muslim country but contains a significant Shia community, the Hazara. The Iranians have always exerted a strong political and cultural influence there. Its position astride the ancient Silk Routes connected it to the cultures of the Middle and Far East and made it one of the world's natural highways for trade, invasion and migration. Zoroastrian 'fire-worship', the state religion of Iran for over twelve centuries prior to the Islamic conquest, is believed to have originated here. Alexander the Great briefly occupied the region, and Buddhism flourished for several centuries. Some of its greatest monuments, including the Buddhas of Bamiyan, were destroyed by the Taliban in the early twenty-first century as representing a pre-Islamic culture that was 'an affront to the true religion'. Endlessly fought over, the political history of the modern state of Afghanistan really began with the Hotak and Durrani dynasties of the 1700s, following centuries of occupation by and division between Mongols, Hindus, Muslims, the khanates of Central Asia and the Persians. In the nineteenth century Afghanistan became a buffer state in the 'Great Game' between British India and the Russian Empire. The British, advancing across the Indian sub-continent, were confronted with how best to defend the Raj from a potential Russian invasion through Afghanistan. Did they sit back on the great river lines of the Indus and Sutlej? Did they advance to the border highlands and hold the mountain passes of Khyber and Khojak? Or did they adopt a 'forward policy' and dominate the Afghan capital of Kabul, 'ruling' through a client monarch? The British chose the latter, thereby initiating a lengthy period of complicated, sanguinary, expensive and frustrating relations with that country. Three wars and the imposition of an arbitrary border, the 'Durand Line', between Afghanistan and what would become Pakistan, left a legacy of distrust and suspicion, most particularly among the dominant Pashtun tribes. This history would colour local attitudes to Britain's re-engagement with the country after 9/11.

In 1919, King Amanullah Khan had declared Afghanistan a fully sovereign and independent country, taking his lead from the Versailles Conference and President Woodrow Wilson's principles of 'nationhood' and 'self-determination'. The King moved to end Afghanistan's traditional political isolation by establishing diplomatic relations with other states. He also undertook a lengthy overseas tour and attempted to introduce reforms intended to modernize the country. In a trend that would be replicated across the Muslim world, right up to the modern day, his 'modernizing' reforms, especially those relating to women and education, provoked a violent backlash from religious and tribal leaders and from socially conservative elements in society. After an abdication and two royal assassinations, Mohammed Zahir Khan succeeded to the throne in 1933, ruling until 1973, when his cousin and Prime Minister, Daoud Khan, overthrew him in a bloodless coup and made himself first President of the new Republic of Afghanistan.

During and after the Second World War, Daoud Khan established close links with the Soviet Union, and Afghanistan was a great beneficiary of Soviet aid. He initiated the vast Helmand Valley project, importing people from across Afghanistan and creating a complex web of family, clan and tribal politics that the British would have considerable problems understanding during their operations there half a century later. He also stirred up problems with Pakistan along the Durand Line, the boundary which may have made strategic sense to the British in the late nineteenth century but which had effectively drawn an international border straight through the Pashtun community. When Daoud Khan made himself President in 1973, the longstanding tension between Afghanistan and Pakistan escalated. The Pakistani Prime Minister, Ali Bhutto, began using the Inter-Services Intelligence Agency (ISI) to conduct a proxy war with Afghanistan, taking advantage of the lawless 'tribal areas' bordering Afghanistan to train and support such terrorist groups and leaders as the Haqqanis and Gulbuddin Hekmatyar, who opposed President Daoud Khan. These 'players', with their complex agendas and their ruthless modus operandi, would become a major thorn in the side of Western policy-makers and planners in the years after the fall of the Taliban in 2001. President Daoud Khan, having initiated the confrontation with Pakistan, now began to worry about increasing Soviet interference in his country via their influence in the People's Democratic Party of Afghanistan (PDPA). Seeking to lessen Soviet influence, and balance Pakistani enmity, he turned to Egypt, Saudi Arabia and India for assistance. However, in April 1978, a PDPA-inspired coup, led by Mohammed Taraki and Haffizullah Amin, probably supported by the Soviets and Ali Bhutto of Pakistan, overthrew the President. Daoud Khan and almost all of his family were killed. Only in 2008 were the bodies discovered, in two mass graves, and Daoud Khan himself was given a state funeral in March 2009 in Kabul.

The plotters did not exactly thrive. Their subsequent draconian rule led to the execution of around 30,000 political prisoners and open revolt across much of the country. Overthrown in a military coup himself, Ali Bhutto was hanged in April 1979. Mohammed Taraki was assassinated by Haffizullah Amin in September, and in his turn Amin was killed by Soviet special forces as the Fortieth Army used Christmas Eve to thunder through the Kalang Pass and occupy Kabul. A Soviet-organized government led by Babrak Kamal now took control in Afghanistan. As a 23-year-old subaltern stationed in West Germany, I may have missed some of these twists and turns, but although it was clear by the start of 1980 that the West was facing serious challenges, it soon became apparent that the Soviets were, too. The Red Army had assumed that local Afghan government forces loyal to Babrak Kamal would do most of the fighting against internal opposition. The same problems that dogged the later NATO International Security Assistance Force (ISAF) thwarted these Soviet 'heroic assumptions'. The Afghan forces were ill-trained and ill-equipped, they were poorly-motivated, their leadership was often weak and corrupt, and they increasingly relied on Soviet support, particularly airpower, if they were to stand and fight. While Babrak Kamal's government could hold on to the major population centres and the main highways and arterial routes, the opposition forces to all intents and purposes dominated eighty per cent of the country. A brutal cycle of atrocity and reprisal thrived in this environment. Afghan insurgents also began to receive massive amounts of aid and training in neighbouring Pakistan, and even in China, largely paid for by America and the Arab monarchies of the Gulf, particularly Saudi Arabia. The United States saw a great opportunity to pay the Soviets back for the debacle in Vietnam and their humiliation in Iran, while Saudi Arabia, scarred by the recent siege of the Grand Mosque, now saw a fertile market for their Wahhabi philosophy. They therefore accompanied their support for the war against the 'infidel' with generous funding for mosques, Islamic schools, *madrassas* and imams, in both Pakistan and Afghanistan. The West saw the conflict primarily through the ideological prism of the Cold War and the opposing ideals of liberal democracy and communism. The mujahideen, the 'holy warriors', saw it as a religious confrontation, in which they could accept the help of the Western 'infidel', who at least were 'people of the book', in order to defeat the godless Soviets and their compromising, heretical, secular Afghan supporters. When they had achieved that victory they intended to build on it to galvanize the *umma* to take up with them the eternal Islamic struggle, turning on their 'temporary' Western supporters.

In Europe and America we watched with fascination and awe as 'Johnny Pathan', of imperial notoriety, took the military technology of the West and combined it with the fanaticism of his tribe and religion to humble the great Soviet Empire. We cheered at footage of Russian helicopters, hit by CIA-supplied Stinger missiles, exploding and falling from the skies; we winced as we read of the savagery exhibited by the combatants; and we shuddered at the scale of human misery that was stacking up on both sides of the increasingly brutal struggle. What we did not do, as became increasingly clear in the following decades, was make any provision to build on ultimate success against the Soviets by investing a minute proportion of our military expenditure in Afghanistan's social and economic development. Nor did we fully understand the resonance that the 'Afghan victory' against the Soviets and their 'clients' would have across the whole Islamic world, or that those who had gone to fight alongside the indigenous Afghan insurgents would now seek to return to their own countries inspired, radicalized and looking for further 'Islamic' triumphs. The sheer scale of this new challenge would soon be firmly brought to our attention.

Chapter 11

Lending Style to Vulgar Brawls

Global chaos has got to be pretty extreme to dampen the enthusiasms of youth, and that applied in spades to the young officers of the 15th/19th Hussars in 1980. Age does bring with it rose-tinted spectacles, but those early days in the Army were extraordinarily satisfying and enjoyable, both personally and professionally. The Officers' Mess was full of like-minded souls: enthusiastic, positive, occasionally reckless, always humorous and morally and physically courageous. Our soldiers, mostly Geordies, were a delight and privilege to serve with and to command. The military, particularly the officer corps, was not the place for dull introverts, however talented they may be in other fields. It required self-confidence, which had to be based on professional competence, an outgoing nature, a sense of humour that could be sustained in adversity and a degree of showmanship. It attracted aggressive, risk-taking young men, and a cavalry mess in the 1980s was not for the faint-hearted. It largely remained the preserve of the public schoolboy, with all the best and worst features of that type. A distinctly anti-intellectual attitude prevailed, although many individuals were highly intelligent, if not necessarily marked by academic distinction. The sophisticated, and sometimes not so sophisticated, practical joke was highly prized, and new officers were often faced with elaborately contrived situations, just bordering on the marginally plausible, which tested their good manners and credulity, and which normally ended up with their being thrown in the fish pond. Drink was a routine part of life, as was smoking. In the absence of television, videos or DVDs, a great deal of whisky-fuelled, high-stakes card games were played in the evenings, and no one could go to bed until the senior 'liver-in' had departed, for fear of having his room 'bombed' or its contents defenestrated. The friendships forged in this crucible lasted us for life, and we took the trust, loyalty and laughter with us on exercise, on the sports field, on operations and to war. Girlfriends and wives, and in due course sons and daughters, were absorbed into this 'family', and as our relationships thrived over the decades, so the stories and anecdotes grew and were embellished in the telling.

Every troop, squadron or regiment is 'the best in the Army' to those who serve in it. That, certainly, is how it should feel, if an organization is 'cooking on gas'. War and close combat are at the core of the profession of arms, and everything we did was directed at giving the individual the moral and physical courage to hold his place in the line under fire when every other human instinct might say 'run'. Regimental colours, standards and guidons, battle honours and 'regimental days', honours and awards, military and sporting competitions, squadron dances and regimental balls, everything was designed to generate a shared sense of pride, self-confidence, purpose and endeavour. We expected the officer corps to respond to the call of 'God, Queen and Country', but our soldiers also needed that sense of trust and confidence in the organization, their equipment, their leaders, and above all each other, to underpin the more esoteric appeals to 'loyalty' and 'duty'. It was a robust time, when 'custard soldiers', those deemed to be 'upset by trifles', were disparaged, and tough senior NCOs would exhort the less aggressive officers to just tell the soldiers what to do! 'Good God, Sir, we are here to defend democracy, not practise it'! I loved the Army's combination of hard physical exertion, intellectual challenge and camaraderie. I embraced the 'team spirit', the 'band of brothers' philosophy that made the most tedious or terrifying activities such bonding experiences. It was by no means a 'caste system', indeed the mark of a good regiment and a good mess was precisely its openness and its welcoming hospitality, but it was delightfully 'tribal' in that thoroughly British way that is recognizable but which, at the same time, defies definition.

I had wanted to go to Constantinople, modern Istanbul, ever since my Crusade studies, and in the summer of 1980, between the spring work-up training and the major autumn manoeuvres, I persuaded David Rutherford-Jones, a fellow officer, to come 'rubble-stumbling', as he put it. The Istanbul of 1980 was very much like the city showcased in the James Bond film *From Russia with Love*. Having thoroughly explored the historic capital, which seemed to contain a very heavy and obvious military presence, we travelled to Cappadocia and back, then boarded a car ferry that bounced along the coast to Izmir and then to Bodrum, Marmaris, Fethiye and Antalya. These places are now huge and thriving tourist destinations, but in 1980 they were mostly sleepy fishing villages. I am not sure what we thought we were playing at, but we had brought our dinner jackets along for the ride, as any young cavalry officer would. On the first night at sea, we sent a bottle of champagne ahead to be chilled and, after a swift slug of Famous Grouse whisky, made our 'grand entrance' into the restaurant. The assembled diners, mostly attired in shorts and T-shirts, took in this extraordinary vision, fell silent and then started clapping. Slightly self-consciously, we took our seats. The waiter opened the champagne with a flourish saying, 'The captain did not know you were coming, otherwise he would have been here to greet you himself.' We never found out exactly who it was that the captain thought was on board. Back in the Mess some days later, another fellow officer grabbed me.

'You and David were in Turkey the other day. Have you seen that they have just had a military coup?'

That explained the soldiers across Istanbul, and it provoked in me an even greater interest in that country. Ten days later, Saddam Hussein invaded Iran, trying to take advantage of the turmoil of the Islamic revolution.

In the October of the same year, David R-J and I took about a dozen soldiers on an 'adventure training' trip to the Atlas Mountains of Morocco. Before we left Germany, I had learnt that Field Marshal Sir Claude Auchinleck, the famous 'Auk', former Middle East Commander-in-Chief in the Second World War, twice Commander-in-Chief in India and writer of a nice letter to my grandfather, had retired to Marrakech. I had written to him to ask if we could take a cup of tea off him, and David and I received a charming invitation back. We scrubbed up in the local campsite as best we could and went to visit the great man. Ninety years old, he could not have been more welcoming. As we swapped notes regarding the finer points of soldiering, I asked him what branch of the Indian Army he had joined.

'I was in a Punjab infantry battalion', he said.

'David and I are in the 15th/19th Hussars', I stated proudly.

'Cavalry officers, eh?' he smiled. 'Good of you to let me talk to you.'

I still have a rather poor photo of the occasion, but I remember it vividly. The Field Marshal died only three months later, although I do not think that sad event and our visit were in any way connected.

In 2017, the Democracy Index deemed Morocco to be a 'hybrid regime', a definition which acknowledged the constitutional reforms initiated by King Mohammed VI in the wake of the Arab Spring of 2011. In 1980, Morocco was still very much an autocracy, although French influence and tourism had made it a very agreeable country to visit, and our expedition to the Atlas and the Jebel Toubkal was a great success, especially for our soldiers, most of whom were drawn from Newcastle and the mining villages of Northumberland. Known in Arabic as *Al Maghreb*, the place the sun sets, the Berber population of Morocco had converted to Islam early on in the Muslim expansion, and it was from Tangier that the conquest of Iberia was launched. The last of the Ummayads had fled here, after the Abbasids massacred the rest of the clan, and in due course two powerful Muslim dynasties arose, the Almoravids and the Almohads, the latter marked by the aggressively fundamentalist nature of their rule. When the Muslim rulers were finally expelled from Spain in 1492, this Arab-Berber kingdom managed to remain outside both the Christian orbit and the expansionist ambitions of the Ottoman Empire, and the disparate parts were eventually united in 1631 under the Alaouite dynasty, which has remained the ruling house of Morocco to the present day. France showed a keen interest in Morocco from 1830, largely because of its border with Algeria, which they had recently prised from the Ottomans, but also because of its Atlantic and Mediterranean coastlines. France established a controversial 'Protectorate', which she held on to throughout both World Wars, but in 1956, in the face of growing political resistance and rising violence, the Protectorate ended and the new Kingdom of Morocco was formed under its old ruling family. While there was always some degree of political tension, which had sometimes toppled over into violence, the country remained stable, even through the volatile period of the Arab Spring, and Mohammed VI cautiously and judiciously managed the political and economic reforms required to sustain this stability.

Loitering in RHQ some months after our return from the Atlas Mountains, the Adjutant called me in and asked if I would like to be run for the job of ADC to the Corps Commander, Lieutenant General Sir Nigel Bagnall, the senior officer in charge of all the British Army formations and units based in Germany. I leapt at the opportunity. Nigel Bagnall was probably the foremost soldier of his day. He thought deeply about his profession and was a devoted family man. He had intelligence, honesty and a level of professional integrity and standards that made him highly respected, and although he could be uncomfortable company for the 'less gifted', he was generous, kind and thoughtful. His close friends and colleagues admired him hugely, as did I. His first words to me in my initial interview were 'Why on earth would you want this job?' He had little time for what he saw as the 'flummery' of military service, loathed dressing up and often referred to the burden of 'having to put on my f–king jewellery'. Twice decorated for gallantry, he had had his first Military Cross sent to him in the post, and only his mother, determined to go to Buckingham Palace, had persuaded him to pick up the second in person. He later told me he had tried the same approach to his knighthood but, as he said, 'It was made very clear to me that better men than I had bent the knee to their monarch, and I had better do the same.'

Over the next fourteen months I carried out all the usual ADC functions of managing the General's diary and social calendar, accompanying him on those visits the Military Assistant felt were 'beneath him' and 'pushing around the small eats' at cocktail parties. But I was also privy to high-level political and military discussions and exposed to the type of prioritizations, trade-offs and compromises that were necessary in order to command and manage an organization as complex as 1st British Corps. Nigel Bagnall saw ADC appointments as not simply providing functions that made his own daily life easier, but as a vehicle for the professional development of young officers. So it was that I was privileged to sit at the back of conference rooms and offices while the brightest and best of that generation of senior and mid-ranking officers kicked around concepts and ideas, built them into exercise programmes and embarked on educating and training the Army to a new and higher professional standard. Nigel Bagnall was a great student of German armoured manoeuvre during the Second World War, and particularly of their operations on the Eastern Front, where smaller German units and formations had consistently defeated far larger Soviet forces. On the basis of this study, he sought to change the way the British Army, indeed NATO in general, thought about large-scale manoeuvre warfare in the face of superior Soviet numbers. He was later selected to be the Chief of the General Staff (CGS), professional head of the British Army, and was able to keep advancing his programme of Army-wide professional development. It was largely the Army that he shaped and led that was to serve us so well in the deserts of Iraq on Operation Desert Storm and later in the complexities of the Balkan conflicts. He should by rights have become CDS, but he and Margaret Thatcher had parted company over the issue of the British nuclear deterrent.

On 2 April 1982, while the British Army was still focused on the intellectual challenge of reshaping our military response to potential Soviet aggression, Argentina invaded and occupied the Falkland Islands. It was a desperate attempt by the Argentine junta of General Galtieri to shore up its faltering domestic support. The ensuing drama is a well-known story, which had significant consequences for British domestic politics, for Britain's place in the world and for the organization and management of Britain's armed forces. With the decisiveness that defined her premiership, Margaret Thatcher sanctioned the deployment of a naval Task Force to take back the

Islands and to restore British sovereignty. In a ten-week operation, full of calculated risk, daring and heroism, carried out against the backdrop of complex political and diplomatic manoeuvring, the Falkland Islands were retaken. The British press adopted a gung-ho attitude that was mercilessly parodied for years afterwards, with headlines like 'Stick it up your Junta', in response to Argentine diplomatic offers, and the more controversial 'Gotcha!', when HMS *Conqueror* sank the battleship *Belgrano*. There were other heart-stopping moments in the campaign, but with the retaking of Port Stanley a ceasefire was eventually declared on the morning of 14 June, and the Argentine commander surrendered to Major General Jeremy Moore later that day. It had been a Wellingtonian 'near-run thing', but what it did for the morale of the British nation, and of the Armed Forces, is difficult to overstate, even now. It genuinely seemed to signal a renaissance of British power, influence and reputation. That victory, the turnaround of the British economy and the palpable sense of direction and control that Margaret Thatcher exuded secured her election victory in 1983. On the back of that campaign, she forged an extraordinarily close relationship with President Reagan which was to bear remarkable geopolitical fruit in helping bring down the Soviet Union. Whatever people's views of her were and are, the significance of her achievements cannot be denied.

Back in the office, the Military Assistant often spoke about his time on Loan Service to the Sultan of Oman and his experiences in the Dhofar War of the early 1970s in the south of that country.

'You need to get some sand between your toes', he exhorted me, bringing back childhood memories of time in Aden, and feeding a sense of restlessness that had only been exacerbated by stories of derring-do from the recent Falklands campaign.

With the blessing and encouragement of Nigel Bagnall, I put my name into the system, knowing that such an opportunity might not come for several years yet. I went to see Major General John Waters, who I would work for some years later, during a NATO appointment. On my application form he wrote, 'Approved. This officer wants adventure and excitement. Exactly what we all joined the Army for.' It would indeed be a couple more years before I did 'get sand between my toes', but when I did, it was to be one of the most satisfying periods of my career, indeed of my life.

While these personal and career events were playing out, the situation in the Middle East had been taking further twists, feeding off old ethnic and confessional enmities and laying down new sources of fear and hatred. In the bloody Ottoman-Safavid wars of the sixteenth and seventeenth centuries there had always been conflict over control of the Shatt-al-Arab, a 200km stretch of water in Basra Province formed by the confluence of the Tigris and Euphrates rivers and discharging into the Persian Gulf. While the Safavids had held it for a while, the 1639 Treaty of Zuhab had given permanent control to the Ottomans, a status confirmed by subsequent wars and new treaties. After the First World War and the carving-up of the Ottoman Empire, the British managed to make the waterway bi-national by using the European *thalweg* principle, whereby the border was drawn in the middle of the navigable channel. In 1937, after the British mandate in Baghdad had run out, Iran and the newly-independent Iraq signed a treaty that seemed to have settled the dispute. The provisions of the Treaty favoured Iraq, but in 1969, as Iran became more powerful and militarily assertive, the Shah publicly abrogated it and challenged the Iraqis to respond, which they were unable to do. After the assassination of King Feisal II in 1958, Iraq had gone through a period of political turmoil, during which the Iraqi Ba'ath Party, an offshoot of the Syrian version, had risen to prominence in the establishment of the new republic. A key figure was Saddam Hussein, a political street thug from the Iraqi Sunni heartland town of Tikrit, also the birthplace of the great Saladin. In 1968 the Ba'athists took power in Baghdad and, ever conscious of the fractious nature of politics and society in Iraq, instituted a dual policy of widespread repression against any opposition among the Shia majority and countrywide social and economic reform. During this period many of the Shia politicians who would come to prominence after the 2003 invasion and occupation of Iraq took refuge in Iran, thereby incurring a 'debt of honour' to the Iranians, an obligation that would have to be repaid in time. In 1971, as the British departed the Gulf and the Iranians seized the Emirati islands, the Iraqi Ba'ath government broke off all diplomatic relations with Tehran, and the Iranians responded by becoming the main sponsors of those Iraqi Kurdish groups fighting for independence from Baghdad. This tit-for-tat confrontation was ended by the 1975 Algiers Agreement, whereby the Shah stopped supporting the Kurds, leaving them at the mercy of the Ba'athists and the increasingly powerful Saddam Hussein, but it left a simmering antagonism and mistrust between the two regional powers.

Saddam Hussein and many Iraqis – Sunnis, but also those secular and educated Shia who identified more closely with their citizenship and ethnicity than with their religion – had initially welcomed the upheaval in Iran and the overthrow of Mohammed Reza Shah in 1979. However, it soon became clear that Ayatollah Khomeini had wider ambitions than merely revolution in Iran, and that he intended to espouse a doctrine of pan-Islamism, reaching out to both Sunnis and Shia over the heads of the leaders of Arab republics and monarchies, across the Muslim world. This constituted a major challenge, not least to those who were propagating pan-Arabism and Arab nationalism. Khomeini called on Iraqis to overthrow the secular, impious Ba'athist government, but Saddam, although alarmed by Khomeini's aspiration to be the champion of Iraq's majority Shia population, continued to praise the Iranian Revolution and issued a call for 'mutual non-interference'. Khomeini rejected this olive branch and continued to call for Islamic revolution, including in Iraq. Through 1980 Saddam, President since the previous year, watched the political turmoil in Iran, including the apparent collapse of the Iranian armed forces, and his calculations changed. Like Saudi Arabia and Iran, Iraq had taken advantage of the steep rise in oil prices and invested heavily in the military since 1975. Saddam now saw a successful military campaign against an Iran in turmoil as potentially achieving several objectives: reversing the 1975 Algiers Agreement with regard to the Shatt-al-Arab; dealing with a regional rival and stamping out the pretensions of the Islamic revolution; seizing Khuzestan, which included some of Iran's richest oil fields and which had a largely Arab population; replacing Egypt, partly isolated as a result of the agreement with Israel, as the leader of the Arab world; and establishing Iraqi hegemony in the Gulf. One side-result of all this destabilizing activity in the region was the seizure of the Iranian Embassy in London, in May 1980, by Iranian Arabs from Khuzestan, later revealed to have been trained by the Iraqis. In the resulting siege, and the successful SAS assault, Margaret Thatcher usefully honed her 'Iron Lady' image. Anglo-Iranian wrangling over who should pay for the damage incurred went on until 1993, and the only surviving gunman was released from a British prison in 2008.

After several months of border skirmishing and political posturing, Iraq launched a full-scale invasion of Iran on 22 September 1980, attempting unsuccessfully to destroy the Iranian airforce. The ground invasion followed the next day, largely in an attempt to seize the Iranian side of the Shatt-al-Arab and take the significant oil towns of Abadan and Khorramshahr. In the north, the Iraqis established a strong defensive position around the Kurdish city of Sulemaniya in order to defend the important oil fields around Kirkuk. While the Iraqis did not face well-led or well-coordinated Iranian resistance, they were surprised at its strength and resilience. Early on, Khomeini had established the Iranian Revolutionary Guard Corps (IRGC), whose Qods Force was to become such an effective instrument of Iranian 'foreign policy' in later years. This organization, and the paramilitary *basij*, provided a mass of ideologically and nationally motivated manpower that fought alongside the regular Iranian armed forces and put 'backbone' into the fight, albeit at an horrendous cost in casualties. By 7 December, despite having taken Khorramshahr, the Iraqi strategic reserves had been depleted, and Saddam Hussein announced that Iraq was 'going on the defensive'. For the next eight months there would be stalemate, as the fighting evolved into Great War-style trench warfare, in which all manoeuvre was hampered by minefields, fortifications, waterways and mountains. Chemical weapons were used for the first time in the conflict, Iranian air attacks were made on the Iraqi Osirak nuclear reactor, later destroyed in 1981 by an Israeli airstrike, and Saddam initiated the 'Battle of the Cities' by launching Scud missiles at Tehran. In the meantime, the Iranians compensated for their lack of infantry heavy weapons by using 'human wave assaults' to try and swamp the Iraqi defences.

Having conducted several highly attritional operations, the Iranians did eventually retake Khorramshahr in May 1982, although Britain's, and much of the rest of the world's, attention was by now focused on the Falkland Islands. The month before, Iraq's rival Ba'athist regime in Syria, an Arab country but with close ties to Iran through the shared Shi'ism of the leadership, cut off the Iraqi pipeline to the Mediterranean, starving Iraq of the funds to finance the war. At this stage the Gulf monarchies, with no love of Saddam Hussein but fearing Iranian ambition and Shia fundamentalism even more, weighed in with large subsidies to keep Iraq in the fight. Iraq also began to receive aid from America, from some Western European countries and from the Soviet Union, who were engaged in their own fight with Islamists in Afghanistan. Ronald Reagan declared that 'the US could not allow Iraq to lose the war to Iran', although Henry Kissinger cynically remarked that 'it was a pity they could not both lose'. Reagan's inauguration present from Iran in January 1981 had been the release of the fifty-two American embassy hostages.

In June 1982, about a week after British victory in the Falklands War, Saddam sued for peace, but Khomeini proclaimed he would not halt Iranian operations until the Iraqi Ba'athist regime had fallen, and he told his generals to plan for the invasion of Iraq. As part of this ambition he supported the formation of an Iraqi 'government-in-exile' based around a number of prominent Iraqi Shia clerics and politicians, and he anticipated an uprising among the Shia and Kurdish populations of Iraq, in which hope he was only partly successful. At a cabinet meeting in Baghdad, the Minister of Health suggested Saddam might step down, temporarily, in order to facilitate a ceasefire. Having ascertained that no one else agreed with this suggestion, Saddam took the hapless Minister into the next room and shot him.

For the most part, Iraq would remain on the defensive for the next six years, unable to mass enough strength to mount any major operations, while Iran launched no fewer that seventy offensives, some of them the largest since the Second World War. On and off, much of the area around Basra, Al Amarah and the Arab marshlands became the scene of intense, bloody and indecisive combat. This was the area that the British would occupy between 2003 and 2009, and evidence of the scale and ferocity of this fighting remained very obvious. The Iranians also cut off Iraqi access to the Gulf, rendering Iraq effectively landlocked and requiring her to ship any oil out via Kuwait. In 1984, having absorbed multiple Iranian assaults, Saddam initiated the so-called 'Tanker War' by attacking the oil terminal and tankers at Kharg Island, hoping the Iranians might retaliate by closing the Straits of Hormuz, thereby inciting US intervention. In a sporadic campaign that lasted until 1987, the US eventually agreed to 're-flag' oil tankers in order to try and deter Iranian retaliation. In 1986, the Iranians at last took the Al Faw peninsula in Southern Iraq, having forced a crossing on the Shatt-al-Arab. Saddam's response was to attempt to counterbalance Iranian Shia religious fervour by emphasizing Iraqi nationalism and Arab ethnic identity, while he simultaneously increased the 'Islamization' of his words and behaviour. At the same time, he initiated the notorious *Al Anfal* campaign to crush the Kurds, with widespread use of chemical weapons. The war ground on, and Basra was largely destroyed, although it was not taken by the Iranians.

By 1987 Iran looked to be gaining the upper hand, but at great cost; the Iranians were becoming war-weary, while their economy was coming under increasing pressure. On 20 July, the UN Security Council passed Resolution 598, calling for an end to hostilities and a return to pre-war boundaries. In the meantime, it was Iraq who had re-equipped and re-armed, since it was able to replace lost equipment in a way that Iran, sanctioned or rejected by most of the world, could not. In early 1988 Saddam began a new 'war of the cities', raining down Scud missiles on many Iranian population centres. He also halted an Iranian assault on the water and power centres in the Kurdish region by massive use of chemical weapons, including on the Kurdish village of Halabja, and he retook the Al Faw in a well-executed operation, again using chemical weapons, which had by now become a regular feature of Iraqi tactics. At this stage, Hashemi

Rafsanjani, who later became very well-known on the international stage, was appointed Supreme Commander of the Iranian Armed Forces, setting up a joint central command to unify the IRGC, the *basij*, the regular forces and some Kurdish *peshmerga* allies. This had little effect on the fighting at the time, but it was significant for the future. In July 1988, with the threat of major chemical assault on Iranian cities, and an almost total lack of international support, which seemed to be confirmed when the USS *Vincennes* shot down Iran Flight 655 to muted international reaction, Rafsanjani persuaded Khomeini to accept UNSCR 598 exactly a year after it had been passed. A statement from Khomeini was read out on state radio: 'Happy are those who have departed through martyrdom. Happy are those who have lost their lives in this convoy of light. Unhappy am I that I still survive, and that I have drunk the poisoned chalice . . . ' The news was greeted with wild celebrations in Baghdad, and with sombre resignation in Tehran. Although greatly exaggerated casualty figures were bandied about, the conservative estimates were quite bad enough. Iraq was deemed to have lost 120,000–200,000 killed, 400,000 wounded and 70,000 taken prisoner, Iran up to 260,000 dead on the battlefield and countless others in the attacks on the cities. It therefore came as a complete shock to the West when, in August 1990, after all this bloodshed, loss and economic dislocation, and while still negotiating an end to hostilities with Iran, Saddam Hussein embarked on the invasion and occupation of Kuwait, with even loftier ambitions regarding Saudi Arabia after that.

On 3 June 1982, again while we had been preoccupied with the South Atlantic, the Israeli ambassador to Britain, Shlomo Argov, was shot and wounded in London. Although this hit had, in fact, been ordered by Iraqi intelligence, it was the excuse that the Israeli Prime Minister, Menachem Begin, and his Defence Minister, Ariel Sharon, a former hero of the Yom Kippur War, needed to launch an invasion of Lebanon, with the intention of rooting out the PLO. This organization had been founded in 1964, but its violent campaign against Israel was accelerated by the Six Day War. In the wake of the Israeli seizure of the West Bank in 1967 many Palestinian fighters had moved their bases into Jordan, from where they continued to attack Israel, while openly starting to call for the overthrow of the Jordanian Hashemite monarchy. After several terrorist incidents, including the hijacking and blowing up of civilian airliners at Dawson's Field and two assassination attempts on King Hussein, the Jordanian Armed Forces moved against them in a major set of violent confrontations collectively known as 'Black September', although the actions actually lasted from September

1970 to July 1971. At this stage King Hussein, now holding the upper hand, had permitted the PLO fighters to depart for Lebanon.

In Lebanon, the PLO, as they had done in Jordan, soon established a 'state-within-a state'. They used the country as a base for continuing strikes on Israel and to organize the highly-publicized attack on the Munich Olympics in 1972. Lebanon was a creation of France, as part of the post-First World War settlement, and designed to favour the Christian Maronite community, to the advantage of the French. The French had departed in 1946, and the demographic balance between Christians and Muslims and between Sunnis and Shias had been altered by birth-rate and migration. The PLO presence added to an already flammable mix, which included a large, and increasingly resented, Syrian military presence, positioned there by Hafez al Assad. A deeply unpleasant civil war between Sunni, Shia and Christian militias had already been rumbling on since 1975, inflamed by external sponsors, that routine hallmark of Middle East politics. In 1978 Israel had launched Operation Litani in order to establish a security zone in Southern Lebanon, in loose alliance with the Christian militias, who by now were engaged in their own fight with the PLO. This intervention had led to the insertion of the United Nations Interim Force in Lebanon (UNIFIL), still active today. In the intervening years, Israel strengthened its relationship with the Christians, in particular with the Maronite Phalange movement of Bashar Gemayel, who shared the Israelis' antagonism to the PLO.

On 6 June 1982, the Israelis launched Operation 'Peace for Galilee' with 60,000 soldiers and 800 tanks, supported by amphibious forces. By 14 June, the same day as the surrender of Port Stanley, the Israelis had cut the Damascus-Beirut highway, halting the arrival of any further Syrian reinforcements, achieved air superiority and surrounded Beirut. They maintained this siege of the city until August, when an international agreement led to the evacuation of the PLO leadership to Tunis and, with them, 14,000 PLO combatants. Others went elsewhere in the region, to continue the fight against Israel and, once again, to complicate the domestic politics of their hosts. An uneasy ceasefire was subsequently monitored by the Multinational Force in Lebanon (MNF), with troops drawn from America, France, Italy and the UK. The British contingent was formed around a squadron of the Queen's Dragoon Guards, who were based in the 'Tobacco Factory' in Beirut. While they were there, Bashar Gemayel was assassinated, and the Israelis 'facilitated' a Phalangist group to enter the refugee camps of Sabra and Shatila, resulting in the deaths of several hundred Palestinians and numbers of Shia Arabs. While the British troops were largely left in peace, the US embassy was bombed in April 1983, and in October of the same year, suicide bombers from a group called 'Islamic Jihad' hit the US Marine and the French paratrooper barracks, with a combined loss of over 300 lives. It was a worrying sign of what was to come. MNF withdrew soon afterwards, and the Israelis largely withdrew from the South in 1985. An intervention by the US in 1993, this time into Somalia, well captured in the film *Black Hawk Down*, would see a similar cycle of worthy optimism, confusion about the realities of tribal complexity, bloody retaliation by local militia groups and a damaging withdrawal. The MNF departure now left a security vacuum in Lebanon that would again be filled by the Syrians, and which would also lead to the establishment of the Shia-dominated Hezbollah ('Party of God'), who would come to completely dominate Southern Lebanon from 2000. Meanwhile, the Lebanese Civil War resumed its downward spiral of violence and atrocity, leading to the emigration of nearly one million Christians, most of whom would not return. It would come to a stuttering halt in 1990, having claimed around 120,000 lives. The only 'up-side' was that the memories of these dark times would act as a significant brake on violence in Lebanon during the bloody Syrian conflict that followed the Arab Spring, and would help to mitigate the potentially violent consequences of a large-scale refugee problem.

In the months before I was due to finish as ADC, I had been told that I was due to go to Australia on a six-month exchange posting. I was very excited by this prospect. Thanking the Adjutant for this news, I asked who his own replacement was to be. 'Matt Straker', was the answer. Matt was another good friend, a first-class soldier, a Special Forces officer and altogether a rather 'loose cannon' in the very finest traditions of the British Army. I had first met him in Cyprus on one of my University attachments, when he had managed to put a hire car into the top branches of a large tree, having lost traction on a bend.

'That's an interesting choice', I said, using the English euphemism for 'what the hell are you thinking of', and thereby sealing my own fate. 'But a good one', I continued, not quickly enough.

'You are right', said Robert Webb Bowen, 'the Colonel is just trying to keep Matt in the Army. You should be adjutant, and Matt should go to Australia.'

How true it is that 'no good turn ever goes unpunished'. I finished as ADC early in 1983 to go to the Junior Division of the Staff College, mandatory for all captains and vital for those going to take up appointments in regimental headquarters. The Commandant was Brigadier Arthur Gooch, whose dog, Mustapha, could often be relied upon to give a painfully honest critique of any speaker's presentation by pacing out into the middle of the lecture theatre and yawning in a rather ostentatious manner. It was also here that Charles Trevelyan, a small, blond, 'perfectly formed' officer from the Royal Scots Dragoon Guards, launched a memorable put-down. A strong believer in the old adage that the role of cavalry in modern warfare is 'to lend style to what would otherwise be a mere vulgar brawl', he was giving a talk on the armoured corps.

One officer, clearly irritated by his manner, stood up in question time and rather pointedly asked, 'Is it true that everybody in your regiment has a private income?'

'Oh come on, don't be so silly', replied Charles innocently. 'Only the officers.'

There was a split-second pause before the auditorium erupted with laughter. Charles had been the officer at Staff College who, having been complimented on his academic strengths by an earnest member of the Directing Staff, was then asked to identify his weaknesses. Charles, not known for his lack of self-confidence, had a stab at answering the question: 'Probably Ferraris . . . and Belgian chocolates'.

I soon found myself, once again, headed for the Channel ferry to return to Germany. I enjoyed being adjutant, responsible to the Commanding Officer for all the personnel issues of the Regiment, including postings, promotions, manning and discipline. It was a demanding appointment, but very satisfying. Peter Hervey, the Commanding Officer, was a delight to work for, possessing that combination of confidence, competence and good humour that always appeals to officers and soldiers alike. Once one of the squadron leaders rang me to say he could not find the Regimental Training Directive for that year. I drew this to the attention of the commanding officer. Leaning back in his chair, and taking a long drag on his cigarette, he said, 'Tell him it's more of the same.' He then paused, ' . . . only better'. That may have seemed appropriate at the time, and several years later when the world had been turned upside down, we would sorely miss some of the comforting certainties of the Cold War era.

Towards the middle of 1984, I was told there was a vacancy in the following year for an 'acting' major to command an armoured squadron in the Sultan of Oman's Armoured Regiment (SOAR). I had recently passed the exams required for the Army's Staff College, but my first shot at a place would not be until 1988. I had been confronted with finding a suitable appointment for the next three years, but I now knew exactly what I would do: get sand between my toes.

Chapter 12

Soldier in the Sand

Oman is in the Gulf Co-operation Council (GCC), but is not an altogether comfortable member of it. Founded in 1981, the GCC is an intergovernmental political and economic union. It contains all six Gulf monarchies, but Saudi Arabia is understandably the predominant member, and Saudi Wahhabism does not fit well with the moderate, tolerant Ibadi Islam of Oman, while the political activism of the UAE did not appeal to the late Sultan Qaboos. A 2011 Saudi proposal to transform the GCC into a 'Gulf Union', with tighter economic, political and military coordination, partly to counter increasing Iranian influence, was rejected by Oman. The Arab Spring, especially the sharply different attitudes to events in Egypt and Libya, with Saudi Arabia and the UAE on one side and Qatar on the other, has also made relationships within the GCC increasingly fractious, while in the 2017 'blockade' of Qatar, Oman stood firmly in the neutral camp, along with Kuwait. Saudi Arabia's increasingly long, messy and complex intervention in Yemen, Oman's westward neighbour, has further increased the pressure on regional relationships.

Oman is, in many ways, more an Indian Ocean state than a Gulf one (see Map 8). Like Yemen, its history and preoccupations are different from the other occupants of the Arabian Peninsula. Oman does have Bedouin tribesmen, and camels and deserts, but it also has ocean coastlines, a long seafaring history, a keen curiosity about the outside world, mountains ranging up to 10,000ft and a distinct, monsoonal micro-climate in the mountainous southern Dhofar region. Sinbad the Sailor was an Omani, from the port of Sohar on the Batinah coast, and it was Omani and Yemeni traders who took the religion of Islam east to the Indies, implanting it in the Malayan peninsula and Indonesian archipelago. Oman dominated the Swahili coast from Mombasa to Zanzibar for several centuries, with a separate capital in Dar-es-Salaam, and the Omanis also held the coastal areas of what is now the Pakistani province of Baluchistan, only relinquishing them in 1958. This knowledge of the outside world, and the military, diplomatic and commercial contacts and interactions that went with it, gave Omanis a very different view of the world from that of the pearl-fishers, pirates and camel-herders of much of the rest of the Arabian Peninsula, certainly prior to the collapse of the Ottomans and the discovery of oil.

Oman's close connection with Iran is both geographical and historical; from Sohar to Sur, and down to Ras al Hadd, the country was dominated by the Parthians, and later the Sassanians, until the advent of Islam, brought to the country by an expedition sent by the Prophet Mohammed. Oman eventually adopted a branch of Islam called Ibadism, named after its founder, Abdullah bin Ibadh al Tamimi. Although Ibadism developed from the *Kharijite* breakaway movement, it rejected the *Kharijite* belief that those Muslims holding differing viewpoints were automatically 'apostates' and 'heretics' and therefore subject to jihad. Given philosophical depth in Basra, Ibadism spread widely, but its alienation from the dominant Sunni and Shia sects put it under pressure and it consolidated only in Oman, although small pockets can also be found in the Maghreb countries of Algeria, Libya and Tunisia. The differences between Ibadism and the mainstream Muslim sects may seem esoteric to modern Western eyes, but they are significant and, combined with Oman's exposure to the wider world over the centuries, have generated a society that is both more tolerant and more pragmatic than those of her larger neighbours to the north and east. Sultan Qaboos, the autocratic but enlightened ruler since 1970, forbade any Omani to join the mujahideen in Afghanistan during the fight against Soviet occupation. He was convinced, rightly as we have seen, that those that did pursue jihad in Central Asia would return to their home countries radicalized and dangerous. No Omani has subsequently been identified on the contemporary battlegrounds of Afghanistan, Iraq and Syria, or serving in Al Qa'eda, IS or similar *takfiri* groups.

When the Portuguese broke into the Indian Ocean, after Vasco da Gama's successful voyage around the Cape of Good Hope in 1498, they occupied the Omani coastal capital of Muscat for nearly 150 years, and their forts of Jalali and Mulali still stand watch over the harbour. During the struggle for supremacy between the Portuguese and the Ottomans, the Omanis regained their independence and established a powerful regional empire. A last spasm of Persian ambition in Oman was defeated in 1749, when the Al Said dynasty, which rules Oman to this day, came to power. In this period the Sultan moved to Zanzibar, which was then, and for a long time afterwards, a major centre of the slave trade and a generator of great wealth. Through the nineteenth century, the Sultan of Oman and the British routinely clashed as the British sought to suppress this trade. In the same period, Britain was consolidating its position in the Gulf with the establishment of the 'Perpetual Truce' and the Trucial States. In 1913, tension within Oman led to a split in the country, between the Imam in the interior and the Sultan in Muscat. Brokered by the British in 1920, the Treaty of Seeb formalized this position, although leaving the Sultan with responsibility for external affairs. This situation pertained throughout both World Wars, and it was only to be challenged over the issue of exploratory oil-drilling concessions at a desert location called Fahud. The Sultan, by then Said bin Timur, claimed primacy as negotiation with foreigners was involved, but the Imam claimed it as an internal matter since the oil finds were on his territory. Conflict ensued, and in 1955 the Sultan sent troops to occupy the centres of population in the interior. They did not have a happy time of it, but in 1957 the Sultan was able to call on the assistance of the British Army and the RAF to suppress the rebellion. At this stage the Imam and his forces retreated to the inaccessible Jebel Akhdar mountains, but a daring operation in early 1959 by the SAS, whose exploits both here and in the Malaya Emergency reprieved them from possible disbandment, secured the Jebel, although the rebel leadership escaped to Saudi Arabia, where they continued to promote their cause until the 1970s. One of the SAS officers in that operation was Johnnie Watts, who was the senior officer in the Sultan's Armed Forces (SAF) when I went to Oman in 1985.

In 1965, just after oil was first discovered, another rebellion began, this time in Dhofar, inspired by the separatist tendencies of the south but also by the pan-Arab rhetoric of Nasser and incitement from the NLF and FLOSY in neighbouring Yemen. The province of Dhofar consists of an intermittent, narrow, fertile coastal plain, on which stands the provincial capital, Salalah. Behind are the rugged hills of the Jebel Dhofar. From June to September each year, the Jebel receives the moisture-laden winds of the *Khareef* monsoon and is shrouded in cloud. As a result, it is heavily vegetated and for much of the year is lush and green. In modern times, its local climate, in such dramatic contrast to the rest of the Arabian Peninsula, has made the Dhofar a major tourist destination, including for many visitors from neighbouring Gulf states escaping from the stifling heat and coastal humidity of an Arabian summer. North of the Jebel, the hills slope down, via rough *wadis* and cliffs, to extensive gravel plains that eventually feed into the desert sand seas of the Rub al Khali, the Empty Quarter, and the border with Saudi Arabia. In 1965 the Dhofar was a private fiefdom of the Sultan.

The British had had a close relationship with Oman since the nineteenth century, and since the Jebel Akhdar War significant numbers of British Army officers and NCOs had served on secondment with the Sultan's Armed Forces. It was exciting soldiering, for those who could put up with the austere conditions, but also frustrating, for Sultan Said bin Timur would not invest in his small military, for fear of an internal coup, and was therefore ill-prepared and ill-equipped to face a rebellion in the south. The Dhofar Liberation Front (DLF) first mounted small hit-and-run raids but they were significantly emboldened in 1967 by Arab failure in the Six Day War, which radicalized opinion throughout the Arab world, and by the withdrawal of the British from Aden and South Yemen. At this stage the Chinese began to send arms and aid to the rebels. In 1968 the DLF had become the People's Front for the Liberation of the Arabian Gulf (PFLOAG), with much wider regional ambitions, although the splits in the organization between the ideologues and those fighting for local autonomy would prove to be a critical weakness when the new Sultan adopted a much more sophisticated approach to countering the insurgency. The rebels were universally referred to as the *adoo* ('enemy'), and that is how I always heard former British officers in SAF talk about them. By 1970 the *adoo* largely controlled the whole Jebel, using terror tactics to break up the traditional Dhofari tribal structures. In that year, on 23 July, Sultan Said's son, Qaboos, overthrew his father, with the knowledge and complicity of the British government, who could see that there was no hope of reversing the PFLOAG successes without a root-and-branch transformation of Omani society. Only Qaboos, trained at Sandhurst while also receiving a British education in many other aspects of government and administration, offered this opportunity. The coup was almost bloodless, although Sultan Said managed to shoot himself in the foot, when he mishandled a machine gun. The new Sultan packed his father off to spend the rest of his days in the Dorchester Hotel in London, while unveiling a new 'five-point plan' for Dhofar, the result of much thought and application, undertaken as he had watched the unravelling of his birthright. There would be a general amnesty for all those who had opposed his father, and a vigorous military campaign against those who rejected it, enabled by significant new investment in the SAF. The Dhofar would now be fully incorporated into Oman. Indeed, Sultan Qaboos's mother was a Dhofari, which undoubtedly helped him to gain the loyalty of many of the locals. He would initiate an extensive nationwide programme of development, focussing on healthcare and education, and beginning with such simple initiatives as well-digging

Above: 1917 – My grandmother (seated second left) with staff of St George's Hospital, Malta.

Below: 1944 – My grandfather (in white suit) inspecting Cochin harbour with Field Marshal Sir Claude Auchinleck.

Above left: 1916 – My grandmother in the Royal Army Medical Corps. No badges of rank.

Above right: 1929 – My mother with her amah in Cochin.

Left: 1951 – My mother's publicity photo for the West End stage.

Above left: 1951 – My father as a newly commissioned officer in the Royal Air Force Regiment.

Above right: 1953 – My parents' wedding day at Brompton Oratory, London.

Right: 1959 – Crater, Aden. My mother holding my brother Mark, while I stand beside her. Behind us is the Armed Aden Police barracks, scene of the 1967 mutiny.

1956 – Colonel Gamal Abdel Nasser, Egyptian leader and champion of pan-Arabism.

1960 – My father (left) commanding an Honour Guard for Lord Louis Mountbatten.

1960 – My grandmother (third left), my mother (centre) and my father (second right) enjoying life in Aden.

1960 – My father's Blackburn Beverley, of 84 Squadron RAF, offloading supplies at Makerios, Aden.

1967 – British troops in Aden during the campaign against NLF and FLOSY.

1971 – Abu Dhabi at the time of the British withdrawal from East of Suez.

Abu Dhabi today.

1973 – Regular Commissions Board, Westbury. 'Come in Number 34, your time is up'.

1979 – 'Young blades' in the 15th/19th Hussars. Self (left) and David A'hern.

1979 – Soviet troops on the road to Kabul, Afghanistan.

Top left: 1977 – My father, as Station Commander, receives the Prince of Wales at RAF Northolt.

Top right: 1980 – Tea with Field Marshal Sir Claude Auchinleck in Marrakesh.

Above: 1982 – (L to R) Justin, our father, Mark, self, at Justin's Oxford graduation.

Right: 1985 – Sultan Qaboos al Said, ruler of Oman since 1970, at a Sultan's Armed Forces parade.

1986 – E Squadron, Sultan of Oman's Armoured Regiment, on Safrat ad Dawh ranges. My 2iC, Abdullah al Ghallani, is on the left.

1986 – 'Troop trialling' the new Land Cruisers in the Wahiba Sands, Oman.

1986 – The joys of command. E Squadron soldiers in the Wadi Muaydin, Jebel Akhdar.

Above left: 1990/91 – Major General Rupert Smith, GOC 1ˢᵗ (UK) Armoured Division in the Gulf War and later GOC Northern Ireland.

Above right: 1990/91 – General Norman Schwarzkopf ('Stormin' Norman'), Commander of the US-led Coalition, and General Colin Powell, Chairman of the Combined Joint Chiefs of Staff. Two veterans of the Vietnam War.

1991 – The 'Highway of Death', images of which did much to influence the decision to suspend combat operations.

Lieutenant General Peter de la Billière (centre) and Prince Khalid bin Sultan of Saudi Arabia, Deputy Coalition Commander (right).

1987 – With Jamie Mackeness (left) in the Karakoram, Pakistan.

2000 – A short ride in the Hindu Kush. Richard Holmes (second left), self, Evelyn Webb-Carter (front right).

2000 – The Cavalry and Guards Club on tour. Captain Charles Elwell (late Grenadier Guards) and Colonel Simon Mayall (late QDG) entertain the locals in the Hindu Kush.

2001 – President Saddam Hussein of Iraq and Chairman Yasser Arafat of the Palestine Liberation Organisation, Baghdad.

Above left: 2003 – The fall of Saddam Hussein's statue in Firdos Square, Baghdad.

Above right: 2003 – Saddam Hussein after his capture.

2006 – Al Faw Palace, near Baghdad International Airport, headquarters of MNC-I. My 'villa' is at top left.

Initial military success for the Coalition soon turned into long, complex and violent counter-terrorism and counter-insurgency campaigns.

2006 – With Lieutenant General Peter Chiarelli (right), Commanding General MNC-I.

Right: 2006 – Briefing Iraqi Prime Minister Nouri al Maliki (centre) through my interpreter Nico (left).

Below: 2007 – Planning another phase of the Baghdad Security Plan with Brigadier Joe Anderson (left), later Commander ISAF, Afghanistan, and Major General Reeadh (centre) of the Iraqi Security Forces.

2008 – An uneasy partnership. President George W. Bush (centre) with President Musharraf of Pakistan (left) and President Hamid Karzai of Afghanistan.

Above left: 2010 – General David Petraeus welcomes Ed Miliband, leader of the British Labour Party, to HQ ISAF.

Above right: 2011 – In discussion with Major General Hamad Ali al Attiyah of Qatar about the situation in Libya and Syria.

Below: 2012 – An audience with King Abdullah II of Jordan (right). Peter Millett, HM Ambassador, is seated left.

2014 – Caliph Ibrahim, Abu Bakr al Baghdadi, announces the formation of Islamic State from the *minbar* in Mosul's Grand Mosque.

2014 – Islamic State fighters pose for a propaganda video.

2015 – Presenting a certificate to the 1,000th *peshmerga* soldier to be trained by the British Army.

2019 – With General Ahmed Harith of Oman, marking the 40th anniversary of our commissioning from the Royal Military Academy Sandhurst.

2019 – The opening of 'Mayall Square' in the Royal Navy's Support Facility in Bahrain.

2019 – With Prince Charles, Colonel in Chief of the Queen's Dragoon Guards, at Cavalry Memorial. General Sir Richard Shirreff in the centre.

in the villages and mobile first-aid clinics. He also launched a major diplomatic effort to gain global support, conscious that both the Soviet Union and China would seek to thwart his plans.

Within hours of the coup, British SAS teams were on the ground, and with them, Royal Engineer detachments. Edward Heath, who had hoped to reverse Wilson's decision to withdraw from East of Suez, saw support of Sultan Qaboos as a way of continuing to show British engagement in the region. The initial phases of the operations to counter the insurgency revolved around convincing the local Dhofaris that their interests were best served by supporting the new Sultan, and therefore focused on enhancing the civil administration and providing medical and veterinary assistance, while gathering and collating intelligence. The command structure was overhauled, and a sophisticated information operations campaign was initiated that sought to counter communist propaganda by appealing to Islamic belief and traditional tribal values and customs. There was a satisfying response to the Sultan's amnesty offer, and many former rebels were incorporated into SAF as *firqat*, irregular units. They were highly effective in their own way, but were a source of despair to many British soldiers due to their cavalier approach to 'good military discipline'. As SAF grew, so did the numbers of British officers and soldiers in the force. Many of these came on 'loan service', which did what it said on the tin, and it had been one of those officers who had exhorted me 'to get some sand between my toes'. Those of us fortunate enough to serve in SAF in the later years were rather envious of those who had done the 'hard yards' in the Dhofar War, but we all found our own satisfaction in serving in the ranks of the Sultan's military. In addition to the 'loan service' personnel, there were a number of other officers and senior ranks who had served in the British Army and Royal Marines, subsequently left regular service and now served 'on contract', hired directly by the Sultan. Several of these were still around in my time, and they could always be relied upon to 'pull up a sandbag' and regale you with tales of Operation Jaguar, the Hornbeam Line, the Shershitti Caves and the fight for Sarfait.

The British land contingent supporting the 10,000 SAF soldiers, and the growing numbers of *firqat*, was about 500, with a further 500 from the Royal Air Force. There was also a contingent of nearly 4,000 from the Imperial Iranian Armed Forces, who took responsibility for guarding some of the major arterial routes and military bases, as well as a small contingent from Jordan. The former contribution reflected the longstanding relationship between Iran and Oman, but was also part of the Shah's wider ambition for the Iranians to replace the British as the traditional 'policemen of the Gulf', although many Sunni Arabs in the region rejected any Persian assumption of this role. The Dhofar War wound on until October 1975, when a final offensive succeeded in cutting the *adoo* off from their supply bases, at which stage most rebels either surrendered or sought sanctuary in Yemen. It had been a highly successful campaign, and an important one, given the Soviet and Chinese ambition to capitalize on the British withdrawal from the Gulf. It took the lessons of 'hearts and minds' from the equally successful Malaya campaign and applied them in a sophisticated and well-coordinated manner that decisively split the opposition, thereby robbing them of their support bases and recruitment pools.

Key to success was the imagination, drive and honesty of the new Sultan, who offered a vision of the future that did much to make the military successes possible and then politically sustainable. In my own career, I saw all too often, to reverse Clausewitz's dictum, that 'politics is the continuation of war by other means', and that if a campaign is conducted with viable and appealing political objectives, it minimizes the need to fight and can make the military 'line of operation' easier and much more effective. Thus military success can deliver a lasting and durable political outcome, which is what the objective of war should be. Despite its success, which Sultan Qaboos continued to build on in the following decades, the Dhofar War was not well known in Britain. Partly this was because the British Government chose not to publicize it, partly because it was a campaign fought many thousands of miles away from home and far from the intrusion of the media, and partly because back home the 'Troubles' in Northern Ireland captured much of the attention of the British government and public.

Much had changed in Oman between the Sultan's accession in 1970 and the time I touched down at Seeb Airport on 6 June 1985, but one thing that hadn't was the heat of the sun in midsummer, even early in the morning, and with it the effect of 90° humidity on the carefully starched collar of a Jermyn Street shirt. By the time I had descended the steps of Gulf Air Flight 007 I was already feeling rather uncomfortable, but nothing could suppress my excitement at being back in Arabia. With those happy memories of past times in Aden, I felt instantly at home as I sat down for breakfast in the officers' mess on that first morning. I had spent the last three months learning Arabic at the Defence School of Languages in Beaconsfield. The 'colloquial Arabic' course at Beaconsfield was intensive, and rightly so. We had language tests every morning, and each evening we were given between thirty and fifty new words to learn. By the time we left we had a working vocabulary of nearly 1,500 words, the capacity to string together several useful, if stylized, sentences, and the ability to conduct basic, if stilted, conversations. I was on my way to command E Squadron of the Sultan of Oman's Armoured Regiment (SOAR), and the majority of the squadron could speak no English. During the Dhofar War, Omani units had had up to twenty or more British officers and senior ranks in each regiment. While this had continued for some years afterwards, the Sultan had, quite understandably, begun a measured programme of 'Omanization', in which the Omani officer cadre had grown incrementally and British 'loan service' and 'contract' numbers had steadily declined.

By 1985, most Omani infantry units had only a single British officer, largely responsible for the training programme. In the armoured, artillery and engineer regiments, British numbers remained thicker on the ground, because of the technical demands of those elements. SOAR had a British commanding officer, Richard Kinsella-Bevan, second-in-command, adjutant, operations officer and signals officer, as well as the Regimental Sergeant Major. It had five 'sabre squadrons'. Three of these were equipped with British armoured reconnaissance vehicles, familiar to those of us from Germany, and were commanded by Omanis, with British deputies. The other two, one fielding rather old American M60 tanks, and E Squadron with the British Chieftain tank, had British commanders, Howard Elston, an old friend, and myself. The Quartermaster's department was also still very anglicized. Captain Mick Harding had formerly been in the Household Cavalry until, as he told me later, 'I went around the corner for rock salmon and chips and decided not to come back.' He was known, affectionately, by the Omanis, as *Abu lihya* ('father of the beard') for his impressive facial hair which, combined with a formidable girth, made him resemble Santa Claus. Most Omani men, like most Muslim men, sport some form of beard in emulation of the Prophet. The longer the beard, the greater the piety. Omanis did not understand the British penchant for being clean-shaven, even when we explained that we did so because it was against British Army regulations to grow anything but a moustache, unless one was a pioneer sergeant in an infantry battalion which, self-evidently, none of us were. Mick Harding loved his bon mots. Once, when we had a visit from the People's Liberation Army of China, he theatrically stormed into a briefing.

'This delegation cannot go on to the tank park', he declared.

'Why not?' said the Commanding Officer, falling neatly into Mick's carefully laid trap.

'Because we don't want any Chinks in our armour', he said, to huge applause from the British officers, total bemusement from our Omani colleagues and a crinkly smile from the CO.

While loan service officers and senior ranks were mostly career soldiers who sought the excitement and 'romance' of Beau Geste-style soldiering, the 'contract' personnel came in a greater variety of shapes and sizes. Sometimes unkindly characterized as being there because of 'debt, drink or divorce', many were also outstanding soldiers who had chafed against the restraints of regular soldiering or civilian life. A number had served in the Dhofar war and stayed on, attracted by the pay and the lifestyle. Many just kept their heads down, did their work and saved money. Some did have personal issues which they sublimated in a routine of lonely desert and *jebel* deployments, particularly in the south, followed by hedonistic periods of 'leave'. One, a great friend from Sandhurst, was in Oman to enable himself to go to business school and get an MBA. Another was a foremost scholar of Omani tribal culture and a great Arabic linguist. A third had already served in the Royal Green Jackets and the French Foreign Legion. Another officer, not typical, thank goodness, came back in from the desert and, walking into a fellow officer's room, pulled out a pistol saying, 'This will give you something to talk about in the Mess' and shot himself.

There were also my delightful fellow Omani officers, courteous to a fault and wholly welcoming. Among them was Ahmed Harith al Nabhani, who would go on to be Chief of Staff of the Sultan's Armed Forces (COSSAF) and who was already identified as 'the coming man'. His uncle had been killed in an RAF bombing raid during the Jebel Akhdar War but, remarkably, he and his family did not seem to bear a grudge against the British. In 1971, aged fifteen, he had descended from the Jebel to join the SAF and to fight in Dhofar. Posted to the Armoured Car Squadron, Robin Searby, who would later return as the Senior British Loan Service Officer in Oman, spotted his potential, and when the war ended, recommended him to the young Sultan as a man who should go to Sandhurst. Ahmed spent a year with a family in Broadstairs learning English and, unbeknownst to each other, he and I had both passed out from the Royal Military Academy in early 1979, a 40th anniversary we celebrated together at the Academy in 2019. He would go on to command the Armoured Regiment, before becoming the Army Commander in 2003. In 2007, when his predecessor was killed in an unfortunate road accident, the Sultan appointed him as COSSAF. It was quite a journey for the young man who had clambered down the Wadi al Muadin nearly forty years earlier to answer the Sultan's call to arms, but it was, in many ways, typical of the way Oman was developing under the guidance of Sultan Qaboos.

After that first breakfast I went, by way of a charming oval swimming pool, in and around which we all spent a good deal of time, to my air-conditioned bungalow. It was like a little tropical oasis, built under a jacaranda tree and surrounded by bougainvillea. I was given the keys to my white Toyota Corolla, and then went to get 'kitted out' in Omani uniform, for although we were British officers, we were serving the Sultan and we wore the uniform of his Army: stone-coloured barrack dress and brown suede boots for the office; green tank coveralls and green suede boots for exercise and gunnery camp; the green beret of the armoured regiment. We were also given the prized *jaish* (Army) *shemargh*, that multi-purpose black and green cotton square designed to be wrapped tightly around your head, but also good for use as a towel, a sun-shade, a face veil and a pillow. The more fashion-conscious officers customized their *shemarghs* with tassels. Every British officer was strongly advised not to be seen or photographed in a *shemargh* before they had got the hang of tying and wearing it properly, for fear of exciting ridicule.

The next day, for the first time, I stood on the tank park watching E Squadron form up under Sergeant Major Ali Nasser. I had been up since 5.00 am, as we were every working day, and the sun was still low on the horizon, although it had already cleared away any slight coolness from the night before. He and I had met the previous evening to discuss personalities in the squadron, and the training programme. He had been in the *jaish* since Dhofar, had been on several courses in the UK and spoke reasonable English. Like almost every Omani I met, he was hugely likeable, and we managed to communicate quite well. As I stood off to the side, he called the squadron to attention.

'*Sareea Khamsa . . . taheer!*' ('E Squadron . . . attention!')

In good British drill style, a hundred left feet crashed onto the tarmac in unison. Ali Nasser spun to face me. I marched on to the parade ground, halted and we exchanged salutes, and smiles.

'*Sareea Khamsa. Kull a wahid majoodeen, wa jihazeen, seedee.*' ('The squadron is all present and correct, Sir.')

With my fourteen tanks as backdrop, I took over the parade and, in carefully rehearsed Arabic, stood the squadron at ease, called it to attention, summoned the squadron officers to take up their positions, stood them all at ease again and introduced myself to my new command. I was twenty-nine and a major in the Sultan of Oman's Armed Forces. I would not have been anywhere else.

After a normal squadron parade in the British Army, everyone falls out and gets on with the business of the day, while the squadron leader drifts among his soldiers, catching up on the state of the vehicles and joshing with his command team, before going to the office to deal with the usual plethora of paperwork that accompanies daily life in a regiment. In Oman this routine was the same, but different. On being ordered to 'carry on', literally everyone would come over to shake hands, reflecting the democratic nature of traditional Arab culture, where all are equal before God, even if God chooses to place different individuals in different positions in society. It was part of the Muslim philosophy of life summed up in the expression '*inshallah*', 'God wills it' or 'it is the will of God'. It was also used as an almost reflex response to any statement or order, from 'good luck' to 'turn left here'. The Omanis had a great sense of humour, and a self-confidence bred of their longstanding and successful engagement with the wider world. To be confronted with a hundred smiling faces and outstretched hands at 6.30 in the morning was just a delight, and very good for the process of trying to remember names. '*Asalaam waalaykum, seedee*', '*kayfhaalak seedee*', 'welcome, sir', 'how are you, sir.' '*Bikhayr, shukraan*', '*mabsoot jiddan, shukraan*', 'I am well thank you', 'I am very happy, thank you.' '*Wa anta Ali* (or *Khamis, Mohammed, Marzooq, Hamad, Ahmed*) *kayfhaalak, wa kayfahlatak?*' 'And you, Ali (or Khamis, etc), how are you, and how is your family?' A really pleasurable ritual, performed every day, and at almost every subsequent meeting. It was such a sincere and delightful experience that it never felt like 'just going through the motions'.

It was a huge privilege to command Omanis. The country had been, until recently, very underdeveloped, it was not blessed with the energy wealth of its neighbours and it had fought a demanding six-year war in the south. I loved being in the British Army, but that was a well-oiled and well-honed machine, where progress came incrementally, on the back of long experience and practice. Oman, and with it the armed forces, was by no means a *tabula rasa*, but the learning curve was always going to be steeper and sharper. In one generation, many Omanis had come out of the desert or the *jebel*, from ways of life largely unchanged for centuries, into an environment of rapid technological advance, to be confronted by a spectrum of new and challenging assumptions about what constituted 'modernity'. Organization, administration, discipline and technology, those hallmarks of modern Western military structures, were not necessarily a comfortable fit with the independently-spirited Omanis, particularly the Bedouin. Many of my older soldiers had not grown up with electricity, cars or roads. Most had never tied a bootlace before joining the army. Some could only read or write in the most rudimentary manner. Now they were faced with the complexity of a main battle tank, including an 'integrated fire control system' that, frankly, left many British soldiers baffled.

However, things were changing fast. A senior Omani officer, a pilot in the Sultan's air force, said he found it almost impossible to explain to his children the circumstances of his own childhood in Sur, where he had lived in a palm-frond hut, walked five miles to school every day and had had to set sail to visit the capital because there were no coastal roads. Sultan Qaboos saw his armed forces as a highly effective vehicle for social mobility, via education and training, and continued to use them as an essential part of his plans for national development. It was to Sultan Qaboos's eternal credit that he recognized both the strengths and the limitations of his country and society, seeking to give Oman the place it deserved in the region and the wider world, while carefully managing the speed at which change took place. The result was an ever-modernizing society, but one which avoided some of the excesses of Oman's neighbours. Loan service personnel had a key role to play in this development agenda, and our expertise and enthusiasm was vital in raising standards, in line with the Sultan's ambitions. This was matched by a willingness to learn and an equal enthusiasm on the part of the Omanis, and we came far further, far faster, than we might have done with similar raw material, in similar circumstances, back in Britain. This palpable sense of contributing to a country that deserved and welcomed our assistance gave us all a real feeling of achievement.

Although all my tank soldiers were Omanis, my logistical and adminis-trative staff was mostly from India, Pakistan and Sri Lanka. The Chief Clerk was an impressive Pashtun called Rab Nawaz. He, like others from the sub-continent, had six weeks' annual holiday, when he went back home to a wife and family that he did not see for the rest of the year. This could sometimes be extended by using the Muslim religious festivals of Eid al Fitr, the Feast of the Breaking of the Fast, held at the end of Ramadan, and Eid al Adha, the Feast of the Sacrifice, marking the end of the *hajj* season. It was a tough regimen but, like many other 'ex-pat' workers across the Gulf, he had made a conscious decision to seek well-paid employment at the expense of family life, given the economic situation back home. On the back of their efforts, the next generation would have far greater opportunities. Rab and I used to play out a little ritual when he came back from leave. He would come into my office, with great stamping of feet and saluting. After my asking after his family, he would present me with a gift, normally onyx cups or the like, although once I was given a fine pair of embroidered slippers. I would thank him profusely, and he would go out. I would then sit down and look at my watch. Almost exactly ten minutes later, he would re-enter, with more foot-stamping and saluting.

'I have a problem in my village, sir. Could I trouble you for some more leave?'

'But Rab', I would say, 'you have only just come back from leave. What would His Majesty say? We are here to serve the Sultan, and he pays us well.'

After some more to-ing and fro-ing in this vein, I would knock him down from a month to a week, and he would depart with words to the effect that I was 'mother and father to the squadron'. Honour was satisfied, his work was excellent and we both seemed to enjoy our 'stately dance'. Just before I left Oman in 1987, I asked him about Benazir Bhutto's chances of becoming Prime Minister in the next year's election in Pakistan. Benazir had been President of the Oxford Union during my time at Oxford, in the year that her father had been ousted in a military coup.

Rab looked at me pityingly: 'In Pakistan we do not let our women run the house. We would not let one run the country.'

In December 1988, Benazir Bhutto became the first female Prime Minister of Pakistan. She was fated to be killed in a bombing attack in 2007.

We spent a good deal of time in the desert, on exercises and at gunnery camp. There was always one reconnaissance squadron on rotation in the south, supporting the Omani infantry battalions on their own rotations up on the *jebel*, or in the outposts of Ramlat Shuwait and Makeenat Shehan on the Yemeni border. The tank squadrons stayed in the north, except in 1987, when we also deployed south to confront a Yemeni border incursion, which was broken up by some sharp flying and shooting by the Sultan of Oman's Air Force. Our usual military 'playground' was the plains and water-cut channels of the Wadi Khalfain. This area also encompassed our live-fire gunnery ranges of Safwat ad Dawh, where every day we had to chase camels out of the firing 'template' and occasionally recover the target number boards from the Bedouin, who used them to build huts. There were several notable advantages to soldiering in Oman, in contrast to West Germany. It was warm, it was dry and we did not face a nuclear, biological or chemical threat, so there was no requirement for the dreaded chemical suit and respirator. We also had 'secure' radios, which obviated the need for laborious coding and decoding, and we rarely operated at night, because either complete darkness, or the 'flat light' from a full moon, combined with the sheer scale and profusion of *wadis*, made it mighty dangerous for mounted crews, in either tanks or 'soft-skinned' vehicles like Land Rovers or lorries. Sometimes we carried out reconnaissance missions into the less inhabited quarters of the country, and once I spent five delightful days striking south through the deserts to the Indian Ocean, then along the coast and across the extensive gravel plains to the southern base of Thumrait. Sipping whisky and smoking cheroots by a campfire; grilling locally-caught fish; drinking strong, bitter, cardamom-infused coffee from minute *finjaan* cups; watching with amusement as a fellow officer took an ill-considered swig from the finger-bowl provided by our Bedouin hosts. On another occasion we spent a blissful week in the dunes of the Sharqia Sands trialling the new Land Cruiser Desert Patrol vehicles. How much better could it get? It may sound like a cliché, but every desert morning, as the sun breached the horizon to the east, one could not help but mutter Omar Khayyam's evocative verse under one's breath:

Awake! For Morning in the Bowl of Night
Has flung the Stone that puts the Stars to Flight:
And Lo! The Hunter of the East has caught
The Sultan's Turret in a Noose of Light

In the summer months we left the tanks in the hangars, and spent two glorious weeks in a tented training camp up in the Jebel Akdhar, away from the humidity and the air-conditioners. It was all the stuff of memories. We could hardly believe that we were doing all this and being paid for our trouble. Although my parents were back from Canada, I think I only returned to England once in my three years in Oman. My holidays were spent in Kenya, hiking up the Karakoram Highway in Pakistan with Jamie Mackeness, butterfly-hunting, golfing and shooting wild pig with Howard Elston in Sri Lanka, or visiting my brother in Hong Kong.

My tank crew, Khamis Masoud, Hamad Ali and Abdullah Hassan, were outstanding, and all were excellent cooks, although Omani food was not noted for its variety, at least not in the *jaish*. We had various permutations of tinned tuna, chicken or goat with rice, and great bowls of dhal, seasoned with hot pepper sauce and scooped up in large chapattis. The Omanis favoured a hot beverage called *karak*, which was fundamentally very strong, very milky and heavily-sugared tea, laced with cardamom and cinnamon. At daybreak the crews would light fires by the vehicles and put a large cooking-pot on to boil. They would then thread together a couple of dozen Lipton teabags and drop them in the pot, accompanied by several tins of condensed milk, a box or two of sugar lumps and a handful of spices. It was too much for me, although other British officers loved it. Along with my lack of a beard, my crew were also visibly disappointed when, after putting up with *karak* for several exercises, I asked them to make '*chai inglesi, wa kaleel haleeb, wa bidoon sukkar*' ('English tea, with a small amount of milk, and no sugar'). My Arabic grew considerably more workmanlike over the months, aided by Ali Nasser and Khamis Masoud. There had been no time to learn to read and write the language at Beaconsfield, and we had been taught phonetically, using 'crash cards' with the English word on one side and a phonetic translation on the other. I always regretted not using my time in Oman more efficiently in order to become more fluent in Arabic, but I could give orders face-to-face or over the radio quite effectively enough, although my English accent and pronunciation never really left me.

In late 1986 we conducted one of the largest exercises in the region, *Saif Sareea* (Swift Sword), alongside the Royal Marines and the British paratroopers of 5 Airborne Brigade. The scenario was the UK reinforcement of a key Gulf ally threatened with aggression. The plan envisaged an amphibious landing on a coastline held by friendly forces, and an advance to hold, then repel, the enemy. We had a chain of command and a streamlined planning process that was relevant and appropriate for a major joint-force operation with allies. Everything reflected the hard-won operational lessons of the Falklands. Initially, the weather was foul, as it can occasionally be in the region, and 40 Commando were almost washed into the Indian Ocean as rain cascaded off the rocky low hills and a flash flood swept through the *wadi* they were occupying. I was commanding the Omani armour contingent attached to the British brigade and spent several days with the soldiers of the Parachute Regiment, and all their equipment, draped over my tanks, as we ferried them from one engagement to another, until the enemy had been 'repulsed' from Omani territory. At this point, we staged an elaborate firepower demonstration for the Sultan and other visiting dignitaries. I had met the Sultan briefly on a couple of previous occasions, including during the fifteenth National Day celebrations the year before, and it was a privilege to escort him along the ranks of the dismounted E Squadron crews and to sing their praises to him. The young soldiers were clearly delighted to exchange salutes, handshakes and words with their monarch.

In barracks, our days finished at 1.00 pm, except during Ramadan, when we began work an hour earlier but gave up the unequal struggle against fasting and the sun by 11.00 am. It was during one of these periods that I used to commute to the Sultan's Armed Forces Aqua Club, open to all officers but largely used by the British, where I gained my sub-aqua diving qualifications. Ramadan or not, most afternoons, and certainly most weekends, we would go to the Club. The manager was Bill Foxton, that contract officer who had been in the Royal Green Jackets and Foreign Legion and who had lost a hand in a mortar incident during the Dhofar War. He was a great raconteur, and I would often change for the beach but then spend all afternoon in his air-conditioned office drinking Foster's lager and 'shooting the breeze'. He eventually left Oman and found his way to the Balkans in the 1990s. Our paths briefly crossed again in Kosovo in 2002, when I was commanding my Brigade there.

A normal loan service posting was for twenty-four months, but since I already had a place at Staff College for January 1988 I was able to extend my time in Oman until October 1987. By this stage the Armoured Regiment had decamped from our comfortable billet near Muscat and moved to a brand new base on the far side of the Jebel Akhdar, near to the old interior capital of Nizwa. This move was part of the continuing development of the Sultan's Armed Forces, in preparation for expansion to a brigade-sized organization of three regiments. There was a large turnover of personnel at this stage. 'Omanization' was continuing, loan service posts were declining and 'contracts' were no longer being renewed. Most of my close friends from the early days had departed, and by a process of elimination I ended up as the last British officer directly commanding Omanis in the field. While there were still deputies at various levels, along with advisers, trainers and staff officers, the days of British command were coming to an end. Whilst sad, it also reflected our success. The Omanis were taking over with confidence and competence and, I believed, a keen sense of gratitude to the British. It had been a mutual 'love affair', and strong personal and professional bonds had been formed. As in all relationships, however, these needed constant attention, and over the years, back in the UK and working in the MoD, I would often despair at the shortsightedness of officials and policy-makers, as they weighed small sums of money in the balance against our strategic interests in a country that actively welcomed our presence and engagement.

I was torn, as my departure date approached. I had loved my time in Oman but I could not apply for another loan service appointment, and the 'contract' world was coming to an end. A private security company offered me the chance to command a company of soldiers in Mozambique, helping to guard the Beria railway. However, this was still the period of Soviet interference in Southern Africa, and being the only European in a military organization of suspect loyalty, while being responsible for the security of a fixed target, did not look like an attractive option. As the autumn weather got better in Oman, and worse in Britain, I contemplated losing my command and rank, taking a hefty cut in pay and spending a year 'back at school'. In my mind's eye, while doing my farewell rounds, I was composing my resignation letter. Thank goodness, that plan didn't work out.

Chapter 13

'New World Order' – Part II (1989)

W hen I flew back into Heathrow in October 1987 I was still uncertain what I wanted to do, and rather unsettled. I was due to go to Staff College in the New Year, and I mistakenly thought my best soldiering days were behind me. Margaret Thatcher had won her third election earlier in that year; the 'special relationship' with the US was thriving; NATO solidarity had been sustained through the Cruise and Pershing Missile political crisis; and the Soviets were daily being ground down in the crucible of Afghanistan. In the Middle East, the Iran-Iraq War continued to be a sanguinary stalemate, while the Gulf States were parlaying their increasing wealth into massive building projects and large defence purchases, of which the huge British-Saudi Arabian *Al Yamamah* deal for substantial numbers of Tornado multi-role combat aircraft was among the most notable. Israel's 1982 invasion of Lebanon, and their long-term occupation of the Shia south of the country, had catalysed the formation of Hezbollah, supported by both the Shia Alawite regime of Hafez Assad and, where their death-struggle against Saddam Hussein allowed, the Ayatollahs of Iran.

This was also the era of hostage-taking in Beirut, when between 1982 and 1992 militants took captive 104 people, including Terry Waite, Charles Glass and the CIA head of station, William Buckley, who was murdered, as were several others. Ronald Reagan had been drawn into this situation, hoping to secure the release of US hostages in Lebanon by using the good offices of 'responsible elements' in Iran. The search for such 'moderate Iranian elements' would continue to the present day, with persistent disappointment and frustration. The US plan was for the Israelis to ship weapons, mostly anti-tank missiles, but also ground-to-air missiles, to the Iranians, who would then use them in the fight against the Iraqis who were also being armed by the Americans. The Israelis would then be re-supplied by the Americans and, in another twist, their payments would go to finance the anti-communist forces, the Contras, in Central America. It was incredibly convoluted, duplicitous, illegal under US law and embarrassing when it came out, as the US had been actively campaigning against all arms and spares transfers to the Islamic Republic. The whole affair degenerated into an undignified 'arms-for-hostages' deal that was only partly successful and which sent an appalling message that there was a 'market' in hostages. Hostage-taking would become an enduring hallmark of terrorist fundraising in later years. American audiences, and the wider world, were gripped by the subsequent trial of Colonel Oliver North and the revelations about his secretary, Fawn Hall, who had been shredding huge quantities of incriminating material in the Pentagon while apparently shipping out equal amounts of evidence in her underwear.

The previous year, in my absence abroad, my father had finished his last posting in the RAF, as Air Officer Commanding Cadets, and had been awarded a CBE for his thirty-seven years of distinguished service. At the time of my return, my parents were commuting between Camberley and Southern Spain, where they had bought a small retirement property. I was due to join them, but not before I had lunch in London with my old boss, now Chief of the General Staff, Nigel Bagnall. The day before, on Tuesday 13 October, Michael Fish, the well-known television weatherman, famously said, 'Earlier on today, apparently, a woman rang the BBC and said she heard a hurricane was on its way. Well, if you are watching, don't worry, there isn't.' That evening, the worst storm for three centuries hit South-East England, causing record levels of damage, devastating the Ashdown Forest and killing nineteen people. When I woke on the 14th, only vaguely aware of the tumult of the night before, I found a scene of devastation. The trip to London took nearly three times as long as usual, with roads blocked at every turn by fallen trees, with distraught drivers examining crushed cars. It was a delightful reunion with Nigel and Anna Bagnall. I expressed my professional concerns, and he gently encouraged me to think carefully about my decision. He made no predictions about the future, or promotion prospects, but I knew he believed I was in a career whose core purpose I understood and valued, one that I clearly enjoyed and one which suited my temperament.

The next day, I flew to Spain, leaving my car parked well away from any large trees. Unbeknownst to me, the decision to stay in or to leave the Army was about to be taken out of my hands. As oil prices had begun to decline in the 1980s, OPEC sought to cut production to keep those prices up. Saudi Arabia went from 10 million barrels a day to just 2.3 million, but other oil producers, not least Iran and Iraq, locked in their death-struggle, continued to increase production. In 1985, Saudi Arabia abandoned a strategy of trying to prop up prices, and instead sought to increase its market share at the expense of other producers. By July 1987 the price of OPEC crude had fallen from over $23 a barrel to just under $10 in only six months. Although some of this fall in energy prices helped Western economies, it created an atmosphere of financial uncertainty. While the stock markets had boomed, the underlying fundamentals were now fragile. On Thursday, 15 October, as I was landing in Malaga, Iran hit two of the 'US-flagged' oil supertankers in the Gulf, provoking a robust American response and raising the prospect of a widening conflict in the Middle East and closure of the Straits of Hormuz. That element of a potential crisis passed but, with the UK stock market still closed because of the 'great storm', the Dow Jones in New York fell by about seven per cent. On Friday, 16 October, with the London stock market still largely closed, the Dow fell even further. By 19 October, 'Black Monday', global markets were in free-fall, with collapses in the stock markets of leading industrial countries ranging from the mid-twenties per cent in the US and UK to forty-five per cent in Hong Kong and nearly sixty per cent in New Zealand. It was long before the advent of 24-hour news so, either sat in a Spanish restaurant or lounging on a Costa del Sol beach that weekend, I was blissfully unaware that my small investment in Clogau Gold was heading south fast, along with the rest of the UK economy.

A year earlier, when the British economy was booming, I believe I would have had very little difficulty finding suitable employment in the expanding financial sector. Whether I would have enjoyed it, or found it satisfying, is a different matter. Now, when I went to see a number of ex-Army officers who had done well in second careers, all of them said largely the same thing: 'This is not a good time to be looking for a job in the City. We are laying people off, not taking them on.' All were helpful, but honest: 'If you do leave the Army, get back in touch with us and we will see how the land lies.' David Rosier, who I would later work with closely when I was Colonel of the Queen's Dragoon Guards, also commented, 'I do not get the feeling you really want to leave the Army.' He was right.

I also took a look at the Secret Intelligence Service (SIS). Nowadays, MI6 advertises in the broadsheets and on the internet, but in 1987, although we did not know how quickly its demise would be upon us, the Soviet Union and its espionage activities still constituted the primary threat to the UK, and the SIS remained the shadowy organization of legend and hearsay. It was an intriguing prospect, and after several days weighing up the options, I presented myself at a Carlton Gardens address for an exploratory interview. I liked what I heard and saw, and my high regard for the Service has only grown over the intervening years, as I have worked ever more closely with them, particularly in the period after 9/11. However, I could see that it was not for me. The Armed Forces and the Security Services share a deep commitment to public service, to British national interest and to the security of the United Kingdom, but I knew what levels of patience, secrecy and discretion were required for good intelligence work. I also had enough self-awareness to know that, while I was not materially acquisitive, I did enjoy the overt trappings of career success in public service. In December I took my draft letter of resignation and consigned it to the waste-paper bin. Reluctantly, but definitely for the best, I turned my attention to the Staff College reading list.

For most of us, Staff College occupied a full year, of which the first three months were spent on technical training at Shrivenham, before we all went to Camberley. Once again, there was a delightful reunion of fellow officers, although many old friends had either completed their Short Service Commissions and left, or had wrestled with a similar dilemma to mine and, often motivated by the demands of marriage and children, had chosen civilian life. Almost everyone I had rated in the Army did well outside of it, but some, I always knew, at heart regretted their choice to leave. The hundred or so British students represented the top twenty-five per cent of their age-cohort, having passed the promotion exam at the requisite level for Staff College entry. The other thirty or so students were, as at Sandhurst, from close, historical allies of Britain, including the Gulf. Once more we were formed into syndicates, which changed from term to term. My time on the technical phase was not an undiluted success. In my last piece of set work I gave a presentation on the 'attack helicopter', which was about to become a staple of the British Army's inventory with the introduction of the Apache. I chose this topic because it enabled me to start with a lengthy clip from the film *Apocalypse Now*, which went down well with my class-mates. This early triumph was negated when I put up a picture of the interior of an Apache cockpit.

'This is a highly complex piece of equipment'. I said portentously. 'As you can see, the cockpit is full of . . . ' There was a long pause as I sought the right technical term and the class leaned in to sup of my wisdom, '. . . knobs.'

It was all I could think of to say, and the class responded with the derisive laughter that my explanation deserved.

The syllabus of the main course was akin to that of the Junior Division of Staff College, but reflected our age, our experience and the appointments we were now being trained to fill. There remained a twin focus: all-arms manoeuvre for a war in Central Europe; and the counter-terrorism and counter-insurgency campaigns in Northern Ireland that still dominated the domestic news. It was, quite rightly, another demanding course, but it inevitably had its lighter moments. Many senior people, from all walks of life, came to impart their wisdom. One of them was Sir Dennis Rook, the Chairman of the multinational energy giant British Gas. At the conclusion of his talk the industrial titan stood expectantly waiting for astute and piercing questions. Auberon Ashbrooke, a bright, balding, rotund cavalry officer, often saluted by the unsuspecting at Sandhurst because he had already looked like a brigadier by the age of twenty, stood up. The first question always made people feel better, because it gave others the time to formulate their own. Such questions were occasionally actually designed to elicit knowledge, but more often to impress the Commandant, particularly close to report-writing time. The officer cleared his throat.

'Sir Dennis', he said, 'I have a small flat in Chelsea with gas central heating, and I have noticed a funny knocking sound coming from my boiler. Can you offer any advice?'

Sir Dennis looked suitably unamused and the Commandant exuded exasperation, but the student body rocked with laughter.

Among the overseas students we had two Pakistani officers and two from India. They got on well enough with each other in this environment, but in individual conversations the deep enmity between their countries showed through. The President of India at the time was Rajiv Gandhi, who had succeeded his mother, Indira Gandhi, after her assassination in 1984 and who would himself be assassinated in 1991. The President of Pakistan was General Muhammed Zia al Haq, who had assumed the presidency in 1978 after deposing Prime Minister Ali Bhutto and subsequently hanging him. Zia al Haq was a very conservative, even fundamentalist Muslim, who had progressively 'Islamized' his country, out of both conviction and political calculation. He had also systematically coordinated the Afghan mujahideen campaign against the Soviet Union's occupation of that country, using the powerful state organization of the ISI, elements of the Pakistani armed forces and the vast sums of Saudi money from both the Kingdom itself and individuals. In this endeavour he was initially strongly supported by the Americans, who were clear about the risk from communism but who, despite the experience of Iran, failed, and would continue to fail, to grasp the scale of the challenge from Islamism. While Zia al Haq's efforts would make a major contribution to the eventual Soviet withdrawal, they also led to the arrival of millions of refugees, who brought heroin, weapons and radicalized Islam into the frontier provinces of Pakistan. At the same time, Zia al Haq was pursuing an atomic weapons programme that would further inflame tensions on the sub-continent. In August 1988, when we were in the middle of one of our major exercises, the Pakistani officers came into the Mess, visibly shaken, to announce that President Zia had been killed in an aircraft crash, along with the US ambassador to Pakistan. His legacy, in Pakistan, Afghanistan and the Middle East, through his support of Arab foreign fighters among the mujahideen, was to be toxic and long-lasting.

As we neared the end of our course, the atmosphere lightened. We had either 'made our mark' by then, or not, and the die was largely cast as to our first post-Staff College appointments. A Colonel from the Directing Staff decided to test our knowledge of nuclear, biological and chemical warfare by hauling unsuspecting students off the street and subjecting them to a snap test, recorded on video. Several of us were ambushed, and the limitations of our knowledge were sharply exposed. In the resulting film, which was shown in the lecture hall to huge public amusement, a languid and well-connected Household Cavalry officer, whose focus was very much more on central London than on the Central Front, appeared as one of the interviewees. The Colonel challenged him with a 'killer question':

'You are shopping in Bagshot, when you hear an enormous explosion and you see a mushroom cloud over Bracknell . . . '

Before he could complete the interrogation, the Household Cavalryman snapped back: 'Stop right there, Colonel. I can conceive of no possible circumstances under which I would be shopping in Bagshot.'

If ever a student played to type, this was it. Shortly afterwards, I learnt that I was to be posted to be a staff officer in the Ministry of Defence, in Army Staff Duties, the branch responsible for Army organizational policy. In late 1988 my assumption was that I would subsequently return to West Germany and to Regimental Duty on the NATO front line, to continue facing down the Russian Bear.

In March 1985 Mikhail Gorbachev had been elected General Secretary of the Soviet Communist Party and therefore de facto leader of the Soviet Union. Seeking to reform the economy, in order to revitalize a Communist system that was being challenged by growing Western economic and military might, he embraced *perestroika* ('rebuilding') and *glasnost* ('openness'). This 'liberalization by stealth' served to foster nationalism and generate ethnic disputes within the Soviet Union. In the Baltic States, and in the Muslim Central Asian republics, new nationalist movements began to grow and challenge the authority of the central government. Meanwhile, the drain on Russian blood and treasure in Afghanistan continued, and Gorbachev sought disengagement from this costly foreign adventure, while trying to salvage his country's reputation.

In June 1987, while I was still in Oman, Ronald Reagan had gone to Berlin's Brandenburg Gate, long a symbol of the East-West stand-off, for the 750th anniversary of that city. Here, going 'off-script', he issued a challenge to the Soviet Union:

> General Secretary Gorbachev, if you seek peace, if you seek prosperity, if you seek liberalization, come here to this gate.
> Mr Gorbachev, open this gate. Mr Gorbachev, tear down this wall.

In November 1988 Reagan completed his second term as President, to be succeeded by his Vice President, George H. W. Bush.

During spring 1989, as I was settling into the MoD and my new life in London, the pace of events continued to quicken. Elections, political reform and accompanying uncertainty continued in the Soviet Union, the last Soviet troops pulled out of Afghanistan while the Chinese Government brutally suppressed the student 'uprisings' in Tiananmen Square. The MoD, with its mix of politicians, civil servants and officers from all three services, could be a frustrating place, but it was also a fascinating environment to be working in, and when I was not in command appointments, or on operations, I was to spend many years 'in Whitehall'. 'Defence' is a ferociously complex business, and despite the frustrations and the irritations, it is demanding and stimulating to be at the heart of the cut and thrust of government, trying to help the Chiefs exercise their responsibilities for the 'morale and fighting effectiveness of their service'. Years later, when I was Colonel Army Plans, we had become bogged down for several hours in some committee or another. During a welcome coffee break, John Deverell, a fellow Colonel, bounded up to me.

'Well, Simon', he said, 'this is all great fun. Don't you think that the motto of the MoD should be, "Wait, there is a harder way".'

He had a point.

The Soviet withdrawal from Afghanistan left behind a weak, divided and beleaguered regime. This Afghan government would not survive long after the withdrawal of Soviet military support. Their weakness and subsequent fall paved the way for mujahideen success in 1992 and, ultimately, the rise of the Taliban and, with them, Al Qa'eda. By mid-1989 the Soviet 'empire' was being shaken by the election of the first non-Communist government in Poland and the prospect of a similar result in Hungary. Dismantling the fence with Austria led to 13,000 East Germans 'escaping'. In an extraordinary climax to these events, Erich Honecker of East Germany, who had only recently predicted that the Berlin Wall would stand 'for another fifty or a hundred years', resigned, and on 9 November, faced with the pressures of mass demonstrations in East Berlin, the authorities opened the gates to allow unrestricted movement between the two halves of the city. The unofficial demolition of the Wall began that very night. A mere eleven months later, on 3 November 1990, Germany was reunited.

The day the Wall fell, I had been staying with military friends near Telford, and we were all stunned by the news. The pointers must all have been there, but no one seemed to have joined up the dots. It may not have been a failure of intelligence, but it seemed to have been a colossal failure of imagination. The world as we knew it had been turned on its head, and the legacy of those heady days was to have a very distorting effect on later Western policy approaches, when politicians and officials were trying to formulate coherent responses to the Arab Spring and when many of them, inappropriately, drew on the experience of 'Berlin 1989' for inspiration and hope during 'Cairo 2011'. There was more to come. Through 1990 and into 1991, there were further challenges to Gorbachev, as his reforms provoked clashes between reformers and conservatives, including many hard-line officers in the KGB. An attempted coup in August 1991 was thwarted, but on 25 December 1991 Gorbachev resigned, ceding all powers, including control of the nuclear arsenal, to Boris Yeltsin. The Russian Federation, a new sovereign state, was formed, and the Soviet flag was lowered from the Kremlin for the last time. Gorbachev ruefully defended his record on economic reform and relationships with the wider world, but conceded that 'the old system collapsed before a new one had time to start working'. There would be significant consequences, not least because of the manner in which America and the West chose to take advantage of this period of relative Russian weakness. Fifteen new states now stood where one mighty superpower had recently held sway. It had been a world-defining period. On 9 November 1989, as the Berlin Wall had been coming down, a desolate Lieutenant Colonel Vladimir Putin could have been found in the gardens of the Soviet Consulate in Dresden, burning KGB documents.

The British Government's immediate response to the fall of the Berlin Wall had been to initiate a Defence Review entitled 'Options for Change', which in line with almost every other Western country now sought to pocket a 'peace dividend' from major reductions in military spending in the wake of the collapse of the Soviet and Warsaw Pact threats. Defence expenditure, which had risen to nearly 5 per cent of gross domestic product in 1985, would now fall back progressively to around 2 per cent or less, and there would be substantial cuts in all three Services. For the Army, this would entail finding manpower reductions of nearly 20 per cent, cutting strength from 155,000 to 116,000. All of this turmoil should have been quite enough to keep policy-makers, pundits, analysts and commentators, not to mention harassed MoD staff officers, fully occupied, but then, in the midst of all this geopolitical upheaval in Eastern Europe, the Middle East erupted again, as Saddam Hussein's tanks drove across the Kuwaiti border.

Chapter 14

Eastward Ho! – The Liberation of Kuwait

In 2007, when I had recently returned from my operational tour in Baghdad as the Deputy Commanding General of Multi-National Corps-Iraq (MNC-I), I attended a dinner at the Cavalry and Guards Club in Piccadilly. The guest of honour that night was Lady Thatcher. This was the first time I had met her in the flesh, and by coffee time I had made it my business to be sitting next to her.

'I have waited sixteen years to ask you this, Baroness', I said. 'If you had still been Prime Minister in 1991, would we have stopped the war with Saddam when we did?'

'Absolutely not', she said. 'We had not finished the job!'

In 2003, when I was attending the Royal College of Defence Studies, at the same time that the contentious US-led invasion and occupation of Iraq was taking place, I had put a similar proposition to a senior government minister of the period. His reaction was interestingly defensive, his contention being that we had reached the limits of our 'permissions' under the 1990 UN Security Council Resolution, which was all about the liberation of Kuwait. In addition, he contended, the extraordinarily broad coalition put together by President Bush would not have survived any extension of operations to encompass the overthrow of Saddam Hussein. He did, however, confirm the cavalier way that the decision to end combat operations had been taken by President Bush's 'war cabinet'. On the afternoon of 27 February 1991 he had been leaning against the door in the Oval Office when General Colin Powell, at that time the Chairman of the Joint Chiefs of Staff, had entered to tell the President that the commanders on the ground were becoming unsettled by the scale of the destruction being inflicted on the Iraqi armed forces. This reporting had been compounded by early images of the notorious 'Highway of Death' and the 'traffic jam from Hell' on the road from Kuwait City to Basra. The President said words to the effect of 'Then it's time to bring this to a close. Tell General Schwarzkopf to tell the Iraqis that we will implement a ceasefire from 0800 hours local time tomorrow morning.' And that was it. At a critical moment of history, in the middle of one of the largest military operations of the twentieth century, which I was in the middle of at the time, a major strategic decision had been taken, almost on a whim, which would have huge implications for the Middle East and the future of Western involvement in the region.

Several years after both these encounters, I was asked to give a talk on modern Middle East politics to the Advisory Board of a major global risk-analysis company. Surveying the situation in Iraq at that time, I once again contended that we had finished operations too early. I acknowledged that there would have been a different set of political consequences and complications as a result of completing the destruction of the Iraqi Republican Guard, but suggested that we would have saved ourselves a great deal of trouble by ensuring that Saddam Hussein himself came to the peace-table to sign a proper peace settlement. By not doing so, and by imposing only a half-hearted ceasefire, we had ultimately left him free to construct a narrative claiming that the Coalition had halted its operations because it had been defeated. Incredible as it might seem to Western audiences, Saddam had thereby been able to pose as a hero to many across the Sunni Arab world. In addition, the flawed ceasefire provisions, particularly with regard to helicopters, left Saddam with the military wherewithal to crush the Shia and Kurd uprisings which we did so much to encourage. While I did not contend we should have gone on to Baghdad, I did argue that we should have imposed a formal peace agreement, publicly signed by Saddam Hussein in the full glare of the world's media, and with no Coalition withdrawal from Iraq until all provisions had been met, including reparations to Kuwait and the return of all prisoners, civilian and military. It was a course of action I was certain Margaret Thatcher would have vigorously advocated, and this seemed to have been confirmed for me at that 2007 dinner. I believed that Thatcher would have had the strategic vision, and the moral authority, to urge President Bush, for a second time, 'not to go wobbly'. Tragically, by the end of operations in late February 1991 she was, courtesy of her own party, no longer in power.

I was in my second year as a staff officer in the MoD when Saddam Hussein invaded Kuwait on 2 August 1990. August is always a bad time for a crisis because, despite the best of good intentions, people's attentions turn to school holidays and family vacations. As a bachelor, I had volunteered to cover the July/August period in order to allow my married colleagues to get away. This was not totally altruistic. Not only did I anticipate an idle few weeks in London, but I was confident that my being on holiday in September would save me from my Branch Colonel's holiday-fuelled set of new initiatives. Consequently, I was in a rather empty MoD when the news of the invasion broke, and with it, the first images of Iraqi tanks streaming south into Kuwait City. In a gross failure of diplomacy and intelligence, we had not seen this coming, and even in retrospect it seems extraordinary that the West, and the US in particular, could have given Saddam the slightest impression that we would ignore threats to, let alone an invasion of, Kuwait. Saddam achieved surprise at every level. This may be anecdotal, but Kuwaitis, with their well-honed black humour, said later that the Saudi border guards were uncertain as to which constituted the bigger challenge to the Kingdom: Saddam's tanks driving south, or Kuwaiti women drivers escaping the invaders. In any case, Kuwait's long nightmare of brutal occupation had begun. Intelligence staffs now predicted a rapid Iraqi drive to seize the major Saudi oilfields, broadly concentrated in the important Eastern Province, with its predominantly Shia population.

Motivations are strange things. As the global community reacted, diplomatically and militarily, to this grotesque breach of international law, I could only feel that it was, at a very parochial, personal and selfish level, an opportunity. Bizarre as this can sometimes seem to civilian friends, I know that I was not alone. As an armoured corps officer in the British Army, my primary responsibility had been to face down the Soviet hordes in Central Europe. While I was fascinated by politics, history and international affairs, the military cohort of the 1980s really needed only to be tactically and technically competent enough to fight our part of any conventional war against the Soviets. Despite operating in the 'grey areas' of the demanding Northern Ireland campaign, many of our skills in 'expeditionary warfare', so critical in our long and successful overseas presence, and in executing our well-managed retreat from Empire, had been allowed to atrophy. The longevity of appointments, the familiarity with religions, cultures and tribal dynamics, let alone languages, had been neglected, even in the Arabic-speaking world, where we had once held such a dominant position. If any large-scale military operation was to be undertaken, we anticipated that it would be on the Central Front, conducted under the threat of nuclear holocaust. I had missed the Falklands War in 1982, as had most of the armoured corps, and we had rarely taken part in the long-running and bitter campaign in Northern Ireland. We all knew how tough the Falklands conflict had been, and at what cost success had been achieved, but we were young, and those of us who had not yet taken part in operations had felt a palpable sense of 'them and us'. We had envied our fellow officers in the Parachute Regiments, the Royal Marines, the Guards Brigade and the

Gurkhas, as they told their stories of Goose Green, Tumbledown Mountain and Wireless Ridge, and we had admired their fresh, watery-blue, green and white Falklands medal ribbons.

So this seemed to be our moment, and I felt that my three years' tank service in the Sultan of Oman's Armoured Regiment was an additional strong argument for being part of the UK's military contribution. I knew the region, I spoke Arabic and I had commanded armour in the desert. Already the Royal Scots Dragoon Guards and the Queen's Royal Irish Hussars were on their way, as part of 7th Armoured Brigade, the famous 'Desert Rats'. The 14th/20th King's Hussars were now also going, including among their number an old friend from Oxford, Richard Shirreff. He and I had first met in the queue for the film *Jaws* in 1976, both of us predicting, thankfully wrongly, 'five years in the Army, then off to the City to make some money'. However, I was in an MoD appointment, and my own Regiment, the 15th/19thHussars, was equipped with Chieftain rather than the newer Challenger tanks. They had been tasked with the important, but unglamorous, role of delivering pre-deployment training. No desert glory for them. In the time-honoured way, as notably pursued by Winston Churchill, I began canvassing to get myself sent to the forthcoming war in the Middle East. I was not alone. All over the Army, people were to be found crouched behind photocopiers and the like, pleading to be allowed to return to regimental duty or to fill any of the additional staff and liaison appointments that always spring up in the course of a major operation. This was a period well before the advent of mobile phones, emails or the internet, and conducting a clandestine campaign to get sent on operations was as tricky as conducting a love affair from Germany with only the single telephone in the Officers' Mess at your disposal.

By this stage it was late October. All my efforts had so far been in vain, but many friends were already in the Gulf, or en route to the region, to join the vast Coalition effort that would eventually top over half a million servicemen and women, including many from across the Middle East. Saddam Hussein could not have chosen his moment more poorly, despite his initial successes. With the fall of the Berlin Wall, the Americans, under President George Bush, and the Russians, then still under Gorbachev, had found a rare moment of unity on the UN Security Council, and both supported a UN Resolution calling for the 'use of all necessary measures' to evict Saddam from Kuwait. The US had already been planning to move thousands of military vehicles, and vast quantities of stores, back to the United States. These were now simply diverted directly to the Saudi ports of Dharhan and Al Jubayl, as the initial military response, based around the US Marines and the Airborne Divisions, was reinforced with the heavy formations of the US Army, their deployment covered by an 'air-armada' of a scale that only the Americans could generate. At the same time, the Arab states of the GCC also stepped up to the plate, under the leadership of King Fahd of Saudi Arabia. This bold commitment was not without controversy, and it would have long-term implications. A young man of Yemeni and Saudi descent, freshly returned from the successes of the Afghanistan mujahideen against the Soviets, now pledged his 'holy warriors' to the defence of Saudi Arabia, rather than allowing 'infidel' soldiers to 'defile' the Kingdom of the 'Custodian of the Two Holy Places'. King Fahd and his closest advisers chose otherwise. Osama bin Laden, scion of the great Saudi construction company of the same name, withdrew to consider his options and his response to this snub. It would not be long in coming.

Saddam Hussein, like Nasser before him, had had dreams of uniting and leading the Arab Middle East, and in 1989, at the end of the war with Iran, he had established the Arab Cooperation Council (ACC), promoting Iraq as the main rival to Saudi Arabia and the GCC. He had persuaded Egypt and Jordan to join this organization, and also North Yemen, which after the assassination of two previous Presidents was now led by a military officer from the important Sanhan tribe, Ali Abdullah Saleh. Remarkably, by May 1990 Saleh had succeeded in uniting the two very distinct and very fractious parts of Yemen. It was never to be a happy marriage. Alongside the GCC states were now also contingents from Egypt, supposedly aligned with Iraq in the ACC, and from Syria, an old Cold War adversary of America but also a long-time regional rival of Iraq. While expressing their support in terms of Arab and Muslim solidarity, these countries also saw an opportunity to ingratiate themselves with the Americans, while they waited to see what the long-term implications of the end of the Cold War would be. However, Yasser Arafat of the PLO, from his new base in Tunisia, declared his support for Saddam. He reflected a view, widely held on the 'Arab street', that Saddam had been a far stauncher supporter of the Palestinian struggle against Israel than the Gulf monarchies. This may have been true, but Arafat's was an ill-judged gesture that came at a price when nearly half a million Palestinians were evicted from the Gulf States after the liberation of Kuwait. King Hussein of Jordan, whose Kingdom's economy was so closely tied to that of Iraq, attempted to adopt a position of neutrality. The newly united Republic of Yemen also tried to sit on the fence. For President Saleh's failure to condemn Iraq, Saudi Arabia 'repatriated' 800,000 Yemenis and, with them, the millions of dollars of remittances they sent home each year, while for their failure to support the UN Security Council Resolution the US cut their $70 million annual development aid package with the words, 'That was the most expensive "no" vote you ever cast.'

On 25 November I was still stuck in the MoD, and getting fed up with stories and images of the growing Coalition build-up in the Gulf, when the phone rang. It was Jamie Mackeness from my Oman days. Was I going to the Sultan's Armed Forces Dinner that night? I was not, but I was not doing anything else, either, so I would try to get a late ticket and join him there. In the nature of these reunions, the 'war stories' of service in Oman flowed, as did commentary on the situation in Kuwait. I found myself with General Johnnie Watts, the gallant SAS officer who had been the Chief of Defence in Oman during my time. The whisky was flowing and, in that period before smoking indoors was banned, the air was thick with cigar fumes. I aired the complaint that my 'talents' were not being usefully employed by the British Government, and Johnnie Watts wrote my name on a scrap of paper and put it in his dinner jacket pocket, saying:

'Peter de la Billière [then the senior British officer in Riyadh] has always been my second-in-command in the SAS. I will tell him to get you out there. As soon as Diane goes through my pockets and asks me why I have your name on this piece of paper, I shall remember to write him a letter.'

The next morning, I woke up with the traditional SAF Dinner hangover, to be confronted with headlines from Brigadier Patrick Cordingly, commander of the 'Desert Rats', predicting the possibility of 25,000 Coalition casualties. It was with slightly diminished martial ardour that I returned to the MoD on Monday, although I did say to my Branch Colonel, Ashley Truluck, that I felt it was only a matter of time before my fitness for deployment was recognized.

Nothing happened for a further three weeks. At last I could take the suspense no longer and I rang Johnnie Watts. I got Diane. Had the General contacted Peter de la Billiere? She had found the note with my name on it later than usual, but General Johnnie had been as good as his word. She hoped I still wanted to get out to the Gulf.

'Oh, rather!' I said, trusting that Patrick Cordingly was just being gloomy regarding casualties.

'Good', she said. 'Johnnie has rather implied to Peter he can't win the war without you!'

I put down the phone both elated and apprehensive. Two weeks later, Ashley Truluck called me in.

'This is a very odd way to staff such issues', he said, 'but I have a signal here from General de la Billière's office saying you are to report to General Rupert Smith's (GOC 1st UK Armoured Division) headquarters within the next two weeks.'

'I thought the system would sooner or later recall my Arabic qualifications', I said, disingenuously, as I withdrew from his office, grinning from ear to ear.

As I had been watching the mighty military enterprise unfold, waiting to deploy, another drama was taking place in British politics. Like the central player in a Victorian bear-baiting spectacle, Margaret Thatcher, victor of the Falklands War, 'hammer' of the unions, the geo-strategic partner of President Ronald Reagan in orchestrating the collapse of the Soviet Union, the winner of three General Elections, was being dragged down by malcontents in her own party. The British military, staunchly apolitical in terms of our relationship with the state, had a huge regard and affection for Thatcher. We saw in her a firm guardian of British national interest, and a politician with a great and justifiable sense of ambition for her country. She instinctively understood, and sincerely believed in, the importance of a strong and credible military to underpin the rhetoric of politicians, particularly those leading a country with global responsibilities and reach. She spoke to the heart of those core assumptions that all ranks in the military held dear, regarding service to their country and the concept of 'unlimited liability'. It was therefore with incredulity that, as we prepared to send overseas to war the largest military force since 1945, members of her own party were prepared to unseat the most successful Prime Minister of modern times. Our allies were similarly incredulous. Her replacement was John Major, a decent and intelligent enough man, but largely unknown to the Americans and lacking the experience, the confidence and perhaps the personality, to influence the President and US decision-makers at that critical time. He would go on to win the 1992 General Election, but the consequences and the manner of Thatcher's demise would haunt the Tory Party for years to come and, in my opinion, severely affected the outcome of the war.

Thanks to the thoughtfulness of a girlfriend, I would depart for 'the front' armed with a lovely silver Asprey's cigarette case that, she romantically declared, was to be worn in my left breast pocket in order to 'deflect' any stray Iraqi Kalashnikov rounds. What could possibly go wrong?

Chapter 15

Iraq: Round One

I eventually landed at Al Jubayl, in a sandstorm, in early December, after a suitably haphazard administrative process. I was rather incongruously dressed in Omani desert fatigues, sporting a totally unnecessary bayonet on my belt, with no proper winter or wet-weather clothing but with my Asprey's 'mini-flak jacket' in my top pocket. I was not alone in sporting a 'customized' uniform. The lack of proper desert kit, and a natural thespian instinct in the British officer corps, had provoked a frantic rummaging around in dressing-up boxes and cupboards and the deployment of various leather jerkins, crummocks, cravats and cricket sweaters. Rupert Smith turned a 'Nelsonian blind eye' to this display, as had his desert predecessor General Bernard Montgomery, but I could see our better-resourced and more strictly uniformed American allies found it a shade unnerving. In 1940s war films it was just about all right, but half a century on, prior to Saddam's 'Mother of all Battles', the jury was firmly out in some quarters of the US military.

I was not particularly inspired by this bleak but prominent oil town perched on the eastern coast of the vast desert plain of northern Saudi Arabia. It was about three weeks before Christmas and about forty days before K-Day, the expiry of the UN deadline for Saddam to withdraw from Kuwait. However, whatever the drabness of the surroundings, it was difficult not to be impressed by the scale of manpower and materiel pouring into this nondescript place by land, sea and air in preparation for the execution of a military option in the event that UN sanctions failed to shift Saddam from Kuwait, the so-called 'nineteenth province of Iraq'. The US military build-up was continuing apace, in line with the Colin Powell 'doctrine', forged from the disappointments and disillusionment of the Vietnam War. The painstaking rebuilding of the US Army as an all-volunteer force, 'the Army of Excellence', was now accompanied by a determination that it should not be used except to bring to bear 'overwhelming force' in pursuit of well defined policy objectives. Powell's intentions had been made perfectly clear: 'Our strategy is very, very clear.

We are going to cut the Iraqi Army off, and kill it.' In conventional war-fighting, where the destruction or defeat of the main body of the enemy is the prelude to a political resolution, this was fine; however, such confident certainties would be tested to destruction in the later, more complex 'wars of 9/11', in Iraq and Afghanistan. However, in Iraq in 1990, we were hugely encouraged by the Americans' determination. We were firm NATO allies, and we knew just how much we owed to the US for their conventional presence in Europe and their ultimate nuclear guarantees against the Soviets. However, few of us had ever worked closely with them. From then on, we have never stopped working alongside them and, whatever the political strains in the period after 2003, the military experience has always been positive. There is a danger in making sweeping generalizations about a great country, and about a very large military cohort, but my experience with the US Armed Forces has been extensive and always positive. They were then, and they remain, big-hearted, welcoming and generous, consummately professional, intelligent and empathetic, imbued with a deep sense of patriotism and public service and courageous to a fault, both morally and physically.

I subsequently served with Americans in Bosnia, Kosovo, Iraq and Afghanistan, in command and on staff appointments, and I believe our military interests were nearly always best served when we hugged them closely, and poorly served when we sought to plough a 'UK-only' furrow. The first Gulf War was the start of the modern US-UK military 'special relationship', within which so many British officers developed those professional and personal relationships that are the core lubricant of coalition operations. If there are weaknesses, they are, paradoxically, in the Americans' innate sense of self-confidence, so refreshing and positive but a potential limitation when they operate amongst other cultures, particularly when allied to a lack of 'curiosity' about the outside world, about 'the other'. Here is where Britain's global historical experience can sometimes be valuable, if deployed tactfully. It is perhaps what made them grasp with such enthusiasm the thesis of Francis Fukuyama that the West, and by extension the US, had won the global battle of ideas with the fall of the Berlin Wall. Cynical Europeans, more attuned to the lengthy shadows that history can cast, would often give more credence to the gloomier proposition put forward by Samuel Huntington. I was one of the latter. These positive American traits are an understandable product of the history and founding principles of the Republic, and of the huge success of the US since 1945. However, in the Middle East, that deeply complex cockpit of historical entitlement, inspiration and grievance, such attitudes can generate frustration, anger and sometimes violent resistance. American assumptions about 'equality' and 'rights' do not necessarily strike a positive chord in very conservative societies, where cultural norms are often underpinned by strict religious observance. This was less of an issue in 1990 than it was in 2003, but the coming rise of Al Qa'eda would draw much of its self-justification from the strong 'infidel' Western presence in Saudi Arabia at that time.

Arriving to take up the post of a divisional flank liaison officer, I was quickly informed that I was now to be the Operations Officer at one of the two headquarters from which General Rupert Smith would deploy, train and command the British ground contribution to Operation Desert Storm. Having focused on Germany for so long, it is difficult to convey how extraordinary it then seemed to be planning to advance across the Arabian deserts, alongside the Americans, in the sort of sweeping movements, unhindered by physical obstacles, of which a cavalryman could normally only dream. In some ways, unsurprisingly, we were singularly unprepared for our new circumstances. Our tank tracks were not designed for the harsh erosion of fine sand, our engine filters were not up to the job, we had no desert combat uniform or boots and we were ill-informed about how cold and wet the Northern Gulf could be in winter. Global Positioning Satellites were in their infancy, and although this was to be the first war of the new cruise missiles, which so entranced television audiences as they appeared to navigate themselves around the street layout of Baghdad, this was not a luxury the ground forces yet had. We were also short of body-armour, notwithstanding my own elegant personal solution; such supplies as the British Army did have were still committed to operations in Northern Ireland. Despite this, few of us had any moral or psychological problems with our presence in the Gulf, or our likely mission, and we knew that titanic efforts were being made to address these deficiencies before we started operations. One of the more irritating aspects of the operation, however, was the determination of some elements of the British press to emphasize the supposed Iraqi military capability and to speculate on casualty figures. This remained a sobering thought throughout our preparations, and even more so for families back home. Such intrusion on operations and speculation would only become more pronounced as the years passed.

I spent the night of Christmas Eve with Arthur Denaro and his Regiment, the Queen's Royal Irish Hussars, and we celebrated the Nativity with a carol service and midnight mass underneath the stars. At thirty-four, my youthful assumptions about immortality remained, but as I looked across the ranks of young men singing of their confidence in 'peace on Earth, good will to all men', it seemed impossible, if we were called on to fight, that all of us would not have some close friend or comrade killed or badly wounded. Shortly after Christmas, in recognition of the fact that we might well be in for a period of lengthy diplomacy, we instituted a closely–controlled furlough programme for the Division, and three of us found ourselves in the Diplomat Hotel in Bahrain over New Year, singing Auld Lang Syne to a Filipino band. My fellow New Year revellers included Captain Tom Beckett, who would succeed me as the Defence Senior Adviser Middle East a quarter of a century later. Right up to the last days before the ground offensive began, the military postal system continued to deliver letters and parcels. We were overwhelmed by 'tuck boxes' and an extraordinary range of letters and 'goodies' that arrived from friends, family and often just members of the public, addressed simply to 'a soldier in the desert'. Several marriages resulted from these missives. On the night-shift the briefing map, better known as 'the bird-table', often served a useful secondary function as a picnic table for remarkably exotic 'midnight feasts'. I was sent a copy of William Dalrymple's book *In Xanadu*, which I subsequently swapped for an American camp-cot in one of the great trades of the Gulf War. There was a sustained flow of morale-boosting contributions to the war effort, although it took me a while to work out, in seeking to bypass the strictures against alcohol in Saudi Arabia, that the bottles of 'baby lotion' and 'shampoo' were for imbibing, not for personal hygiene. At one stage a whole side of salmon arrived, although the prize for the least useful present of all went to a Queen's Dragoon Guard officer, 'Spook' Pittman, who took delivery of a three-piece blue pinstripe suit just prior to our advance into Iraq.

Originally we had been deployed to bolster the US Marine Corps directly south of Kuwait, but by New Year we were well into executing General Schwarzkopf's brilliant deception plan and beginning to move the bulk of the Coalition ground forces to the west, in order to carry out the powerful 'left hook' (see Map 9). 'Any news?' was the constant refrain of those coming on shift as we approached and finally crossed the UN deadline of 15 January. By this stage we were dug in some 40km north of Al Jubayl, and the bitter weather, which was to be a feature of the campaign, had locked in. I was sat in the command post at around two o'clock in the morning of 16 January, cursing myself for not having brought enough warm clothing with me and discussing whether a swift victory and a skiing holiday remained an option, when the secure line from General de la Billière's HQ in Riyadh rang.

In a voice simultaneously anxious, excited and breathless, his military assistant said, 'Simon, you should know that fifteen minutes ago the US launched a hundred cruise missiles at Iraqi positions, and Allied Air Forces are now bombing Baghdad. Could you inform General Rupert?'

As I turned to my fellow staff officers there was an anticipatory silence, almost tangible in its intensity.

'It's begun', I declared, in the absence of anything more profound to say.

Tension there may have been, but there was also a palpable sense of relief. The Coalition governments had crossed the political minefield to this decision point with exemplary confidence. We were not now to be left impotent in the desert, awaiting some fudged, face-saving deal. The outcome, given the overwhelming forces arrayed against them, was now clear, and the Iraqi Army had two options: withdraw, or be destroyed where they stood.

All through the rest of January we continued to close up with the bulk of our superior formation, the US 7th Corps, to the west of the Wadi al Batin. G-Day, the beginning of the ground offensive, remained a closely guarded secret as we worked to build up the maximum combat power for an assault on the well-prepared and heavily-defended Iraqi positions. I ran the Divisional HQ by night, as the primary staff officer, handing over to my daytime opposite number after the early morning updates. Life was a constant series of operational and intelligence briefings and training exercises, both with our own forces and with the Americans, particularly in preparation for the deliberate breaching of the border sand defences, the 'berm', and the extensive Iraqi minefields. The arrival and stockpiling of equipment and ammunition were continually monitored. All this took place against the backdrop of the Iraqi Scud campaign and its increasingly apparent impotence, the continuing devastating air offensive and the sudden and doomed Iraqi assault on Ras al Khafji. We were constantly looking for any indication in the Iraqis' dispositions that might indicate they had identified our move west, and we stood by in anticipation of chemical strikes or spoiling attacks that could unbalance our preparations. We were well briefed on the Iraqi use of chemical weapons in their conflict with Iran. Our respirators went everywhere with us and no one was heard with more pleasure at the daily briefings than the chemical defence officer with his 'Nothing to report'. That said, in the early days we stood-to, in our respirators, at every 'Scud-alert'. When it became clear that the Iraqis could not even hit Riyadh, and that a strike on our well-protected

HQ in the middle of the desert would just be sheer bad luck, we became rather more cavalier in our response. This was not so when we had to bunch up, in due course, in order to move through the breach in the Iraqi defensive positions, at which time our justifiable concern went right back up.

In retrospect, there is no doubt that the Coalition ground forces could have struck earlier, with the same ultimate result, but we were well aware of the political imperative to keep Coalition casualties to a minimum, an aspiration we all heartily endorsed. By the middle of February, firm details of the ground plan were being unveiled, and we noticed that the emphasis of the air campaign was switching from deep interdiction of Iraqi command and control nodes, and the logistic supply routes, to the Iraqi positions directly to the north of us. The weather continued cold and wet and, in this unseasonable climate, even long-dormant grass seeds were germinating, giving a green sheen to the desert. Indeed, one day we emerged from the night shift to find the rising sun glinting off a thin layer of ice.

As I ran the night-shift operations staff, I normally had the days 'off'. Although we usually tried to sleep, at least to doze, until early afternoon, professional curiosity made many of us anxious to see whatever we could of this mighty military enterprise. One day, another Sandhurst and Camberley friend, Richard Folkes, visited the HQ in his Lynx helicopter. Would I like to come with him to visit an American aviation battalion? I leapt at the opportunity, as did Jim Baxter. As we sat in the briefing tent with Colonel Mooray and a cup of what, in those days, passed for coffee in America, a staff officer ran in with a new mission for the unit.

'Got to go', said the Colonel darting for the door. He checked himself. 'Say, do you guys want to come along?'

'Yes', I said.

Richard looked less certain. 'What about my helicopter?'

'Look, Richard', I replied, 'if we get shot down that will be the least of your worries, and if we don't, your Lynx will still be here when we get back.'

So it was that at one moment we were in the relative safety of Saudi Arabia, the next, strapped into a Blackhawk helicopter, we were thundering into Iraq at about 130 knots, 30ft above the desert and hell-bent on the destruction of an Iraqi radar site. The SAS were already deployed within Iraq on their 'Scud-hunting' mission, but as the first rockets exploded on the position, there was some exhilaration in knowing we were among the first British soldiers to see live rounds fired in anger, although tempered by the knowledge that real people, with real families, were on the receiving end.

Needless to say, our mutual 'bond of secrecy' did not survive beyond the first ten minutes of later interrogation by colleagues.

Meanwhile, back in the UK, an older military campaign was still active. On his retirement, my father had become Security Adviser to the Cabinet Office. On 7 February 1990, when he had presciently just submitted a report that said it was impossible to fully guarantee the security of Whitehall without turning it into a pedestrian-only 'fortress', an IRA mortar attack on Downing Street almost killed John Major and his cabinet. My father's windows were blown in, but fortunately he was not in the office at the time.

Standing outside 'the bunker' at night, watching the flashes on the horizon from bombing missions, or going forward to the border berm to monitor the massive firepower of the artillery strikes alongside the likes of Kate Adie, Robert Fox and other journalists, we felt genuine sympathy for the Iraqi soldiers, in all probability conscripted from the repressed Shia majority, possibly veterans of the murderous Iran-Iraq War, crouched in their cold, wet trenches, poorly fed and equipped, awaiting the inevitable onslaught. However, it was our firm conviction that, while our mission was the liberation of Kuwait, we also had to inflict a comprehensive defeat on Saddam Hussein's military, in particular on the Iraqi Republican Guard, not simply the best equipped, trained and motivated of the Iraqi forces, but the backbone, alongside the brutal intelligence services, of Saddam's murderous Ba'athist regime. Napoleon stated that 'the moral is to the physical as three is to one', and we believed that the more demoralized the Iraqi soldier was, the more limited his resistance would be when the ground forces clashed.

Two days before G-Day, now set for 24 February, it looked as though Saddam had suddenly capitulated, and news of a set of Russian 'peace proposals' sent a wave of mixed emotions through the Coalition. Human emotions pulled us in conflicting directions, not least those with families, but most saw in the disingenuous Russian initiative that face-saving fudge we had all feared, and we could not help feeling that to stop operations at this stage would simply be to condemn ourselves to undertake a similar operation at a later date, very possibly in less advantageous circumstances. Similar emotions, under different circumstances, would mark the preparations for invasion in 2003.

Saddam's 'rivers of blood' speech therefore came as something of both a surprise and a relief. Both we, and, it transpired, most Iraqi generals, had believed that the Iraqi President would play a long game and withdraw from Kuwait in order to preserve his army and his power base. Within hours of the expiry of a follow-up ultimatum by President Bush, the largest bombardment since 1945 began, and the Coalition ground forces sprung the trap. The unfolding of the ground war is well-told history by now: the pitch-black nights; the driving rain; the unexpectedly brief resistance; the expected chemical attacks that did not take place; and the waves of relieved prisoners of war. No one slept as we strove to balance the requirement to maintain momentum against the logistic strains imposed by the speed of our advance and the long distances. We were moving the divisional HQ every six hours, rather than the planned twenty-four, as we sought to keep close contact with the leading troops.

We had gone through the breach in the border berm in a huge, nose-to-tail column of vehicles, in our chemical defence suits, festooned with helmets, side-arms and respirators, pumped full of nerve-agent pre-treatment tablets, and with our arms aching from anthrax injections, although I had politely passed up the offer from an enthusiastic medic of an anti-plague injection as well. As reports kept flooding in of short, sharp, violent and successful engagements, we began to experience a growing realization that, God willing, we were going to survive this event, that the casualty lists would not be full of familiar names and that we were taking part in one of the most spectacularly successful advances in military history. It was at that stage, on the evening of 27 February, that the secure phone to Riyadh rang yet again.

'Simon, please inform General Rupert there will be a ceasefire tomorrow morning at 0800 hours.'

'You are joking', I said. 'You know as well as I do that we have not finished this business. All reports from the US flanking formations tell us that the Republican Guard is battered, but still a credible fighting force.'

'I know that, Simon', said a weary voice. 'That is how we all see the situation here as well, but that is the direction from Washington to Schwarzkopf.'

I woke Rupert Smith from a snatched slumber, to break the news: 'We are declaring a ceasefire for tomorrow morning.' I saw by his face that he, too, felt this was premature.

By eight o'clock on the morning of 28 February, the ceasefire offered to Saddam by the Americans, without full consultation with allies, was in force, and the 'hundred hours war' was complete. We had just crossed the Iraq-Kuwait border and were driving on to Kuwait City in a final attempt to halt any further Iraqi withdrawal. The mood was therefore one of gritty and weary exuberance, tempered by our grim surroundings. Burning, burnt and destroyed vehicles were scattered across the landscape, bodies lay in the grotesque awkwardness of death, smoke was rising and ammunition continued to 'cook off' and explode at intermittent intervals. Over the drab, featureless landscape a milky sun was just visible through the low black cloud cover created by the oilfield fires lit by the withdrawing Iraqis in a last, spiteful gesture and fanned by an onshore wind.

A reporter expressed himself surprised – indeed, he actually sounded a little disappointed – by the effectiveness of the operation. I apologised to him, ironically, that we had not made it more difficult for ourselves.

'A "bad" war for journalists', I said, 'normally implies that it has been a "good" one for the soldiers who actually have to do the fighting. This is what you taxpayers have been paying for. For all its deficiencies, this was the Army with which we were going to fight the Third World War. You and your colleagues may have been misled by amateur assessments of Iraqi capability, and relative military strengths, but no professional should seriously have doubted the military outcome.'

Clearly, he felt it would have been 'fairer' if we had taken more casualties. In *Quartered Safe Out Here*, George McDonald Fraser's outstanding book on the grinding experience of junior leadership in the Burma campaign, he writes of encountering a similar attitude at the end of the Pacific War. This time it was people decrying the use of the atomic bomb to bring the war with Japan to an end, completely unsympathetic to the number of Allied casualties that would have been incurred in a conventional invasion.

The Divisional HQ moved into the Mutla Farm date plantation, a rare oasis of greenery up on the Mutla Ridge, a feature rising a few hundred feet above the capital city. The formations and units of the Division were spread out along and on either side of the Kuwait City–Basra road. In 2014 a Kuwaiti friend took me back to the Mutla Farm, and it was slightly eerie to walk the tracks in the plantation, trying to conjure up again in my mind how it had all looked in early March 1991. Needless to say, there was no longer any evidence of our occupation, and anything we may have left had long been covered by sand. My thirty-fifth birthday fell on 7 March, and here, coming all the way through the logistic chain, and hot on the heels of our military success, was a brandy-soaked birthday cake, with eight whisky 'miniatures' baked into it. A small, discreet operations-staff party marked the occasion. The pace remained frantic, although the focus had changed. We had to support those putting out the oilfield fires; to feed, tend, house and secure tens of thousands of Iraqi prisoners; to start clearing mines; to bury bodies; to prepare our own, mercifully few, dead for repatriation; to collect and destroy enemy weapons and ammunition; to repair and recover our own battered vehicles; and to bring up food, water, fuel and lubricants. There was a small residual threat of enemy action, for which we had to be prepared, and we still had a very extended logistic chain, going back west to where we had breached the berm. To shorten this line of communication, General Rupert asked me, as an Arabic speaker, to negotiate a new supply route with the Egyptian and Syrian forces which were then straddling the road stretching west from Kuwait City back into Saudi Arabia. To do this I had to make my way through a minefield gap that had been cleared to the west of the 'Highway of Death', the images of which we held partly responsible for the premature end to the military operations. It was certainly a sea of carnage, but the reality was that, when the head and tail of the column of fleeing Iraqis had been hit, those in the main body of the traffic jam had read the writing on the wall. Unable to leave the road due to the minefields on either side, they had abandoned their cars, and their loot, and most had fled safely back into Kuwait City. But the damage to the prospect of a decisive end to the campaign had already been done.

We opened the new Divisional logistic route, and then began to deal with the plethora of visitors, while planning our own extraction back to the UK and Germany. An early arrival was the new Prime Minister, John Major. He was already looking towards the election of 1992 and he wanted to capitalize on our 'victory', and 'get our boys home', fast. It was an understandable sentiment, shared by many of us, although we were disquieted by the unseemly haste to disengage. We were aware of similar pressures on Norman Schwarzkopf. George Bush also had an election to fight. Despite his huge popularity at the time, his fatal declaration, 'Read my lips! No new taxes', a pledge he would be forced to break, would deliver the presidency to Bill Clinton. The absence of George Bush would have important implications for how the West handled Russia in the 1990s, with their immense sense of loss and humiliation at the collapse of their 'Empire'. I was responsible for the programme of John Major's visit, and it was heavily dependent on helicopters. On the morning of his arrival in Kuwait I came out of the HQ to see a rare clear sky. With the sound of helicopters starting up at the nearby helipad, I was in a good mood.

'Call me a cock-eyed optimist', I said to Chris Sexton, a fellow officer, 'but this looks like a fly-programme to me', something which would include visits to UK troops.

At that very moment a pilot ran round the corner shouting, rather theatrically, 'Abort, abort, abort!'

Apparently the oilfield smoke had chosen this day of all days to settle across Kuwait City, thereby limiting the PM's visit to the politicos and those units, mostly American, he could get to by vehicle. For years afterwards Chris and I would greet each other with a cry of 'Abort, abort, abort!' accompanied by frantic chopping motions across the throat and much laughter. We certainly found it funny, but maybe you had to have been there.

Gradually, the speed of withdrawal gathered pace; the combat troops departing first, then the supporting elements and lastly the coordinating headquarters. The US chose to hold on longer and to implement a full repair, maintenance and repainting programme for their vehicle fleet. We were pleased to be on our way home, but our professional instincts told us that their approach was the correct one, and we were to be proved right. We wasted, or lost, vast quantities of assets and stores, and we allowed a degradation of vehicles, over the months it would take to load, ship and unload them again in Germany, that it would take tens of millions of pounds to rectify. More importantly, the same domestic imperatives to get us out quickly impacted on the negotiations at Safwan. These left major deficiencies in the final agreement, which was not subject to the right level of scrutiny and which contributed to Saddam remaining in power, and to further misery for the Iraqi people and the region. The decade-long no-fly zones of Operation Provide Comfort (later Northern Watch) and Southern Watch were unsatisfactory mitigation for our failure to conclude the campaign decisively. In 1998 President Clinton was forced to initiate Operation Desert Fox, a barrage of cruise missiles, in order to 'punish' the Saddam regime for its infringements of the ceasefire arrangements, its continuing attempt to breach UN sanctions and its apparent attempts to revive its weapons of mass destruction (WMD) programmes. Five years later, we were back again on the road to Basra, but this time we went all the way to Baghdad.

Chapter 16

The Mould Breaks

Istayed in and around the Gulf for several weeks after the end of the campaign. From my previous time in Oman I had many friends in the area, and the RAF seemed to be running a rather convenient 'shuttle service' up and down the coast. As I breezed through Bahrain for the third time and once again gave my name, rank and serial number to the young Flight Lieutenant, I noted over her shoulder that under the heading 'Sponsor' she had simply written 'God knows'!

While I do not think the new Commanding Officer of my Regiment was over-anxious to see me, he was clearly beginning to wonder what 'vital task' I was engaged on that required me to stay in the Middle East so long after Kuwait had been liberated. I reappeared in London, in time for the May Cavalry Memorial Parade, to be met with the usual derision and joshing from those who feel that any time spent away from regimental duty, even for a war, must be a 'jolly'. Sadly, the work we had begun in 1990 on cuts to the Army was now about to be implemented. We had naively believed that the Gulf War might make the Major government think again, if only out of a sense of gratitude for the sacrifices made. We should have known better; Her Majesty's Treasury had already banked the savings from the so-called 'peace dividend', long before we had even crossed the 'line of departure' into Iraq. The 15th/19th Hussars, last amalgamated in 1922, were now to be merged with the 13th/18th Hussars to form a new entity, the 'Light Dragoons'.

I was returning to regimental duty as a tank squadron leader, and we had a packed programme. We were due to go to Canada on Exercise Medicine Man, the demanding live-fire and manoeuvre training programme which was the great 'measuring-stick' for armoured competence and confidence. We did commendably well. Soon after that, we were to prepare for a six-month operational deployment to Cyprus as part of the longstanding UN presence on the island. It would be our 'last hurrah' as a Regiment before amalgamation in late 1992. The British Army occupied permanent bases in Episkopi and Dhekalia, and the RAF had the important airbase of

Akrotiri. However, since the Turkish invasion of the north in 1974, the British had also taken on a battalion-sized responsibility for a section of the Green Line, the UN-monitored division between the Turks and the Greek Cypriots. I had been there in 1976, during one of my university visits to the 15th/19th Hussars, when the Regiment had had an armoured car squadron in Nicosia supporting the infantry. I had not returned since, but had always hoped to. Back in the MoD, before we had both deployed to Iraq, my old pilot friend, Richard Folkes, had been responsible for helping determine the Army's operational tour plot. Just before the fall of the Berlin Wall, I had asked him about the possibility of my Regiment escaping from Germany for a while. Some months later, he had breezed into my office.

'Got any plans for the first half of 1992, old chum?'

'I didn't until now', I said. 'Is this your way of telling me that the 15th/19th Hussars are to take up the burden of defending the rules-based international world order in the Eastern Med?'

'It is', he replied.

'In that case you are worthy of a very large glass of red at Gordon's Wine Bar.'

Only now is it safe to reveal such secrets of the Cold War, and the scientific way in which the Army's operational deployments were determined.

The UN Force in Cyprus (UNFICYP) was not an 'operational tour' as it would have been viewed by those in Northern Ireland, let alone those who had served in the Falklands or the Gulf, but it was an important commitment, and by December 1991 we were back on the Line, with the Regimental headquarters at the old Nicosia Airport, unused since the Turkish invasion. David R-J had the Western Squadron, based in the 'Box Factory', with an area of responsibility that ran across 20km of farmland. I had the Eastern Squadron, headquartered in an old primary school, with my left flank close to the deserted Nicosia 'Grammar School', which overlooked us, and opposite Wayne's Keep, an old military graveyard. My right flank ran up to the Canadian positions near the old Ledra Palace Hotel, where the major UN north-south crossing point was. The Canadian area then ran through the centre of Nicosia City. The whole line followed the ceasefire limits of 1974. While the opposing forces were, in some places, over a mile apart, in others the UN presence was like a sliver of ham in a sandwich, the Turkish and Greek-Cypriot positions being so close to each other. While there was little direct danger to UN troops, the scope for local flare-ups was significant and highly charged politically.

Cyprus is a beautiful island, as anyone who has been there will testify. Its location and climate has made it the site of human settlement from earliest times. It was under Byzantine rule for 800 years, and subject to periodic and devastating Muslim raids until the Crusading period. In 1191, Richard the Lionheart seized the island from a renegade Byzantine 'emperor' who was foolish enough to threaten the Lionheart's fiancée, Berengaria, and his sister, Queen Joanna of Sicily, when they were shipwrecked off the island on their way to Acre and the Third Crusade. Richard and Berengaria were married in Limassol. A year later, Richard sold Cyprus to the Knights Templar, who in turn sold it to the disgraced King Guy de Lusignan, architect of the Crusader defeat at the Horns of Hattin. Thousands of Christians fled here after the fall of Acre in 1291. In the fifteenth century, the Republic of Venice took control of the island, at a time when the battle for control of the Eastern Mediterranean was at its height, and the galleys of Venice, Pisa, Genoa and the Knights Hospitaller of Rhodes were fighting the battle fleets of the Ottomans and their Barbary Coast allies. In 1570, between the successful defence of Malta and Don Juan's naval victory at Lepanto, the Ottomans took control of Cyprus, despite fierce resistance by the cities of Nicosia and Famagusta. In the latter siege, the Venetian commander, Marco Bragadin, was rewarded for his gallant defence of the city, in which the son of the Ottoman commander had been killed, by being flayed alive.

Ottoman rule was at times indifferent and at others oppressive, and this combination led to a gradual economic decline over 250 years, with the populations of the Muslim and Christian communities fluctuating throughout this time. During the Greek War of Independence in the 1820s, and after this long period of Ottoman neglect or harshness, the idea of *enosis*, or 'union' with the newly independent Greece, became firmly rooted among Greek Cypriots. At the 1878 Congress of Berlin, in the aftermath of yet another Russo-Turkish War, Cyprus was 'leased' to the British, although in terms of sovereignty the island, like British-controlled Egypt, technically remained *de jure* Ottoman territory until the outbreak of the Great War.

Ataturk's new Turkish Republic relinquished all claims to the island under the 1923 Treaty of Lausanne, and Cyprus became a British 'crown colony' in 1925. The island remained a vital possession in the Second World War and, although the Axis Powers challenged Malta and captured Crete, Cyprus was not significantly threatened. Post-war, the Greeks and some Greek Cypriots again raised the idea of *enosis*. The British administrators moved slowly to respond to this challenge, and the Greeks sought to internationalize the issue through the UN. The Turks, in a fit of neo-Ottomanism, also called for annexation of the island and then, in view of a population ratio that favoured the Greeks, suggested a division of the island. A sad and nasty little war ended up being fought by the British Army against the Greek Cypriot EOKA movement, the National Organization of Cypriot Fighters, which bitterly divided the island, polarized the two communities further and left the British in yet another unenviable and uncomfortable political position. This sombre period was well captured in Lawrence Durrell's book, *Bitter Lemons of Cyprus*.

In August 1960, just prior to our return from Aden, Cyprus had attained independence under President Archbishop Makarios as a result of the London Agreement between Britain, Greece and Turkey. Friction and discontent on all sides was not long in resurfacing, and inter-communal violence erupted again in December 1963, resulting in death, displacement and deep distrust. Communities retreated into ethnic enclaves, and the UN imposed the Green Line in Nicosia and set up UNFICYP. In 1964, Turkey, a member of NATO along with Greece since 1952, threatened to invade the island to defend Turkish Cypriots, but President Johnson forestalled this by threatening to withdraw US guarantees to Turkey in the event of a Soviet incursion. In the meantime, Greece dispatched 10,000 troops to the island. In July 1974, the Greek military junta inspired a *coup d'état* in Cyprus, overthrowing President Makarios and installing the local nationalist leader, Nikos Sampson. It should really have come as no surprise to anyone when, just five days later, the Turkish Army invaded, citing as justification breaches of the guarantees in the 1960 London Agreement. By December 1974 a ceasefire was in place, and the UN now extended the Nicosia Green Line across the whole island, while also extending the UNFICYP mandate. Thirty thousand Turkish soldiers were now on the island, and 36 per cent of Cyprus was under Turkish control. A hundred and eighty thousand Greeks had been evicted from the north, and 50,000 Turkish Cypriots had moved from the south to occupy their properties. In the next few years, a further 150,000 Turks from the mainland would join their compatriots and co-religionists.

By 1992 the extended Green Line had been in place for eighteen years, and the land either side of it remained much as it had been at the time of the original ceasefire. Its course was marked by a series of blue-and-white painted oil drums, interspersed with UN watch-towers. In that time, one soldier, in the Austrian sector, had been in his observation-post on eighteen six-month tours, a total of nine years, and had actually tried to purchase the site from the Greek-Cypriot government. Each troop of about thirty soldiers had a 'troop house', from which they sallied forth each day, and occasionally at night, to man the Line and ensure neither side had encroached on the other or violated the ceasefire conditions. Since we were close to Nicosia, the capital, we had many visitors, and the soldiers routinely had to give 'orientation briefs' to a range of military and diplomatic dignitaries. Having deployed just before Christmas, again, I was glad when the 'festive season' was over, as many of the soldiers in the Regiment had young wives and families and felt the separation keenly. On later operations, particularly in Iraq and Afghanistan, we would put a huge effort into forming strong 'Rear Operations Groups', back at the home-base, in order to do all we could to help those families left behind and thereby take any additional pressures off the husbands in the front-line, who needed to concentrate on looking after themselves and their fellow soldiers.

The UN tour in Cyprus was not demanding, although it carried significant reputational risk if good military discipline was not maintained, and we managed to fit in a fair amount of sport, fitness and 'adventure training'. One of our more significant achievements was to install lighting in deserted urban areas where the Turk and Greek Cypriot positions were close, as a way of building confidence. It was only a small step forward, but it took a level of sensitive negotiation that would have done credit to the Versailles Conference. As UN troops, we could go freely either side of the Green Line, and the officers routinely crossed the Pentadactyl spine of mountains to visit the old Venetian port of Kyrenia to drink brandy-sours or to dine at the lovely Kybele Restaurant in Bellapais Abbey. In many ways we found it easier to get on with the Turkish military than with the Greek Cypriots, who bore a huge sense of grievance and who felt the UN were far too 'even-handed'. At one point, David R-J and I were invited to an 'official dinner' by the senior Turkish officers. It was a fairly sumptuous affair, with lots of raki and plenty of good Turkish wine and kebabs. After some toasts and speeches, a belly-dancer appeared and made several circuits of the assembled officers.

'Time to deploy my Turkish linguistic skills', I informed David, and said, '*Mukemmel. Cokguzel*' ('Excellent. Very lovely'), while making exaggerated thumbs-up signs and giving a warm smile, which to observers probably looked more like a lascivious leer.

'Why thank you', the dancer said in a broad northern British accent, as she swept past me again, to the usual discordant Eastern music, navel gyrating, and thumb-cymbals clattering. 'Actually, I'm from Scunthorpe.'

C-plus, for effort.

For my mid-tour leave I chose to go to Syria and visit more Crusader castles. Syria in the early 1990s was a society in transition. Since the French departure in 1946 it had usually aligned itself with the Soviet Union, but the collapse of that 'Empire' had imposed a rethink on Hafez Assad, and he had seen an opportunity, in the Coalition operation to liberate Kuwait, to make overtures to the US. He also hoped, as a bonus, to give his rival, Saddam Hussein, a good kicking. He had achieved both, and Syria was 'coming in from the cold'. His suppression of the Muslim Brotherhood in Hama in 1982, when up to 25,000 people were killed, was conveniently overlooked. The brutality of this operation had given rise to the military term 'Hama Rules', meaning the complete, large-scale destruction of a military target. Hama would become an epicentre of opposition to Bashar al Assad during the Arab Spring, and its inhabitants would again suffer a similar fate. That was in the future. In 1992 I was superbly looked after in Damascus, and I often found myself smoking hubble-bubble pipes in the shadow of the wonderful Umayyad Mosque. The mosque was built on the site of a Christian basilica dedicated to St John the Baptist, and legend had it that the building contained his head. It was believed by Muslims to be the place to which Jesus would return at the 'End of Days', and its mausoleum contained the tomb of the great Saladin which General Gouraud had reportedly kicked in 1920. Visiting the covered market, with bullet-holes still in the roof from a French assault on the city in 1926, 'Straight Street' with the fabled 'Eye of the Needle', and roof-top garden restaurants, all made my stay exotic and fun. I rented a car and drove out to Palmyra, the great oasis capital of Queen Zenobia, who had launched a doomed revolt against the Romans, staying in the small hotel named after her. At dawn and dusk I strolled, almost alone, through the glories of Tadmur and sat looking down on this architectural marvel of the Roman period, from the Ottoman fort on a nearby hill. In 2016, all of this wonderful site would be subject to the barbarous iconoclasm of Islamic State, when they joined the other great 'destroyers' of history in attempting to expunge some of the world's greatest monuments and drain humanity's well of artistic achievement.

From Palmyra I drove to Aleppo, with its famous Baron Hotel, where so many Levant travellers, including T. E. Lawrence, Agatha Christie, Freya Stark, Gertrude Bell and Vita Sackville West, had stayed. Whether the historic visitors' book, now including Major Simon Mayall's signature, has survived the horrors of the Syrian civil war, I do not know, but the destruction of that great centre of civilization is yet another tragic story of the modern

Middle East. Aleppo is one of the oldest continuously inhabited cities in the world. It had an ambivalent political role during the Crusading period, as it sought to retain its independence from Baghdad, and it was outside its gates that the Ottomans defeated the Mamluks in 1516, and the caliphate was transferred from Cairo to Istanbul. It was the third largest city in the Ottoman Empire, and its importance as a trading centre only really began to decline with the opening of the Suez Canal. In view of the pictures that have dominated our television screens since 2012, it is difficult to believe that in 2006 Aleppo won the title of 'Islamic Capital of Culture'. From Aleppo, I went to the extraordinary castle of Sahyun, also known as Qalat Salah ad-Din (the castle of Saladin) with its dry moat and a drawbridge support column carved from live rock, and then to Qalat al Marqab, the vast Hospitaller castle on the coast. Finally, I visited the mighty Crac des Chevaliers that dominates the passes from the Syrian Highlands to the eastern plains beyond. This was also a Hospitaller castle, built on an existing fort and completed in 1170. Capable of housing a garrison of up to 2,000, it was strong enough to remain in Crusader hands through the destruction of the Kingdom of Jerusalem in 1187. During the long thirteenth century decline of the residual Crusader Kingdom, Crac finally fell to the Mamluks and Sultan Baibars in 1271, supposedly as the result of a forged letter, purportedly from the Grand Master of the Hospital, telling the garrison to surrender. While Sahyun and Qalat al Marqab are still accessible to the public, Crac des Chevaliers, and the town that nestles in its shadows, have been badly damaged in the Syrian civil war, although in 2020 it is firmly back in territory controlled by the Assad regime.

On my return to Cyprus I was informed that I had been fortunate enough to 'catch the selector's eye' for early inclusion on the 'Pink List', named for the colour of the paper on which it was printed, which listed those majors who would be promoted to Lieutenant Colonel over the next year. I returned to Germany to be second-in-command of the newly amalgamated Regiment, the Light Dragoons, which was standing up with Andrew Stewart, formerly of the 13th/18th Hussars, as the first commanding officer. All amalgamations are difficult, but this one had been as successful as it was possible to be in the circumstances, by dint of everyone being determined to make it so. It was also helped by having the focus of an early operational deployment to the Balkans, where the violence accompanying the long-anticipated collapse of Yugoslavia was now spiralling out of control. After a few months, I got a letter informing me that I was to go to Army Staff

College as a member of the Directing Staff. However, as I was making my arrangements I was directed to go and see General Sir John Waters, the commander who had signed off my application for Loan Service in Oman. I was to be interviewed for the post of Military Assistant to the Deputy Supreme Allied Commander, Europe (DSACEUR), the appointment he was due to take up in early 1993. I was successful, and there could not have been a more interesting time to be taking up a NATO appointment. The Cold War was over, the Soviet Union and the Warsaw Pact had collapsed and the Gulf War had utterly altered the political landscape in the Middle East. However, President George Bush, a key architect of those victories, had unexpectedly lost to Bill Clinton in the 1992 US presidential election. With the Balkans now collapsing into chaos, what was to become of the 'New World Order' that George Bush had told us we were on the threshold of?

Chapter 17

Belgium and the Balkans

'The Balkans' is both a geographical and, possibly, a linguistic term. Geographically, it refers to the large European peninsula separated from Asia by the Dardanelles, the Sea of Marmara and the Bosphorus. It is bounded by the Adriatic Sea to the west, the Aegean and Mediterranean Seas to the south, the Black Sea to the east and, very broadly speaking, the River Danube to the north. In Turkish, *Balkan* means 'a chain of wooded mountains', and in Persian *balk* means 'mud'. The area has both, in large quantities. Its geographical position has made it another of the world's great crossroads of migration, culture and conflict. It has been the junction between the Latin and Greek elements of the Roman Empire, and by extension, the dividing line between Catholicism and Eastern Orthodoxy. It has been the destination for massive successive influxes of 'pagans' from the east, both from the steppes of Russia and the plateau of Anatolia, and was one of the great historical fault-lines between Islam and Christianity.

Progressive Ottoman decline from the seventeenth century, and their precipitous collapse in the Great War, left a cauldron of unresolved ethnic and religious feuds and confrontations, between Catholics, Orthodox Christians and Muslims, and between Slavs, Turks and those Slavs who had converted, many centuries earlier, to Islam. Ottoman Muslim domination of the Balkans had lasted the best part of 400 years, and as a result of centuries of war and isolation from the mainstream of economic advance in the West, the Balkans suffered huge demographic decline and became the least developed part of Europe.

After the Great War, the idea of a 'Yugoslavia', a Union of South Slavs, was revived, and the Kingdom of Yugoslavia was formed in 1929. It was a majority Christian entity, but split between rival and antagonistic Catholic and Orthodox communities and containing a large Muslim minority, based mostly, but not exclusively, in the Austro-Hungarian province of Bosnia-Herzegovina. Muslim Albania became a separate state. The rise of the Fascist dictators put pressure on the divided loyalties of the country, and in 1941 Germany invaded, setting up an independent state of Croatia and occupying Bosnia and parts of Serbia. A Yugoslav resistance force arose, but it was riven from the outset by visceral loathing between its various elements. The blood-letting was widespread and conducted with shocking Balkan brutality. Allied attempts to get the various groups, Communist and Royalist, Croat and Serb, to concentrate on attacking the Germans and Italians rather than each other met with mixed fortunes.

In the 1945 Yugoslav elections only the Communists appeared on the ballot papers. Unsurprisingly, they won all the seats, and Josef Broz, better known as Tito, whose highly effective partisan actions during the war had made him hugely popular, became President of a new Yugoslavia. Tito's achievement was remarkable, given both the history and the geography of the constituent parts of a federal Yugoslavia. However, his success relied on repressive state structures and it bore heavily on the ethnic Albanians of the country, whose own nationalist ambitions, and their Muslim identity, made them doubly suspect. In 1980, Tito began to suffer blood circulation problems, his left leg was incompetently amputated and he died of gangrene.

On his death, ethnic tensions, always present, began to grow, and historical Serb ambition came to the fore again during the period of Soviet collapse. By late 1991 the longstanding centrifugal tensions in Yugoslavia had spilled over into inter-communal violence between Croats and Serbs, and by both sets of Christian Slavs against the Muslim communities. While the Croatian War of Independence lasted from 1991 to 1995 and was marked by the siege and bombardment of Dubrovnik, it was overshadowed by the Bosnian War that raged alongside it. In the face of this ethnic and religious conflict, the UN Security Council unanimously agreed to the deployment of peacekeeping troops in the Balkans. The United Nations Protection Force (UNPROFOR), eventually numbering 39,000 troops from forty-two countries, increasingly became focused on protecting Bosnian Muslims against a systematic programme of ethnic cleansing by the Bosnian Serbs under Radovan Karadzic. In spite of hostile actions by the Serbs, UNPROFOR successfully kept Sarajevo airport open, using it to distribute humanitarian aid. In April and May 1993, as I arrived to take up my NATO appointment, the UN had designated the Muslim towns of Srebrenica and Gorazde as 'safe areas', which were to be 'free from armed attack or any other hostile act'.

While the politico-military headquarters of NATO itself is in Brussels, the operational headquarters, Supreme Headquarters Allied Powers Europe (SHAPE), is in Mons. In 1993, the Supreme Allied Commander (SACEUR), who also doubled up as the Commander of all US forces in Europe, was

General John Shalikashvili. The British held the DSACEUR appointment, now filled by General Sir John Waters, and a German general, Peter Carstens, was the Chief of Staff. The headquarters had a rather American feel to it, but it was manned by officers and staff from across the alliance, although, at that time, the outer offices of the senior commanders were filled on a national basis.

I have mentioned before the tribal nature of the British Army, and this is nowhere more prominently reflected than in the variety of uniforms worn. On the first Friday of our handover, the outgoing MA, Hughie Monro, was wearing his Highlander rig of red and blue tartan, a blue jersey, a sporran, a dirk and glengarry headgear, with accompanying feathers. I was sporting Light Dragoon barrack-dress of jodhpur-boots, cavalry twill trousers, a pastel green pullover and a red side-hat, while also carrying a riding crop.

Colonel Rob Weber, a US naval aviator who worked for SACEUR, chanced upon us loitering in the corridor. He stopped, looked us up and down and said, 'My goodness, the thing I love about you Brits is your roll-your-own uniforms.'

Some months later, as I was sauntering down the 'nobs' corridor, recognizable as such because of the wood panelling, Rob was standing outside his boss's office speaking to another US officer.

'Hey, John', he said to his companion, 'I don't think you've met Simon Mayall yet. He's the DSACEUR's golf pro.'

SHAPE was a fascinating headquarters to work in, with an endlessly varied programme, and much travel. We were dealing with NATO 'Transformation' after the end of the Cold War, the NATO contribution to mitigating the horrors of the Balkan crisis and how the West should deal with Russia and the other new states that had emerged from the collapse of the Soviet Union. I often had to remind people that George Bush's declaration of a 'New World Order' had been, in many ways, a statement of fact, not necessarily carrying any moral weighting. The word 'new' did not automatically imply 'better', I said, it often just meant 'different'. It would be up to us, and the decisions we made, whether the global situation improved or not.

This was the era of the writings of Fukuyama and Huntington, and the battle of ideas between the liberal 'idealists', proclaiming the triumph of Western liberal democracy, and the 'realists', warning of the power of identity politics to wreck our assumptions. I increasingly believed that if George H.W. Bush had won the 1992 Presidential election we would have handled the consequences of the collapse of the Soviet Union much more effectively, although the instincts and behaviour of Boris Yeltsin, and the naked greed of the 'oligarchs', might very well have thwarted the best-intentioned of American leaders. President Bill Clinton, and many others in his administration, had a distinctly American and liberal-left disdain for history and its enduring influence, particularly when it was channelled through the prism of strongly-held religious identities. They could not envisage a time when the West might not be dominant, when the appeal of liberal democracy would not prevail against social conservatism and religious piety, and when the universalism of 'freedom' would not trump the particularism of ethnicity and religious identity. They did not see that so many cherished characteristics of Western society could often be viewed by other cultures and societies with suspicion and fear, and sometimes with a complex combination of attraction and repulsion. This latter ambivalence would progressively transmit itself to the large Muslim immigrant populations that began significantly to alter the demographics of Western Europe in this period, creating new fault-lines that would be brutally exposed in the decades after 9/11. Russia at this stage looked weak, and she had been the 'enemy' for so long that the idea of helping her manage her catastrophic sense of national loss was not a high priority for Western policy-makers, despite the evident long-term advantages of seeking a new model of partnership, rather than contributing to an already strong sense of resentment and revanchism. In the Balkans and the Eastern Mediterranean, Russia felt a strong sense of historical responsibility towards Orthodox Christians, not least the Serbs. To ride roughshod over these sensitivities was to store up problems for the future. America, Europe, NATO and the European Union continued, insensitively, to take advantage of Russia for nearly two decades after the collapse of the Soviet Union. At this stage, failures in Iraq, the financial crash of 2008, political unrest in Ukraine and the stumbling Western response to the Arab Spring and civil war in Syria gave Russia the opportunity to regain her self-confidence and self-respect, and to behave and operate in a manner wholly unhelpful to Western interests.

I travelled extensively with DSACEUR, including to the Caucasus, where the antagonism between Christian Armenia, Christian Georgia and Muslim Azerbaijan was still raw, and to the new Muslim Turkic Republics of Central Asia. These were fascinating visits from every point of view. With General John Waters, and then General Jeremy Mackenzie, both of whom were the greatest fun to work for, we were on the wilder frontiers of military diplomacy. In Kyrgyzstan we supped on effervescent mare's milk, while in Turkmenistan we only just avoided being 'gifted' a horse.

We watched General Moldabeyev pitch forward into his soup and vanish under the table, a victim of his own hospitality, while in Kazakhstan we held discussions with General Nuramgambetov, who held the award of Hero of the Soviet Union for his part in storming the Reichstag in 1945. In Azerbaijan we drove back from a visit to a run-down air defence base. There had been a typically long, vodka-fuelled lunch, and I was having difficulty staying awake. Jeremy Mackenzie was in the back with the Azeri Chief of Staff, sitting three abreast, with a rather large and perspiring interpreter between him and his counterpart. Noticing my soporific state, every time his host asked him a question, Mackenzie would mischievously say, loudly, 'What do you think, Simon?' giving me repetitive whiplash as I was hauled back out of my slumbers. Halfway to our destination, our host, through the interpreter, opened up a new front.

'The General says he earns $40 a month. What does the DSACEUR earn?'

I could have had a stab at what a four-star NATO officer was clearing, but I did not have faith in the Azerbaijan health service's ability to reach us in time to deal with our host's seizure.

Jeremy Mackenzie hesitated and, in a master class of tact, diplomacy and half-truth, said, 'Tell the General that I earn more than $100 a month.'

Even this evasive response almost caused the vehicle to leave the road. 'That is a ridiculous amount of money. How does he spend it all?'

Expectations may have risen in Azerbaijan in the last twenty years. One of our last visits together was to Tblisi in Georgia. Here, *tamadan*, a delightful tradition of eating, drinking, singing and reciting poetry together, had been hijacked in the Soviet era to become a form of social control, by concentrating on the drinking element. In 1995 the pendulum had not yet swung back to the traditional style, and we were well and truly ambushed, as toast after toast was proposed and 'no' would not be taken for an answer. Wives, parents, children, girlfriends, flags, battles, Presidents, the Queen, all were enlisted to keep the party going with a swing. DSACEUR and the rest of his delegation, resembling by this stage the last, shattered remnants of the Ninth Crusade, at last retired to the Metechi Palace Hotel, with its encouraging sign exhorting visitors to 'Please deposit your weapons with Reception, for the comfort and safety of other guests.'

When we returned from overseas trips, the General's driver would meet us with a 'Return to Work' brief from the office and any personal mail. Coming back from Canada, sometime in 1994, I opened a letter from the 'Colonel' of the Light Dragoons. In it he informed me that the Regiment had selected a fellow officer of mine to be the next Commanding Officer.

It was a blow. Command is the great milestone in a professional officer's career, and in 'single cap-badge' regiments there was normally only one shot at that appointment. John Waters fully understood my personal disappointment at this news and, with it, the potential career implications. He could not have been more solicitous. 1st The Queen's Dragoon Guards (QDG) might possibly have a gap for a commanding officer from another regiment on the next rotation, but that would not be until 1996. I must be patient. He was confident the system would 'rally round'. The word 'crisis' has an almost totally negative connotation in English, but in Chinese the equivalent concept is encapsulated in a bigram that contains the ideas of both 'danger' and 'opportunity'. It felt best to 'go Chinese' at this stage, and to accentuate the positive. Even if I was fortunate enough to be selected to command the QDGs, I would still have to wait a year after my MA appointment was over, which still had a year to run. I had always hankered to go back to university and, with John Waters' blessing, I now applied for a Defence Fellowship at St Antony's College, Oxford, with a view to writing a study on Turkey's security policy and challenges in the aftermath of the end of the Cold War. Inspired by memories of the 1980 military coup in Turkey, I felt that a study would be interesting and appropriate. Inevitably it would also include some examination of the Balkans, our current focus. Fortunately, the MoD agreed. Meanwhile it was 'back to the war'.

By early 1994 the Serbs were besieging both Gorazde and Srebrenica, and fewer and fewer UN supply convoys were getting into these 'safe areas'. To the Islamic world, the West seemed to be failing to protect the Bosnian Muslims, while to the Russians we were interfering in an area of historical interest to them and siding with Muslims against their Christian, indeed Orthodox, co-religionists. Both impressions would become unhelpfully engrained, despite our worthy intentions. In July 1995, the Serbs moved on Srebrenica and, sensing weakness in the UN response, took the town, killing around 8,000 Bosnian Muslim men and boys. These actions at last catalysed a major NATO air campaign against Serbian and Bosnian-Serb troops, and led to the Dayton Conference and Dayton Peace Accords of late 1995. By this time I was back at Oxford, and once again merely a bystander. In due course, the International Criminal Court in the Hague would bring successful war-crime indictments against many of the Serb and Croat leaders of this period.

Chapter 18

Scholar to Soldier, Again

S t Antony's College is a postgraduate institution founded in 1950 by a Frenchman, Antonin Besse. He had set up a highly successful trading company in Aden in the early twentieth century, and his sons and my grandfather knew each other when Alec was undertaking his construction work in Aden in the 1950s. I was now attached to the Middle East Centre as a Senior Associate Member. When I applied to the MoD to write a thesis on Turkey I was uncertain about what angle I would approach this important country from. It was a Muslim state, it had been an Empire, it occupied a strategically significant geographical position, it was an awkward member of NATO, not least because of its antagonism with Greece, it 'faced' in several different directions, due to geography, religion and history and it had a strong sense of 'historical entitlement' that made it a difficult partner. I knew about Constantinople, the Ottomans, the sieges of Malta and Vienna, the Crimean War and Gallipoli, and I knew of the significance of Ataturk from my initial visit in 1980 and from my time at SHAPE. However, I did not have a clear idea of the nature of Turkish society, its grievances and inspirations, its fears and ambitions.

Ataturk and Erdogan, the current President, are carved from the same adamantine material but have charted different courses to secure Turkey's place in the region and the world. In doing so, they both reflect the fundamental tensions that lie within all Muslim polities and societies. Ataturk, imbued with the spirit of the 'Young Turks', sought to wrench the new young Republic from the atavistic roots of its imperial past and its Islamic underpinning. Having defeated the Allied Powers' ambition to partition among themselves not just the Ottoman scraps but Anatolia itself, he had overseen one of the largest demographic shifts in modern history. The Greek population of Turkey fell from 1.8 million to 120,000, and the Armenian from 1.3 million to 100,000. He abolished both the sultanate and the caliphate, and tried to bind the new citizens of the Republic by imposing a new identity, that of 'Turk', despite the heterogeneous nature of the population, with its Sunni majority, many Balkan refugees, large numbers of Shia Alawites and a substantial population of Kurds. This 'transcendental' idea of politics, in which the community takes priority over the individual and has an 'interest' that is deemed to be distinct and separate from that of its citizens, is in marked contrast to the 'instrumentalism' of Western democracies, which seeks to manage and triangulate the competing interests of state, individuals and groups. Communist, nationalist, Islamic and Islamist countries all embrace a degree of this 'transcendentalism', exhibiting a confidence and certainty that liberal democracies have difficulty understanding or confronting.

Ataturk had a single overriding national mission: to raise the Turkish people to the level of contemporary 'civilization', identified as that of the West. Modernization was the solution. In instituting an economic, social and cultural revolution, he would seek to achieve recognition of Turkey as an 'equal' nation. Given the parlous state of Turkey in the 1920s, it was a Herculean task, and only someone with the authority and reputation of Ataturk could have even attempted it, in the face of the treble challenge of social conservatism, religious piety and ethnic diversity. In due course 'Kemalism', as it came to be known, would rely heavily on the vested interests of the state structures to sustain it, in particular the senior military leadership, who were staunchly nationalist and secular. Circumstances would change as Turkey wrestled with her multiple identities as a Balkan, European, Middle Eastern and Caucasian power. When those state structures, so important for stabilizing Turkey in a volatile region, were usurped by the AK (Truth and Justice) Party and its Islamist-leaning leadership, most notably Erdogan, Turkey's ever-closer alignment with the West and, with it, the increasing adoption of European norms, began to falter. Once again, Western policy-makers initially listened to those who looked and sounded like them and who told them what they wanted to hear, while ignoring the attitudes and prejudices of Anatolian peasants and workers, as they did those of the Egyptian *fellahin* and the Iranian ayatollahs. Erdogan's national ambition was similar to that of Ataturk, to establish Turkey as a major power, but he was fundamentally aligned to the Muslim Brotherhood, and his vision was of an Islamic state, not a liberal democratic one. For Erdogan, Islam, not reform or modernity, would be the solution.

That was in the future. In 1995, Turkey was at a new apogee of enthusiasm for the West. With the collapse of the Soviet Union, an historical threat seemed to have been lifted and, as the strategic centre of gravity shifted from Central Europe, observers had great hopes for this pivotal country with its important political, historical, religious and ethnic links to so many other areas. Through its membership of NATO, and its aspirations to join the European Union, people expected great things of Turkey, particularly when they noted the continuing influence of the secular military, and as they listened to the words of such politicians as Turget Ozal, Tansu Ciller, 'the Margaret Thatcher of the Near East', and Cem Boyner, all of whom seemed to confirm Turkey's destiny as a full-blown 'European country'. However, the more I studied Turkey, the more conservative I found her to be. The high-flown language of the politicians was firmly mitigated by the caution of the Ministry of Foreign Affairs and the senior officers of the Turkish General Staff. Exciting regional prospects raised concern rather than enthusiasm, and the constraints on the Turkish room for manoeuvre became more obvious, the more people I spoke to. I recalled British commentators opining that 'Margaret Thatcher was more ambitious for the British people than they were for themselves.' I sensed a similar mood in Turkey and in due course I entitled my thesis, 'Turkey, Thwarted Ambition?' The question mark was supposed to draw the reader's attention to this national ambivalence. In due course, when the thesis was published in America, the editors removed it and made 'thwarted ambition' a statement, not a question.

I used to go to Turkey regularly, often staying with great friends, Shannan and Hannah Stevenson, in their remarkable house, the 'Pasha's Library'. This sat on the high banks of the Bosphorus, next to the castle of Rumeli Hissar built by Mehmet the Conqueror, prior to besieging Constantinople, in order to cut off the prospect of Byzantine re-supply from the Black Sea. To sit in the garden smoking a *narghile* pipe, high above one of the great waterways of the world, watching warships and tankers passing from Odessa and Sebastopol to the Aegean, was an enchanting experience. At one stage I was in Ankara, visiting the British Embassy and interviewing a range of political leaders. One of these was Abdullah Gul, then Chairman of the Islamic Refah Party, the forerunner of the later AK. He would go on to be both Prime Minister and President of Turkey, until he fell out with Erdogan. In a private conversation we discussed the role of Islam in the Army, and he asked me if I felt it was fair, in a 'democracy', that officers and soldiers who displayed overtly Muslim leanings should be dismissed. I said that it was a pity one's religion and one's patriotism were deemed to be in conflict. I told him that I was a Catholic and that, until relatively recently, the British state had considered Catholics to have potentially dangerous split loyalties. Now, I said, there was no question about the commitment of Catholics in the British Army or their loyalty to 'God, Queen and Country'. I hoped Turkey would, in time, also be able to square this circle. His English was excellent, the interview went on twice as long as scheduled, and I went away very satisfied.

The next morning, my complacency was pricked. When I arrived at the Embassy, the Defence Attaché met me with a slightly harassed look on his face.

'I've been misquoted', I said pre-emptively, completely blindsided about what the issue was, but trying to get my retaliation in early.

'That is what the Ambassador wants to know', he replied, hustling me down the corridor to see Brendan Prendergast.

On the Ambassador's desk was a copy of *Milliyet*, a daily newspaper with one of the highest circulations in the country. It must have been a slow news day, because the headline, translated for my benefit, read 'Inconvenient Visit by British Army Officer'. Abdullah Gul had helpfully implied to a journalist that my comments on the role of religion in the military had been made at a 'press conference', not in the privacy of his office. The Turkish General Staff had picked this comment up and used Turkey's equivalent of the *Daily Express* to put a 'shot across my bows', those of the British Embassy and the Refah Party itself. Brendan Prendergast was an old hand in the region and, when I explained myself, just commented that I had been used in the growing stand-off between the Turkish 'establishment' and those who were increasingly challenging the pillars of Kemalism. I met Abdullah Gul many years later at a Fenerbahce-Galatasaray football match in Istanbul, and I reminded him of our conversation and its outcome. AK was by then firmly in the ascendancy, although Gul personally was out of favour with Erdogan. He roared with laughter. I could only join in.

Shortly after this episode, I went with Robin Hardy, an old friend from Balliol, to visit Trebizond, the great Byzantine city on the southern shore of the Black Sea that had survived for a further eight years after the 1453 fall of Constantinople. From Trebizond we went to the cliff-face monastery of Sumelia and then to the ancient Armenian capital of Ani, which lies close to the modern Armenian border and in sight of Mount Ararat, the supposed resting place of Noah's Ark. From here we travelled to see the isolated, lonely and lovely twelfth century Georgian churches in the remote hills and valleys of the region. It was at this stage that I became aware that we were being followed, as I kept seeing the same white Fiat with an Istanbul number plate. Robin was dismissive of my suspicions, but I recalled my brush with the authorities in Ankara. I was also rather aware that the north-east of Turkey was quite some way from the population centres of Istanbul and Izmir, let alone the tourist beach-resorts of the Turquoise Coast. There had been several reports of journalists 'going missing' in the area, and there were regular reports of Armenian or Kurdish 'terrorism'. At last, driving back to Artvin, it became clear to us both that we were under surveillance. As we came around the corner of the switchback road leading to the town, we ran into 'roadworks' and were directed off onto a dirt track. 'This is it', I was thinking, still consoling myself with the thought that I was a Lieutenant Colonel in the British Army and that the Embassy knew I was in the country. Several hundred yards later, we popped out again on to the main road. Yes, we were being followed, but no, the diversion had not been an elaborate ploy to give me some sort of 'shakedown'. Many years before, the academic, Robert Byron, visited ancient sites in Central Asia and in his book, *The Road to Oxiana*, related hearing his guide ask a companion, 'Why do you think the British secret service are interested in this cave?' I rather felt the Turkish General Staff had similarly mistaken my innocent and academic interest in the medieval religious buildings of the Caucasus for something more sinister.

Towards the end of our trip, we had overstayed our time at another site and were driving back in the dark, when we encountered a '*Gendarma*' roadblock. The young soldier, nervous but polite, asked for our passports.

'*Ingles?*' he asked.

'Yes', I replied, 'English. Number One.'

He seemed to absorb this for a moment then, leaning into the car, and looking concerned, he said, '*Carlesh*'.

'Not quite getting your drift, old boy', I said.

'*Carlesh*', he said again, his fellow soldier nodding vigorously. '*Carlesh*'.

Then he changed tack. '*Carlesh . . . and Diana.*'

The scales dropped from my eyes.

'*Cok problem*', he continued sympathetically.

'Oh yes', I agreed, 'very *cok problem!*'

It had been rather a surreal moment, keeping a weather eye open for a terrorist attack, while discussing the contents of *Hello* magazine.

When I got back to Oxford I received a letter from General Robert Ward, the 'Colonel' of the Queen's Dragoon Guards, inviting me to the Cavalry and Guards Club. At the conclusion of our lunch he confirmed that I would be the next commanding officer of his Regiment, taking over from Hamish McDonald. I was both hugely gratified and mightily relieved. I was enjoying being a student again, but I really wanted a full-time career as a soldier and the chance to pitch for the higher echelons. I was now 'back in the game', and I had been offered a wonderful opportunity to command a marvellous Regiment.

In early 1997, having submitted my thesis on Turkey, I drove through the gates of Athlone Barracks in Sennelager to take over command of 1ˢᵗ The Queen's Dragoon Guards, the senior cavalry regiment of 'the line', formed from a 1959 amalgamation of 1ˢᵗ King's Dragoon Guards and 2ⁿᵈ Dragoon Guards (Queen's Bays). We wore the Habsburg eagle as our cap-badge, since Queen Victoria had invited the Austro-Hungarian Emperor Franz Joseph to be our 'Colonel in Chief' in 1895, and we flew the Habsburg 'spread eagle' flag over our barracks, alongside the Union Flag and the flag of the Principality of Wales, reflecting our strong Welsh links. Our battle honours covered almost every major conflict that the British Army had been involved in since the seventeenth century, less the Falklands, and even there we had deployed one officer. A reinforced squadron had deployed to the 1990–1 Gulf War, and the Regiment had just returned from Bosnia. I would take them to Northern Ireland, and in the years after 9/11, the Regiment would undertake three operational tours of Iraq, and a further three tours in Afghanistan, conducting themselves with great professionalism and gallantry. Early in my command tour, we had a visit from a Russian delegation as part of the 'Conventional Forces in Europe' Agreement. While the ostensible reason for their visit was to check on the fifty-eight Challenger tanks I had within my barracks, I could tell that what really exercised their interest was the Imperial-white Habsburg flag flying at the gate, the Habsburg eagle on every soldier's beret, the huge portrait of the Emperor Franz Joseph in the Officers' Mess, the champagne at lunch and the Mess staff looking splendid in their 'Regimentals'. Goodness knows what they put in their report.

Command of a regiment is one of the highlights of any career, and whatever happens after that is a bonus. For many years, in true British 'Corinthian spirit', many officers had little interest in professional life after 'command'. The nature of imperial and colonial soldiering encouraged this attitude, and it took the salutary experiences of the Boer War, and then the sanguinary horrors of the First World War, to force the British Army to take their tactical and technical excellence at unit-level and raise their game to the formation-level. The doctrinal mantra had always been that the 'nature' of conflict was enduring and that war was always a violent contest of wills. It would remain a mix of chance, risk and policy, whose underlying nature was human, thereby making it inherently volatile. However, due to political change, societal evolution and advances in technology, experience and experimentation, the 'character' of conflict was dynamic and constantly changing. The realities of the Afghanistan and Iraq campaigns, post 9/11, would starkly expose, once again, the timeless tension between the 'enduring nature' of conflict and its 'dynamic character'.

The training programme, during my time in command, reflected the changing defence priorities of the late 1990s. We had cut the Army by a third since the Gulf War, and we had closed many of the familiar bases in Germany which had once supported a British military population, soldiers and families, of around 100,000. Despite this, we still stood by our belief that the UK needed an Army that continued to be capable of 'joined up war-fighting' at large-scale, most probably within a larger US-led coalition, as in the Gulf. Nowhere was this felt more strongly than in an armoured regiment. Therefore, in my first year I took the Regiment back to Canada to be put through our paces again on our great, live-fire training area in Suffield, Alberta. It was a gruelling, demanding and professionally satisfying experience, as it was designed to be, highlighting strengths, or revealing weaknesses, in individuals and organizations, commanders and subordinates, processes and procedures and training methods and equipment. We had, however, also learnt much from the complexity of recent multinational peacekeeping operations in such fractured countries as Bosnia, and there remained a continuing requirement for military support to the Royal Ulster Constabulary.

Therefore, whilst we put ourselves through our paces for our primary role as an armoured regiment, we also had an eye on Northern Ireland, since we had been 'stood up' to go to the Province in 1998 in the dismounted infantry role. After winning the 1997 general election, Tony Blair had initiated a further full-scale Defence Review, while also re-invigorating the Northern Ireland peace process. Northern Ireland and the 'Troubles' had been part of the political backdrop to most of my youth and all of my Army career. We all knew of the Ardoyne, the Shankill Road, South Armagh, the Maze Prison, Crossmaglen and Warrenpoint, and most of our infantry colleagues had spent interminable stretches of time in Ulster. It was becoming clear that weariness, political accommodation and economic success, north and south of the border, were at last marginalizing the hardline elements among both Nationalists and Unionists, and creating the conditions for a political settlement. This was, however, bringing into question the requirement for the routine deployment of additional troops. The Regiment wanted to go, as did I, and I wrote a letter to General Rupert Smith, who I had served under in the Gulf War and who was now the Northern Ireland commander. I told him that QDG had begun their training, that they relished the prospect of the tour and that it would be a huge blow to the Regiment to be now stood down. I said that we were happy to serve in any role, in any location and under any chain of command, and urged him to continue to support our deployment. In due course, a typically gracious response arrived, handwritten, in which Rupert Smith said that he fully understood my sentiments, that he could not actively advocate the QDG deployment on the basis of a personal friendship, but that he had no intention, as the senior commander, of making any recommendation that suggested QDG were not needed. I could not have asked for anything more, and the Regiment continued to train for the challenges of riots, snipers and bombs, while conscious that the political landscape, and with it the security demands, were changing fast.

We did eventually deploy to Northern Ireland, in May 1998, coinciding with the implementation of the Good Friday Agreement, and our organization, lay-down and tactics reflected these changing circumstances. We guarded the Maze Prison, with its mixed population of terrorists and ODCs ('ordinary decent criminals'), conducted endless patrols, cordons, checkpoints and searches, policed marches and demonstrations and stood patiently in the 'shield-wall' and alongside our lightly armoured vehicles, the infamous 'Snatch' Land Rovers of so many later Iraq inquests and inquiries, while the 'boyos' of both communities pelted us with bricks and petrol bombs. It was very light stuff compared to the experiences of our military and police forebears at the height of the 'Troubles', but it was an outstanding experience for young soldiers and commanders and another reminder of the flexibility and versatility required of modern armies. Britain had finished with National Service in the 1960s, and time and again we were reminded how difficult it would have been to sustain operations in Northern Ireland, or to have deployed effectively on 'wars of discretion' like Operation Desert Storm, or to the Balkans, with a conscript army. There had been an exponential rise in the prevalence of mass media and social media, and increasing judicial challenge. This was allied to a new generation of politicians and public who closely questioned the political and legal justifications for war, and the circumstances of casualties. In this environment, modern civilian and military leaders found themselves under ever-increasing scrutiny. These were all trends that would only gather momentum, and they would reach a crescendo in the Iraq and Afghanistan campaigns that soon confronted us.

The long experience of Northern Ireland should perhaps have prepared us much better for the complexity and nuances of Iraq in 2003, and later. We could have been better and more useful friends to the Americans in highlighting for them the multi-layered complexity that was likely to confront us all in the Middle East and Central Asia. We did take with us many of the lessons from our long campaign in the Province, but we remained unprepared to address or confront the enduring power and influence of ethnic, tribal or religious sectarianism. The Balkans should have been a further reminder of how violent ethnic and religious bigotry could be, how it fed on historical experiences of inferiority and oppression, of grievance and entitlement, and how much identification with one group or another determined the division of spoils in a society. To do so went against the zeitgeist of the West, our assumptions of 'universal values' and our determination not to be 'judgemental' about other cultures. In doing so, or not doing so, we actually displayed the worst type of Western patronizing attitudes, with disastrous results for our interventions, and particularly for the people of Iraq. It was in pressing for a clear-eyed, historical, 'realist' understanding of the religious and ethnic complexity of Iraq that Britain could have made a major contribution to the Coalition.

In January 1999, with a sense of sadness that no amount of anticipation can prepare you for, I relinquished command of QDG and handed over to my successor, Patrick Andrews. The Army had kindly sweetened the bitter pill by selecting me for promotion to full Colonel, and early in 1999 I re-entered the MoD as Colonel Army Plans, an appointment responsible for helping shape Defence policy on the size, shape and structure of the British Army.

Chapter 19

Rise of the Jihadists

A s we approached the new century, there was another turn of the wheel in the Balkans, this time in the Serbian province of Kosovo, with its large Muslim majority. The Dayton Agreement of 1995 had largely halted the three-way blood-letting between Croats, Serbs and Bosnian Muslims, but it had not addressed the issue of Kosovo, and soon political resistance there to Belgrade turned violent, leading to the formation of the Kosovan Liberation Army (KLA). A ceasefire had been brokered, but it collapsed just as I was returning to the MoD. The media were again full of stories of Serb brutality and atrocities against Muslims, and again, in the spirit of the times, international opinion called for intervention, although without being able to garner a UN Security Council Resolution, due to a Russian veto. The Serbs had come to be 'bogey-men' for the West, but they had long been aligned to Russia, by virtue of history, ethnicity and religion. China, whose Belgrade embassy would unfortunately be struck by a NATO missile, also voted against intervention, thus splitting the Security Council 3-2, although this now represented more a traditional power-play than the ideological division of the Cold War. Russia disliked Western high-handedness and continued to resent her loss of great power status. She was also concerned at any encouragement to secessionism and state break-up. This attitude would display itself again in the wake of Western intervention in the Middle East and during the chaos of the Arab Spring, Western failures in Libya, the rise and spread of Islamic State and the civil war in Syria. In the meantime, about a million Kosovo Albanians were displaced. A politically decisive, although militarily ineffective, bombing campaign was conducted between March and June 1999, at which point President Milosevic, in Belgrade, agreed to the presence of foreign troops in Kosovo and the withdrawal of Serb forces.

He had undoubtedly been influenced by the assembly of a NATO ground force in neighbouring Macedonia, although this had been a source of great friction with Greece, a NATO ally, but one who also had religious and historical reasons for siding with their fellow Orthodox Christians in

Serbia and Russia. At this stage, the population flows began to shift in the other direction, as Kosovans returned and Serbs now fled from avenging Muslims. On 10 June 1999, while we were still building up the force in Macedonia, UNSCR 1244 was passed, allowing the NATO-led peacekeeping force into Kosovo. Although Russia had acquiesced in this, she had also skilfully sent a small force to 'seize' the airport at Pristina. This resulted in a stand-off between General Wes Clark, the American NATO commander who wanted the Russians confronted and turned out, and General Mike Jackson, the British general in charge of the ground forces in the Balkans, who famously said that he was 'not prepared to initiate World War Three' over this Russian move. It was not a happy time for Alliance solidarity, and the Americans, the major stakeholders in NATO, felt understandably aggrieved, particularly when this contretemps went public.

The consequences of this successful intervention were to have a profound effect on subsequent calls for the international community to 'do something', not least in the wake of 9/11. In April 1999, a month after the bombing campaign opened, Tony Blair had made a speech in Chicago setting out the case for 'humanitarian intervention', while trying to steer a fine line between the consistent US desire to preserve its freedom of unilateral manoeuvre and the UN Charter, which allowed for interventions only in very specific circumstances, such as reversing aggression, as in Kuwait in 1990–1. Indeed, Article 2 of the Charter stated, 'All Members shall refrain in their international relations from the threat of force against the territorial integrity or political independence of any other state.' Blair outlined his five proposed rules for intervention: be sure of your case; exhaust all other options first; check if you are confident military operations can be successful; prepare for the long term; and identify if your interests are involved. Ideally, the UN would lead the way, but he implied that individual countries should, could and would act if the UN did not. The perennial problem here was that of who is the guardian of the definitions. As one man's 'terrorist' is another man's 'freedom fighter', so one man's 'intervention' can easily be seen, or characterized, as another's 'aggression'. Such distinctions would become painfully clear during the invasion and occupation of Iraq and in the international responses to the Arab Spring. It would be at this stage that US and Western war-weariness, and disillusionment with intervention, would be confronted by a resurgent, more self-confident and ambitious Russia. That was in the future. In the meantime, Tony Blair and President Bill Clinton were visiting Kosovo, where the adoring cries of 'Tonee, Tonee, Tonee!' would have been enough to turn anyone's head.

In November 2000, George W. Bush, son of the former President, won the US presidential election. With that result, whatever the institutional strengths of the British–American 'special relationship', Tony Blair seemed to have lost his key ally in the White House. Where Bill Clinton had been a liberal, multilateral internationalist, the new President seemed less convinced by 'liberal intervention' and much more determined to focus on American domestic and economic agendas. However, in the words of P. G. Wodehouse, 'fate has a nasty habit of sneaking up behind you with a cosh.'

In our enthusiasm for the 'New World Order' and the 'liberal interventions' of the mid to late 1990s, our attention had unhelpfully slipped from events in the Middle East and Central Asia. With the collapse of the Soviet Union, Russian backing for the Afghan government had fallen away, and the Pakistani ISI had helped manoeuvre to put the mujahideen in power. In the ensuing instability, militias formed, warlords thrived, along with criminals, state structures collapsed and the divisions between the Pashtun, Uzbek and Tajik communities were exacerbated. In 1994, the Taliban (literally 'students'), a movement originating among young Afghan refugees in Pakistan, well-funded and ideologically motivated by Saudi Arabia, developed as a politico–religious force, rapidly taking control of Southern Afghanistan and the Pashtun heartlands. At the same time, in the north, the Tajik leader, Ahmad Shah Masoud, took control of Kabul. In 1996, as an uneasy peace descended on the Balkans, the Taliban, backed by Pakistan and Saudi Arabia, prepared for a major offensive against Kabul, and Masoud withdrew to his stronghold of the Panjshir Valley in the north-east. The Taliban established the 'Islamic Emirate of Afghanistan' and imposed a strict form of sharia law that was probably only exceeded in its application of methodical violence and brutal control with the advent of Islamic State. Afghanistan became the proxy battleground for Arabs, Iranians and Pakistanis, with horrendous levels of violence, death and displacement. The war against the Soviet Union and the Afghan Marxist government had attracted several thousand ideologically motivated recruits from across the Islamic world. While many of these had been killed, others, further radicalized by their experiences, went 'home' and, in true *takfiri* style, sought to continue the jihadi struggle. One of these individuals was Ramzi Yousef of Kuwait, who had spent time in training camps in Afghanistan and who had arrived in the US in September 1992, planning to detonate a bomb. Aided by his uncle, Khalid Sheikh Mohammed, later considered to be one of the principal architects of the 9/11 attacks, he aimed to set off an explosion in the basement of Tower One of the World Trade

Centre, with the intention of toppling it into Tower Two, thereby bringing them both down. He estimated that he could inflict 25,000 casualties. In the event, a bomb was detonated that killed six people but failed to achieve its apocalyptic intent. Ramzi Yousef was eventually hunted down and arrested in Islamabad.

Many mujahideen had also chosen to stay on in Afghanistan. These included Osama bin Laden and Ayman al Zawahiri, an Egyptian religious scholar, a leader of the Egyptian Islamic Jihad movement and an avid student of the teachings of Sayyid Qutb of the Muslim Brotherhood. Back in 1984, they had already set up the Maktab al Khidamat (MAK), or 'Services Office', to facilitate international support for the mujahideen. They had a major facility in Peshawar, but also branches in the US, where the continuing focus on the Soviets blinded the Americans to the new threat these two were incubating through innocuous-sounding 'charitable' organizations. A military training camp was set up in Pakistan known as Al Qa'eda (the Base), and this name came to denote the wider foreign-fighter network. Although there is debate about its foundation, it seems likely it was at a meeting in August 1988 that it was agreed to link ideology, money and the existing jihadi network into a more formal structure. At the same time, Al Qa'eda's goal of 'lifting the word of God and making His religion victorious' in Afghanistan was extended to other parts of the world.

In 1990, Osama bin Laden had returned to Saudi Arabia to make his quixotic offer of the mujahideen to defend the Arabian Peninsula against Saddam Hussein. Rebuffed, he was then banished to Sudan, where he nursed a festering grudge against the House of Saud for inviting Western forces into the 'land of the Two Holy Cities', a grudge that was further inflamed by Saudi support for the Israel-Palestinian Oslo Accords of 1993, seen as yet another 'betrayal', on a par with the Egyptian-Israeli peace treaty of 1979. In 1996, after a series of failed and clumsy assassination attempts in Egypt and Sudan, the Al Qa'eda leadership was expelled from Khartoum and relocated again to Afghanistan, to set up their headquarters under the protection of the Taliban. From here they committed themselves to launch the offensive phase of a 'global jihad', with the explicit aim of driving non-Muslims from every Muslim land and imposing 'good Islamic behaviour', as defined by them, on all Muslims, including those in Western countries. In 1996, Osama bin Laden issued a fatwa, a religiously binding edict, which amounted to a declaration of war against the US and its allies.

Neither Osama bin Laden nor Ayman al-Zawahiri in fact had any of the traditional Islamic scholarly qualifications to issue a fatwa, but they were not going to let a small detail like that stand in their way. On 23 February 1998, rejecting the authority of the various institutional *ulema* of the Islamic world, they co-signed a further fatwa calling on Muslims, collectively and individually, to kill Americans, British and others, whenever and wherever they could. Other co-signatories included the leaders of jihadi movements in Egypt, Pakistan and Bangladesh. Under the banner of the 'World Front for Combat against Jews and Crusaders', they set out their case against America and her Western allies, and the Israelis and the Jews, citing: the US military presence in Saudi Arabia since the Gulf War; the use of such bases to attack other Muslim countries; the devastating effect of war and sanctions on the Iraqi people; the humiliation of Muslims and Islam by the 'Crusader-Zionist alliance'; and the occupation of Jerusalem by the 'Jews' petty state'. They finished with this declaration:

> The ruling to kill the Americans and their allies – civilian and military – is an individual duty for every Muslim who can do it, in any country in which it is possible to do so, in order to liberate the al-Aqsa Mosque [in Jerusalem] and the Holy Mosque [in Mecca] from their grip, and in order for their armies to move out of all the lands of Islam, defeated and unable to threaten any Muslim. This is in accordance with the words of Almighty Allah [in the Koran], 'and fight the pagans all together, as they fight you all together', and 'fight them until there is no more tumult or oppression, and there prevail justice and faith in Allah'.

Like the caliphs of the Umayyads and the Abbasids, and the Ottoman Sultans after them, battling the Byzantine or the Holy Roman Empire, Osama bin Laden saw the United States as delaying and thwarting the triumph of Islam.

At about the same time, Khalid Sheikh Mohammed, whose hatred of America and its pro-Israeli policies had been behind his support for the 1993 attack in New York, brought to Osama bin Laden the idea of launching a further attack on the World Trade Centre. Although Bin Laden would initially claim that he was not responsible for the attacks of 9/11, it subsequently became clear that his was the organizing mind behind it. As we approached the turn of the century, still focused on the continuing complexities of the Balkans, while sustaining military and economic pressure on Iraq, the plans that would bring together nineteen terrorist plotters and four aircraft over the skies of Washington and New York on 11 September 2001 were gathering momentum. Although the existence of Al Qa'eda was well known, and there seemed to have been multiple reports that a major terrorist attack was being planned, even that it might involve aircraft, there were gaps in intelligence and a dangerous and debilitating cultural reluctance to share information between intelligence agencies. Meanwhile, Osama bin Laden and al-Zawahiri now took 'ownership' of a plan by the Egyptian Islamic Jihad movement to bomb the US Embassies in Kenya and Tanzania, in retaliation for a range of perceived grievances regarding American involvement in the region. On 7 August 1998, a date chosen by Bin Laden to coincide with the anniversary of the arrival of US troops in Saudi Arabia eight years earlier, two huge truck bombs were detonated, almost simultaneously, killing 224 people, almost all of them locals. It was a dramatic statement of intent by Al Qa'eda. On 20 August President Clinton implemented Operation Infinite Reach, cruise missile attacks on Islamist bases in Sudan and Afghanistan, the American 'response of choice' since the disasters of the 1993 Somalia intervention. These were the first officially acknowledged pre-emptive and retaliatory strikes against non-state actors. Operation Desert Fox, against Iraq, followed some three months later.

Halfway through my time back in the MoD, a friend had mentioned that General Evelyn Webb-Carter, who had been a Colonel during my first incarnation as an MoD 'knife-fighter', was planning a riding trip through the Hindu Kush mountains of the North-West Frontier Province of Pakistan. Although I was something of a faux cavalryman as regards riding prowess, I was absolutely up for an exotic and adventurous trip. A deposit cheque secured my place on the expedition, and I took myself off to the Household Cavalry Barracks at Hyde Park to be put through my paces in the riding school. It was time well spent. The plan was for the eight members of the team to fly to Islamabad and then onto Gilgit, where we would pick up our horses and join the support team that was being organized for us by Maqsood al Mulk, a member of the dominant family of Chitral, our eventual destination. Evelyn had designed the trip to follow the route of the column led by Colonel James Kelly, in April 1895, to relieve the fort at Chitral, which was being besieged by Pashtun tribesmen. It was a somewhat typical story of imperial action on the frontiers of Empire, with the usual ingredients of ferocious local tribesmen, duplicitous internecine tribal politics, plucky young British officers and steadfast local and colonial troops. Just the stuff to get the pulse of any proud Englishman racing. James Kelly had been in the Hunza Valley when news of the siege reached him, along with the orders to raise a relief column. He struck out with about 400 Sikh Pioneers, 900 Hunza 'Irregulars', two mountain guns and an assortment of British junior officers, whose later memoirs made for wonderful reading. Crossing the great Shandur Pass, waist-deep in snow, Kelly relieved the garrison at Chitral on 20 April after a siege of a month and a half. Among the survivors was Captain Charlie Townshend, who would go on to be the ill-fated commander of the British force that surrendered to the Ottomans at Kut-al-Amara in Iraq in 1916.

Our ride was to last nearly three weeks, through 450km of some of the most glorious and impressive scenery in the world, climbing up to the Shandur Plateau with its famous polo pitch, then descending past Fort Mastuj into the Chitral valley. Many of the local population belonged to the Ismaili branch of Islam, whose spiritual leader was the Aga Khan and whose generosity could be seen all along the route. At Fort Mastuj we encountered the formidable Colonel Kushwat, formerly of the Indian Army.

'At this time of the year', he declared, 'I am normally in the Rose and Crown in Salisbury, with my old British comrades. This year, Britain has come to me.'

At a celebratory al fresco dinner that night, in honour of which we had dragged crushed blazers and regimental ties out of our cases, there was dancing. In a large circle, around an enormous fire, the whole village gathered, the women firmly segregated to one side and the children allowed to squat in the front. A series of young men took to the 'dance-floor' and, to the powerful rhythm of the local drums and flutes, performed a series of energetic twirls and leaps. The night was cold, the stars shone, and we could just make out the snow-capped tops of the Pamirs. Colonel Kushwat thought we looked chilly, and we made to move our seats closer to the fire. Not a bit of it. The fire, basically one enormous, flaming tree trunk, was manhandled closer to us. The music and dancing continued, and it was clear that eventually someone was going to have to 'take one for the team' and demonstrate how the British entertained themselves on high days and holidays. Evelyn was the boss, but despite his Sandhurst training, he was not prepared to apply the 'Serve to Lead' principles. Richard Holmes, the noted military historian, had pretended to go into a hypnotic trance, while the girls, Milagros, Jenny and Christina, were clearly exempt. Henry Dallal was taking photographs, and Charles Elwell, another Grenadier Guardsman who had got up to dance on previous occasions, was rather ostentatiously massaging an imaginary 'war wound'. Summoning up the spirit that won an empire, I rose and plunged into the melee. Some moves from *Saturday Night Fever*, some half-remembered steps from a Scottish reeling session, followed by a powerful combination of twist and rock-and-roll manoeuvres, and the 'floor' was handed over to me. These many years later, I like to think that, somewhere in the Chitral Valley, stories are still told of the 'dancing *feringhee*', and that some of those moves may now have been built into the cultural fabric of the North-West Frontier Province.

When we eventually arrived in Chitral we were met by the combined polo clubs of the Valley, and we rode into the town sixty horsemen strong. We were preceded by the band of the Chitrali Scouts, resplendent in tartan, spats and feathers, playing the 'Black Bear' and marching with all the style and swagger of a British State Ceremonial Band. The whole occasion was magnificent and moving. Less than a year later, the events of 9/11 made it unlikely that anyone would risk such an adventure again for a long time.

From Chitral we drove to Peshawar, which had all the feel of a hard frontier town, with its old fashioned, precisely laid-out military cantonment, its chaotic and bustling centre and the sprawling Afghan refugee camps that surrounded it. Looking back on that period, we were surprisingly ill- or un-informed, about the modern significance of Peshawar. We knew of its place in Raj history, but not much about: its pivotal linkage with the mujahideen war against the Soviets; its place in the supply chain of arms, heroin, money and radical Islam; the establishment of the MAK and the ideological campaign that had produced the Taliban; the shadowy role of the Pakistani ISI; and the plans being nurtured by the disenchanted son of a Saudi construction family. All of these would become clearer, to a much wider Western audience, within the year. We drove through the Khyber Pass to the border with Afghanistan, recalling the three Anglo-Afghan Wars and the disaster of the 1842 British retreat from Kabul, so brilliantly captured by George Macdonald Fraser in his first Flashman novel. All along the route, the cap-badges of famous British regiments, some long gone, some still firmly in the order of battle, were carved into the rock. Little did we know that our fourth military foray into Afghanistan was just over the horizon. In the garden of the Officers' Mess of the Khyber Rifles I encountered a large tree wrapped in chains that had long since been absorbed into the bark of its impressive trunk. On a small plaque next to it were written words along the lines of 'I have been chained up on the orders of the Orderly Officer for being unsteady on parade.' It was easy for those of us in the military to imagine two young British officers, miles from home, sat in this frontier fort garden at night, perhaps back from the type of 'butcher and bolt' operation so vividly described by John Masters in *Bugles and a Tiger,* demanding, through whisky-induced double-vision, that the tree 'stand still on parade', then summoning a bemused orderly to 'clap it in irons' for 'insubordination' when it failed to do so.

During our stay in Peshawar I used to frequent the old bazaar and its antique shops, which were normally run by Afghans. I struck up a particularly good relationship with one delightful old man who sported an impressively large hennaed beard and who did his business through an English-speaking grandson. I had purchased a number of his items but, on the last day, he produced a small travelling communion set, in silver. It was only about $50. I had no ready money left, and no time to go to the bank, but I was intrigued by the possible history of this object and wanted to 'rescue' it. We ascertained, from the hallmark, that it dated from 1863. What was it doing in the hands of an Afghan trader in the Pakistan border town of Peshawar? It had an engraved plate on it that implied that it might have been given by a father to his son, and I speculated that the owner might have been a military padre, although I never did find out. I explained my predicament to the young boy and asked if his grandfather would 'trust the word of a British officer' that I would remit the money as soon as I returned to London. The boy relayed my message, and the old gentleman grinned and burst into Pashtun.

'Of course he trusts you', the youngster relayed back. 'He says, "We have fought the British many times, but we always liked them".'

This was going better than I had hoped.

'However', said the youngster gravely, 'he also says . . . ' and I leaned forward to hear what historical qualification was about to be imparted '. . . that it would be easier if you sent a cheque to his brother in Ealing.'

Ah, the joys of globalization. I did so.

Shortly after this expedition, I left the MoD, with a spring in my step, heading for the Higher Command and Staff Course (HCSC) and due to take over 1st Mechanised Brigade in Tidworth, on Salisbury Plain, in May 2001. HCSC was another brainchild of Nigel Bagnall and, since 1988, attendance on it had become mandatory for all Army officers, and for some from the Royal Navy and RAF, who aspired to the higher ranks of the services. While most of the syllabus was taught at the new Joint Services Command and Staff College in Shrivenham, near Swindon, we also went to the US, and had a rather frenetic 'battlefield tour', criss-crossing Northern France in order to study aspects of the Franco-Prussian War and the two World Wars. Our guide was the endlessly engaging Professor Richard Holmes, who had been on our great Hindu Kush trip and who died, far too young, a few years later.

The year 2001 was going to be when Britain returned to the Gulf for a major deployment with the Omanis in Exercise Saif Sareea 2. A few years earlier, the MoD, in its wisdom, had decided that money was tight and that this important joint exercise would have to be cut as a 'savings measure'. Those of us who knew the area, the country and the ruler, were horrified. Sultan Qaboos had been our most steadfast friend in the region for many years, and we had a unique military and intelligence relationship with him. He patiently sustained a large loan service contingent, bought British military equipment and waived many of the usual payments that others made for the use of facilities in his country. He expected us to honour our commitments to him. He had invested a lot of Oman's money in this exercise, other rulers in the Gulf were always looking to judge the strength of the bilateral relationship, and competitors, particularly the US and the French, were ever looking to supplant us in Oman's affections. Geoff Hoon, the Defence Secretary, had dropped in on his way to Australia, to relay the MoD decision to the Sultan. Given the Sultan's legendary politeness, Hoon departed thinking the audience had gone well and that the MoD was now off the hook. In reality, the Sultan was furious, and the 'Friends of Oman', myself included, rallied round to make it clear to the Prime Minister that he was in danger of compromising a vital strategic partnership on the back of appallingly poor judgment by the MoD. Thank goodness, wiser counsels prevailed, the money was found and the Sultan was assured that the exercise would go ahead as planned. Those plans were now in motion, and British troops, armoured vehicles, aircraft and ships were on their way to various ports and airfields in Oman. The Omani land commander was my old friend, now a General, Ahmed Harith al Nabhani. We would soon be very grateful that we had not insulted our old friends in the Sultanate.

On the existing programme, 1st Mechanised Brigade did not have anything substantive scheduled for 2001, although we were due to go on a six-month operational tour to Kosovo in the second half of 2002. The Brigade's headquarters at Tidworth was in a converted medical centre. I had an outstanding Chief of Staff, Patrick Sanders, who claimed to have been born in the office in which he now worked, and a first-class Deputy Chief of Staff, Ewen McLay, along with several bright young captains on their first staff tours. The various regiments and battalions in the Brigade were all commanded by confident, competent commanding officers, and we made a merry 'band of brothers'. As the summer advanced, the Headquarters went through its paces doing command-post exercises, battlefield tours, staff training and small-scale deployments on Salisbury

Plain, while the units went through their own training routines and we looked ahead to our move back to the Balkans. In a Tom Clancy novel, or an episode of *Homeland*, the action would by now have been cutting between the daily routine of 1st Mechanised Brigade, the Al Qa'eda leadership in their base in Afghanistan, the preparations of the jihadi hijackers and the frantic work of the intelligence agencies as they detected that some major terrorist incident was being planned, with the tension rising inexorably for the reader or viewer. That is not how it felt in early September 2001.

On the morning of 11 September I came into the headquarters intending to write some annual confidential reports on officers in the Brigade. Usually I would have been wearing camouflage combat kit and boots, because that uniform was both comfortable and flexible if I decided to go out to visit troops on training. That day, I was consciously in Barrack Dress: highly polished jodhpur-boots, pressed barrack dress trousers with a QDG stable belt, a white shirt with rank slides and the red tabs of a General Staff officer, a service dress hat with a broad red stripe around it, and carrying a riding crop, the regimental mark of a cavalry officer. I was hosting a dinner party at my residence that night and planned to be away at a sensible time.

I beavered away all morning, drafting reports and amending those my excellent PA, Carol, had already managed to type up. I had no computer in my office, and we had no TV-feed in the headquarters. The phone rang occasionally, calls the PA intercepted, and the Chief of Staff, normally puffing on a hand-rolled cigarette, came in at judicious moments if he needed any direction or clarification, or simply to share a joke. At just shy of two o'clock in the afternoon, the Chief Clerk entered and said that I might want to be aware that a plane seemed to have crashed into the North Tower of the World Trade Centre in New York. I was only half-listening, and mentally processed it as a freak aviation accident. I suspect that I was not alone. Not fifteen minutes later, a retired officer in the headquarters who had a tiny black-and-white television in his office for watching cricket, rushed in to say that a second aircraft had now been flown into the South Tower. Life was never to be quite the same again.

The third and fourth aircraft we only learned about later. In the meantime, I told Patrick Sanders to inform the brigade units, and Ewen McLay to make an assessment of what transport and logistic assets we had at high readiness. I was convinced that the attacks in New York, horrendous, daring and sophisticated as they were, were going to be part of a wider, sustained attack on the West, and that London was a sure-fire next target. In my brigade area I had Boscombe Down airfield, which was designated as an 'emergency aerodrome' and whose runway was long enough to accommodate a Space Shuttle, if one should ever have overshot Cape Canaveral. The phone rang, and an officer in the MoD informed me that US airspace was now closed, and that the two hundred commercial aircraft that had not yet reached the point of 'no-return' over the Atlantic were being recovered back to UK. If the major civilian airports could not handle them, they would land at Boscombe Down, among other contingency airfields. RAF Typhoon aircraft had been scrambled and were already flying combat air patrols, with orders to prepare to shoot down any airliner that failed to respond to instructions. I was to go and 'secure' Boscombe Down. Totally inappropriately dressed for this national emergency, while fulfilling every RAF stereotype of a cavalry officer, I breezed onto the airbase with Ewen McLay to examine the logistic implications of several large airliners arriving, back-to-back, in the next couple of hours. The RAF were the experts at handling aircraft, but we had the assets to deal with the feeding, baggage-handling, and onward movement of large numbers of people. We made our plans and dispositions, and we waited. Soon it became clear that the civilian airports, with judicious scheduling and sequencing, would be able to handle the returning air-armada, and we stood down. Only then did we begin to comprehend the enormity of what had taken place in America. As a result of the twin impacts, both towers of the World Trade Centre had rapidly collapsed. The west side of the Pentagon had sustained significant damage from the third strike, while the fourth aircraft had plunged into a field in Pennsylvania, after the passengers had heroically attempted to wrest back control from the hijackers. Nearly 3,000 people had been killed, and over 6,000 injured. It could have been so much worse, but important lessons in fire-fighting and mass evacuation had been learned from the 1993 terrorist attack on the building. Subsequent investigation revealed that fifteen of the nineteen hijackers were of Saudi Arabian origin, nine of them from the traditionally radical Saudi provinces bordering Yemen.

With the country and the military on high alert, and anticipating that Al Qa'eda was planning further atrocities, for responsibility had very quickly been attributed to them, we went ahead with the dinner party. In the circumstances it seemed like a small act of defiance. The following morning, the band of the Household Division played 'The Star-Spangled Banner' in the courtyard of Buckingham Palace.

Chapter 20

The Aftermath

On 20 September, President Bush felt confident enough to attribute responsibility for the attacks. He 'pointed the finger' at Al Qa'eda and the Taliban in a speech in which he demanded the Taliban handed over Osama bin Laden and his confederates and close all 'terrorist' training camps. He now petitioned the International Community to back a military operation to overthrow their regime in Afghanistan. While the UN would not sanction this, NATO invoked Article 5, 'An attack on one is an attack on all', and the organization approved the campaign as 'self-defence against armed attack'. On 7 October, after some diplomatic to-ing and fro-ing, a US-led coalition initiated military action, utilizing a bombing campaign and CIA and military special forces acting alongside the local Afghan anti-Taliban forces of the Northern Alliance. On 9 September 2001, just two days before the attacks in New York, Ahmad Shah Masoud, one of their key leaders, had been assassinated by two Arab operatives of Al Qa'eda posing as photographers. The Taliban collapsed far quicker than anticipated, but not before elements of the Pakistani establishment had engineered the evacuation of hundreds of top Al Qa'eda and Taliban leaders and foot soldiers. The Taliban's last stronghold of Kandahar fell on 13 November, but this was to be far from the end of the story.

As the intelligence picture developed, international support was being gathered and military options scoped, I had taken my brigade headquarters out on exercise. While we were on Salisbury Plain, the phone had rung. Brigadier Peter Wall, a future CGS but then the Commander of Joint Force Operations (CJFO), the UK's high-readiness operational HQ, was on the line. He had been due to go to Oman as the controlling HQ for Exercise Saif Sareea 2, while my own HQ had been designated as the 'stand-by' headquarters in case some other operation or crisis had arisen.

'You were the *stand-by* headquarters, Simon', he said. 'You are now the *stand-in* headquarters.'

Peter would be going to the new American airbase at Al Udeid in Qatar to help plan and prosecute operations against the Taliban, while HQ 1st Mechanised Brigade would now go to Oman.

As the UK was preparing to carry out reprisals against Al Qa'eda and the Taliban, while also deploying for the largest overseas exercise in some years, and we, in Tidworth, were reconfiguring ourselves to join the party, the British government was asking Sultan Qaboos for the use of almost all his airfields in order to deploy our aircraft to the region and support air operations over Afghanistan. Once again, the Sultan demonstrated his generosity, but I could only imagine what his reaction might have been if, as planned, we had 'pulled the rug' on this important bilateral exercise. Although the combined activity put a serious strain on the UK's armed forces, both the operation in Afghanistan and the concurrent deployment in Oman were highly successful. Air Marshal Glen Torpy, the Chief of Joint Operations (CJO), had been designated the overall commander of British Forces on exercise in Oman, but his proper 'day job' meant he was also responsible for some of the deployments to support the operations in Afghanistan. As his de facto Chief of Staff in Oman, I had to manoeuvre between describing what we were doing about the fictional opposition in Saif Sareea while also supporting briefings about what was happening to the 'real' enemy in Central Asia. In a slightly surreal manner, the fictional opponents were successfully 'expelled' from Oman at almost exactly the same time that the real enemy, the Taliban, were abandoning their last positions.

In Oman I was able to see many old friends, not least a number of officers and soldiers who had been in my squadron back in the 1980s. They were uniformly happy reunions, and I was delighted to see how many of them had gone on to have successful careers. A great deal of coffee was drunk, dates eaten and goat, chicken and rice consumed. We returned to Tidworth conscious that the context in which we were soon to deploy back to the Balkans had totally changed, and that there were now new and, rightly, more demanding operational priorities. By chance, I would be taking over from David R-J and 20 Armoured Brigade, and we planned for a frictionless handover in May. Meanwhile, in Afghanistan, an Afghan Interim Administration had been formed under Hamid Karzai, a leading member of an historically prominent Pashtun tribe and family, and the UN had now established the International Security Assistance Force (ISAF) to support the new administration and provide security in Kabul. Britain had followed up the expulsion of the Taliban by joining in the hunt for Osama bin

Laden and other Al Qa'eda commanders and fighters in the mountains of eastern Afghanistan. Although initially scaled back at the end of this phase, the British contribution would expand incrementally from 2002 under the codename Operation Herrick, particularly after the resurgence of the Taliban threatened the new Afghan government, giving us reason to believe that the country could once again become a haven for international Islamist terrorists.

Kosovo Force (KFOR) had been formed immediately after the adoption of UNSCR 1244, with a mission to deter threats from Serbia, provide a safe and secure environment and disarm the Kosovo Liberation Army who, some considered, were almost as culpable in the inter-communal violence as the Serbs. The campaign against Milosevic had been controversial, not least because it had no UN mandate, while the Russians had been very publicly sidelined, other than in their bold move to occupy Pristina airport. Indeed, back in 1999, some Republican partisans in America had even gone as far as accusing President Clinton of initiating the Kosovo operation in order to drive the Monica Lewinsky scandal off the front pages. KFOR was organized into five multinational brigade areas, with the French in the north, the Americans in the east with their huge BONDSTEEL military base, the Germans to the south, the Italians to the west, and the British in the centre. The Area of Responsibility for Multi-National Brigade (Centre), as we were known, included: the capital city, Pristina; the international airport; Headquarters KFOR itself; the historic Serbian town of Gracinica; and the site of the 1389 Battle of Kosovo–Polje, the infamous 'Field of Blackbirds'. When Serbs used to rail against the Muslim presence and influence in the Balkans, I would remind them of their own decisive role in helping the Ottomans defeat the Burgundian–Hungarian crusaders at Nicopolis in 1396, thereby helping establish Ottoman dominance. Historical sensitivities were never far below the surface of any conversation in the Balkans. The NATO Military Committee, a body composed of senior military representatives from all the Alliance countries, including Turkey, came to visit my Brigade. Included in the programme was a visit to the battlefield of Kosovo–Polje. I had vetted all aspects of the visit, except the script for the explanation of the events of 1389! All was going well until the Norwegian officer finished his presentation by referring to the '400 years of brutal, heavy-handed Ottoman rule' that had followed the Serbian defeat. The Turkish general immediately raised a red card, demanded an apology and wrote a lengthy letter about the benefits of Ottoman rule, in particular their religious tolerance, which had to be sent to all KFOR units.

In the British-led multinational brigade there were two British battle-groups and Swedish, Norwegian, Finnish and joint Czech-Slovak battalions. Our commander was a French general, Marcel Valentin, and I had excellent fellow sector commanders, including Brigadier General Doug Lute, an American cavalryman who would go on to be the US ambassador to NATO and with whom I spent many an amusing hour. The Americans were operating under General Order Number One, no alcohol on operations, but Doug often managed to bring his 'magic glass' with him when he came to visit my headquarters – the one that 'turned anything you poured into it non-alcoholic'. The Europeans were far more flexible about alcohol and, unlike in Iraq or Afghanistan, there was scope in the Balkans to use food and drink at the 'operational level' in order to help lubricate the complex and frustrating day-to-day interactions with the Kosovans and Serbs. It was often needed.

Before our deployment, I had visited all the capitals of the contingents I had under command, in order to introduce myself, explain how I saw the situation in Kosovo and set out what I hoped we might collectively achieve. We assessed that there was no longer a direct security threat from Serbia, but the deep historical ethnic and religious antagonisms within the country could always spill over into localized violence, which we had to guard against. In my view, the greatest threat to the long-term success of Kosovo came from a cultural disregard for the 'rule of law', common in parts of the world where state institutions have been historically viewed with contempt, suspicion or fear. This was particularly so where former members of the Kosovo Liberation Army were concerned. They had now become the Kosovo Protection Corps (KPC), but some of them were choosing to use their 'war hero' status to pursue lucrative criminal activities and to operate as a 'mafia' organization. They needed to be brought firmly within the new state structures and purged of their worst elements, whilst avoiding a potential public backlash against the UN and KFOR. We aimed to put 'respect for the rule of law' at the centre of our campaign, and in due course we managed to jail several leading 'mafia' figures. For these operations we had to put together special 'Task Forces' that could play to the strengths of the individual contingents and which could thereby avoid breaching anyone's national political or military 'red lines'.

We adopted the 'Al Capone' approach to getting these criminals off the streets. In other words, while we would have loved to arrest and jail them for murder and other acts of violence, we were more confident that we could nail them on tax evasion charges or the like. While they were put under surveillance, in order to gather evidence of their movements and activities, we had a UN judge and prosecutor appointed to the case. When we felt we had a good enough case, we would arrest them. The British could only conduct surveillance in uniform, the Swedes had a national dispensation to conduct some operations in civilian clothes, the Italian Carabinieri could do 'hard-arrest' operations, while the Americans could detain suspects at Camp BONDSTEEL. It was a marriage made in heaven. Concurrently with the arrests, we would release a raft of news stories that implicated the individuals in a range of nefarious activities. By the time they had been tried, convicted and incarcerated, no one with the slightest sense of civic responsibility was prepared to take to the streets on their behalf.

We were always very conscious that the attention of policy-makers in Washington and London remained firmly on Afghanistan and Central Asia, but we were already detecting the growing influence of Al Qa'eda among some of the more radical Muslim elements in the Balkans. As Operation Enduring Freedom continued its mission to track down and kill Osama bin Laden and other Al Qa'eda leaders, we were aware of how vulnerable coalition troops in Kosovo might be to terrorist attacks, and we expanded our intelligence efforts accordingly. We were always rather poor in countering the Islamist propaganda that portrayed us as anti-Muslim, when much of our collective effort in the Balkans, for nearly a decade, had been focused on defending Muslim populations against Christian Serbs and Croats. We were painfully slow at getting this message out there and, unsurprisingly, Al Qa'eda and its sympathisers had little interest in helping us do so. Some years later, when I was the Senior Mentor for the Army Generalship Course, we held a discussion with women from some Muslim communities in Nottingham. I commented to them that it was depressing that more British Muslims had joined Islamic State than had joined the British Army or the armed forces of their adopted country. They countered with a general contention that 'the British state was fighting Islam'. I acknowledged their perceptions, but then listed my service in the Middle East and Balkans, where I had commanded Omani Arabs, helped liberate the Kuwaitis, protected Muslims from Croats and Serbs, served alongside Iraqi and Afghan Muslims and had a part in many efforts, however clumsily conducted, to save Muslims from being killed by other Muslims.

'Nobody tells us this', they said.

'It is not in the interests of some people in your communities to do so', I countered, 'and others have often been singularly ineffective in getting this message and narrative out.'

We continued to provide 'a safe and secure environment' in Kosovo through the long hot summer of 2002, which saw the British contingent celebrating Queen Elizabeth II's Golden Jubilee by lighting a chain of beacons across our brigade area and, as a gift to the Kosovan people, saving Pristina's only working power station from burning down. However, during that time we became increasingly aware that the subject of Iraq was appearing in operational briefings from London. Some years before, in October 1998, removing Saddam Hussein had become official US foreign policy with the passing of the Iraq Liberation Act. This had been enacted after Saddam's expulsion of the UN weapons inspectors, who had been ploughing their lonely and frustrating furrow since the suspension of hostilities way back in 1991. In December 1998, Operation Desert Fox had been launched, ostensibly to hamper Saddam's attempts to develop WMD, but also in retribution for his assumed complicity in the bombing of the US embassies in East Africa. In 2000, with the election of George W. Bush, US policy towards Iraq had become more overtly aggressive and began to be expressed in terms of 'regime change'. Opinion is divided on whether invasion was a foreign policy objective from Bush's inauguration, but his Secretary of Defense, Donald Rumsfeld, had certainly been quick to search for linkages between Saddam Hussein and Osama bin Laden in the wake of 9/11. The rhetorical question, 'Can we risk allowing WMD to fall into the hands of international terrorists?' certainly had a powerful resonance among those beginning to advocate military action in the Middle East. On 20 September 2001 Bush had announced his 'War on Terror' which, along with the commitment to 'pre-emptive' military action, was later to be termed the 'Bush Doctrine'. Some of this rationale and rhetoric would dovetail with the case for intervention laid out in Blair's 1999 Chicago speech.

Even as the Taliban regime was being toppled, some Bush advisers were arguing for an immediate invasion of Iraq, putting forward a cocktail of good reasons to use the catalyst of 9/11 to remove the Saddam Hussein 'thorn' from their collective sides. In his State of the Union address on 29 January 2002, President Bush used the phrase 'axis of evil' for the first time, to describe foreign governments that sponsored terrorism and sought WMD. He named North Korea and Iran, unhelpfully for any moderate reformist movements in the latter, but reserved most criticism for Iraq. As early as July 2002, the CIA was putting teams into the Kurdish region of Iraq, taking advantage of the Kurds' justifiable antipathy towards Baghdad. These teams were tasked with cooperating with the *peshmerga*, Kurdish fighters who would soon rise to prominence. Other advisers advocated building a new international coalition and obtaining UN authorization, as Bush Senior had so effectively done in 1990. George W. Bush chose to follow a dual-track approach. He directed Donald Rumsfeld to prepare the US military for war in Iraq, while continuing to prosecute operations in Afghanistan, and he went to the UN on 12 September 2002 to make the legal case for the removal of Saddam Hussein. International opinion was split, with the UK and Tony Blair supportive, while France's President Chirac, Germany's Chancellor Schröder and Russia, under the then relatively unknown President Putin, were sceptical or actively opposed to military action.

In October 2002 the US Congress passed the 'Iraq Resolution', which authorized the President to 'use any means necessary' against Iraq. On 8 November, after considerable debate, the UN Security Council adopted a compromise resolution, UNSCR 1441, which authorized the resumption of weapons inspections, while promising 'serious consequences' for non-compliance. France and Russia made it clear that they did not view such 'consequences' as including the use of force to overthrow the regime. Both John Negroponte and Jeremy Greenstock, the US and UK ambassadors to the UN, assured the Security Council that Resolution 1441 did not provide any 'automaticity' or 'hidden triggers' for an invasion without further consultation. On 13 November, Saddam accepted the Resolution, and the United Nations Monitoring, Verification and Inspection Commission (UNMOVIC) and the International Atomic Energy Agency (IAEA) returned to Iraq under the direction of the UNMOVIC Chairman, Hans Blix, and the Director General of IAEA, Mohammed al Baradei. By February 2003 the IAEA 'had found no evidence or plausible indication of the revival of a nuclear weapons programme in Iraq', while UNMOVIC stated that it would take 'months' fully to verify Iraqi compliance with Resolution 1441. The issue of whether Saddam did, or did not, have WMD, and whether, if he did, they constituted a 'clear and present danger', as the British Government would assert, would prove to be politically toxic, both at the time and as the campaign of invasion and occupation unfolded.

Much of this passed us by in Pristina. The US forces in Kosovo were commanded through their European HQ in Stuttgart, while Afghanistan and Iraq fell under Central Command, with its Headquarters in Tampa, Florida, so the Americans in the Balkans were also largely 'out of the loop', while the French and Germans had no intention of taking part in any military action in the Middle East. In Britain, Tony Blair was wrestling with his desire to support the Americans, both politically and militarily, the antipathy of many in his New Labour Party to 'warmongering' and widespread public scepticism about further embroilment in the Muslim world, even in the wake of 9/11. Blair therefore had no intention yet of publicly signalling his predisposition to join in an invasion.

In the meantime, I knew my time commanding 1st Mechanised Brigade was coming to an end, and in November 2002 I handed over responsibilty for Multi-National Brigade (Centre) to 12 Mechanised Brigade, commanded by Jonathan Shaw, and 1st Mechanised Brigade itself to another Parachute Regiment officer, Andrew Kennett. As I was doing so, Erdogan's AK party in Turkey, only founded a year earlier and increasingly to be identified with neo-Ottoman pretensions and the Muslim Brotherhood, won its first of many national elections. Kosovo had not been a 'dangerous' operation, but it had been a professionally challenging and satisfying time. We had achieved all that we had been asked to and had kept Kosovo quiet, out of the news and on a path to greater stability, while events of more substance were preoccupying our political and military masters in London. We had conducted a sensitive and nuanced operation that had made a substantive contribution to reducing tensions in a complex and difficult part of the world. Our young officers and soldiers, from all the nations I had under command, had shown a commendable sensitivity to the historical antipathies of the region and to its multiplicity of entrenched ethnic and religious differences.

Chapter 21

Crisis on the Tigris

In early 2003, I joined around eighty other 'members', from fifty different countries, at the Royal College of Defence Studies (RCDS) in Seaford House, Belgrave Square. We were largely a mixture of military and diplomatic officials, with a leavening of academics and business leaders. Many of the overseas members were again from traditional friends and allies of the United Kingdom in the Gulf and the Commonwealth, but there were also participants from Eastern Europe, including Russia, from the Far East, including China, and a first officer from Syria. It made for lively discussion and debate. RCDS was the successor to the Imperial Defence College, set up by Winston Churchill in 1927 as a result of the scars he carried from the ill-fated Gallipoli campaign. Its aim, from the outset, had been to educate senior military officers and civil servants alongside each other, thereby exposing both cohorts to the complexity of political decision-making and the equal complexity of aligning military planning and actions to political objectives. Our campaigns in the Middle East and Central Asia, over the next decade and a half, would sometimes test those ambitions to destruction.

The course aimed to develop 'strategic leadership skills'. It was designed to be 'grown up', with a leisurely start, some first-rate lectures, seminar discussions, plenty of time for the overseas members and their families to enjoy their year in London and for all of us to read, mix, discuss and debate. The Commandant was Lieutenant General Sir Christopher Wallace, who ran the whole programme with a delightful combination of acerbic wit, ironic observation and clarity of thought.

The opening months of the course coincided with the political, diplomatic and military drumbeats that accompanied the preparations for a showdown with Iraq and Saddam Hussein. Our Arab colleagues had expressed early concerns and real nervousness about this course of action and the aims and objectives of our plans for yet another chapter of conflict in the Middle East. They had no love for Saddam, and many of them had served in the Coalition forces in the first Gulf War, but they were Sunni Arabs, and they were deeply worried about the consequences of the overthrow of the

Saddam regime, the empowerment of the Iraqi Shia majority and thereby the potential for increased Iranian influence and interference in the region. It is easy to understand Muslim attachment to Arabia and the two Holy Cities but, except for the century of Umayyad dominance in Damascus, the centre of the Sunni Arab Islamic world, and of many of its major achievements, was in Iraq, and the Abbasid capital, Baghdad, had been the seat of the caliphate for half a millennium. Despite its diminished status under the Ottomans, and while containing a large Shia Arab population, it had always remained a Sunni-dominated city and of great significance to all Muslims. Our Gulf friends were telling us this in 2003, but our policy-makers, beset by so many other pressures, were not necessarily listening.

The toppling of Saddam and the imposition of Western-style democracy on a country where 60 per cent of the population were oppressed Shia and another 20 per cent were Kurds would inevitably doom the Iraqi Sunni Arabs to a position of perpetual inferiority. They had every right to be concerned, as future events proved, but a strong case for war was being made, albeit on flimsy evidence and compromised intelligence. Even those of us who instinctively supported standing by the Americans on this major foreign policy issue were not altogether swayed by the intelligence case. Given the origins of Al Qa'eda, with its ideology that despised 'apostate' regimes, the claims of complicity between Saddam Hussein and Osama bin Laden, on anything but a very tactical and opportunistic level, seemed doubtful. Those of us who had been involved in the Iraq War of 1990–1 did believe that Saddam very probably had some residual WMD stockpiles, but we were very sceptical of their strategic significance, and Tony Blair's '45 minute' claim was viewed as very dubious. The Prime Minister had had the potential political consequences of an invasion set out to him by academics who had stressed the ethnic, religious and confessional complexity of Iraq. However, his response had been, broadly, 'But Saddam is a very nasty man, isn't he?' In 1588, on being informed that the Spanish Armada was not in very good shape for the proposed invasion of England, the Duke of Medina Sidonia, the overall commander of the expedition, had declared, 'We are sailing in the confident hope of a miracle.' Blair seemed to have adopted a similar mindset.

We could see which way the wind was blowing. As professional soldiers we had few concerns about the ability of a US-led Coalition to defeat the Iraqi Army and take Baghdad. However, we also assumed, or at least profoundly hoped, that the post-conflict phase had been as meticulously thought through, and that military competence and success would transition, seamlessly, into an equally competent governmental and administrative performance. While we avidly read the papers and watched the news, we were blissfully unaware of the internal debates going on in Washington between the White House, the Department of Defense under Donald Rumsfeld, the Pentagon and the Joint Chiefs, Central Command, which would execute the campaign, and the State Department under Colin Powell, himself the former Chairman of the Joint Chiefs during the first Gulf War.

On 5 February 2003 Colin Powell made his ill-fated presentation to the UN General Assembly regarding the 'evidence' for Saddam Hussein's WMD programme, his supposed linkages with Al Qa'eda and the 'likelihood' of his complicity in the 9/11 attacks. Powell's personal reputation played an important part in persuading many people of the credibility of his claims. Despite this, the attempts by the US to gain the UN authorization they sought for military action looked likely to fail. On 15 February, the anti-war movement mobilized between six and ten million people in demonstrations in more than 800 cities around the world. Nonetheless, preparations for the invasion were going ahead. On 17 March, having failed to get a second UN resolution in support of military action, President Bush went on television to issue an ultimatum, giving Saddam Hussein, and his sons Uday and Qusay, 48 hours to leave the country. There were, by now, around 200,000 US, British and allied troops in the region, poised for action. British public opinion was sharply divided. The British military were also concerned about the 'legality' of any conflict, and the CDS, Admiral Sir Mike Boyce, had to obtain a written guarantee that British forces would be operating within International Law. Without any explicit UN authorization, the preparatory bombing of targets in Iraq began on 18 March, 24 hours before the ultimatum President Bush had given to Saddam Hussein ran out. That same day, Tony Blair made the case for war in the House of Commons. In a powerful and compelling speech, he cited systematic breaches of UN Resolutions from the period of the Liberation of Kuwait, and the 'authorization' for the use of force granted by UN Resolution 1441, despite its ambiguity. He also drew heavily on a British intelligence report, soon to be dubbed 'the dodgy dossier' for its 'sexed-up' and dubious claims of a 'strategic threat' and '45 minutes from Armageddon'. The government motion was approved by 419 votes to 149, but three Labour ministers, including Robin Cook, the Foreign Secretary, resigned. There was an extraordinary mood across the country, indeed the world, and the roots of much future friction, turmoil and violence were put down in those days.

Turkey, worried about the consequences of Iraqi collapse and embroiled in its own, decades-long, internal conflict with the Kurds, had refused to allow the US to open a northern front, although American Special Forces were already operating within the Kurdish region of Iraq. In the early hours of 19 March, intelligence reports led to a strike on the Dora Farms outside Baghdad, in an attempt to kill Saddam and his sons. The intelligence was faulty. That night, operations began in earnest with a bombing campaign based on 'shock and awe', a phrase that swiftly entered the modern military lexicon. At roughly the same time, the ground forces of the 'Coalition of the Willing' crossed from Kuwait into Iraq. The invasion was swift, leading to the collapse of the Iraqi military and government within about three weeks. The US 3rd Infantry Division moved west, then north to Baghdad, while 1st Marine Expeditionary Force (MEF) drove up through the centre of the country. 1st (UK) Armoured Division, part of a 45,000-man overall British contribution to the Coalition, took the southern city of Basra and the Al Faw peninsula, the scene of horrendous fighting in the Iran-Iraq War, while also securing the key oil fields of Rumaila. The media once again demonstrated a complete lack of understanding of modern warfare, reporting routine operational pauses for logistic re-supply as 'the advance getting bogged down', and issuing dire warnings of the Iraqis preparing to make Baghdad into a 'second Stalingrad'. In reality, one or two 'thunder runs' by US armoured columns swiftly took the Coalition to the heart of the Iraqi capital. Many of us were watching the television as 'Comical Ali', the Iraqi government spokesman, talked of American forces being annihilated by the Republican Guard, while over his shoulder viewers could see US tanks already manoeuvring across the Tigris bridges.

On 9 April Baghdad was formally occupied by Coalition forces, and on the same day came the symbolic toppling of Saddam's statue in Firdos [Paradise] Square. The Stars and Stripes, initially placed over the statue's head, was rapidly replaced by the Iraqi flag, and images of Iraqis beating the statue with their shoes were beamed around the world. By 12 April all fighting by regular forces had ceased, and that was when the trouble really began. The fall of Baghdad, far from bringing peace, saw a country-wide outbreak of regional and sectarian violence as Iraqi tribes, even cities, immediately came to blows over old grudges and animosities. While the Coalition forces looked for Saddam, his sons and the senior Ba'ath leadership, and sought to uncover the WMD stocks that had been the most compelling justification for the invasion, Iraqis embarked on a spree of looting and revenge killings, as Arabs and Kurds, Sunni and Shia struggled to dominate the shattered remains of the Iraqi state. The assumption that Iraqis would unite in the wake of Saddam's fall proved illusory, as could have been predicted. Television screens were full of pictures of bemused US soldiers standing at barriers, while around them various ministries, shops and the National Museum were comprehensively plundered. 'Stuff happens', said Donald Rumsfeld, following the long line of civilian leaders, in many countries, who have viewed military manpower, particularly in the Army, as an 'overhead' not a 'capability'. In his own internal fight with the Pentagon he had been anxious to prove that modern weaponry, born out of the so-called 'Revolution in Military Affairs' that followed the Liberation of Kuwait in 1991, accompanied by agility and manoeuvre, could win a rapid victory without the requirement for the large numbers of troops that had characterized former conflicts. It could, but the overthrow of Saddam was supposed to be a 'preliminary operation' that would enable nothing less than the 'reshaping of the Middle East', and this level of ambition required an extensive Coalition footprint across the country, and in depth. General Rick Shinseki, a former US Army Chief, had argued that a force of 'several hundred thousand' would be needed to secure Iraq, even allowing for plans to co-opt the assistance of willing members of the Iraqi security forces. He was side-lined for his pains. General Tommy Franks, the overall Coalition commander, had little time for the post-conflict objectives and was content to concentrate on the 'war-fighting' phase. In this he had been brilliantly successful, but remarkably he failed to take into account Clausewitz's admonition that 'war is the continuation of politics by other means'. The realities of Iraq and the region would simply not align with Coalition hopes and dreams. Another of Clausewitz's most enduring observations was, 'The first, the supreme, the most far-reaching act of judgement that the statesman and commander have to make is to establish the kind of war on which they are embarking; neither mistaking it for, nor trying to turn it into something that is alien to its nature.' While intervention in Afghanistan in 2001 had had a clear logic and an easily explicable narrative, the political and legal arguments for the invasion of Iraq had had as much to do with internal US political dynamics as it did with the stated *casus belli* regarding WMD and Saddam Hussein's links to Al Qa'eda. The image of President Bush on board the aircraft carrier USS *Abraham Lincoln* on 1 May declaring 'major combat operations over', with a banner proclaiming 'Mission Accomplished' behind him, would come back to haunt him and others, as Iraq descended into chaos and Iraqi and Coalition Force casualty levels rose inexorably.

The chain of command was confused from the start, as was the legal status of the occupying forces. Normally, post-invasion, the military would seek rapidly to hand over responsibility to civilian political leaders, institutions and agencies and move into a supporting role. This did not happen in Iraq, where the internecine battles between Rumsfeld and Powell left the responsibility for Iraq in the hands of the Department of Defense, and Paul 'Jerry' Bremer, the new head of the Coalition Provisional Authority (CPA), worked directly to President Bush, through Rumsfeld. The State Department had had a comprehensive plan for transition, but they had been sidelined, and the Organization for Reconstruction and Humanitarian Assistance, under retired General Jay Warner, was under-gunned and soon lost credibility and any traction. General Tommy Franks' retirement was posted on 22 May, and the very next day, Jerry Bremer issued CPA Orders Number One and Two announcing the de-Ba'athification of Iraqi society and the disbandment of the Iraqi Army. Much of the Iraqi Army had already gone home, although their salaries continued to be paid, while senior Iraqi officers had been promised they would have a role to play 'in building the new Iraq'. At a stroke, Bremer, who had not consulted the military, let alone allies in the Coalition, kicked over an almighty hornet's nest. Humiliation is a dangerous game in the Middle East, where issues of shame and personal dignity are so important. The Coalition did not have enough troops to secure barracks and arms depots while trying to maintain order, restore basic services and uncover any WMD sites and stockpiles. The dissolution of the Iraqi Army led to immediate rioting among former soldiers, many of them the only breadwinners in poor families. Unemployment sky-rocketed as Ba'ath Party members, all those civil servants, engineers, rubbish collectors, academics and teachers, the people who ran almost all important bureaucratic and administrative functions in the country, were laid off in their thousands. As resistance to Coalition occupation stiffened, the military reaction, often heavy-handed, reinforced this growing sense of Iraqi humiliation. Lieutenant General 'Rick' Sanchez took over Coalition command in June. For this mission, on which so much of America's ambition and reputation in the Middle East rested, Bush and Rumsfeld chose a newly promoted and untested Lieutenant General. Sanchez was confronted by a lack of 'command authority', an under-resourced staff, conflicting orders from Washington, growing civil disorder, a failure to get basic power supplies back on line as the summer temperatures soared, and a poisonous relationship between himself and Bremer, which communicated itself to both the military and the civil personnel.

Despite the finding and killing of Saddam's sons in July 2003, Ba'ath Party loyalists, former Iraqi military personnel and increasing numbers of foreign fighters, who saw Iraq as the new battleground after their eviction from Afghanistan, ignited an eight-year violent insurgency. As the fruitless search for WMD became more desperate, and the situation on the ground looked more confused, public support for the whole venture began to waver, with political consequences in the home countries. At round the same time, reports began to filter out of widespread prisoner abuse by US troops at Abu Ghraib prison, a notorious facility since Saddam's time, further fanning the flames of opposition. It fuelled ever greater resentment and resistance among the Sunnis of Mosul, in the 'Triangle of Death' centred around Saddam's birthplace of Tikrit, and along the Euphrates Valley, including in the main towns of the Sunni-dominated Anbar province, Fallujah and Ramadi. The actual pictures of the abuse, when they came out in April 2004, rightly shocked the world and did huge damage to the Coalition cause. For jihadists and socially conservative Sunnis alike, the images of the degradation and humiliation of Iraqis by laughing 'infidels', including female soldiers, starkly confirmed their worst impressions of Coalition attitudes and intentions. Needless to say, these images were ruthlessly exploited for their propaganda value by countless Islamist websites and social media outlets.

On 19 August, the UN Special Representative, the highly-respected Sergio de Mello, was killed, along with another twenty-two UN personnel, when a car-bomb destroyed the UN headquarters in Baghdad. On 12 November, another huge car-bomb killed eighteen Italian troops and Carabinieri in Nasiriyah, almost killing Colonel Georgio di Pauli, an old colleague from Kosovo. The Coalition forces were beginning to retire behind the wire and entering into an ever more confrontational and violent relationship with many local Sunni Iraqis, but increasingly the Shia as well. Saddam himself was captured in December 2003, but that did little to dampen the Sunni insurgency, while the majority Shia began to flex their muscles and confront the Coalition forces. Even in Basra, Shia-dominated and with little sectarian tension, the British began to have a harder time of it. The invasion of Iraq, and the subsequent 'success' in delivering democracy, was supposed to have cowed the neighbouring Iranians, 'putting them on notice' regarding their activities in the region. Some of the more ambitious neo-Conservatives who had dominated the debates about the wisdom or otherwise of invading Iraq had even envisaged reaching Baghdad, then 'turning right' and going on to topple the Ayatollahs in Tehran. As Coalition woes multiplied, Iran began to support Shia resistance to the Americans and British more aggressively and to confront the US more openly. It was in November 2003 that an IAEA investigation concluded that the Islamic Republic of Iran had systematically failed to report on its nuclear programme in line with its obligations under the Nuclear Proliferation Treaty. While there was no evidence of an overt Iranian nuclear weapons programme yet, the issue of Iran's nuclear ambitions grew in urgency in the coming years, particularly when seen from Washington, Riyadh and Tel Aviv.

A major feature of RCDS was its famed 'world tour', on which groups of a dozen or so 'members' would spend a month in a particular part of the world examining the political, economic and social aspects of a region, in order to identify the issues and challenges faced and the policies being pursued to address them. In the summer of 2003, while the post-invasion situation in Iraq was unfolding, my syndicate had departed for an intensive trip to Pakistan, India and Sri Lanka. These visits had been meticulously planned by the RCDS staff, and by the British High Commissions in each capital. We enjoyed extraordinarily high-level access in all three countries, meeting politicians, diplomats, academics and senior members of the armed forces. Many were sporting their own RCDS ties, from earlier courses, including President Pervez Musharraf of Pakistan. It was another very clear example, if any was needed, of the benefits to the United Kingdom of investing in important instruments of 'soft power', with their long-term potential to oil the wheels of diplomacy.

In Pakistan, we sensed the ambivalence of that country to events in Afghanistan, and the way in which long-term antagonism to India influenced attitudes to the Pashtun population on either side of the border. This also affected attitudes to the 'tribal areas', and to the 'terrorist' groups who espoused violence in the name of Islam and had launched attacks in India and Afghanistan, but also inside Pakistan. The country had its own Sunni-Shia split, which often flared into violence, while India had a Muslim population almost as large as the population of Pakistan itself. The calculations of the Pakistani political classes, the armed forces and the Inter-Services Intelligence agency towards Islamic extremism were extremely difficult to unravel, particularly given the scale of internal violence. We went up to the 'disputed line' in Kashmir, where we were reassured to hear that the Indian Army, a valley away, had been informed of our visit, in case they intended to launch some routine, 'speculative' artillery shelling. In Peshawar we visited the Afghan refugee camps, which were beginning to empty as people returned to their own country in the wake of the overthrow of the Taliban; and while I was unable to visit my old friend with the brother in Ealing,

I did revisit the 'chained' tree in the Officers' Mess garden of the Khyber Rifles.

I also experienced a blinding flash of enlightenment when we visited an Islamic school, a *madrassa*. Here we saw a classroom full of bright, enthusiastic young Pakistani boys, rocking to and fro as they recited their Koranic lessons. This may well have been one of those schools funded by Saudi Arabia, with a curriculum based on Wahhabi fundamentalist teachings, which had been set up as part of the Saudi assistance to the mujahideen during the war with the Soviets. I opined to the mullah who was taking the class that, as Christians, we read the Bible and learned and understood the teachings, the stories and the parables, but that we did not feel the need to learn it off by heart. He reminded me of the difference between the Bible, a human record of Christ's life and teachings, and the Koran, the received word of God, merely 'recited' by the prophet Mohammed, and therefore worthy of being learnt by heart. Whilst I considered this distinction I recalled that in 'orthodox' Islam the Koran cannot be translated from Arabic into another language, and that therefore these young Pakistani boys were learning by rote a book whose contents they could not actually understand. It was as if a young English boy was memorizing the Bible in Latin. It would be the mullah's role, in due course, to explain the message behind the readings, and the mullah's own upbringing and educational influences would determine what he chose to emphasise and what to ignore. The implications were obvious and, in a country where there were such poor public educational facilities and *madrassas* were the only option for many poor Pakistanis, the scope for exercising a substantial and possibly malign influence on large numbers of young minds was very apparent. This phenomenon was not limited to the Islamic world itself, but was also becoming apparent in the growing Muslim communities of the West. Here, the shortcomings of Western government policies on integration left many Muslim youths vulnerable to the appeal of extremist ideology, taught by people using a very selective interpretation of Koranic verses and increasingly magnified in its effect through the sophisticated use of social media.

The size and scale of India was daunting for a two-week 'wave-top' tour, but in that time we managed to visit: New Delhi; Leh and Srinagar in Kashmir; Mumbai, where I hunted down my grandparents' marriage entry in St John's Cathedral; Bangalore and Hyderabad, the 'Silicon Valley' hotspots of India; Calcutta, with its magnificent Raj buildings; and the Hindu holy city of Benares. It was a fascinating trip, although two weeks hardly did justice to the 'world's largest democracy', with its multi-faceted history, culture, religion and civilization, let alone its ambitious plans for the future. It was easy to understand the fascination that India had held for my grandparents, and for the many British who had made that country their professional focus, and their home, over so many generations.

Other RCDS 'highlights' had been extended visits to regions of the United Kingdom, a 20,000-word dissertation, the chance to undertake an MA course at King's College London and the diplomatic 'war game' at the end of the third term. Teased by a fellow member who declared, 'I think we can be certain that Simon Mayall won't be volunteering for any extra work', I actually found myself the only British member signed up for the MA. However, I enjoyed the opportunity to read more widely and to experience again that old frisson evoked by the words, 'Gentlemen, you may now turn your exam papers over.' The dissertation formed an important part of the MA course, and I felt that, given the current political circumstances, my background and interests, I would continue to concentrate on issues in the Middle East. Since 9/11, much new work had been written about the nature of conflict between Islam and the West, some of it building on Samuel Huntington's book *Clash of Civilizations*, whose observations regarding the Islamic world were looking to be all too prescient by this time, and whose thesis regarding identity politics would look ever more valid as Russia and China increasingly began to 'flex their muscles'. There had also been a renewed interest in the crusading period, and a fresh concentration on Muslim interpretations of jihad. While it was easy to identify the historical antagonisms between Arabs, Persians and Turks, and those between Sunni and Shia, what I had not really focused on previously was just how much violence there also was within the Islamic world by Sunni Muslims against other Sunni Muslims, and how the same jihadi philosophy used to inspire attacks on the 'crusaders and Zionists' was also deployed to justify the assault on other Muslims. Therefore, with a nod to Samuel Huntington, I entitled my work, 'Jihad and the Clash *within* Civilisation'.

In the 1980s, the West had been convinced that the rise of Islamism in Iran had been a 'bad thing', particularly since it had contributed significantly to the fall of the Shah. However, the same policy-makers, at the same time, seemed to believe that the success of that same fundamentalist ideology in Afghanistan, albeit a Sunni version, was a 'good thing', since confronting the Soviet Union and communist ideology was the West's Cold War priority. The climactic years of that dramatic campaign had been the catalyst for Osama bin Laden to set up Al Qa'eda, a new and much more potent manifestation of Islamist extremism and terror. This version of Islamism went much wider than merely confronting the 'infidel'. It now combined this with the Islamist challenge to many modern Muslim countries and 'regimes', particularly the Kingdom of Saudi Arabia. Al Qa'eda postulated an ideologically coherent narrative that, relying on very selective inspiration and grievance, demanded and received a particularly high level of commitment and sacrifice from its adherents. 'Betrayal' by Saudi Arabia during the Gulf War now generated a new strategy for the expansion of Islamic fundamentalism. In this plan, the 'Far Enemy', the West and particularly America, would be subjected to a spectacular strike. This would, inevitably, provoke a massive response against targets in the Middle East or Central Asia, which in turn would cause a tidal wave of violent Muslim reaction, much of it against the West, but also against 'false' governments in the Muslim world. However improbable it seemed at the time, the perceived consequences would be: an overthrow of the 'Near Enemy', defined as the corrupted and illegitimate autocracies and monarchies of the region; the spontaneous revival of the universal Muslim community, the *umma*; and the restoration of the caliphate – all under the strict application of sharia law. Having launched this strategy with the 9/11 attacks, thereby provoking the Coalition invasion of Iraq, Osama bin Laden did not live to see the grander elements of his plan for the Muslim world implemented. But Caliph Ibrahim and Islamic State would have another bloody attempt at it.

Although evident during the last decades of the Ottoman Empire, the confrontation between Islamists and nationalists, reformers and secularists, had really come to the forefront of Middle East politics with the collapse of the Empire and the caliphate, and with the formation of new countries and states in the aftermath of the First World War. The ensuing tension had raised again the possibility of legitimate, indeed obligatory, jihad against domestic Muslim regimes that were viewed as straying from 'Islamic virtue'. In the Western world, the basic unit of human organization had become the nation state, which was seen as being sub-divided in various ways, one of which was by religion. Islamist fundamentalists, but also many other Muslims, identified with their religion first and chose to see their world as a religious unity illegitimately sub-divided into nations. Islamists therefore see the legitimacy of the *umma* as being oppressed and corrupted by regimes that conspire to undermine a shared Muslim identity. The reality of Middle East politics, particularly since the Second World War, has generated strange sets of alliances. Reformers and conservatives have sought to sustain the new states and make them stronger. Intellectuals and the peasant classes have become united in calls for a renewal of Islamic values. Islamists and elements of the military have joined forces to overthrow monarchical regimes. Muslims and communists have joined in recognizing ostensibly shared values of social justice and resistance to oppression. Repressive, authoritarian regimes and Western liberal democrats have made common cause to thwart Islamists, in order to address their own security concerns and maintain an unrestricted flow of energy supplies. In this potpourri of motivation and rationale, the oppression of, or compromise with, Islamists has become both an alibi, and a genuine reason, for not embracing or implementing long-required political, social or economic reforms.

The effect of these ideological and physical confrontations and compacts has been crippling for the development of Muslim states in the Middle East. Where governments have attempted to liberalize, they have been attacked on theological and sharia grounds, and the Islamists have gained credibility and strength. Where governments have sought to suppress the Islamists, they have merely fed their status as 'martyrs' and further radicalized elements of the population. Where governments have sought accommodation with the Islamists, they have undermined the growth of political reform movements and any attempts to liberalize and develop their economies. Governments have been forced to confront the pressures of operating in a globalized world economy, with its growing social and cultural assumptions about the primacy of the individual, while facing down internal unrest from movements committed to a vision of society built on sharia and the primacy of the *umma*.

Some commentators have discerned a continuity between the modern manifestation of Islamist extremism, as exemplified by Al Qa'eda and IS, and the secular, totalitarian philosophies of the twentieth century, together with aspects of the millenarianism of medieval Europe. Key common features are: an assumption of 'corruption' within societies; an assault by corrupting external 'satanic forces'; resistance by 'the faithful'; and leadership by a vanguard of 'the chosen'. In victory, a 'reign of purity' will be established in a one–party state with a charismatic leader. Nazism, Bolshevism, Maoism and extremist manifestations of Islamism, all have at their heart an attack on modern concepts of 'liberalism', with the definition of the 'enemy' lying in the hands of the 'vanguard' and the language of discourse becoming increasingly violent, with increasing insensitivity to the shedding of blood. Indeed, violence almost becomes an end in itself, as more and more 'enemies' are identified. In the years leading to 9/11, interpretations of jihad were used to justify war against the West and the state of Israel, against the 'godless' Soviets, against 'heretical' Shia and secular Ba'athists and against the 'impious' military government of Egypt and the monarchical regimes of the Gulf. In time, almost anyone who questioned the fundamentalist interpretation of the Koran could be deemed to be 'heretical'. This trend, whereby *takfiri* Islamists continually redefine the enemy in order to sustain their narrative and inspire their followers, would become further marked in the years following the fall of Saddam Hussein in Iraq in 2003, and in the wake of the Arab Spring of 2011.

In addition, while these major political and social shifts had been taking place across the Muslim Middle East, there had been a corresponding growth of first- and second-generation Muslim communities in many Western countries, bringing with it increasing levels of disenfranchisement, alienation and resentment among both the host and the immigrant populations. Theoretically, these Muslims now lived in the *dar al-Harb*, the House of War, but they were in a 'state of truce' while they had freedom to practise their religion. Within this construct an Islamic fatwa had no legal status, as these were only valid within the *dar al-Salam*, the House of Peace. In 1979, when Grand Ayatollah Khomeini issued his fatwa against Salman Rushdie, a British citizen, in the wake of the publication of *The Satanic Verses*, he was making a bold new assertion: seeking to transcend the traditional definition of the frontiers of Islam and claiming jurisdiction over Muslim immigrant populations abroad, both Sunni and Shia, treating them as 'citizens' of the global *umma*. His intervention was a dramatic, revolutionary and deeply damaging development. It sparked a new consciousness in the Muslim diaspora of a 'neo-fundamentalism' that, although it came from an Iranian Shia leader, dovetailed very neatly with Sunni-inspired Islamism. It was from this broad theological and intellectual background and tendency that many of the 9/11 hijackers were drawn.

Osama bin Laden and Ayman al Zawahiri, his Egyptian-born ideologue, drank deep at this well and took violence and never-ending conflict, as implied by the more radical interpretations of Islamism, to new heights, particularly in their assault on the 'heretics' and 'apostates' of their own religion. Although the attacks on US and European targets and interests attracted most attention in the West, the scale of death and suffering in Muslim countries, dealt by both Muslim regimes and Islamist attackers, was and continues to be at a dramatically higher level. Abdullah Azzam, a Palestinian who studied in Egypt and Saudi Arabia, was an early mentor of Osama bin Laden and was known as the 'Father of Global Jihad'. He was another who espoused the ideological 'vanguard' theory, proclaiming,

'History does not write its lines except in blood. Glory does not build its edifices except with skulls. Honour and respect cannot be established except on the foundations of cripples and corpses.' He was killed in a car-bomb attack in Pakistan in 1989. Despite all the challenges and setbacks to Islamism in the years following 9/11, whether by military action, the spread of democracy and global wealth, social media or the developing role of women in Muslim societies, the core messages of such groups as Al Qa'eda and IS still command remarkable levels of loyalty, including the willingness to make sacrifices and to commit atrocities.

Chapter 22

Jihad versus 'the Surge' –
a Clash of Strategies

B y the time I had put my pen down at the end of the final three-hour MA exam, promising myself that this was the last set of examinations I would ever sit, my military fate had been decided. I was to return to the Ministry of Defence as the Director of Army Resources and Plans (D Army RP), a step up from my previous post as Colonel Army Plans and an appointment that, in truth, suited me well, with its powerful responsibilities for continuing to help Defence, and the CGS, determine the size, shape and structure of the Army, while wrestling with the perennial problem of lack of money. The issues, the frictions and the challenges were familiar enough, although daily life had been made slightly more difficult by the MoD staff being distributed between the Old War Office, the Metropole Building and Northumberland House, while the original Ministry of Defence building itself was being gutted and modernized. The pace of work was frenetic, as it was becoming daily clearer that we were going to have to take further cuts to structure and manpower, and the CGS, General Mike Jackson, had now determined that the Army would use this opportunity to rationalize the organization of the infantry under an initiative known as the Future Infantry Structure (FIS). This was to prove a highly controversial and emotive subject, given the importance and role of the 'regimental system' and the 'tribal' nature of the combat arms. Army RP were at the centre of many of these debates, in which emotions ran high and much 'crockery was broken', not least in Scotland, as the various staffs tried to determine the principles under which battalions would be amalgamated and new identities forged, and while the 'old and bold', those former senior officers with strong regimental affiliations, made their many representations, not always helpfully. All our work, in 2004 and 2005, important and demanding though it was, took place against an ever-worsening security situation in Iraq, where the combination of poor planning and 'heroically optimistic' early assumptions had left the

Coalition soldiers on the ground in an increasingly beleaguered position, and the civilian population at the mercy of sectarian militias and the ensuing chaos and violence. In April 2004, a large and impressive group of former ambassadors, not all from the 'camel corps', as Foreign Office Arabists were often called, wrote to Blair expressing significant disquiet at the UK's policies in the Middle East. Primarily they criticised the Iraq campaign, but they also drew attention to the way the 'Two-State Solution' at the heart of any potential Israel-Palestine peace agreement was being undermined by people turning a blind eye to the continuing major 'settler' incursions in the West Bank and East Jerusalem.

The months of April to June 2004 represented the bloodiest period of fighting since the fall of Baghdad. The limited transfer of power from the CPA to an interim 'caretaker' government, who immediately began the trial of Saddam, did not diminish the violence. Bremer announced the transfer two days earlier than advertised, and then departed Iraq, along with his trademark Timberland boots. It did not look like the actions of someone who was leaving on the back of a 'job well done'. At the same time, the military organization was completely overhauled, with the establishment of Multi-National Force-Iraq (MNF-I) to handle 'strategic'-level issues, and Multi-National Corps-Iraq (MNC-I) tasked to manage the day-to-day military campaign, which inevitably included a good deal of interaction with a range of civilian agencies. Multi-National Security Transition Command-Iraq (MNSTC-I) was also set up, with responsibility for the reconstruction of the Iraqi Security Forces (ISF). It was an acknowledgement of the impossible position Rick Sanchez had been put in. In effect, he was to be replaced by both General George Casey and Lieutenant General Tom Metz. It was analogous to General Auchinleck being replaced by the combination of Generals Alexander and Montgomery in the Western Desert in 1942.

By late 2004 the Americans, provoked by the well-publicized murder of four Blackwater civilian contractors, had determined on an operation against the Sunni stronghold of Fallujah, but also on confronting the new Shia-based *Jaish al Mahdi* (JAM), the 'Mahdi Army', in Najaf. Modern Najaf contains the ancient city of Kufa, which was the original power-base of Caliph Ali and his sons Hassan and Hussein. The JAM, a large sectarian militia, was led by the popular Shia religious firebrand, Muqtada al Sadr, whose father had been a prominent cleric executed by Saddam. He had a strong following in Sadr City, the great, unprepossessing and dilapidated Shia quarter of Baghdad to the east of the Tigris. He represented the 'activist' branch of Shi'ism, in contrast to the influential Ayatollah Ali Sistani in Najaf, who was the epitome of the 'quietist' tradition. Sistani's influence had been vital in trying to help align Coalition objectives with those of the majority Shia, and regular reports of his poor health, at several stages even of his death, were greeted with grave concern by the Coalition. Both US operations had only limited long-term success, given the fractious and sectarian nature of Iraqi politics. The US tried a limited assault in Fallujah, turned the town over to the nascent ISF as part of a 'local deal' and, when that predictably failed, had another go, before turning their attention to Najaf. When the Americans had begun to experience trouble in Baghdad, there had been discussions about sending the British 16 Air Assault Brigade to assist, on the premise that the British Army had great competence in dealing with the complexity of urban operations among a civilian population as a result of long experience in Northern Ireland. However, at an early stage the Iraq War was already provoking domestic repercussions in the UK, and there was no political appetite for extending British responsibilities. The US had hoped to bring their force levels down to 30,000 by late 2003, and the British had assumed they would be down to 6,000 troops in the same period. However, in late 2004 there were still over 150,000 Coalition military personnel in the country, as well as tens of thousands of civilian contractors. Huge amounts of money were being spent in keeping the operation going, not just on men and materiel, but with the likes of Kellogg Brown Root and Halliburton charging around $100 per person per day to house, feed and water this vast occupation force.

In November 2004, as the rate and sophistication of insurgent attacks grew, the interim government tried to find its feet and the battle for infrastructure and basic services continued, the US launched a new, full-scale assault on Fallujah, and a parallel operation in Mosul alongside the Kurdish *peshmerga*. The casualty levels were high, even by the standards of Iraq, and deficiencies in equipment, particularly among Coalition light-armour vehicles like the Humvee and the British 'Snatch' Land Rover, were beginning to be reported regularly in the Western media. Pictures of improvised explosive devices (IEDs) blowing up Coalition vehicles and soldiers were also appearing daily on jihadi websites and further fuelling the influx of Sunni foreign fighters. These made their way to Syria, under the Assad government's watchful eye, and then infiltrated across the long open border or along the Euphrates Valley. There was also a significant rise in the incidence of suicide bombings, a particularly unsettling development for Coalition Forces. There were over 400 such attacks in 2004 alone.

Although 'martyrdom' has a long and honourable tradition among the Shia, stretching back to Ali and his sons, the suicide bomb and the suicide car-bomb were a distinctly Sunni jihadist phenomenon. An election in January 2005, which most Sunnis boycotted, gave only temporary respite from the violence, and any hopes of large-scale troop reductions were soon dashed. In August, the *Washington Post* quoted an anonymous senior US official as saying, 'The United States no longer expects to see a model new democracy, a self-supporting oil industry or a society in which the majority of people are free from serious security or economic challenges. What we expected to achieve was never realistic given the timetable, or what unfolded on the ground.' It was a starkly pessimistic assessment, and things were going to get much worse before they got better.

In the summer of 2005, the annual British Army Conference was held at Warminster, and among the usual cast of British speakers Major General Peter Chiarelli of the US Army also came to give a presentation. This was not long after the 7/7 bombings of buses and underground trains in London which had killed fifty-six people, including the four bombers, all British-born Muslims, and wounded hundreds more. Peter Chiarelli had commanded 1st Cavalry Division in Baghdad the year before, and his formation had been very heavily involved in a significant fight against JAM in Sadr City. When JAM launched their attacks, Chiarelli had had to commit his troops to a major urban operation, alongside the still-nascent new ISF, in order to regain control of the area. By all accounts, it had been a vicious and bloody affair, and '1st Cav' had lost scores of tanks and armoured vehicles and over 100 dead in the close urban fighting. His experience had convinced him that the 'day of the tank' was not yet over, despite ever-increasing enthusiasm for UAVs and 'precision strikes', nor was the enduring requirement for tough, resilient and brave officers and soldiers prepared to engage in the lethal demands of close combat. Robert Gates, who would replace Donald Rumsfeld as Defense Secretary, serving both President Bush and President Obama, would later say:

> Never neglect the psychological, cultural, political, and human dimensions of warfare, which is inevitably tragic, inefficient, and uncertain. Be sceptical of systems-analysis, computer models, game theories, or doctrines that suggest otherwise. Look askance at idealized, triumphalist, or ethnocentric notions of future conflict that aspire to up-end the immutable principles of war: where the enemy is killed, but our troops and innocent civilians are spared.

Where adversaries can be cowed, shocked, or awed into submission, instead of being tracked down, hilltop by hilltop, house by house, block by bloody block.

This echoed the sentiments of General William Tecumseh Sherman ('Every attempt to make war easy and safe will result in humiliation and disaster') and of General 'Vinegar Joe' Stilwell ('No matter how a war starts, it ends in mud. It has to be slugged out – there are no trick solutions or cheap shortcuts'). Wise words.

Peter Chiarelli's story of combat was a sobering one, but of equal interest was his approach to dealing with the aftermath. He had discerned that much of the violence stemmed from those areas in Sadr City notable for high unemployment and dreadful public services. Despite the risks, and to considerable scepticism from his superiors and some of his subordinates, he had initiated a wide-ranging works programme that offered the locals employment, and tackled the issues of sewerage, water, electricity and trash collection – his SWET projects. In very short order, he was able to prove that this had substantially reduced levels of violence, and that his soldiers were increasingly patrolling Sadr City with the willing consent of the local inhabitants. One brigade commander did not suffer a single further casualty in the rest of the tour. There were setbacks, but in the context of mostly unremittingly bad news from Iraq, his work gave some grounds for optimism. Some months later, we learnt that he was returning to Baghdad, with a third star, as the Commander of MNC-I, with the opportunity to apply his methods on a nationwide canvas. At about the same time, General Mike Jackson called me into his office. I, too, had caught the selectors' eye, for promotion to Major General and an exit from the MoD. Disappointingly, I was not going to get command of a British division, a position we all aspired to, but I was going to be Deputy Commanding General (DCG) for MNC-I, succeeding Major General Peter Everson. This was a senior Coalition appointment that the UK held in recognition of the force levels and the specialist capabilities we were contributing to the campaign. Among these were our highly effective Special Forces, who were doing tremendous work in Basra and Baghdad. I would be taking up the appointment in the late summer of 2006, working for Peter Chiarelli. In the meantime, I was to finish my work in Army RP, brush up my Arabic and go to Fort Hood in Texas to work with Lieutenant General Ray Odierno of 5 US Corps, who would be replacing Chiarelli and his HQ 3 US Corps in around nine months' time. I would straddle the tenure of both Commanders, and provide continuity in HQ MNC-I. While I was on my way to Texas, Hezbollah fighters attacked an Israeli border patrol and took two soldiers hostage, provoking another Israeli assault into South Lebanon. Given the unprecedented level of Iranian support for Hezbollah in this confrontation, some considered this bloody 34-day conflict to be the first round of an Israeli-Iranian 'proxy war' rather than a continuation of the long-running Arab-Israeli conflict. The next decade would see this new dimension of Middle East political tension become increasingly more pronounced, as the Shia Iranians positioned themselves as the most vocal supporters of the Palestinians, and as the Sunni Arabs appeared to lose interest in their cause.

Ray Odierno was a markedly different character from Peter Chiarelli and equally impressive. He was a very large, bullet-headed artilleryman, thoughtful and taciturn. It was difficult to imagine his equivalent in my own Army. His son had lost an arm in a fire-fight in Afghanistan, and he was not the only American or British senior officer to know the true personal cost of our operations. He had previously commanded 4th Infantry Division in Central Iraq, where the writer and journalist Tom Ricks, in his book *Fiasco*, unfavourably compared his 'hard-driving' style of command, and his very 'kinetic' approach to operations, to General David Petraeus's more nuanced style of leadership of 101st Airborne Division in Northern Iraq. Among Odierno's talented command team was Britain's Emma Sky as his trusted Political Adviser, or POLAD. They were an unlikely pairing. The one a bull of a military man from central casting, the other a slight, liberal NGO activist, they had met in Kirkuk and had formed a 'combative-collaborative' partnership, both committed to trying to salvage something from the current operational wreckage. Odierno would often refer to her as 'my very own insurgent'. One 'serial' in the 'Main Events List' for the 'work-up' training was dealing with a crisis involving the Mosul Dam, whose poor initial construction had always made it liable to catastrophic failure, with potentially huge downstream consequences as far south as Baghdad. Judicious daily maintenance would sustain its structural integrity for some years, but the issue raised its head again in 2014, when IS took Mosul and maintenance work ground to a halt, until the Iraqi Special Operations Force secured the dam, in an early success against the jihadists.

The situation continued to deteriorate in Iraq. Casualties were mounting, the public were losing confidence and the political hubris of the early days of occupation had long since dissipated as the catalogue of political and military miscalculation and failure escalated. Iraq was sucking all the oxygen out of politics, nowhere more so than in the UK, where the fault-lines between Tony Blair and his Chancellor, Gordon Brown, were becoming increasingly exposed. In the meantime, the effort that could have gone into Afghanistan to capitalize on the successes of 2001, 2002 and 2003 did not materialize. The security picture in Afghanistan was patchy at best, and the opportunity to put the Afghan economy on some form of long-term, sustainable basis, which might have thwarted its development as a 'narco-state', was wasted. Napoleon once said, 'I may have lost a battle, but I never lost a minute.' The international community 'lost' four, maybe five, years in Afghanistan because of the intervention in Iraq, and they never really made up the time. In early 2006, as I was preparing to take up my appointment in Baghdad, Sunni insurgents, masterminded by Abu Musa al Zarqawi, a psychotic Jordanian jihadist, had launched a large-scale, sophisticated, destructive attack on the iconic Shia 'Golden Mosque' of Samarra. It was an outrage deliberately designed to stir up the worst elements of sectarian hatred, and it pitted Sunni and Shia against each other in another episode of the historical cycle of violence that transcended, and long pre-dated, any antipathy towards the Americans and their allies.

In the aftermath of the attack, the multicultural city of Baghdad was subject to levels of violence and scenes of ethnic cleansing not seen since the Balkans, and the 'death squads' of both sects matched atrocity for atrocity. The Sunni gangs favoured decapitation, while the Shia killers opted for the extensive use of power-tools on their victims. The Ministry of Health and the municipal hospitals were in the hands of JAM supporters, and no Sunni could go there with any hope of getting out alive. The police, national and local, were often complicit, and each daybreak would reveal scores of bodies tortured, killed and dumped on the roadside, or thrown into the Tigris, where they would gather in the bend of the river at Kut-al-Amara, scene of the British disaster of 1916. Trying to purge the ISF and Iraqi Police leadership of sectarianism would be a task of Augean proportions. Criticism of US and British policy was becoming ever more pronounced, and in 2006 some high-ranking retired American officers began publicly to demand the resignation of Donald Rumsfeld for his mismanagement of the war.

In June 2006, Nouri al Maliki, leader of the Shia Al Dawa party, became Prime Minister. He had been in exile for over 24 years and had spent most of those years in Damascus, Tehran or Lebanon among his Shia co-religionists. He was widely perceived to be close to the Iranian regime, as were many of the Shia political leadership. How could it be otherwise, given their experiences, their sense of indebtedness and their pathological fear of a

Sunni revival? His elevation was contentious and broadly negative, while the sectarian nature of many of his attitudes and policies made it difficult to prosecute an even-handed approach to terrorism and the insurgency, establish genuinely 'national' security forces or build the foundations of any lasting national reconciliation strategy.

The sheer complexity of the burgeoning chaos in Iraq had taken a long time to be properly understood, while the formulation of a coherent strategy to address it was only just slowly unfolding. It would involve embracing new assumptions regarding time and effort, and uncomfortable political and military compromises. As the old expression has it, 'When you are up to your arms in crocodiles, it is sometimes difficult to remember that your original plan had been to drain the swamp.' Sun Tsu had attributed to him the maxim, 'Strategy without tactics is the slowest path to victory. Tactics without strategy is the noise before defeat.' Rick Shinseki, the former US Army Chief who had argued for much higher force-levels in Iraq, also once said, 'If you do not like change, you will like irrelevance even less.' In the second half of 2006, neither our strategy nor our tactics seemed to be truly relevant to the scale of the problems we faced. An Iraqi, a virulent opponent of Saddam, living in exile, captured the ambivalence of Iraqis towards the Coalition efforts when he wrote: 'The sense that our people, our country, our culture, our history were being spat on by US soldiers, themselves pitifully lacking in history, education, culture and respect, was too much to bear.' This was a harsh observation, but one containing a valuable insight.

By 2006 there were three major identifiable groups of insurgents, although they were often violently opposed to each other and routinely split among themselves. The most obvious were the large contingent of 'secular' Sunnis. These comprised disenfranchised Ba'athists, ex-Iraqi Army personnel, ex-members of Saddam's security forces and radicalized citizens, all with the twin targets of the Coalition Forces and the newly empowered Shia. In the Sunni majority areas of Anbar and the Euphrates Valley, and the Saddam heartlands of Tikrit, they had at an early stage infiltrated the re-forming ISF, particularly the police. Although divided by ideology, they had formed ad hoc coalitions with the Sunni jihadist and Islamist groups that had begun to stream in through the porous Syrian border, financed and facilitated by a range of sympathisers, not least the Syrian Assad regime. Sunni resistance was further inflamed by Arab concepts of honour, retribution and retaliation, especially in the tribal areas of Anbar in western Iraq. It was too easy either to ignore the strength of this feeling of humiliation or, unhelpfully, to confuse or conflate it with the ideological zealotry of the jihadists.

The second group were the Islamists and jihadists themselves, who coalesced around Al Zarqawi and his Al Qa'eda in Iraq (AQI) movement, all of them broadly committed to the establishment of an Islamic state in Iraq, having expelled the invaders and suppressed the 'heretical' and treasonous Shia. Al Zarqawi had given his *bayat*, the oath of allegiance, to Osama bin Laden in late 2004, but his political ambition was all too obvious, and by 2006 he had been instructed by bin Laden to confine himself to military matters and not to try and usurp the ideological leadership. His overall strategy appeared to have four strands: to isolate the US and erode its legitimacy by attacking international bodies, NGOs and US allies; to prevent any Iraqis from co-operating with the occupiers, with a series of attacks on army and police recruit centres and targeted assassinations and bombings of those to whom the CPA planned to transfer power; to commit atrocities that drove out foreigners and hampered attempts to reconstruct Iraq and deliver basic services; and to foment sectarian conflict by targeting the Shia. In all this Al Zarqawi was murderously successful, making life for the Coalition Forces tough and deadly, and comprehensively dashing whatever hopes the US had had of a swift and clean extraction. His disdain for Americans, Shias and secularists was matched by his contempt for the US goal of 'democracy'. He saw democracy as not just empowering the Shia 'heretics' but as heresy in its own right, saying, 'We are totally opposed to democracy. Democracy implies choice, including choice in religion, and therefore is *haram*, forbidden.'

The third group comprised the Shia resistance movements. In US planning, the Shia had been seen as the net beneficiaries of the invasion and therefore as having the most reason to co-operate with Coalition Forces. Shia *émigrés* like Ahmed al Chalabi, with an eye on gaining power in a 'liberated' Iraq, had made a compelling case in Washington that this would be the reality of invasion. However, a mixture of memories of the 'betrayal' of 1991, genuine Iraqi nationalism, Shia disdain for America's Gulf Sunni friends, Iranian influence and Coalition miscalculations led to a stand-off with JAM and thwarted these hopes. This put the Coalition and JAM into a state of persistent confrontation, which diverted resources while making the establishment of a common front against the Sunni insurgents and jihadists very difficult. The status, role and influence of the JAM was further complicated by the tendency of the Shia-dominated government, led by Nouri al Maliki, only to see threats from the Sunni groups and to restrain Coalition operations against the malign activities of Shia militias. It also enabled ever-increasing levels of Iranian influence in the country.

Among these violent groups and seething tensions, large numbers of Iraqis simply sought to keep their heads below the parapet, trying to steer clear of the violence aimed at the Coalition Forces, the Coalition's own counter-insurgency campaign, the battles between competing Sunni and Shia militia and the increasingly fractious relationship between Al Zarqawi's foreign jihadists and the indigenous Sunni insurgents. Criminals also thrived, as they always do in such situations. The only element of Iraqi society that remained relatively immune from this witches' brew of violence were the Kurds in their mountain fastness in the north, although their own ambitions for a Greater Kurdistan brought them into sporadic conflict with the Shia-dominated government and the Sunni insurgents, both of whom contested their aspirations. They were not immune, either, from the suspicions of their Turkish neighbours, who had their own long-standing problems with their large Kurdish minority.

The Samarra attack acted as an accelerant for all the violent tensions competing for prominence in Iraq at that time, creating a security situation that teetered on the brink of all-out civil war. While acts of violence and casualties rose inexorably through 2006, along with the temperature, the Coalition Forces tried to prosecute a counter-insurgency campaign, protect civilians, stand between the militias, support reconstruction and build the new ISF. The Coalition Forces increasingly consisted of only the US and UK, as the other allied contingents either withdrew or hunkered down defensively in their fortified outposts, reflecting their governments' lack of enthusiasm for an operation that had started controversially and then gone wildly off-script. In many cases the ISF, notably the Army, acted bravely and admirably, but their performance understandably reflected their short independent existence, the speed of their expansion, their lack of capability and the complexity of the sectarian 'soup' in which we were all swimming.

By late 2006, identifying a coherent military strategy that would underpin the stated, but frayed, policy objective of 'supporting a new, democratic Iraqi government, that would govern in the interests of all its citizens and not be a threat to the region' remained the highest political and military priority of the US Government. This became even more urgent as the Bush Presidency moved towards its last quarter and the Republicans got caned in the Congressional elections of that year. The reality was that America was facing a strategic defeat potentially greater than Vietnam. All excuses had been exhausted, and the language of 'victory' was being quietly dropped in favour of the lower ambition of 'withdrawal with honour'.

Chapter 23

Lawrence Redux

HQ MNC-I was situated within the vast Camp Victory. The headquarters had requisitioned the Saddam-era Al Faw Palace, close to Baghdad International Airport. It was surrounded by an artificial lake, around which were attractive guest villas now occupied by senior Coalition officers. I shared one of these, known as Glubb Pasha House, with my ADC, Tom 'Smokey' Robinson, my 'house sergeant', Corporal Welch of the Royal Engineers, and members of my highly professional Close Protection team. The Palace itself was approached across a two-lane causeway, and the vast atrium was dominated by a 'three-storey' crystal chandelier. The Operations Room was like a multiplex cinema, on a scale and of a sophistication only the Americans can achieve, with banked staff positions and a vast wall of television screens relaying a mix of CNN, NBC, interactive maps and 'Predator' UAV down-links from across Iraq. My own office, around the corner from the Commanding General, was generously proportioned and looked out over the lake. There was a nearby balcony, where I shared 'strategy conversations', and the occasional cigarette, with Peter Chiarelli. It was certainly a step up from the converted medical centre of Tidworth or the portakabin complex of Pristina. There was a daily morning 'battle rhythm' that extended until about ten o'clock, when all the routine briefings, the updates and the senior get-togethers were completed (see Map 10). After that, General Chiarelli and I would cover a range of meetings and engagements, often having to take a helicopter into the 'Green Zone' two or three times a day to meet political and diplomatic leaders, MNF-I senior leadership, Iraqi military and police chiefs or those civilian contractors charged with attempting to address the infrastructure problems. If there were no helicopters available, or the weather was too bad, we dashed to the Green Zone in convoy along Route Irish, which at one stage was deemed 'the most dangerous four miles in the world'. Field Marshal Charles Guthrie came to visit one time, as 'Colonel' of the SAS, and claimed to have been shot at while in transit. General Graeme Lamb, the British Deputy for MNF-I, also Special Forces, quizzed him.

'Were you injured?'

'No.'

'Was your vehicle hit?'

'No.'

'Was any other vehicle hit?'

'No.'

'Well, it doesn't count then.'

Flying over Baghdad, by day and by night, was memorable. Helmets, Osprey body armour and ballistic glasses on. Door guns swung out, all weapons 'locked and loaded', the gunners in full-face visors. The whirr of rotors and the vibration of the Black Hawk. A radio check. A hover, as the weight comes off the wheels. Both helicopters poised above the lake, then a dipping plunge followed by a fast ascent, and out over the wire and across the roof-tops of Baghdad's suburbs. In the distance, Saddam's half-finished mega-mosque with the only visible construction cranes in the capital, and below, the chaos of the Baghdad traffic, until the Green Zone came into sight. A hard bank over the Tigris River and its bridges, and a sweep across the iconic Baghdad parade-ground with the massive crossed swords held in arms and hands modelled on Saddam's own, the ground studded with helmets taken in the war against Iran. Then a spiralling dive and a flared landing at Forward Operating Base Liberty. In amongst the boredom, the filth and the routine horrors of war, one should never underestimate the attractive power and the murderous glamour of soldiering.

The Green Zone was a small town in itself, originally the Saddam regime's centre of power, occupying a bend in the River Tigris. It was easy to forget that it was actually completely cut off, by walls, barbed wire, and the river itself, from the rest of Baghdad, the so-called 'Red Zone'. Here were all the embassies, the Iraqi Government and Parliament, and a very large ISF presence, which reflected the prevailing paranoia but made these troops unavailable for other operations. There was also a multitude of private military security companies manned by personnel drawn from Nepal, Colombia, San Salvador, Liberia, Uganda, or by 'retired' UK and US Special Forces. The bomb damage of 2003 was still very evident, and while some half-hearted attempts had been made to plant flowers on roundabouts, the whole area was a maze of barbed wire, anti-blast walls, checkpoints, barriers and sentry boxes. There was rubbish everywhere, and a thick coating of dust on most surfaces. Rockets fired by the Shia militia from Sadr City would routinely land somewhere in this huge sprawling compound. The British Ambassador was another old Oxford friend, Dominic Asquith, whose residence provided a great watering hole for weary military commanders, including Americans, who were subject to General Order Number One but who welcomed occasional relief from the enormous operational burdens they carried. The other notable watering hole was Maude House, the residence of Graeme Lamb and the weekly rendezvous point for the various British personnel in the Green Zone. The administrative 'anarchy', captured so well in Ravi Chandrasekaran's book, *Imperial Life in the Emerald City*, had gone, but so too had that earlier optimism and enthusiasm. This was now 'hard pounding', and the various political milestones and tactical successes since 2003 had all proved to be false dawns. Trying to 'bump-start' my Arabic again, I had used an old Iraqi textbook with conversational lessons that usually involved going to a picturesque restaurant on Abu Nawas Street overlooking the River Tigris, accompanied by the lovely Basima. There we would eat fish and salad, fruit and honeyed baklava, while listening to Iraqi music and possibly 'tripping the light fantastic' on the dance floor. By late 2006, any Westerner seeking that type of entertainment in downtown Baghdad would very quickly have been shot, blown up or kidnapped.

MNC-I had divided Iraq into six multinational division (MND) areas of responsibility (AOR), although the US Marines insisted on calling theirs, in Anbar, a Multi-National Force (MNF). MND (North-East) covered the Kurdish region and was commanded by the South Koreans. They had not had a single casualty since arriving, but their AOR had a border with Turkey, who nursed their perennial suspicions of the Kurds, and Iran, who were always keen to dabble in Iraqi politics and in the internal Kurdish antipathies between the Barzanis of Erbil and the Talabanis of Suleymaniyah. Some years later, I would be David Cameron's Security Envoy to the Kurds, after the fall of Mosul to Islamic State, and I would get to know the region, its leaders and its people, considerably better. However, in 2006, given the security priorities in the rest of Iraq, I only visited the Kurdish region and the South Koreans once. I used to fly to various points in Iraq on a C12 aircraft generously provided by the Americans, and this time I was 'waved off' by a female Captain from South Carolina who was the protocol officer for the day. This flight was on a delightful, clear Mesopotamian morning. We flew north, with the two great rivers beneath us, struck by the greenery and scale of cultivation between them and then the sudden line of the desert to the west of the Euphrates and the broken and hilly ground to the east of the Tigris, where it rose up to meet the Zagros Mountains and the Iranian border. We landed at Erbil, which felt very like any small airport somewhere in Southern Europe. The landscape was totally different, and there was little evidence of the security trappings of Baghdad or any other town in Iraq. The Kurds, the great beneficiaries of the fall of Saddam, had been largely self-governing since 2003. The economy was booming, construction was taking place and there was no requirement for helmets and body-armour. A travel poster for Lufthansa announced, 'Come and visit Kurdistan – the other Iraq.' How true. At HQ MND (NE) I was exposed to a surreal video of South Koreans and Kurds dancing and practising martial arts together, all to the Michael Jackson song, 'Build the World, Make it a Better Place'. After kimchi and noodles in the canteen, I visited the hospital, which was almost entirely full of Kurds and where, for some reason, I was presented with a huge bunch of flowers. I could see that the South Korean commander needed little advice from me about counter-insurgency operations in his area. As we landed back in Baghdad, after the usual plummeting descent to avoid ground-fire, I saw the same protocol officer 'on parade'. Grinning at the ADC, I leapt down the aircraft steps and, as she snapped up a salute, thrust the bunch of flowers into her hands.

Without pausing, she said, 'If it's chocolates next time, General, you've got yourself a date!'

MND (North) was under US command and included the Sunni 'badlands' around Saddam's birthplace of Tikrit, the city of Mosul, the ruins of ancient Nineveh, which would later be desecrated by Islamic State, and the important oil refinery of Bayji which, like the Iraqi oil outlets in the Gulf, looked like the set of a *Mad Max* movie rather than the vital infrastructure facilities of a modern state. Their condition reflected the effects of years of sanctions, but also chronic under-investment. The whole energy sector was riddled with corruption, and there were somewhere in the region of 160 'illegal' filling stations between Bayji and Baghdad, with much of the fruits of this 'black economy' helping to fuel the insurgency. The AOR also held the disputed oil town of Kirkuk, claimed by the Kurds, who had been promised a referendum on the issue. Saddam had tried to forcibly alter the demographic balance by filling the city with Sunni Arabs. These had been driven out, and Kirkuk was now a flashpoint of contention between the Kurds and a population of Shia Arabs, some of whom were refugees from Saddam's clearance of the southern marshes. The AOR also included the area of Tal Afar with its large Turkmen Shia population, which made it of interest to the Turks, and Mount Sinjar, where there was a substantial concentration of Yazidis, who would endure appalling atrocities a few years later at the hands of IS. These locations were close to the Iraqi-Syrian border, whose border posts and sand 'berm' IS would so symbolically bulldoze in 2014, to represent the destruction of the 'illegitimate' partition of the *umma*. Peter Macfarlane, a bright and thoughtful US brigade commander who would go on to command Coalition forces in the fight against IS several years later, told of an event that had had a significant effect on his thinking and his understanding of the complexity of our situation. On the international border he had asked a local shepherd why, as an 'Iraqi', he kept moving his sheep into Syria and back. The shepherd patiently explained that his family had been living and farming in the area for generations, throughout Ottoman times, when no 'states' had existed within the caliphate.

'Why did you put this border through my sheep', asked the shepherd.

MND (Centre South) was based around Kut-al-Amara, downstream from Baghdad on the Tigris, and shared a border with Iran. Commanded by the Poles, it contained the site of the ancient Sassanian capital of Ctesiphon. It also included the National Police Training Centre at Numaniyah, the scene of a mass 'poisoning' during my time, although it may well just have been the food. The Centre became the focus of successive frustrating attempts to recast a sectarian and corrupt organization as an effective and 'impersonal' national institution.

MNF (West) covered the Euphrates Valley from the outskirts of Baghdad to the Syrian border, and the vast desert wastes of Anbar, with its almost exclusively Sunni population. It included the fractious urban centres of Ramadi, Fallujah, Hit and Haditha, and it had a complex tribal make-up that had proved as tricky to manage for the British, during the early Mandate days, and Saddam, as it did for the Coalition now. In 2006 this was, in many ways, the heart of the insurgency, fuelled by the complicity of the Syrian regime of Bashar al Assad and consistently stretching its violent tentacles into Baghdad itself, through a murderous campaign of car-bombings. Anbar was largely the preserve of the US Marines, one of whose commanders, General Jim Mattis, a hard, thoughtful and intellectual senior officer, would go on to be Defense Secretary for President Trump, before resigning in frustration after a year in the job. Somehow he had got a copy of my RCDS paper on *takfirism* and the Sunni 'civil war', and we had a long and useful discussion trying to identify fault-lines in the diverse Sunni elements of the insurgency. Anbar, with its complex tribal politics, was a tough 'paper round', and the Marines were having a demanding time of it. In an experience reminiscent of Vietnam, they would win every tactical battle, but campaign success was slipping out of their grasp. In September 2006, the southern province of Muthanna was being handed back to full Iraqi control, while in Anbar over 700 IED attacks on Coalition Forces took place in that month alone. A candid assessment of the situation in the west by Colonel Peter Devlin was leaked to the *Washington Post*. He basically said that, despite the gallantry of the Marines and elements of the ISF, security was so bad that no reconstruction or political development could take place in Anbar. It was a bleak report. However, it was also to be here that the security tide would begin to turn, as General Stan McChrystal's special forces' 'intelligence-strike' network wore down the AQI leadership and bombing facilitators, while at the same time the relentless brutality of the jihadists alienated the local population, who at last began to see salvation, and advantage, in supporting the Government and the Coalition.

If 'the legitimacy of the Government of Iraq' was the political focus of the Coalition, then supporting the efforts of MND (Baghdad) was the military 'main effort' in 2006. If security could not be provided in the capital city, and with it, a basic level of services, the credibility of the US, the Coalition Forces and the Iraqi Government would continue to be undermined. Since 2003 it had proved nigh-on impossible to improve the electricity supply. Where we had done so, the explosion of 'white goods' coming into the country, including vast numbers of air-conditioners, meant that demand always outstripped supply. The power cuts, the blackouts, the electricity shortages, all fed into the insurgency narrative, leading some to hark back nostalgically to the brutal certainties of Saddam's rule. AQI knew this, as did their Sunni Ba'athist allies, hence their multi-faceted, sophisticated and deadly campaign to wreck our ambitions, which included regular attacks on the power grid. General 'JD' Thurman, the 'Thurmanator', was the Commanding General of 4th Infantry Division, which was bearing the brunt of this assault. He was a large Texan, with a great heart and a great desire to help the Iraqi people. Helping to drive the growth of the ISF, in numbers and capability, he found it almost impossible to get the Iraqis to wear body armour and helmets at checkpoints or on patrol. This left them vulnerable to car-bombs, snipers and IEDs. JD could not work out if this was Muslim fatalism, a cultural dislike of military discipline and authority or merely a desire to be more comfortable in the hot weather. Returning from another visit to the Baghdad 'Security Perimeter', he said, in frustration, 'I honestly think that we are the only people actually trying to hold this country together.' He repatriated 235 US soldiers killed in action during his year-long tour, and Joe Fil, his successor with the 1st Cavalry Division, had a further 160 KIA. This was a relentless toll for officers and soldiers on their second or third year-long tour. The operational model was to 'Clear, Hold and Build', but the Coalition Force levels were never high enough to do that effectively. They could 'clear' and 'hold' areas, but rarely for long enough for a sustainable 'build' programme to be initiated, something badly needed to give confidence to the citizens of Baghdad.

MND (South-East) was the British AOR, controlling Basra and the important oilfields of the south, and including the Shatt al-Arab waterway and the vital riverine exits to the Gulf. Ninety per cent of Iraq's total revenues were dependent on the continued working of two 'gimcrack' offshore oil facilities operating in a confined stretch of the Gulf, sandwiched between Iranian and Kuwaiti waters. It was the scene of regular brushes with the Iranian Republican Guard Corps, including the notorious incident in 2007 involving Iranian abduction of British personnel from HMS *Cornwall*. A narrow channel also took ships up to the Iraqi port of Umm al Qasr. Geoff Hoon once compared this port to Southampton. A journalist hunted down some soldiers from Hampshire and asked them what they thought of the comparison.

'He's obviously never been to Umm al Qasr, or to Southampton', said one.

'It's got no booze, no women, and there is a good chance of getting shot at', said the other. He paused for a moment, 'I think it's rather more like Portsmouth.'

The British divisional HQ was located at Shaibah, the old RAF airfield into which my father had flown back in the 1960s, with the HQ of the operational brigade and many other elements of the British contribution in the Basra Palace. There were other Forward Operating Bases (FOBs) in the city itself. The security situation was becoming more fraught, and the Iranians, who shared a long border with MND (SE), the various Shia militias and the criminal gangs could sense that the British 'heart' was no longer in the operation. The UK had increasingly opted to run the operation in the south almost separately from the overall Coalition effort. We would make a similar mistake in Helmand in Afghanistan, until it was clear we needed US and Afghan reinforcement. Some of this approach was a function of the distance from Baghdad and the absence of a major sectarian fault-line in the south, but some of it was simply unhelpful Coalition 'behaviour'. The advantage of having a higher headquarters is that you can ask for more resources if you feel that you are being over-faced by the situation on the ground or that your efforts should be prioritized over those of other areas of the battlefield. The British commander in MND (SE) had, of course, like all subordinate Coalition commanders, two 'higher headquarters'. One was the national, political one in London, which was being battered by daily stories of British casualties, body repatriations through Wotton Bassett, equipment deficiencies, particularly centring on the 'Snatch' Land Rover, the reverberations of the 'dodgy dossier' and an approaching change of Labour Government leadership. This was also the depressing and scandalous period of Phil Shiner and Public Interest Lawyers, who made a discreditable industry out of bringing trumped-up allegations of 'abuse' and 'brutality' against thousands of British soldiers. Fuelled by public money, 'pay-offs', official complicity and government weakness, this dreadful episode lasted for nearly a decade before almost every one of the allegations was deemed to have no merit and Mr Shiner was 'struck off' as a practising lawyer.

The other higher headquarters was HQ MNC-I in Baghdad. The US civil and military leadership was wrestling with similar problems to their Coalition partners, but the US President and the military had so much more 'skin in the game' and could not contemplate failure. London, including the Chancellor, Gordon Brown, who would succeed Tony Blair as Prime Minister in 2007, had by this stage no desire for the British commander in the south to engage more closely with the American chain of command. That would draw the UK further into a campaign from which they now wished to withdraw, although still wishing to claim 'job done'. The trouble was that the UK commander, Major General Richard Shirreff, did not have the wherewithal to re-establish a sustainable British dominance in Basra and the south. He had put up an imaginative plan to tackle the worsening situation, Operation Salamanca, but because it was aimed at the Shia militia and their Iranian backers, the Iraqi Prime Minister would not give it his support.

In Baghdad, General Graeme Lamb and I found ourselves in an awkward position. We were 'believers' in the Coalition mission and wanted to 'lean into it' in order to find a way through the chaos and violence. We could see what disasters would unfold if the Coalition was seen to be 'defeated' and we simply walked away from Mesopotamia. We had both established excellent working relationships with our respective US commanders and their staffs, and our voices were heard in the US-dominated discussions. Unfortunately, UK political and public support for the mission was waning, and this had communicated itself to the MoD and to PJHQ. Consequently, we were both largely excluded from the debates in London and Northwood, and our relationship with MND (SE) was strained as a result. In the meantime, General Richard Dannatt had taken over from General Mike Jackson as CGS. In October 2006, in an interview with Sarah Sands of the *Daily Mail*, he was drawn into giving opinions about UK policy in Iraq, the causes of our intervention and whether our presence in Basra was now helping or hindering the security situation. The British and international media were full of the story all day, and my US colleagues demanded to know if we 'Brits' were 'on or off the bus'. My calls to London and Basra made things no clearer. Matters later came to a head when Richard Shirreff and General Nick Houghton, the Chief of Joint Operations (CJO) and a future CDS, came to Baghdad to give a brief on Operation Sinbad, which was a revision of Operation Salamanca and included the role that the local Iraqi 10ᵗʰ Division were expected to play. It was patently clear that UK and US intentions were now diverging. Peter Chiarelli was tired and irritable.

Before the briefing had even begun, he said, 'This is how I see it. You want to go to Afghanistan, and you are dressing up the situation in Basra to justify getting out. I see no evidence, whatsoever, that the 10ᵗʰ Iraqi Division will confront JAM.'

Operation Sinbad went ahead, but it could only ever be a 'band-aid' solution, and Chiarelli's doubts about the Iraqi forces at this stage were probably correct. The British would stay on in Basra until a full withdrawal in 2009, but our capacity to 'make the operational weather' was increasingly constrained by political risk-aversion and the shift of focus to Afghanistan, increasingly deemed, in London, to be 'the good war'. In due course, Nouri al Maliki would initiate Operation Charge of the Knights, as even he became frustrated by the pretensions of the Shia militias in Basra. This would also draw the US into the south. It was largely a fuller, more determined implementation of the Richard Shirreff's original Operation Salamanca, but political nervousness, and chain-of-command issues, meant that the British initially found themselves consigned to the role of observers. By the time we entered the fray in a convincing manner, the reputational damage had been done and the narrative of 'failure in Basra' had been established. Sometime after this, a deal was done with the JAM leadership, whereby Shia militia prisoners were released, while the British relinquished their presence in the city in return for attacks on British forces ceasing. It was a modern and rather disreputable form of Danegeld, but it also demonstrated a recognition of the stark realities of the situation in Southern Iraq.

Involved in all this Coalition Force activity were the nascent, but developing, ISF. There were many patriotic Iraqis among the population, of all sects, but CPA Order Number 2 had been a disaster in removing from the Coalition equation an Iraqi military structure and chain of command upon which to build new capabilities. The old analogy of 'building an aircraft while you are also trying to fly it' was raised on innumerable occasions. The sectarian situation meant that most Sunnis were totally alienated and either had no desire to enlist in what they perceived to be, and was, a Shia-dominated organization, or they actively joined the insurgency. The Shia officers and soldiers were ill-disposed to any Sunni recruits, and many of them had close links to JAM. As Arabs, many Iraqis resented Iranian interference, but others were bound to them by a shared Shia faith and justifiable paranoia about a revived Sunni power base. As we had seen in Northern Ireland and the Balkans, in uncertain times people looked to their own communities for security, not to the state.

Many military units and checkpoints blatantly flew the Husainiyah flags that celebrated the 'martyrdom' of Ali and his sons. It was a failure of ISF leadership that these flags were not removed. Given the Muslim prohibition on depicting the human form, I was intrigued by this manifestation of visual art, which was anathema to most Sunnis, let alone the jihadists of AQI. It appeared that, in the twelfth century, the Shia villagers of South Lebanon had been strongly influenced by the votive banners of Christ and the Virgin Mary carried by the Crusaders, and this had been transmitted, through Shia communities, all the way to Iran. These flagrant displays of sectarianism in the army had the capacity, indeed were often designed, to raise communal tension. The police were often in an even worse state. Recruited locally, they could not be trusted or expected to behave as officials of an 'impersonal institution'. The Kurds and the *peshmerga* stayed close to home, although there were many attempts to get them to come south to reinforce security in Baghdad. Despite this, progress was being made, much of it based on good training, some operational experience and success, and Coalition support. This support included the Coalition's many Military Training Teams, whose presence was vital in order to give the Iraqis confidence, increase their competence and 'keep them honest'. The key was to 'train, assist and accompany'. The third element was crucial to inspire people in a 'shame-based' culture, but it was also self-evidently central to our plans to hand off responsibility. The moral and confidence-boosting power of saying, 'Come on' rather than 'Off you go' cannot be overestimated. It was a model the British would drop when returning to Iraq in 2014 as part of a new coalition to defeat IS. By then the political and public risk- and casualty-aversion occasioned by our experiences in Iraq and Afghanistan meant that our officers and soldiers were constrained from going beyond the wire and were unable to go into combat alongside the local troops they had trained. It caused bewilderment among our military protégés and huge embarrassment and frustration among our own officers and soldiers. Our reputation suffered for it.

I was also tasked with developing the Headquarters of the Iraqi Ground Forces Command (IGFC). This had been built within Camp Victory, but was on the landside of the causeway, facing the Al Faw Palace across the lake. The commander was General Ali, a Shia, his deputy was General Reeadh, a Sunni, and his Chief of Staff was General Adnan. They had all served in Saddam's army and fought against the Iranians in the 1980s and the Coalition Forces in 1991 and 2003. Through them I met many other Iraqi commanders, who one could quickly classify as 'the good, the bad and the ugly'. General Ali would be commanding in Northern Iraq when IS took Mosul in 2014, by which time the corruption and sectarianism of Nouri al Maliki had gutted the ISF. He would make a hasty and inglorious departure from the battlefield, hastening the collapse of the ISF, whose Shia soldiers were certainly not going to stand and fight the Sunni jihadists if their own officers were leading the retreat. Reeadh would lead a gallant, well-publicized action in Baghdad in 2007, although by staff college standards he was probably a little far forward for a senior commander; while Adnan took several days off, at one stage, in order to 'recover' his daughter from a kidnapping incident. He was fortunate to get her back. I often ate with them, and they would occasionally come to Glubb Pasha House for dinner. On the first occasion I laid on food from the Coalition Forces dining facility, the DFAC, and proudly produced my 'hubble-bubble' pipe. Very culturally attuned. Disdaining Western food, my Iraqi guests arrived bearing the famous *masgouf* fish from the Tigris, and all helped themselves to my cigars.

At one stage, General Abdul Aziz, commanding the 6th Division in Baghdad, said, 'We have a saying in Iraq, Simon. When two fish fight in the Tigris, the British are behind it.'

'Oh that we were still that clever', I lamented. 'But we still hold the position of the "little Satan" in Iran, although I fear that may also be a bit of an historical hangover.'

One evening, the ammunition dump at Forward Operating Base Falcon received a lucky hit from one militia or another and blew up in a quite spectacular manner. On a subsequent night, they managed to drop a rocket into the Camp Victory lake and another into our vehicle-tyre depot. A few days earlier, they might have hit the river folk from Nasariyah, who had come up from the south to clear the aquatic weeds. On a third occasion, we thought that the Iraqi equivalent of the Tet Offensive had begun. It turned out to be a rare display of Iraqi unity and ecumenicalism, when the national football side beat Qatar and, irrespective of sect or militia, everyone came out into the streets to fire their weapon into the air. History does not relate how many of Baghdad's citizens were killed by spent falling rounds. Several times I went on patrol in the capital, and in Kirkuk, Fallujah and Baquba. It was good to be seen on the ground, although it put a burden on the local troops, and we were keen not to give a propaganda victory to the many factions who would have liked to kill a British general. On one occasion I ended up praying in a 'pre-match' group-huddle with a US Army patrol, seeking God's protection for ourselves and the strength and wherewithal to blast any opposition we met to kingdom come. Amen to that. The weather got colder as the year advanced, proving that the winter of 1990–1 had not been an aberration, and the odd Christmas tree began to appear in the Headquarters and in FOBs across Iraq. It was my second Noel on operations in biblical lands, and I spent the festive season with Graeme Lamb at a Special Forces base, watching a 'live-feed' from a drone as 'Raad the bomb-maker', a notorious manufacturer of IEDs, had his own festive plans monumentally disrupted.

One day, I went to visit the Officer Training Academy in Rustamyah, on the outskirts of Baghdad. The British had responsibility for this institution, and you could see the influence of Sandhurst immediately. The Iraqis had a high regard for the American military, but like many in the Arab world they felt a greater affinity to the British, probably because the origins of their country and their army were more closely linked to our own history. They also found the pragmatic approach of the British easier to work with than the more regimented style of the US. Iraq was already sending some of its best cadets to Sandhurst, and these had returned to be the new platoon instructors, although they might have been better employed leading troops in the field. The quality and enthusiasm of the cadets was certainly encouraging.

Sometime later, I flew to Kisik, near Tal Afar, to assess the readiness of a formation to deploy to the capital. The occasion was crowned by the soldiers breaking into a song-and-dance routine, the refrain of which seemed to be 'We're all going to Baghdad! We are going to kill the terrorists!' I felt suitably buoyed up by this display of martial enthusiasm but, needless to say, when the formation eventually did get to Baghdad many of the soldiers had absconded, and they had little or no serviceable equipment left. General Marty Dempsey, who was the head of MNSTC-I and a very competent singer of Irish ballads, confessed that he had handed out equipment to the

ISF worth about $12 billion, but he was not sure he could account for much of it and had very few receipts to prove his largesse. As a consequence, he thought that he might be pursued to his grave by the US government auditors. In fact, he became the US Army Chief of Staff. Given the parlous security situation, and the rate of attrition in the ISF, we were having to deploy Iraqi soldiers into the fight almost as soon as they were recruited and had been given rudimentary infantry training. Consequently, some key aspects of capability, like personnel management, logistic support and equipment husbandry, were miles behind their basic infantry skills, and it showed. The Coalition would need to provide assistance in these areas for some years to come. We were already encountering the same problems in Afghanistan with the Afghan National Security Forces (ANSF).

The 'deputy' role in a coalition can be a difficult one, and much depends on the relationship with the commander. Where it is good, the rest of the staff bring you naturally into the 'circle of knowledge' and the decision-making process. Where it is bad, people go through the motions, but you can quickly find yourself marginalized. Like most of the British deputies, I was fortunate to have had excellent relationships with the US commanders, which enabled me to engage constructively in their thinking and planning. At one stage we were getting badly hit by Explosively Formed Projectiles (EFPs). These weapons were industrially prepared, and they were considerably more lethal against armoured vehicles than the IEDs being put together in Iraqi garages and backstreets. We knew many of them were coming from Iran, facilitated by Qassim Suleimani and the Qods Force. Feelings were naturally running high about Iranian complicity and the one-sided nature of Nouri al Maliki's targeting decisions, which blatantly favoured the Shia militia. Stan McChrystal even felt that his Special Forces teams were, in reality, acting as 'shock-troops' for JAM, as they were almost exclusively targeting Sunni insurgents. The staff had put up a 'mission' for the commanding general's consideration. It was 'To destroy Iranian influence in Iraq'. I looked at it, Peter Chiarelli looked at me, the briefing officers looked at us both.

'Well', I said, tentatively. 'I fully understand the frustrations of the staff, and these EFPs are undoubtedly coming from Iran. However, "destroy" has a particularly kinetic military connotation, and I do not think that that is a viable military task as set out in the Mission Statement. This is a majority Shia country', I continued, 'whose leadership, from top to bottom, has close relationships, connections and "blood debts" to the Iranians. Iranian influence runs through the religion, politics, history, architecture, even the cuisine of the Iraqis, while hundreds of thousands of Iranians make the annual pilgrimage to Najaf and Karbala, and enormous amounts of legitimate trade flow across the border, among it, admittedly, much contraband. I think we need to give more nuanced guidance and direction to our commanders and soldiers regarding countering Iran.'

I was most certainly not trying to be clever, but I did worry about the consequences of troops on the ground, already under immense pressure, applying a literal interpretation of this mission. The mission statement was amended to read, 'To contribute to the defeat of malign Iranian influence in Iraq'.

At another memorable meeting, Peter Chiarelli received an operational update at which the Intelligence Officer gave an assessment that there were 'about 15,000 insurgents active in Iraq'. The Commander held up his hand.

'When I was here in 2004', he said tersely, 'the intelligence assessment was "about 15,000 insurgents". We have killed, or captured, well over 15,000 insurgents since then, but the assessment is still "15,000 insurgents". Whatever else it is we are doing, we appear to be growing insurgents.'

It was an insightful and gloomy observation, but it captured the complexity of counter-insurgency, where tactical military successes not linked to parallel political advances can often exacerbate the threat you are combating. Many of the captured 'insurgents', inevitably mostly Sunni, were held in Camp Bucca in the south, a much more stringently policed and administered facility than Abu Ghraib had been. Conscious of the multiple motivations underlying the insurgency, and the circumstances of our invasion and occupation, I found my visit to the camp rather unsettling, and I tried to avoid staring at the prisoners behind the wire and the bars in their orange 'jump suits'. The whole issue of capture, trial and detention would become a major political and judicial issue in all Coalition countries, and the US detention facility at Guantanamo Bay in Cuba would become a lightning-rod for a range of agendas and for groups who objected to the foreign policy objectives of the US and her allies. Although I did not know it at the time, among the detainees in Camp Bucca was Ibrahim Awad al Samarri. After a later amnesty that saw many detainees released, he would go on to take the name Abu Bakr al Baghdadi and in 2014 would declare the new caliphate from the *minbar* in Mosul's Grand Mosque.

However, through the gloom, some elements of the campaign began to give cause for hope. Americans have a commendable capacity for self-reflection, self-knowledge and self-criticism. In late 2006 President Bush reluctantly admitted the current strategy was not succeeding, and the US military also acknowledged mistakes in their application of military power in this highly complex political and social environment. The leadership of the US military, among them General David Petraeus, but also many of the junior commanders, demanded, and got, a complete overhaul of the doctrine for dealing with an counter-insurgency problem on the scale of that facing the Coalition in 2006 and 2007.

Poring over historical examples, accepting a brutally honest assessment of the situation and taking into account his own experiences as a divisional commander in northern Iraq, Petraeus and a broad-based multi-disciplinary team ruthlessly examined the US experiences over three years: from the successes in Tal Afar and Ramadi to the scandals of the Haditha 'massacre' and the Abu Ghraib abuses, to the current situation of Special Forces operations and the transition of security to the ISF. In re-assessing operational design, training and equipment, Petraeus's team set out a doctrine, strategy and tactics that would give the US administration the confidence to remain politically committed to seeing the operation in Iraq through to a more positive outcome than had appeared possible in 2006. It was at this time that Lawrence of Arabia's dictum gained common currency again: 'Do not try to do too much with your own hands. Better the Arabs do it tolerably, than you do it perfectly. It is their war, and you are here to help them, not to win it for them.' This would be fine and dandy at the tactical level, but the problem here, as it had been for Lawrence, was that many parties in Iraq, the Sunnis and AQI, the Shia and Iran, had a very different idea from the Coalition of what 'winning' looked like. It was against this background that the recommendations of the Baker-Hamilton Report, to transition to ISF control as soon as possible and get out, were superseded by President Bush's brave decision to 'surge' a further five brigade-level combat teams into Iraq. This was a Herculean effort that required some units and formations to extend to fifteen-month tours, and one brigade to be recalled from its recent return to the US.

The UK was a bystander in terms of the debate over the 'surge', both because the US did not seek to engage her in the debate, and because the UK was, by this time, largely set on a path of transition out of an increasingly unpopular conflict, while shifting attention to the neglected and under-resourced campaign in Afghanistan. However, I believe that the UK's influence through this period continued to be important in four areas. The first was the continuing contribution of British Special Forces to the fight against AQI. The second was achieving recognition that, if the

Shia majority could be protected against Sunni and jihadi violence, their militias might be persuaded into an uneasy, but real, state of truce with Coalition Forces. This would leave the Coalition and the ISF to concentrate on Al Qa'eda, who represented the common enemy. Graeme Lamb had argued strongly and effectively for physical barrier measures, akin to those we had used in Northern Ireland, in order to reduce the opportunities for violence against civilians in Baghdad. The Baghdad Security Belt was enhanced, and extensive barriers and checkpoints were erected within the city, which made the job of the suicide and car bombers more difficult, deterred the militia death squads and acted as a check on ethnic and confessional cleansing. This was accompanied by a clear-out of many of the senior leadership of the National Police, thereby removing much of their propensity for sectarian activity. It was to be another eight or nine years before these hastily deployed but effective physical barriers began to be dismantled.

The third key strand was to recognize and acknowledge that Sunni resistance and violence were not monolithic, and that there were real and developing fault-lines between many Iraqi Sunnis and the AQI jihadists and foreign fighters. Under Al Zarqawi the latter had embarked on a spree of violence that drew little distinction between the Coalition Forces, Shias and Sunni 'compromisers', and was indiscriminately killing women and children. In Ramadi, the US had identified this trend and, by protecting the local population, created the conditions for a local rejection of the jihadists that, in time, grew into the 'Sunni Awakening' and the Sunni 'Sons of Iraq'. More importantly, the US high command, and the Shia-dominated government, came to the belief that, despite their distaste, opportunities did exist to engage with elements of the Iraqi Sunni insurgency, particularly among the tribes of Anbar, in order to exploit their growing disaffection with the bloodthirsty and violent Zarqawists. Zarqawi himself had been killed in a strike on his desert hideout in June 2006, but a key turning point came when AQI executed several tribal members and would not then let their families bury the bodies. Sheikh Sattar, a leading tribal figure, who would later be assassinated for his troubles, became a key interlocutor with Graeme Lamb in bringing many of the Anbar tribes 'in from the cold'.

Fourthly, my own contribution was to advocate that, 'surge' or not, a better use of the existing US force levels would be to step back from the daily fire-fights, and 'hug' the ISF ever closer, by increasing the size of the Military Training Teams, by setting up more joint operational bases with the ISF, despite the risks, and by embedding and partnering with the Iraqis more fully at every level. Given the context, and the inevitability of eventual transition, I argued that the ISF would grow more quickly in confidence and competence by closer proximity to the US troops, that their capabilities would develop faster, and that we could more effectively instil a sense of national responsibility, while limiting their capacity or inclination to act in a sectarian manner.

In June 2004, Saddam Hussein had been legally handed over to the Iraqi authorities, although he continued to be held by the US in Camp Cropper. A few weeks later, he was charged with a range of crimes committed over many years. The process went on for a long time, but on 5 November 2006 we learnt that he had now formally been found guilty of 'crimes against humanity' and had been sentenced to death by hanging. The sentence and the verdict had both been appealed, but both appeals were rejected. It was still the month of the *hajj*, but Nouri al Maliki seemed set on carrying out the execution straight away. There was opposition across the Sunni Arab world, demonstrating the continued ambivalence towards Saddam. Twice we prepared to hand him over to the Iraqis, although concerned about a backlash in the Sunni communities, and twice we were stood down. Christmas had come and gone, and we were now about to enter *Eid al Adha*, the great Muslim festival following the end of the *hajj*. We assumed, wrongly, that nothing would now happen until the holiday period was over. On 30 December, as I was in the IGFC headquarters talking with a group of Iraqi officers, Ray Odierno's military assistant rang and asked for me to return across the causeway to MNC-I headquarters. Nouri al Maliki wanted Saddam executed that night and would brook no further delay. The orders were given to the US detention centre to hand the former Iraqi President over, and we alerted the other Coalition contingents as to what was happening. In very short order Saddam was taken from Camp Cropper to Camp Justice, an Iraqi base, and hanged. The initial report was of a dignified end, and the news was greeted with outpourings of celebration in the Shia areas of the country. Saddam's body was flown to Tikrit for burial the next day, in accordance with Muslim tradition, just as video footage of the execution was leaked, appearing to show Saddam being abused and insulted as he climbed the gallows and waited for the drop. Whatever we felt about the man and his execution, we were disappointed that the Iraqi government had not policed the process more effectively, given the great sensitivities in so many quarters.

About halfway through my tour, General Richard Dannatt visited Iraq and, having been to Basra, came to Baghdad to see Generals Casey and

Chiarelli and the British personnel. His whole demeanour reflected the difficult political situation in London, which was affecting all aspects of our military operations at that stage. He told me that the plan, at the end of my tour, was for me 'to be run' for the appointment of Assistant Chief of Defence Staff (Resources and Plans), a powerful, influential and friendless job, dealing with money and 'trampling on people's dreams'. Some weeks later, that plan had changed, and I was instead to be Assistant Chief of the General Staff (ACGS), working directly for Richard Dannatt. It may still have been an MoD posting, but I was now to be the 'champion' of Army ambition, an altogether more attractive proposition.

One of the last, and most vivid, memories of my time in Iraq was attending the Provincial Iraqi Control ceremony in the Shia holy city of Najaf, where security responsibility would be handed over from the Coalition to the ISF. Tom Robinson and I flew down and then transferred to an armoured vehicle to go to the local football stadium. Having passed through extensive security, we found that the ground was full and there was a distinctly holiday atmosphere. Mowafiq Rubaie, the canny political adviser to Nouri al Maliki, was taking the salute at the parade. After his suitably stirring words, the parade began, and a mixture of police cars, 4x4s, fire-engines and military trucks drove past, to huge enthusiasm from the crowd. Then the police themselves marched past, and some units of the ISF, carrying a veritable forest of regimental flags and banners. Bringing up the rear, as a *pièce de resistance*, were some Iraqi Special Forces, who had adopted the impressive high-stepping and high-kicking march that you rarely see at the Queen's Birthday Parade. As they approached the dais they shouted, stopped, and turned to face us. Since almost everyone carried a weapon, wherever we went, Tom and I had developed a degree of Islamic fatalism ourselves. On a cry from the commander, every soldier pulled a frog out of his pocket, alive as far as I could see, bit its head off, and then ate the remainder. The crowd took a moment to absorb this sight, at which point the commander, conscious of a captive audience, produced a rabbit, and a knife the size of Belgium. He decapitated the rabbit and proceeded to gnaw on it, to huge public acclaim. History does not record his role in the later defence of Mosul. I made a mental note to speak to GOC London District about some possible adjustments to State Ceremonial. One sad codicil to this day was that the charming and friendly US Staff Sergeant who had ferried us to and from the helicopter was killed in an IED strike on his way back to Baghdad.

At last it came time to depart from Iraq. Both Tom Robinson and the estimable Corporal Welch, the only British NCO I knew who could commit 'crimes against humanity' with an English fry-up, were going to stay for a further few weeks to support my successor, Major General Gerry Berragan. I made a circuit of farewell calls on my American and Iraqi friends and colleagues and, despite or probably because of their sincere good wishes, I felt rather like a 'war-dodger' to be leaving while this vast and complex conflict still hung in the balance. It had been a huge privilege to have served in Iraq at such a pivotal moment in history, and in due course that sense of privilege was further reinforced when I received the US Legion of Merit. However, as I sat in the C17 aircraft flying from Baghdad down the coast to Bahrain, from where I would return to UK, and as I reflected on the grand ambitions and plans of 2003, I felt angry, disappointed and fearful. Angry at the rationale and intelligence that had been used to convince Western publics of the need for an invasion; at the cavalier manner of the post-conflict planning; at the human cost for the Iraqis; at the naivety of the policy-makers; and at the squandering of opportunities that, if taken, might have resulted in a brighter future for Iraq and for the region. Disappointed at the squandering of Coalition lives, reputation and credibility. And fearful about what I thought might yet happen across the region. While we were trying to rescue something from the firestorm that we had whipped up in Mesopotamia, the Russians, the Chinese, the Iranians and the *takfiri* jihadists all drew their own conclusions, and watched and waited. Their moment would not be long in coming.

Chapter 24

Change of Presidents

If you spend enough time in the MoD, there is little under the sun that comes as a real surprise. Faces change, ministers come and go, civil servants go on forever, closed offices and PAs are swapped for 'open plan' cubicles and DIY staff-work, the sandwich selection in the cafeteria is overhauled. However, most of the issues that confront you on a daily basis are what I would describe as 'old friends with a funny moustache or a false nose on'. In other words, they are the perennial problems associated with high national ambition, which we all applauded, and inadequate resourcing, which remained a constant worry.

I was ACGS from early 2007 until spring 2009, and it was a suitably demanding time to be back in the MoD, although, once more, professionally satisfying. At one stage it even included a visit to Buckingham Palace to update members of the Royal Family about the plans for Prince Harry's 'secret' deployment to Afghanistan, the subject of a sensitive arrangement between the Army, the MoD, the Palace and the more responsible members of the Press. As CGS, Richard Dannatt was very easy to work for. He gave direction, and I, supported by a talented group of peers and subordinates and an effective 'outer-office', delivered on it. He was the Army 'Chief' in a particularly fractious political environment. Tony Blair's political authority had been fatally compromised by the invasion of Iraq, and Gordon Brown, as Chancellor, had shown consistently little interest in Defence or empathy with the Armed Forces. His only intervention of note was as an advocate for the Royal Navy's new aircraft carriers, but this had little to do with military capability and more to do with votes in his constituency, where ship-building was a key industry. Consequently, there was endless skirmishing with the Treasury to justify: the troop levels in Iraq and Afghanistan; new equipment capabilities demanded by the changing threats, not least IEDs; increased and improved training facilities; and a basket of personnel issues ranging from appropriate medical and care provision for the wounded and their families, to 'operational pay and allowances'. I knew this environment well from my previous incarnations in the MoD. It was never a pretty sight at the best of times, but with soldiers being killed and wounded on a depressingly regular basis, it was particularly concerning in 2007.

Inevitably, I continued to take a very close interest in events in Iraq. Although British political and public attention was increasingly focused on Afghanistan, we continued to maintain a substantive force level in Basra, and personnel remained embedded across the Coalition until 2009. In the wake of Coalition Force successes, growing ISF competence and the commitment by President Bush to the 'surge', AQI had launched a ferocious counter-offensive in the middle of 2007, and casualties had continued to rise, testing the nerves of politicians and the military alike and putting further stress on overall Coalition cohesion. However, the potent combination of high-tech intelligence gathering and fusion, well-targeted Special Forces' operations, growing co-operation with the local Sunni tribes and increasingly confident partnered operations with the ISF led to a rapid decimation of the AQI leadership and their networks throughout 2007. With this came an important, albeit reluctant, Iraqi Government agreement to the bankrolling of the 'Sons of Iraq', who had previously been considered by the Shia as the 'enemy'. This combination increased the credibility of the Government, as it did that of the ISF, and with it came greater support among the people, in all parts of Iraqi society, for the legitimate power bases. We all held our breath. And then, suddenly, in autumn 2007, the levels of AQI violence plummeted, and they stayed down.

Blunting the effectiveness of the Sunni insurgency, particularly in Baghdad itself, allowed an uneasy but significant truce to develop with the Shia militias and permitted a greater degree of influence to be exerted over the Maliki government. Although the original high-level strategic objectives of the US-led invasion of Iraq had already been fatally compromised, the new 'strategy' had given the tactical actions of the Coalition the context, coherence, relevance and focus that had previously been lacking. This combination led, at least, to 'operational-level' success that took the pressure off our own troops in Basra, where we pulled down the Union flag in 2009, and it permitted an orderly US draw-down of troops between 2009 and 2011.Unfortunately, much of the American blood and treasure expended in this long and contentious campaign, and with them the prospects for Iraqi peace and stability, was to be squandered. When Barrack Obama became President in 2008, he was determined to withdraw America from what he perceived to be a series of disastrous overseas military entanglements that had diminished US influence and reputation in the world. It was a domestically popular but strategically naïve approach, with long-term negative consequences for American credibility, globally. Obama did not fight hard to sustain a US presence in Iraq after security responsibility had been handed over to the ISF. Undoubtedly, it would have been difficult to achieve a satisfactory Status of Forces Agreement, one that included the legal exemptions for US troops demanded by the Americans, but there was a great deal of tacit support among Iraqis for a residual US presence, even if they could not always say so publicly. Though many of our political and military actions had been poorly thought through and executed, the Coalition had overthrown Saddam, and in doing so had lifted the oppression of the Shia and given a greater sense of security to the Kurds. Notwithstanding this, important Shia politicians, not least the Iraqi Prime Minister, were heavily influenced by the Iranians to make life as difficult as possible for the US and its Coalition partners, and Obama chose to 'take no for an answer' and to commit to withdrawing all US troops in 2011. The consequences were predictable: sectarian politics re-surfaced, the Kurds hunkered down again and the Sunni Arabs nursed a new sense of grievance and fear regarding the Shia and the Iranians. Meanwhile, Nouri al Maliki's combination of paranoia and dependence on Iran led to his reneging on promises made to the Sunni tribal foot soldiers of the 'Sons of Anbar', and he initiated a gradual but critical hollowing-out of ISF competence, credibility and neutrality as a national institution. Their subsequent rout by IS in 2014 was reminiscent of the collapse of the South Vietnamese forces in 1975. That, too, had had its origins in the withdrawal of US commitment and support by an American President, for similar reasons.

Meanwhile, Afghanistan had started to loom larger in the consciousness of British policy-makers, the military and the public. While Hamid Karzai had been elected President of the Islamic Republic of Afghanistan in 2004, the Taliban had swiftly proclaimed they 'were back'. Around the time I was going to serve in Baghdad, ISAF was rolling out a plan to expand its control across the country and, with it, Afghan government presence, including in the contentious south with its majority Pashtun population. The political model adopted for Afghanistan was one of centralized control from Kabul, which ran counter to much historical Afghan experience, and to the long-held Pashtun aversion to political interference from the capital. The new ISAF commander was a British officer, General David Richards, and he was drawn, almost immediately, into a major confrontation with the Taliban to the west of Kandahar. At around the same time, the British took command of the complex province of Helmand, and our troop levels were raised to nearly 8,000. The objectives of the International Community began to become confused, and sometimes conflicting. We were simultaneously trying to conduct counter-terrorism, counter-insurgency, poppy-eradication, nation-building and institutional development, not least that of the ANSF. All these were worthy objectives in their own right but as a combined programme represented a classic case of the victory of hope over expectation. The 'nation-building' agenda, with its emphasis on human rights and female emancipation was important, and indeed harked back to a kinder, gentler time in Afghan political life. However, it also offended many social conservatives in Afghanistan and neighbouring countries, and fed the Taliban narrative that Westerners were occupying the country in order to destroy Afghan culture and undermine the Islamic faith. Once again, we failed to fully comprehend the challenge that our worthy and, to us, self-evidently positive objectives presented to a patriarchal, pious and conservative society. This approach exacerbated the perennial friction between the 'modernizers', often seen and portrayed as 'traitors', and the 'traditionalists', and between the genders and the generations.

In the 'battle of the narratives' the Taliban were proving to be very effective adversaries and highly skilled users of social media, as their insurgent counterparts in Iraq had been. Once again, Afghanistan became a focus for *takfiri* volunteers from across the Muslim world. While the Taliban itself remained a largely Afghan, Sunni, Pashtun movement, they acted as an effective platform for large numbers of fanatical and violent Islamist extremists, as they had done for AQ and a previous generation of foreign fighters, aided and abetted by the continued ambivalence of elements of the Pakistani authorities. Actions along the Durand Line and the start of the US 'drone' campaign against terrorist targets in the Pakistani border areas put great strain on the relationship between Pakistan and the ISAF nations. Since Afghanistan was landlocked, much of the equipment and supplies had to come through or over Pakistan, at considerable cost. Now, late 2008, in the face of public outrage, Pakistan closed those supply routes, and NATO had to negotiate a 'Northern Distribution Network' through Russia and the Central Asian republics. Helped by the visit of President Obama to Moscow in 2009, this was to prove a high-water mark of Russian-Western cooperation, before a combination of international events, including those in the Middle East, conspired to put the relationship back in the 'icebox'. As the 'surge' in Iraq gained traction and then began to wind down, President Obama did agree, reluctantly, to a force uplift in Afghanistan. This included a major troop insertion of US Marines into Helmand, where the British were having a mixed time of it in places like Sangin, Lashkar Ghar and Musa Qala, names increasingly well-known to the British public. US and Coalition policy-makers were being confronted with a similar conundrum to that faced in Vietnam and Iraq. Do you continue to prop up a corrupt and ineffectual government, who cannot command popular loyalty, by committing further forces to a fight that increases local dependency, while losing your domestic support? Or do you cut your losses, put the expenditure of blood and treasure down to experience, accept the reputational damage and anticipate the collapse of your former clients? Was there a credible and sustainable position 'twixt these extremes? We had to wait a while for the answer.

Our operational 'tempo' raised the perennial tension between an army fighting *the* war, Afghanistan, and the same army equipping, preparing and training for *a* war, some future conflict against a 'peer enemy', formerly the Soviet Union. Such a dilemma was made more acute by the reduced size of the Army, the scale of the commitment to Afghanistan, the shortage of critical enablers such as helicopters, the lack of mine-resistant ambush-protected vehicles (MRAPs), the short time between the successive deployments of formations, units and individuals, and the mounting casualty lists. As we concentrated on the current complex expeditionary operations, there grew a belief that state-on-state warfare was now a thing of the past, and that 'hybrid' war between asymmetrical opponents was, and would remain, the enduring military challenge. This was soon to prove a fallacy. Many of the tactics, techniques, procedures and capabilities developed and employed in Iraq and Afghanistan did indeed have enduring relevance, but 'Great Power' rivalry was beginning to raise its ugly head again, with the increasingly aggressive resurgence of Russia, and particularly with the remarkable and rapid growth of Chinese power. Huntington was trumping Fukuyama. However, the political calculation of the 1990s that had given us 'Options for Change' and the 'peace dividend' following the fall of the Berlin Wall, had not gone away. In debt, running a burgeoning deficit, particularly given the 'financial crisis' of 2008 and the range of entitlements and expectations assumed by the Welfare State and the National Health Service, and facing an imminent General Election, a reluctant Gordon Brown had little appetite for increasing Defence spending, to match either the demands of Afghanistan or the implications of a changing geopolitical environment. We were not alone. Britain did at least, just about, continue to meet the declared NATO spending target of 2 per cent of GDP, albeit with some creative accounting, but most NATO allies were falling well short of that. Under President Obama, but especially under President Trump, this perceived 'free-riding', on the back of US tax-payers, would become an increasingly fractious issue.

British 'outer office' staff have always 'listened in' on the telephone calls of their bosses, until told to 'drop off'. It is an effective way of doing business, and it helps the staff to know what to expect, to keep them informed of the way debates and issues are going and to allow them to take some pre-emptive actions. The Americans did not embrace the same protocols, which ensured their personal staff officers were singularly unhelpful in being able to give you a useful steer on any particular topic under discussion. I had been an MA myself, so I was quite used to the idea of four people being 'in on the conversation'. One day we had a call from Evelyn Webb-Carter, whom I knew well from the MoD and from our great equestrian adventures in the Hindu Kush. Evelyn and I occasionally went to smoke an Arabian 'hubble-bubble' pipe in the evening, and after we had completed our formal business we were making some arrangements to catch up in the following week.

'We can have a cocktail at the Garrick Club, and then dinner at Boodles', I said.

'Excellent', he replied. 'Then we might go up the Edgware Road for a hookah.'

He pronounced the last word as 'hooker', and thankfully I suddenly recalled that the MA was still on the line.

'Hooookaaah', I gently corrected him. 'The old water-pipe. See you then.'

I walked out of the office, to be confronted by a grinning staff.

'Let us be very clear what the former GOC London District, General Sir Evelyn Webb-Carter was proposing', I said, fixing them with a steely look.

In May 2009 I was promoted to Lieutenant General, and I took over the appointment of Deputy Chief of Defence Staff (Commitments) (DCDS(C)), the Centre Staff appointment responsible for aligning MoD operational policy with government direction and with the allocated resources. I worked directly to Air Chief Marshal Sir Jock Stirrup, the CDS, another easy and enjoyable relationship. I was the MoD interface with the Cabinet Office, the Foreign Office and the 'Agencies', MI5, MI6 and GCHQ, for operational issues. In addition, I had to keep close links with the Secretary of State for Defence, Ministers, Service Chiefs, the Chief of Joint Operations in Northwood, the Director of Special Forces, who also worked directly to CDS, and the senior commanders on our various operational commitments. The appointment also required spending a good deal of time managing relationships with our allies, not least in Washington where, fortunately, many old friends from Kosovo and Baghdad now held senior positions. It was to be a demanding, fascinating and frustrating appointment, with relentless media and legal attention on our operations, which translated itself into further political anxiety, but I had excellent military and civilian staff and I was very ably supported by two first-class Assistant Chiefs: Andy Pulford, who would go on to be head of the Royal Air Force, and David Capewell, a no-nonsense Royal Marine from Yorkshire who would soon after take up the three-star appointment of CJO.

Early in my tenure, we conducted a strategic stock-take of the state of play across our many operational deployments and an assessment of where the next flashpoints might be. Needless to say, although we were once again being forced to keep an eye on Russia, the majority of existing or potential crises lay across the wider Middle East. In Iraq we had largely handed over security responsibility in Basra to the ISF, although we still retained a small training mission there, and a presence in the Coalition chain of command. That last small, residual military presence would be fully withdrawn, alongside the Americans, in 2011. In Afghanistan, 2009 was seen as a pivotal year. President Hamid Karzai was standing for a second term, security needed to be provided for the elections, and ISAF was having to confront a major increase in Taliban activity, not least in Helmand. Gordon Brown reluctantly agreed to an uplift in force levels to 9,500, but he wanted this reduced again immediately after the Afghan election. In 2006, as the UK deployed into Helmand, the then Defence Secretary, John Reid, had unhappily been quoted as saying that 'We would be happy to leave after three years without firing one shot.' We knew what he meant, but by 2009 we had fired in the region of 12 million shots and had had 196 servicemen and women killed in action, to add to the 179 fatal casualties in Iraq. I knew many of those engaged in these operations, including many young officers who were the sons of friends of mine in the Army. Some of them were killed and some badly wounded, the lot of brave junior commanders across the generations. However, public opinion, staunchly supportive of the military itself, was increasingly questioning the political objectives of our interventions in these complex parts of the world.

At around the same time that we were wrestling with Afghanistan, Washington and Whitehall were becoming increasingly focused on the issue of Iranian nuclear ambition. Iran had been a major, if unintentional and unplanned, beneficiary of the invasion and occupation of Iraq, capitalizing on the splits in the Sunni Arab world and welcoming the installation of a Shia-dominated government in Baghdad. Their regional influence was to grow further when the Arab Spring and subsequent civil war in Syria gave them more opportunities to expand their role. This was not how things should have unfolded, but it should have been clear at an early stage that toppling the Sunni Arab-dominated bulwark of Iraq might well have these consequences. The same conundrum would face the West when it came to confronting Islamic State: how to defeat a Sunni Arab threat without further empowering Iran through her Shia co-religionists across the region. This issue would become even more complex when Russia decisively intervened, alongside Iran, on behalf of Syria's Bashar al Assad. The circle was never properly squared.

At this time, although they denied any ambition to develop nuclear weapons, the Iranians were aggressively pursuing a nuclear programme and a ballistic missile programme in parallel. Many commentators considered that this combination could give them at least the capacity to generate a credible military nuclear capability, although expert opinion disagreed about how long it might take. The Iranians protested that they were only developing a civil nuclear capability, which they had every right to, that they were responsible signatories of the Nuclear Proliferation Treaty, despite the IAEA criticisms of 2003, and that nuclear weapons were prohibited by Islamic teaching. However, their behaviour since the Islamic Revolution of 1979, their bloodthirsty rhetoric, particularly towards America and Israel, and their serial duplicity and secrecy made policy-makers in Washington, Western Europe and especially Tel Aviv highly nervous and suspicious. In 2009, there was a general feeling that if the Iranians did not put a verifiable halt to their nuclear programme, there would exist only a narrow window of opportunity to take military action before we might be confronted with a nuclear-armed opponent in the Gulf. The debate was succinctly summed up as: 'Do we want an Iran with the bomb, or a bombed Iran?' Neither prospect was attractive. A nuclear-armed Iran would catalyse an atomic arms race across the region, with the Sunni states of Saudi Arabia, Egypt and Turkey potentially all pursuing a similar nuclear goal, adding a deadly new dimension to existing historical animosities. It had always been assumed that Saudi Arabia had already made a deal with the Pakistanis to provide them with nuclear warheads in the event of Iran fielding a nuclear capability. However, any pre-emptive strike against Iran would throw up another set of daunting consequences, including an unquantifiable Iranian reaction, a potential environmental catastrophe in the Gulf, severe disruption to energy supplies and widespread destruction. Qatar, with a population of nearly 3 million people, was estimated to have just three days of water supply if its desalination plants were destroyed or even disrupted. These potential consequences would be equally starkly evident during the series of confrontations and alarms in the Gulf in 2019 and 2020.

The Israeli Prime Minister, Benjamin 'Bibi' Netanyahu, was strident about the threat from Iran and what should be done, as he would continue to be nearly a decade later. Policy-makers assessed that an Israeli strike could inflict a major delay on the Iranian programme, although not terminate it, but that Israel might try and manoeuvre the US into joining in on a military option to ensure the job was completed. From these stark and worrying options sprang the lengthy and complex negotiations that would lead to the 2015 Joint Comprehensive Plan of Action (JCPOA), negotiated between the US, the European Union, China, Russia and Iran. Under this agreement, Iran would reverse its nuclear programme and submit itself to a rigorous verification regime, in return for a lifting of sanctions by the US and European powers. However, by the time this agreement came into effect, good in itself although with clear limitations and deficiencies regarding the Iranian ballistic missile programme, the situation in the wider region had changed dramatically. While Iran seemed to be adhering to the letter of the deal regarding its nuclear programme, the leadership in Tehran, and that of the IRGC, had taken full advantage of turmoil across the region to advance Iranian power and influence. In due course, a new, more hawkish administration in Washington under President Trump, supported by the Israelis and the more aggressively inclined of the Sunni Arab states, would seek to overthrow the JCPOA, challenging the assumptions on which it had been signed and causing significant divisions among the original signatories, not least between America and Europe.

Meanwhile, Iraq had stabilized and AQI had largely been defeated. The security gains had yet to be squandered by resurgent sectarianism, but the prevalence of Iranian influence was increasingly obvious. In Syria, the Alawite-dominated Assad regime looked relatively secure and showed some encouraging signs of liberalization. In Egypt, Hosni Mubarak, President for nearly thirty years since Sadat's assassination in 1981, was looking forward to establishing a dynasty through his son, Gamal, and elections were planned for 2010. Along with the military, he seemed to retain a firm grip on the country while both kept a close and watchful eye on the Muslim Brotherhood. In Ankara, President Erdogan continued to consolidate the power of his Truth and Justice Party, breaking with his former allies, the Gulenists, while continuing his campaign to weaken the role of the military in Turkish political life and thereby dilute the secular state established by Ataturk. His suspicion of the Kurds remained as pronounced as ever, despite an ongoing ceasefire, and his support for the Muslim Brotherhood was becoming ever more evident.

Further down the North African coast, Colonel Gaddafi was still enjoying the benefits of renouncing his nuclear, chemical and biological ambitions in the wake of the invasion of Iraq. 'Coming in from the cold', he had become a useful ally in the US 'War on Terror', offering his country as a convenient location for the interrogation and incarceration of 'ne'er-do-wells' picked up on the battlefields of Iraq, Afghanistan and elsewhere. His neighbours were pursuing different paths. In Tunisia, seeking to be a sunshine holiday destination, the corrupt, incompetent but secular government of President Ben Ali continued to exercise inefficient, sporadic and heavy-handed repression. In Algeria, still scarred by the experience of their struggle with France and traumatized by the violent civil war of the 1990s, the 'Pouvoir' (Power) still wielded a sinister and defensive control, presided over by the octogenarian President Bouteflikia and sustained by its energy wealth. Lastly, Morocco, where the monarchy retained a high degree of legitimacy and regard, had been broadly stable for many years. Despite their differences, all these countries were experiencing very high levels of population growth; around 70 per cent of the population was under thirty, and perhaps 30 per cent was under fifteen. However, with poor political, economic and social conditions stimulating the ambitions and aggravating the grievances of a large, restless and disenfranchised youth, who could access the allure of both the West and Al Qa'eda through social media, the scene was set for another major political upheaval. This was not yet necessarily apparent to Western policy-makers. Regimes across the region looked corrupt and controlling, but relatively stable.

This situation suited Western policy objectives, but it did mean turning a blind eye to human rights abuses as well as underestimating the potential for political and social upheaval. Politicians, ambassadors and bureaucrats continued to speak to people who told them what they wanted to hear. There is also a delightful charm and courtesy in the culture of the region that often precludes honest commentary in case it upset visitors or guests. Language problems, travel restrictions, the difficulty of getting out of the cities, the daily pressures of feeding the Whitehall, or Washington, bureaucratic 'beast' – all conspired once again to prevent observers listening to the sermons at Friday prayers, the discussions in the villages, the complaints of housewives and the dissatisfaction of too many unemployed, or under-employed, young men smoking their *narghile* pipes in the tea and coffee houses. Even if the signs were noted, the social conservatism factored in, the growing appeal of *takfiri* ideology acknowledged and the role and influence of religion recognized, it would still have been difficult to anticipate or predict what the spark for an uprising might be, or under what circumstances a spontaneous movement, in a police state, might overwhelm the authorities.

In the Gulf States the situation was somewhat different. As in Morocco and Jordan, the monarchical regimes commanded higher levels of respect, consent and legitimacy, and the state structures were more consistent with historical Arab tradition. These states, the products of the collapse of the Ottoman Empire and the later withdrawal of the British, were a lightning-rod for those critics who wished to work themselves up into a lather about 'patriarchal societies', the 'oppression of women' and the status of guest workers, primarily from the Indian sub-continent. In reality, they enjoyed very high degrees of participatory politics, and social networks that allowed discussion, debate and discord, albeit largely invisible to the foreign observer. The ancient tradition of 'the best man for the job', which had elevated Abu Bakr over Ali, still pertained, and competence was often as highly-valued as ancestry. There was corruption, but there was also a widespread distribution of wealth, through complex networks of family and dependants, that was of a different quality from the brutal sense of entitlement in some of the secular regimes of the Middle East. Elections were rare, although *shura* councils were becoming more common and were supplementing the traditional *majlis* as a forum for deliberation and decision-making. While women could not yet drive in Saudi Arabia, that was coming, and they certainly could in the rest of the Gulf, while the educational and employment opportunities for women were expanding rapidly everywhere. Abuses in the labour market were mitigated by the vast sums of remittance money that were fed into the economies of poor countries and the pockets of poor families. An unhealthy consequence was that, in these wealthy societies where the majority of local people, top to bottom, were on the government payroll, and where daily life was almost completely subsidized, a political philosophy of 'no representation without taxation' pertained, which muted demands for reform. However, with their greater levels of flexibility, adaptability and consent, the Gulf States were much better placed to weather the storm of the Arab Spring, when it eventually broke.

Between the demands of Afghanistan, the worries about Iranian ambition, the perennial Arab-Israeli friction and the longer-term concerns regarding the capacity for timely reform in the region, we also found ourselves confronted by a new manifestation of an old scourge: piracy. Since the collapse of central government in Somalia, foreign fishing trawlers had been exploiting the seas around that country, to the detriment of the local economy. In response, Somali fishing communities formed armed groups to deter, then prey on, these interlopers by hijacking commercial vessels. Very soon this grew into a highly lucrative business, with large numbers of ships, and their crews, being seized, and huge sums of money changing hands. This phenomenon coincided with the growth of Al Qa'eda-affiliated Islamists in Somalia, and rising concerns that money generated by piracy would find its way into the hands of these Al Shabab [Youth] militants. In the event, we detected little read-across between piracy and terrorism, although the keen-eyed did note some major new commercial investments in Nairobi and other towns in Kenya by several Somali businessmen. In 2008 there had been 111 attacks and 42 successful hijackings in the Indian Ocean and the Gulf of Aden, with some ships being seized almost as far away as Sri Lanka. Insurance premiums soared, and ships began to carry sniper teams and to 'blackout' as they approached the areas of high pirate activity. In due course, NATO, the EU and partners implemented an International Maritime Transit Corridor (IMTC) that brought some coherence to the issue of escorts and the tracking of ships. The Tom Hanks film, *Captain Philips*, was a very good depiction of the type of incident that was prevalent at the height of this period. When I took over as DCDS(C) in early 2009, there had already been nearly 100 further attacks, and almost the first live 'crisis' I had to address was the abduction of a British couple, the Chandlers, off their yacht near the Seychelles. The British government had a 'hard' policy of not dealing with terrorists or paying ransom money for hostages, and the couple were held for over a year before a 'private payment' of around £500,000, negotiated through third parties, secured their release. Given that over 30,000 ships pass through the area every year, these incidents may have been relatively small in number, but they were disruptive, and countering them was an intensive, expensive and legally complex business. Warships were not to embark pirates, even if they could apprehend them, for fear they would claim asylum while onboard. It was rather an indictment of the international community that this activity was taking place in the twenty-first century, and it was extremely distressing for the thousand or so seamen held captive at one time or another, and for their families. In due course, international political and military pressure at sea and on land reduced the threat to a manageable level, and by 2017, while much money had changed hands, no ships or seamen were still being held by Somali pirates, and remarkably few people had been killed, on either side. All that said, when I was lecturing on the Queen Mary 2 in 2019, some anti-piracy precautions were still in place.

Afghanistan, inevitably, continued to dominate our thinking and planning throughout 2009. General David McKiernan had been rather abruptly replaced by General Stan McChrystal, whose Special Forces' operations had been so effective in Iraq. Scarred by the consequences of the shocking Abu Ghraib abuse scandal in Iraq, and conscious of the radicalizing effect of civilian casualties, he advocated 'courageous restraint' by ISAF soldiers, in order to minimize the sort of self-defeating military actions that generated resentment and fed an insurgency. The US and Coalition soldiers on the ground, confronted daily by the wily and vicious Taliban fighters, could have been forgiven for being rather ambivalent about a policy that prioritized civilian safety over theirs, however much they understood the thinking behind it. McChrystal was soon locked in a policy battle with the White House, the State Department and the Department of Defense over his assessment of the security situation and the level of forces he believed he required to deliver operational success. With conflicting political agendas and strategy objectives, personality clashes, leaks and media intrusion, these policy battles were often played out in public, to the irritation of all the protagonists. Military commanders hoped that higher troop levels would give them the chance to hold the Taliban on the defensive, while the ANSF were built up and became capable of taking over security responsibility. President Obama did not wish to be backed into a corner and appear to be acquiescing to military pressure for a troop uplift. Vice President Joe Biden had little faith in large-scale conventional operations and felt that, given the corruption of the Afghan government, the poor quality of the ANSF and the duplicity of elements within Pakistan, among other factors, the best the US could do was to conduct a counter-terrorism strategy to keep Al Qa'eda suppressed , while abandoning any wider 'nation-building' ambitions. In the end, McChrystal got much of his troop uplift, because in the wake of Iraq, the military, and the American public, did not want to contemplate 'mission failure'. With greater troop numbers on the ground, the intelligence-led Find-Fix-Finish-Exploit cycle targeted the Taliban leadership, with devastating effect, similar to that in Iraq. However, in June 2010, ill-judged comments by his staff to a journalist were published in *Rolling Stone* magazine, and Stan McChrystal had to resign. He was a soldier and a commander who attracted universal respect, and it was a sad and bitter end to a highly distinguished military career.

McChrystal had been indirectly undone by the Icelandic volcanic eruption of that year which had played havoc with global air travel. Grounded in Paris, his aides had been drinking with the journalist and, lulled into a false sense of security, had made indiscreet and derogatory comments about the US civilian leadership, without insisting their conversation was 'off the record', or not to be recorded at all. I was caught by the same volcanic emissions while on a visit to the Pentagon. For five days I camped with the head of the British Defence Section, Air Vice Marshal Mike Harwood, an old friend from HCSC. At last, we heard that an RAF aircraft, an old VC10, was going to make the trans-Atlantic run, landing at . . . Zaragoza in Spain! The plan was to gather us up along with a combination of British soldiers trying to get home on leave from Afghanistan and several hundred British holiday-makers. From Zaragoza we would travel by coach to Santander, where the good ship HMS *Albion* would 'lift us off the beaches', Dunkirk-style. Well, whatever works. In due course, on a dank, foggy morning we stood around on the quay as one of the Royal Navy's finest warships emerged from the gloom, and we embarked. Due to a funeral, the Captain of the ship had missed this emergency sailing, so as the senior officer on board I occupied his comfortable cabin. Going around the ship I chanced upon Stanley Johnson, a fellow Garrick Club member, along with twelve chief constables returning from America and a whole junior football league's worth of teams, who had been taking part in a competition in Spain. Whether or not the situation justified sending a warship to Spain, the Royal Navy, and the officers and sailors on board, did the country and themselves proud, and we enjoyed a delightful, if unexpected, last leg to our extended return home. Shortly after this episode, President Obama announced that General David Petraeus, the boss of Central Command and one of those US commanders to emerge from Iraq with an enhanced reputation, would take command of operations in Afghanistan. Many of us knew David Petraeus well, and his appointment was greeted by NATO nations with a collective sigh of relief.

David Petraeus continued Stan McChrystal's campaign design in Afgha-nistan, and the military situation stabilized, with the Taliban suffering significant losses. However, aligning ISAF's objectives with those of the Afghan government, and Pakistan, continued to prove difficult. There was a fundamental lack of trust between the major players, and many of the personal relationships were poor. The Taliban continued to recruit and operate, conscious of growing war-weariness among ISAF nations. Old adages such as 'We have watches, they have time' and 'We need to win, they just need to not lose' began to do the rounds.

In May 2010, David Cameron's Conservatives became the largest party in Parliament, although he could only govern in coalition with the Liberal Democrats, which had implications for all aspects of government, Defence included. In September 2010, Ed Miliband was elected leader of the Labour

Party, and it was felt appropriate that he should go to Afghanistan and be briefed on the situation there. Jock Stirrup, who was then handing over to General David Richards as CDS, had 'better things to do' than escort him, so I went with the Labour delegation to Kabul and to Helmand. At HQ ISAF, David Petraeus, who I had last seen in Baghdad, met Ed Miliband and his team at the entrance. Having greeted them, he caught my eye and grinned. I saluted, and grinned back.

'Hey, Simon', he said, 'how are Tottenham Hotspur doing?'

'You are very good, General', I replied, impressed with his memory from the Iraq days, or with his briefing staff. 'They are doing just fine.'

In fact, they weren't.

On 2 May 2011 the US announced that a daring helicopter raid into Pakistan had resulted in the death of Osama bin Laden, who had been identified living in a high-walled residence not far from a major Pakistani military base. To howls of confected protest from Islamabad, the US Navy Seals had descended on Bin Laden's compound and, after a brief fire-fight, shot him dead. Osama bin Laden was positively identified, his body extracted from the house and his remains subsequently deposited in the Indian Ocean, in order to ensure that no jihadi 'shrine' could grow up around any burial site. The architect of 9/11 was dead, but his *takfiri* ideology lived on, as did the Al Qa'eda franchise, which would manifest itself again on the new battlefields of Iraq, Syria, Yemen, Somalia and Nigeria, It would continue to attract another generation of adherents, despite the battering it had taken, and to inspire Islamist movements from Indonesia to Nigeria, the latter in the guise of Boko Haram, that combination of Hausa and Arabic words which encouragingly means, 'Western secular education is forbidden.' It was a sad commentary on the complexity of our efforts in Central Asia that Osama bin Laden was hunted down on the territory of a key partner; there was simply no way that the Pakistani ISI could not have known about his presence there. Indeed, many of the AQ and Taliban senior leadership either had a permanent base in Pakistan or routinely took refuge there. Two weeks after this success, the Taliban in the Kandahar region launched Operation Bad'r, named after an early victory by the Prophet Mohammed, and the operational successes of ISAF could not disguise the continuing shortcomings of the ANSF. In June, President Obama announced the start of the US draw-down, and he was followed by the British, the French and the Canadians, with David Cameron announcing that the British would complete their withdrawal from Helmand in 2014. The political motivation was clear, but the military reaction was as critical as it had been in Iraq.

The opposition would now just wait us out, while the 'staying power' of Western nations was once again called into question.

At this stage I was about to change appointments. When I became DCDS(C) I had hoped to follow that with a last operational tour, as Deputy Commander ISAF, but plans had changed. During my tenure I had formed a close professional relationship with Lord Astor, the Conservative Defence Minister in the House of Lords. The Conservative Party had long been keen to re-energize British relationships in the Arabian Gulf, and in the wider Middle East, after the relative neglect of recent years. In spite of differences with their Liberal Democrat partners, the Government had launched the 'Gulf Initiative', a cross-Government programme of projects and plans designed to capitalize on well-established associations in the region, in an attempt to establish a much more coherent linkage between the UK's security and prosperity agendas. Given the importance of defence and security to the region, and the close bonds generated through the monarchy and the armed forces, Lord Astor saw the opportunity to create a senior military-diplomatic post that could champion elements of this initiative. The appointment would support the efforts of ministers, ambassadors, defence attachés and British industry, not least the important defence companies, both in Whitehall and across the region. It would also help support the activities of the Royal Family in the area, and I often saw, at first-hand, the powerful and positive effect that Her Majesty the Queen, the Prince of Wales and other members of the monarchy had, either on overseas trips, or during reciprocal visits to London. Given my background, experience and knowledge of the Middle East and North Africa, Johnnie Astor felt I was an ideal candidate and, although there was a range of funding and other issues to sort out, he had secured the agreement of Liam Fox, the Defence Secretary, and General David Richards, now CDS, for this initiative. I was delighted. Competition for appointments at the very top of the Services is always fierce, and sometimes the dice do not fall your way. This now seemed to be an opportunity to try and do something strategically significant for my country, and I embraced it enthusiastically.

The creation of the appointment of Defence Senior Adviser Middle East (DSAME) came at an interesting and opportune time. On one early visit to Cairo, I found myself at lunch sitting next to a bright young Egyptian general who was the Director of Military Intelligence, Abdel Fattah el-Sisi. A year later, he would be Defence Minister for President Morsi of the Muslim Brotherhood, and a year after that he would be the new 'Pharaoh', President of the Republic of Egypt, having helped overthrow Morsi and his government. Morsi would die in gaol in 2019. On 17 December 2010, a young Tunisian man, Mohammed Bouazizi, was confronted by a female police officer who demanded to see his licence to sell oranges. When he failed to produce one, she slapped him. In his shame and rage he doused himself in flammable liquid and set himself on fire. He died on 4 January 2011. Social media erupted, and a mere ten days later, in the face of massive, country-wide protests, Zine el Abidine Ben Ali, President of Tunisia for twenty-four years, resigned and fled the country, eventually being given asylum in Saudi Arabia, where he also died in 2019. As we wrestled with the political and military issues thrown up by our operations in Afghanistan, and continued to manage the problems of pirates and Persians, the phenomenon that became known as the Arab Spring swept across the Middle East, presenting Western policy-makers with yet another set of complex situations to challenge, confuse and confound them.

Chapter 25

The Arab Spring

W illiam Wordsworth wrote, about the outbreak of the French
Revolution, 'Bliss it was in that dawn to be alive, but to be young
was very heaven.' His enthusiasm reflected the initially widely-
held view that the subordination of the French crown to 'people power'
would be an unremittingly 'good thing'. Wordsworth had not been alone
in failing to see what dark forces had been unleashed by the events of 1789,
and what headwinds would soon face the reformers and revolutionaries.
Alexis de Tocqueville later commented that despotism, by generating a wide
spectrum of grievances and demands, creates large numbers of people with
little to lose. When the pressure becomes too great, authoritarian regimes
often attempt to buy off sectors of society in order to preserve themselves,
but this creates levels of expectation among other groups that they have
difficulty controlling. As they seek to implement reform they exude an aura
of weakness, desperation or uncertainty, which inspires demands for further
reform, at a faster pace. Once these demands begin to attract widespread
and vocal public support, the regime is faced with capitulation or crack-
down. If it chooses the latter, it must have confidence in the security
forces to carry out its wishes, and unless these forces are mercenaries, the
policemen and soldiers will be drawn from the very population that is now
demanding change. History is littered with examples of the 'guardians of
the state' identifying more closely with the populace than the leadership,
or seeing their own opportunity to seize power. In the nature of these
events, when the leadership does capitulate, or is overthrown, reformers
and revolutionaries quickly find that their only shared interest was change,
and that they now have widely differing views about how to use their new-
found dominance. Meanwhile, other forces in society, as well as external
'players' and predatory neighbours, either see opportunities for themselves
or conspire to reverse the revolution.

So it was during the French and Russian Revolutions, the fall of the
Shah and after the Coalition overthrew Saddam Hussein; and so it would
be during the Arab Spring. Within three years of the Revolution of 1789

France was suffering invasion by foreign powers, was wracked by a multi-faceted civil war and had torn itself apart in an ideological struggle that suppressed both moderate reformers and conservatives and brought with it the 'Terror' of Robespierre and the Jacobins. Exhaustion, reaction and compromise eventually brought Napoleon to the pinnacle of power. Seduced by compelling pictures of young men and women across the Middle East demonstrating for change, Western policy-makers, together with journalists and commentators, chose to ignore the many useful analogies with the French Revolution, and more recent episodes in the Middle East. Instead, they convinced themselves that the Arab Spring was a natural extension of the movements that had led to the fall of the Berlin Wall and the dissolution of the Soviet Union, events which had been historical anomalies in their relative lack of violence. It seemed churlish not to be swept up in these early manifestations of 'people power'. They wished to believe that these upheavals were all about individual liberties, the rights of women and minorities, and the espousal of the 'freedoms' associated with Western democracies. The Arab Spring was indeed highly significant, and it did contribute to the biggest transformation of the Middle East since decolonization, assisted by the consequences of the invasion and occupation of Iraq, but its outcome was not the securing of more democratic political systems or a brighter economic future. Participants were clear what they wanted freedom 'from', but were by no means clear, or unified, about what they wanted freedom 'for'. Despite all our experiences in Iraq, and earlier, we failed once again to factor in historical influences, sectarianism, religion, and culturally different attitudes to identity politics and national loyalty. In our enthusiasm, we demonstrated the sad last gasps of the Fukuyama thesis regarding the inevitable and peaceful triumph of Western-generated 'universal values'.

With the self-immolation of Mohammed Bouazizi, instantly transmitted across the region by social media, waves of unrest struck Jordan, Egypt and Yemen and then spread to other countries, notably Syria and Libya. The largest demonstrations occurred, as usual, after Friday prayers, in the form of 'days of rage'. The sequence of protest, revolution and reaction was different in each country. Tunisia, the smallest of the North African states, became the 'poster boy' of the Arab Spring by managing to negotiate the minefield of conflicting agendas and terror attacks to stage reasonably 'fair and free' democratic elections by 2014. Egypt, the largest and most populous Arab state, also avoided early large-scale violence, as the huge demonstrations in Tahrir Square eventually forced President Mubarak from power, thwarting his hopes of dynastic succession. The Supreme Council of the Armed Forces dissolved the Egyptian Parliament and suspended the constitution. The Americans, who had been firm backers of Mubarak, were left in a quandary. Should they back an old ally in an important country, but appear to be betraying their own 'democratic values', or should they desert him, trust in the democratic instincts that seemed to be on display in Tahrir Square and risk their relationships with key allies in the region, particularly the Kingdom of Saudi Arabia and other Gulf states? Robert Gates, the US Defense Secretary, wrote about this dilemma in his book, *On Duty*. The 'securocrats' argued for caution, while President Obama's young special advisers urged him to 'be on the right side of history'. Obama backed their advice, in line with his previous and future foreign policy moves which combined further to undermine US credibility and influence in the region. Stripped of US backing, Mubarak departed office for hospital and jail on 11 February 2011. Eventually, Mohammed Morsi, strongly backed by a very publicly resurgent Muslim Brotherhood and other Islamists, was elected President in June 2012. In November of that year Morsi issued a constitutional declaration granting himself unlimited powers and the right to legislate without judicial review. A new, hastily drawn-up constitution amounted to a barely-disguised 'Islamist coup', but the Muslim Brotherhood had overplayed their hand. Unlike in Turkey, where Erdogan and the AK Party had progressively neutered the military in order to advance their own Islamist agenda, the Egyptian Muslim Brotherhood had moved too fast. On 3 July 2013, claiming to be responding to widespread protests, the military, led by General Abdel Fattah el-Sisi and cheered on by Saudi Arabia and the UAE, overthrew President Morsi and violently crushed the pro-Brotherhood demonstrations, initiating, in all but name, a military regime. Mohammed Morsi died, still in jail, six years later.

In Yemen, already a fragile and failing state, with a poor economy and a population of around 27 million, fairly evenly divided between Zaidi Shia and Sunnis, mass protests called for the removal of the President, Ali Abdullah Saleh. Yemen had many problems. There had already been a series of 'wars' between the Yemeni state and the Shia Houthis in the north, and there were long-standing tensions between Sana'a, the capital, and the secessionist aspirations of the south, which included the city and port of Aden. In addition, Al Qa'eda in the Arabian Peninsula (AQAP) had taken advantage of the turmoil to establish a powerful and lethal franchise among the Sunni tribes of the south. The US was already operating a counter-terrorism campaign against them, with the backing of both the Yemeni government and Saudi Arabia. Whereas the cruise missile had been the weapon of choice in the late twentieth century, it had now been joined by increasingly sophisticated armed drones, in this instance flown from bases in Djibouti. In due course, Islamic State would also set up a franchise, competing violently not only with the 'heretic' Houthis and the UN-backed 'legitimate' government, but also with AQAP.

Saleh, after twelve years as president of North Yemen and, from 1990, another twenty-two as President of the 'unified' Republic of Yemen, had amassed private wealth estimated at between $30 and $60 million. He often referred to the trials of being President of Yemen as having to 'dance on the heads of snakes', given its complex tribal make-up, the tensions between royalists, republicans, Marxists and Islamists, and the multiplicity of factions vying for money, land, power and influence. With a depleted treasury, and having made too many promises to too many people, his decades-long balancing act, impressive in a country with such a long history of political violence and assassination, was about to come to an end. I had once hosted him at Sandhurst, where his grandson 'passed out' from the Royal Military Academy. He was an awkward guest, difficult to corral and always shooting off to have a cigarette or have a photograph taken with his henchmen. I had also visited him in Sana'a.

'We are the most heavily-armed people on earth', he informed me in the course of the conversation. 'Every man has a rifle, a pistol, a *jambiya* (curved knife) and a sword.'

He paused while we digested these facts.

'Just think what it would be like if we also had alcohol', he continued.

There was a further pause.

'Manchester?' I suggested, to laughter from the President and his advisers.

Resisting the demands of protesters, Saleh was eventually wounded in a bomb attack on the Presidential Palace and airlifted to Riyadh for medical treatment. Even now he could not read the writing on the wall, and to our collective amazement the Saudis permitted him to return to Sana'a, where he continued his Byzantine attempts to retain power. At last, in early 2012 and under great pressure from the GCC, he relinquished authority to his Vice President, Abdulrab al Hadi, who had led the assault on Aden in the 1994 civil war. This new government would struggle on until early 2015, when the Houthis, backed by Iran and now also by the ousted President Saleh as a way of regaining power, seized Sana'a and, along with the capital, political power in the country. Houthi attacks on Saudi Arabia long pre-dated the Arab Spring, and this new civil war, with the Houthis now dominant in Sana'a, would lead to a long and controversial Saudi-led military intervention, and it would weave the internal Yemeni conflict, and the wider campaigns against AQAP and IS, into the regional power struggle between Iran and the Sunni Gulf monarchies. In 2017, Saleh's impressive 'snake-dancing' ended when he tried to play the inter-factional game once too often, and his new Houthi friends killed him.

In Libya, anti-government protests began in February 2011, and the opposition rapidly gained control of most of Benghazi, the second-largest city. In March the rising violence, and the bloodthirsty rhetoric of Colonel Gaddafi, led the UN to authorize a 'no-fly zone' over Libya in order to protect civilians. David Cameron and the French President, Nicolas Sarkozy, appeared to be vying with each other as to who could be more 'forward-leaning' in this new conflict, while President Obama pursued a new, 'unofficial' US doctrine of 'leading from behind'. Libya was an artificial construct put together in 1911, when the Italians took the two Ottoman provinces of Tripolitania and Cyrenaica, with their respective capitals of Tripoli and Benghazi, and formed them into a new entity. The two provinces had little in common, and there are several hundred kilometres of desert coastline between the two major population centres. The south of Libya, the Fezzan, has even less in common with the coastal region, and is ethnically quite distinct, with strong links to the local Tuaregs and to the Muslims of further south. Libya has a population of only 6 million, and its oilfields, with the tenth largest reserves in the world, mean there should be enough wealth for everyone under a half-decent and competent government. In late March 2011, a bombing campaign against Gaddafi's forces began, and in due course a 27-nation coalition joined the intervention. UAE and Qatar were particularly active in supporting rebel groups, although it took us some while to fully discern the differing agendas of the two countries and the political tension that this was bringing to inter-Gulf relationships. The UAE and the Crown Prince of Abu Dhabi, Mohammed bin Zayed, were rabidly opposed to the Muslim Brotherhood and backed the more secular opposition groups, while Qatar appeared to be arming, training and supporting those groups with a more distinctly Islamist tendency. In support of this campaign, the Qataris made a credible case that they were merely backing the most effective and motivated anti-Gaddafi groups, those with the best chance of achieving success. Their explanation had a respectable military logic behind it. The ideological split between two Sunni Gulf monarchies regarding the threat, or otherwise, from 'Political Islam' and the Muslim Brotherhood, would become even more pronounced during the election, the 'Islamist coup' and the military 'counter-coup' in Egypt. These divisions would manifest themselves again throughout the turmoil in Syria. In addition, this major divergence of policy and attitude would be played out through the medium of the Qatari-controlled Al Jazeera television station, whose Islamist leanings were much more evident in their Arabic broadcasts than they were in their English programmes. The combination would eventually lead to a major fissure in the GCC, as if there were not already enough tensions across the Middle East.

In due course, the rebels held Benghazi and then took Tripoli in August, bringing Gaddafi's forty-two years in power to an end. He fled to Sirte, where on 20 October 2011 he was captured and subsequently killed by Qatar-backed militias. Given our misunderstanding of the dynamics of the country, our misplaced optimism and our failure to construct a credible post-conflict stabilization plan, a predictable civil war soon broke out. The early stages of the Libya campaign fell across my last months as DCDS(C) and my first months as DSAME, and in both appointments I was active in trying to help coordinate the Arab contribution to the coalition campaign. I was in the office of the Qatari Chief of Staff, General Hamad Ali Al Attiyah, who distinguished himself at Ras al Khafji in the First Gulf War, when his liaison officer with the rebels in Sirte rang to tell us of Gaddafi's fate. At this stage we were also seeking to bring in an Arab and Muslim 'stabilization force' to help initiate the process of disarming and demobilizing the militia groups and to secure critical national infrastructure, heavy weapons, arms dumps and the like, things we had singularly failed to do in the early stages of the occupation of Iraq. Our hopes rested on the Jordanians who, with well-trained and well-disciplined armed forces, but no money, were always keen to offer troops for UN-sponsored and -paid military tasks. Sadly, the competing agendas both within and outside Libya meant that this initiative failed, and the country entered a squalid and lengthy period of tribal and militia infighting. It was during this period of collapse of central authority, when the lengthy coastline was uncontrolled, that an industrial-scale human trafficking network was established. This would have significant consequences for the domestic politics of several Western European countries, and for European Union institutions and solidarity.

Despite this, I had several later engagements in Libya, where Dominic Asquith was now the British Ambassador in Tripoli, having already navigated the choppy waters of Baghdad during the 'surge' and those of Cairo during the early months of the Arab Spring. As the situation in Libya deteriorated, he was fortunate to escape with his life when his convoy was attacked with rocket-propelled grenades. His US counterpart, John Steven, was not so lucky and was killed by militants in Benghazi in 2012, an incident that became a major headache for Hilary Clinton as Secretary of State.

At this time I met Abdel Hakim bel Haj, who had been a Qatari-sponsored rebel leader in the west of Libya and who, in the period shortly after 9/11, had been the subject of 'extraordinary rendition' to Libya by the CIA, an operation in which MI6 had played a part. The British role in the episode came to light when a handwritten note from a senior British officer was found floating across a burned-out compound in Tripoli. The subsequent legal case would not be settled until 2018. At the time of our meeting, in the Tripoli Intercontinental Hotel, he introduced me to his fellow militia commanders, many of whom, to my surprise, and that of MI5 and the British counter-terrorism agencies, had come from the Libyan community in Manchester. They had all become refugees during the period that Gaddafi had sponsored the IRA, brought down a 747 jumbo jet over Lockerbie and had been responsible for the shooting of WPC Yvonne Fletcher in St James' Square. It was from this same community that the bomber of the Ariana Grande concert, in the Manchester Arena in May 2017, would come.

The 1982 uprising by the Muslim Brotherhood in the city of Hama, brutally put down by Hafez al Assad, had really been the last significant act of opposition to the Syrian Ba'athist government. However, in those same early months of 2011, a series of demonstrations, protests and marches took place in several Syrian towns and cities. Some were driven by poverty and unemployment, a nationwide problem fuelled by water scarcity in the countryside that had driven large numbers of people into urban areas. Some protests were related to genuine demands for political reform, freedom of speech and a halt to the repressive behaviour of the regime. Some were related to a long-held sense of disenfranchisement felt by much of the Sunni majority under the Alawite-dominated regime, and some to a resurgence of the Muslim Brotherhood, with their eye on events taking place in Egypt at the same time. Having watched the unfolding chaos in Yemen, Tunisia, Libya and Egypt, leaders from the Gulf States went to Damascus to urge Bashar al Assad to make some concessions to head off the growing disruption and violence, offering considerable financial support in return. At the time, I was in Qatar with Liam Fox, the Defence Secretary, visiting Emir Tameem, who had recently succeeded to the throne in the wake of an untypically early abdication by his father, Hamad, who had done so much to put the gas-rich state on the map. The new Emir, Sherborne- and Sandhurst-educated, had just returned from Damascus, where Assad had listened to his pleas and inducements, promised to heed them and then, on Tameem's departure, made a public statement of uncompromising harshness towards the opposition. As so often happens with disputes in the Arab world, this volte-face and slight had been taken personally, and the Qataris now implied that they might well support the opposition more actively. They were as good as their word. On 31 July, after a further month of increasingly violent skirmishing, the Syrian Army stormed into several cities, inflicting large numbers of casualties, in an effort to suppress the protests. Their actions failed to cow the rebels, and by the end of 2011 observers were optimistically predicting the imminent fall of the Assad regime, as the opposition, increasingly supported by Turkey, Saudi Arabia, Jordan, UAE and Qatar, made significant gains in the suburbs of Damascus itself and in Aleppo. The US and UK were doing what they could to help co-ordinate the various opposition groups and form them into a militarily effective body that could attract unified international support.

I was now in and out of the region on a very regular basis, still trying to garner support for a 'stabilization force' for Libya, while also trying to discern who was supporting whom among the disparate Syrian opposition groups and their various backers. In mid to late 2011 the international community was still optimistic about the Arab Spring, but they were beginning to note, probably rather late in the day, the growing power and influence of well-armed and ideologically-motivated Sunni Islamist groups in the multiple conflicts across the region. Although there were many superficial similarities between the countries involved, there were distinct and important differences. Libya, an artificial construct, had sprung apart almost as soon as the Gaddafi regime fell. Tunisia was small, both in population and size, and had a relatively 'secular' and cosmopolitan culture. Egypt was religiously homogenous, except for the Coptic Christian community, and ethnically homogeneous with the important exception of the Bedouin in the Sinai Peninsula. The latter were viewed very much as second-class citizens in the eyes of the Nilotic Egyptians. It also had strong state structures, not least the military, and the Egyptian 'deep state' was able to weather the fall of Mubarak and face down the challenge from the Muslim Brotherhood. Yemen was a notoriously tribal country with a propensity for chaotic politics and feudal, internecine warfare. The situation in Syria, however, was very different and bore a number of important similarities to Iraq

The states of Syria and Iraq were products of the post-Ottoman settlement. They contained the great Sunni-Arab Muslim capitals of Damascus and Baghdad and in both, during the fractious mandates of the French and the British, minority communities came to dominate the security forces: the Alawites in Syria, and the Sunnis in Iraq. On independence, these minority groups consolidated their position, gathering in other religious and ethnic minorities and offering them protection against the respective Sunni and Shia majority populations in return for their support. Given the brutal crimes these minority groups had committed in order to retain power, the fall of the Alawites in Syria, or the Sunnis in Iraq, would lead them to a position of permanent subordination and provoke potentially violent reprisals. Saddam had survived war with Iran, uprisings by the Shia and Kurds and catastrophic defeat by the Coalition in 1991, but it was only the full-scale invasion of 2003 that toppled him. In the ensuing chaos and violence, the Iraqi Shia had now consolidated their dominant position, assisted by Iran, while the Sunnis were reaping what they had previously sowed. Assad and the Alawites could see a similar fate awaiting them, so there was no question of their simply throwing in the towel. This 'fight to the last man' attitude should have been identified far earlier than it was. In addition, despite the ambiguous religious status of the Alawites, other Shia forces, most notably from the Iranian Republican Guard Corps under their sinister but highly effective commander, Qassim Suleimani, and Lebanese Hezbollah fighters, began to flood in to support Syrian government forces. Iraqi Shia militia also appeared on the battlefield. In due course, and in the face of Western timidity, the Russians would intervene, and this combination would turn the balance of power decisively in favour of the regime.

Meanwhile, given the increasingly Shia character of the Syrian regime's response, and the very overt assistance of the hated Persians, Syria now became the magnet for Sunni jihadists and militants from across the Arab world. One of the most effective opposition groups was Jabhat al Nusra, inspired by *takfiri* ideology and deemed to be closely associated with Al Qa'eda. This presented Western governments with yet another quandary. They were willing the fall of Assad, but the reality was that, in the absence of a major operation by the Western powers and their Sunni allies, no amount of local opposition supported by *takfiri* foreign fighters, even if well-funded, was likely to succeed. Even if it did succeed, the secular Alawite Ba'athist regime would in all probability then be replaced by an extremist Sunni one. It was no wonder that many Syrians continued to see Assad and the Alawites as a better prospect than the jihadists, whose record of iconoclasm and brutality in Afghanistan and Iraq was well known. Therefore the international community danced on the heads of ideological pins, trying to differentiate between 'moderate' Syrian opposition groups that we could give money and weapons to, and 'extremist' groups who in reality represented a much greater threat to the West and Western interests than Assad did. In the meantime, Syria's ordeal went on, and the casualty toll continued to rise.

While I contributed, where I could, to a better understanding of the region's conflicts, I was also keen to push forward on the Government's commitment to re-engage with old friends in the Gulf, something which, I felt, had a much greater chance of success than our half-hearted interventions in the various manifestations of the Arab Spring. I stated, very publicly, that my intention as DSAME was to interpret the Government's 'Gulf Initiative' as a policy to get Britain back 'East of Suez', certainly as far as the Gulf, if not further, and that I would therefore do all I could to help reverse the misguided British decision to withdraw in 1971. After completing my first set of visits to the Gulf, I reported back that there remained strong affection for Britain in the region, and great opportunities, but that successive British governments had consistently disappointed our friends and allies by failing to commit ourselves to a region that was so patently important to our own security and prosperity. 'When a nation thinks small', I wrote, 'it starts to act small and, in due course, it begins to be treated as small.' National self-interest should have driven our engagement, but many British bureaucrats and officials had made their names and careers in the multilateral arenas of the United Nations and the European Union. Lacking ambition for their own country, unused to displays of overt national self-confidence or self-interest and sometimes unenthusiastic about dealing with autocrats and monarchs, many seemed to have little appetite for capitalizing on the goodwill towards Britain in many areas of former influence. 'We seem to have lost the gift for the grand, generous or gracious gesture', I wrote, contrasting how we did business in the Gulf with how our US and French allies, and rivals, did theirs. I remained convinced of the reality of Britain's global role, reach and influence, while others in Whitehall adopted an attitude that could be summed up as 'We are a small island off the north-west coast of Europe, let us get used to it.' Such an ingrained defeatist attitude was to characterize much of the later approach to Brexit negotiations.

We most certainly did have some outstanding ambassadors in the region, and an expatriate footprint that dwarfed that of all other Western nations put together, but too often we seemed to suffer from a form of collective embarrassment when pushing Britain's interests. The Americans were very obviously the 'biggest dog on the block', so their clout was on a different scale to ours, but we should have exercised a greater competitive advantage over the South Koreans, French, Spanish and Germans in particular, given our long history in the Gulf. A French general once asked if we should coordinate evacuation plans in the UAE, if there was a crisis with Iran. I asked him how many French civilians there were in that country.

'Four thousand', he said.

'We have one hundred and twenty thousand', I replied, to his astonishment. 'We are not going to be lifting that number off the beaches.'

However, despite the difference in historical connections and expatriate numbers, it was the French who had a naval base in UAE with a two-star admiral, a Foreign Legion battalion in the country and a squadron of Rafale jet fighters under UAE command. When the Emiratis sought places on training courses, the French offered them for free, and in English. I believed that an equally forward-leaning posture in UAE might well have helped secure a major Typhoon deal in that country. Due to Treasury rules regarding the charging of fees for all military activity, we were often forced to demand 'full costs' from our friends. In addition, we made little or no provision for any spare capacity within the three Services to meet the substantial, indeed insatiable, international appetite for British military training. The more overt French demonstrations of commitment to Gulf security concerns had resulted in their achieving remarkable commercial success when it came to securing contracts, in all sectors. Whitehall often seemed to be psychologically and intellectually incapable of making the connection between meeting the security needs of our partners in the Gulf, and wider, and thereby serving our own 'prosperity agenda'.

Nor could we appear to find the energy to turn the declared 'Gulf Initiative' into a proper strategy for the region, or to make it 'government policy' in the Middle East. Some of this reflected the realities of coalition government, but much of it was the result of 'foot-dragging' by officials. When the French President, Prime Minister, Foreign or Defence Minister went anywhere in the world, they took senior military officers with them on all occasions, to make very clear their understanding of what was often the highest national priority for their hosts. They also, invariably, arrived in a French government aircraft, not on a commercial aircraft or a charter flight. Their long-term investment in languages, particularly Arabic, was also very evident, allowing them to engage directly with a much wider cross-section of people in the region; not through interpreters, and not solely with those who spoke French or English. When Liam Fox was replaced by Philip Hammond, I briefed the new Defence Secretary on the scale of our engagement in the region and told him how useful the MoD could be in helping secure other British objectives. I urged him to put pressure on the Prime Minister to turn the welcome 'Gulf Initiative' into a 'Gulf Strategy', with some resources behind it.

'We have not had a coherent policy for the Gulf since 1971', I said, 'and the policy then was to get out.'

'I hear you', he replied, 'but despite that, we have been there for the last 40 years.'

'With the greatest respect, Secretary of State', I countered, 'we have actually been in the Gulf for one year, forty times. Our friends have very long memories, and a British policy based on rank short-termism does not look like a firm statement of commitment to the security of our allies.'

Since it was not government 'policy' to have any permanent bases in the Gulf, this meant that we could only deploy there for 'operational' reasons, which then attracted funding from the Treasury, or for programmed training exercises like Saif Sareea, which were always vulnerable to shortages of money within the MoD. Therefore, without a mandated policy of commitment, we could not allocate ships, aircraft, troops or training resources to the region on any permanent basis.

Although there had been minor disturbances in the Gulf monarchies during the early stages of the Arab Spring, only Bahrain had suffered any significant upheavals. Bahrain had been home to the US Fifth Fleet since 1995, and also hosted our own small, rotational, naval presence. The Khalifa royal family are Sunni, but the majority of Bahrainis are Shia. Although there were Shias in governmental positions, and some Shias had been very successful in business, they were excluded from the security forces, and many of them, particularly among the poor and the young, felt disenfranchised or discriminated against. In addition, some Iranian elements, and significant numbers of the local Shia clergy who had close contacts with them, made it their business to encourage and exploit these sentiments. Protests centred around the Pearl Roundabout, where some heavy-handed actions by an ill-prepared police force led to casualties, fuelling a spiral of violence that was played out on social media and internationally. In due course, Saudi and UAE security forces crossed the 'Causeway' into Bahrain, to take over a range of installation-guarding duties, thereby releasing more of the local military and police to take on a public-order role. In Britain and other countries, a predictable coalition of émigré dissidents and human rights groups stirred up an often ill-informed media and political class to criticise the Khalifa royal family. Despite the best efforts of many reform-minded Bahrainis, including the Crown Prince, who made repeated efforts to bridge the sectarian divide,

Shia intransigence and Persian meddling made pragmatic compromise difficult, and opposition continued to simmer. Despite this difficult political environment, in my meetings with King Hamad I encouraged, indeed urged him to take advantage of a Conservative government in Britain in order to 'lock' the UK back into the security architecture of the Gulf on a permanent basis. In due course, the King generously offered to build a new, permanent naval base for the British. Thank goodness that there were enough other advocates of this initiative to get it past the doom-mongers and the nay-sayers in London, and in March 2018, despite several false starts and frustrating delays, Crown Prince Salman and the Duke of York declared HMS *Juffair* 'open', thereby initiating a new period of permanent British presence 'East of Suez'. The new base was a legacy of which I was intensely proud, and its utility and importance were to be well demonstrated in 2019 and 2020, when we needed to increase our maritime presence in the face of Iranian aggression in the Straits of Hormuz. In November 2019, the Royal Navy very generously named the centre of their new base 'Mayall Square'.

Chapter 26

The Rise of Islamic State

In the meantime, the conflict in Syria, which had by now escalated into all-out civil war, was entering a new stage, with long-term consequences for global politics. Russia, which had continued to nurse a deep-rooted resentment against the West, was rediscovering her sense of self-confidence under Vladimir Putin. Patronized and ignored in Bosnia and Kosovo, she had stood by America in the wake of 9/11, only to see her experience and advice regarding Afghanistan dismissed. The Russians had advised against the invasion of Iraq in 2003 and had done what they could to thwart the United Nations sanctioning this intervention. They too had their own problems with Islamist terrorism, and they anticipated, quite rightly in the event, that the invasion and occupation of Iraq would further destabilize an already volatile region and fuel Muslim extremism. Having seen both Afghanistan and Iraq act as magnets for global jihadists, they were astounded that Britain and France, with the US a half-step behind, seemed so enthusiastic to intervene in Libya, and they predicted dire consequences from regime change there, particularly if the post-conflict planning was as ill-thought through as in Iraq. One does not need to be an apologist for Russia or President Putin to suggest the West's own interests would have been better served by managing this important relationship with more finesse. With their own brutal history, and a far stronger sense of national self-interest, the Russians had no stake in proselytizing on behalf of 'universal liberal values'. Like the Chinese, they saw chaos as a far greater threat than authoritarianism, and they demonstrated a clearer-sighted understanding of the political culture of the Middle East and the centrifugal power of sectarianism.

President Obama had no wish to see the US involved in any significant way in the Syrian crisis. Other Western governments willed the fall of Assad, but half-hearted and ambivalent cheering from the side-lines was to prove manifestly ineffective in the face of a determined and brutal stand by the Syrian regime and its allies. There was one last moment at which the Western powers might yet have intervened effectively. In late 2012, the West was confronted with credible allegations that Assad's forces were using chemical weapons against civilians. Obama had strongly implied that verifiable reports of the continued use of such weapons would constitute a 'red line', and that crossing it would be the catalyst for military reprisals. A year later, in August 2013, as the destruction and the death toll continued to rise, and the Syrian opposition became increasingly fragmented and radicalized, there was clear evidence, broadcast on television across the world, of a regime chemical attack in the Ghouta province of Damascus, leading to many casualties. As the world watched what Obama would do, David Cameron led the political charge in the UK to get Parliamentary support for military action. At that time I was in Jordan with the new CDS, General Nick Houghton, to discuss with Coalition partners what further action we could take in Syria. John Kerry, the US Secretary of State, was due to make a statement on behalf of the Obama administration, and we could not work out why David Cameron had chosen to recall Parliament from their summer recess before he had heard the Americans confirm their policy position. In the event, a combination of the prevarication and duplicity of Ed Miliband and the Labour Party, poor party management of Tory MPs and the failure to make a compelling case, meant that Cameron lost the vote. It was a significant failure, a further erosion of the 'royal prerogative' that empowers the executive branch to take tough decisions relating to the use of force, and it undoubtedly contributed to Obama's subsequent failure to observe his own 'red line' and take military action. I sent a note to CDS some days later, saying that we should be in no doubt as to the reputational damage that this domestic political defeat would do to us. A range of allies, partners, friends, rivals, opponents and outright enemies would take note of our timidity and would form their own judgments about our reliability in global affairs. We needed to engage in a robust mitigation strategy to manage the consequences of our lack of action. I do not suggest that Western action at that time would necessarily have altered the military facts on the ground, but I do believe it was the last opportunity for the US and her allies to deliver a coherent punitive gesture, deter Assad from the future use of chemical weapons and, possibly, retain the political initiative with, perhaps, a last serious attempt at a comprehensive political solution. The Russians stepped neatly into this new geopolitical vacuum, promising to act as the 'guarantor' of Syrian chemical disarmament and, in the absence of any other competing military or political initiatives, they now became a major player in the Syrian conflict, and again in the wider Middle East.

Another, albeit lesser, UK public relations disaster was being played out at the same time. In early 2014 when, having failed to generate a 'stabilization force' for that country, Libya had settled into a fractious, intermittently violent, political stalemate, the Cameron government decided that the British military contribution could best be focused on training the nascent Libyan Army. At this stage the Libyan Provisional Government was trying to recruit for the Libyan security forces while at the same time continuing to subsidise the local militias, but bizarrely paying the militias at a higher rate than the 'legitimate' state forces. It was a recipe for disaster, but I could still see how British excellence in military training could have a part to play. To my mind it was obvious that, if the politicians were too risk-adverse to conduct this training in Libya, because of the force-protection issues and therefore cost, we should do it in a third country. To that end I was already sounding out some options, including Jordan, although a similar, earlier programme of military training for Libyans in that country had already ended in a barracks being burned down. Despite this, for the right amount of support and money, Jordan was willing to give this training initiative another go. To my astonishment, the Government decided that the best location for our contribution to Libyan institutional development would be Bassingbourn Camp, in the middle of leafy Cambridgeshire. To no one's surprise, except perhaps that of the politicians, the whole project quickly descended into farce, since British standards of discipline were difficult to enforce on the Libyan recruits, and then almost into tragedy, as trainees broke out of the camp and committed a series of offences, of various degrees of seriousness, in Cambridge. At last, in November, the ill-advised nature of the initiative was acknowledged and, for fear they might make a mass claim for asylum, the Libyans were bundled onto an aircraft and returned home.

Meanwhile, a new crisis was developing in Iraq in the wake of the US withdrawal and the sectarian policies of Nouri al Maliki. This had seen the disbandment of the Sunni militias of the 'Awakening', whose role in the defeat of AQI had been so critical, accompanied by the violent suppression of Sunni protests in the Anbar cities of Fallujah and Ramadi. Al Qa'eda, although weakened, helped to set up a new Sunni jihadist group, Islamic State in the Levant (ISIL), which began to grow, adopting the same *takfiri* ideology as Al Qa'eda, attracting a similar type of adherent and recruit and using social media to similar effect. In the wake of protests and violent disorder in Syria, ISIL then set up a franchise operation in that country under Abu Mohammed al Joulani, called Jabhat al Nusra, which began to gain notoriety for its military prowess and its commitment to the overthrow of Assad. The linkage between Jabhat al Nusra, Al Qa'eda and ISIL was usefully disguised for some time, until in a violent split reminiscent of that between Bolsheviks and Trotskyists, the three organizations broke ranks in 2013, resulting in a further internecine Sunni conflict that killed thousands. Here now was an ideological civil war within a political civil war, with elements of a religious civil war running through them both. It was at this stage that the Syrian regime decisively turned to Iran and Hezbollah for support. Having helped provoke this formal Shia alliance, ISIL could then usefully deploy the age-old narrative of 'defending Sunni-Arab interests against Shia-Persian domination', despite the fact that it was actively attacking other Sunni rebel groups while doing so.

By early 2014, ISIL had largely retaken control of Anbar from the Iraqi government and had established itself in large swathes of eastern Syria, along the Euphrates river valley, having taken Raqqa, which became its HQ, and the oil-rich town of Deir az Zour. Raqqa had been briefly an imperial capital of the Abbasid caliphate under the Caliph Haroun al Rashid, although Baghdad had remained the administrative centre. He had made several pilgrimages to Mecca from here, and much of the action in the fabled *Thousand and One Arabian Nights* takes place in Raqqa. In Iraq, while attention was focused on the familiar Sunni hotspots in Anbar, Western intelligence was not concentrating enough on the campaign of violence, bombings and assassination taking place in Northern Iraq, in and around Mosul. This was progressively undermining the morale and legitimacy of the Iraqi state. On 4 June 2014, an ISIL convoy from Syria entered Mosul. In the chaos that ensued, ISIL 'sleeper cells' were activated, and multiple suicide attacks took place against government buildings and personnel. In the confusion, the Iraqi Security Forces, despite outnumbering ISIL fighters by over fifteen to one, began to desert, often led by their officers. If the leadership would not stand and fight, it was little surprise that the young, predominantly Shia troops would not do so either. In their wake, they left the bodies of their fellow soldiers and policemen and a veritable cornucopia of US-gifted military equipment. In a stroke, a violent, well-disciplined and motivated terror organization had transformed itself into one of the best-armed and best-equipped militaries in the region. The ISIL reputation for violence was further reinforced by the ensuing execution of over 4,000 Iraqi soldiers and policemen. Possibly surprising themselves by this dramatic success, ISIL drove on against Erbil, where they were stopped by the resistance of the Kurdish *peshmerga*, and also south towards Baghdad. In doing so, they reoccupied swathes of Sunni-populated territory, including the old Sunni 'triangle of death', until they were halted by a combination of ISF and a large range of hastily raised Shia militias, who had responded in their thousands to a call to action by Ayatollah Ali Sistani.

On 29 June 2014, the first Friday of Ramadan that year, Abu Bakr al Baghdadi announced the establishment of a 'worldwide caliphate' from the *minbar* of the Grand Mosque in Mosul, and he renamed ISIL as 'Islamic State'. The self-styled new caliph, the first since Ataturk had abolished the title in 1924, announced himself as 'the leader who presides over you' and urged all Muslims to join him to 'make jihad for the sake of Allah'. Under his direction, the Islamic world would be 'returned to dignity, might, right and leadership'. He hailed the jihadi victories in Syria, and now Iraq, which had allowed the restoration of the caliphate in the Sunni Arab world after so many centuries: 'God gave the mujahideen victory after long years of jihad and patience . . . so they have now declared the caliphate, and placed the Caliph in charge.' ISIL maps of the new caliphate covered an area from the Pyrenees, across all of North Africa and well south of the Sahara, through the Middle East and up into the Balkans, the Caucasus, Central Asia and the Indian sub-continent. The bigger maps included great swathes of South-East Asia as well. They basically covered every part of the globe in which Islam, in all its many manifestations, had ever held sway, from the religion's foundation to its current heartlands and fault-lines. They therefore included Spain, lost to Islam since 1492, much of South-East Europe that had long emerged from Ottoman domination, and even Lundy Island, off the North Devon coast, which was claimed to have been occupied by Barbary corsairs in the seventeenth century. Through the power of modern social media and highly sophisticated, seductive and often brutal messaging, they also reached out to the large and growing Muslim populations of Western states.

To many Western observers, much of al Baghdadi's rhetoric may have sounded like a speech from *Game of Thrones*, and the power of the words and images were poorly understood. However, to Muslim listeners, particularly Sunnis and Arabs, the words, like those of Osama bin Laden nearly two decades earlier, struck a powerful chord on many different levels. They appealed to a sense of past greatness, lost opportunities, historical and more recent defeats and humiliations, usurped destinies and potentially brighter futures. They conjured up images of past and present foes, spiritual struggle and physical confrontation, previous great spiritual and military leaders, periods of supremacy and those of subservience. Many in the West could understand neither the abject collapse of the Iraqi Army in the face of a 'rag-tag terrorist organization', nor the appeal of a group already distinguished by the levels of violence they were prepared to employ and to propagate on social media. Very many Muslims did indeed reject its claims, its religious interpretations and its nihilism, and abhorred them. Indeed, to Turks, Iranians, Shias, moderates and professionals, liberals and supporters of women's rights, and to many women themselves, the words, and the sentiments behind them, carried all the menace of a centuries-old religio–cultural war.

However, for more Muslims than we collectively cared to admit, especially those feeling excluded and disenfranchised, or socially and politically emasculated, the attraction of Al Qa'eda and Islamic State should have been easy to grasp: religious certainty, belonging, hyper-masculinity, powerful and seductive imagery, jihadi 'brides', weapons and compelling uniforms, money. It was the same sort of combination that had attracted so many to Bolshevism and Nazism. This was certainly not how the twenty-first century was supposed to unfold.

Having failed to pass his vote for military action in Syria a year earlier, and facing a general election in May 2015, David Cameron had no desire to get further embroiled in the Middle East but felt he had to respond to the latest events in Iraq, not least the start of a genocidal campaign against the Yazidis by Islamic State. The Yazidis are a very distinct ethnic and religious group who live around Mount Sinjar in north-west Iraq. Their religion combines aspects of Christianity, Judaism and Islam. They are monotheists, believing in God the Creator, with a chief protector, the Peacock Angel. IS chose to view them as 'devil worshippers' and began a systematic programme of killing and enslavement, which did, at last, provoke a Western humanitarian response which, along with the efforts of the Kurds, rescued many Yazidis from the horrors of Islamic State. However, for those who did not escape, only death or torment awaited. Captured women were treated as 'sex slaves', sold as 'jihadi brides' and raped, tortured or killed if they refused to convert to Islam. Those that survived were only freed and reunited with their families upon the final, physical destruction of the Islamic State caliphate in 2019.

By August 2014, Philip Hammond had become Foreign Secretary, and Michael Fallon was now at Defence. I had just returned from a routine visit around the Gulf and another instalment of 'Operation Tethered Goat', as I chose to designate the office calls I had with Sheikh Mohammed bin Zayed, the Crown Prince of Abu Dhabi. In these often delightful and interesting exchanges, he routinely took the opportunity to criticise a range of British policies and actions, not least the British Government's attitude to the Muslim Brotherhood, Iranian interference in the region, the Qataris, as well as BBC Arabic editorial policy. It was all 'sporting' stuff, and I often found myself more in agreement with his opinions than with the received wisdom back in London. Returning to the MoD, I was now interested to see the announcement of the appointment of a British 'Security Envoy to the Kurdish Regional Government (KRG)', in acknowledgement of the role the Kurdish *peshmerga* were playing in blunting the IS advance and providing vital security and safety to hundreds of thousands of refugees, mostly Arabs, but also the Yazidis. Who, I wondered, had been selected for this critical, sensitive and potentially thankless task? I was having a drink in the Red Lion pub in Whitehall, a few days later, when the question was answered. An official from No 10 appeared in the doorway.

'Ah, General', he said, 'I've been looking for you.'

'Let me guess', I replied, 'You are trying to find someone to go to Erbil?'

I was due to hand over the appointment of DSAME to General Tom Beckett in January the following year, and I did not want to bring that forward, as I still had several projects I was keen to bring to a successful conclusion, not least my aspirations for the new naval base in Bahrain. Given that it was impossible to isolate what was going on in the KRG from events across Iraq and in the wider region, I was happy to accept the new role but insisted it was double-hatted with the DSAME post for the next several months.

The official announcement of my appointment was made on 24 August 2014, and I left for Iraq the next day to see Prime Minister Haider al Abadi in Baghdad, President Masoud Barzani, and Prime Minister Nechivan Barzani in Erbil, and General Paul Funk, the new US commander in Iraq, whose deputy was now my old Military Assistant, Chris Ghika. I had been knighted in the Queen's Birthday Honours List of June that year, and I received a suitable amount of leg-pulling as I went around greeting old friends, while discussing the dangerous and demoralizing situation in which we now again found ourselves, eleven years after the invasion and occupation of 2003. I had been charged to bring back a report on the situation on the ground, and to give recommendations as to what contribution Britain could usefully make to stabilizing the security situation and reversing IS's gains. It was clear that security across the country was, once again, in a pretty dire condition, although the battle-front had stabilized. It was a depressing state of affairs, given our efforts from the 'surge' onwards, but as we often said, in true military style, 'We are where we are.' Islamic State were unlikely to be able to advance much further into the Shia heartlands of Iraq, but defeating them in Anbar and Mosul was going to be a tough call, particularly given their deep logistic and recruiting roots in Sunni Iraq, and in neighbouring Syria.

The so-called 'caliphate' now held huge swathes of ground across Mesopotamia, and jihadists once again dominated the Euphrates Valley (see Map 11). They had established a reputation for military success, and for brutality, and were well equipped, in no small part thanks to the ISF collapse. The demoralized ISF would need time, training and a huge amount of re-equipping in order to take the fight back to the enemy. In the meantime, IS continued its violent campaign and was beginning its depressing destruction of pre-Islamic historical monuments, true to the spirit of their early Islamist predecessors. In addition, violent *takfiri* rhetoric and imagery were once again dominating social media, urging Sunni Muslims, the world over, to attack the infidel 'Crusaders and Jews' and the heretical Shia. This was once again attracting large numbers of supporters, not least from Muslim communities in Western countries, including Britain. IS was also generating huge amounts of money from oil sales, the trade in antiquities, taxation, extortion and ransoms. Its maximalist pretentions as a caliphate, its large-scale occupation of territory, its impressive organizational structures and resources and its powerful and slick messaging made Islamic State an altogether greater challenge than Al Qa'eda before them.

I returned from a week in theatre with what I considered to be a perfectly respectable set of proposals, in view of the seriousness of the threat, the scale of the challenge in re-constituting the ISF and our own national capabilities and reputation. I recommended: embedding British officers at all levels of the US chain of command; taking responsibility for the counter-IED fight within both the ISF and the Kurdish *peshmerga*; putting British military training teams into the *peshmerga* to accompany those they trained onto the battlefield; and providing the *peshmerga* with appropriate lethal and non-lethal equipment, from machine guns and anti-tank weapons to body armour, bandages and even light-armoured vehicles. This latter recommendation seemed particularly urgent, given the problems the KRG had always had with getting equipment from the central government in Baghdad, who retained their deep and long-standing suspicion of Kurdish ambitions, despite the immediacy of the IS threat. All of this was well within the Government's stated policy, and it seemed to be a package that would be useful to the *peshmerga* and the Coalition, while sending an important message about Britain's commitment. Initially, the Prime Minister seemed to have accepted these recommendations, but from there on in, the Whitehall 'system' conspired to ensure that little of any military significance actually happened on the ground. Coalition politics, Government nervousness about renewed engagement in the Middle

East, particularly after the Syria debacle, and the proximity of a General Election communicated itself to MoD and FCO officialdom. Anxious to avoid bad headlines, let alone casualties, or to explain any proactive activity, the official response was timid, embarrassing and unworthy of Britain. Despite my urging and cajoling, by the time any significant active British support and assistance was given, other nations, including the Germans, French, Danes and Lithuanians, had already 'stepped up to the plate', and we became just one among many countries doing their bit. We did, in due course, deploy officers and soldiers to KRG, and to Iraq, but while they were allowed to 'assist and advise', they were not allowed to 'accompany' those they had trained into the field. The training teams did much useful and important work, but they wholly shared my frustration that they had to remain 'behind the wire'.

In January 2015 I had handed over the DSAME role to my successor, and in May 2015, just prior to the General Election of that year, which David Cameron won, I also relinquished my Envoy role to the KRG. It was with real sadness that I embarked on a series of farewell calls, some to those still firmly engaged 'in the fight', others to rulers, crown princes and political and military leaders with whom I had developed strong personal and professional friendships over the years. These meetings marked the end of this fascinating role, but also the end of my forty years in the Army, so often spent at the centre of great global events. It had been the most wonderful four decades in uniform, eventful and full of variety, colour, fun, laughter and friendship. I can sincerely state that I would not have missed a single day of it. A small consolation was to be asked by Richard Dannatt to join him at the Tower of London, as Lieutenant of the Tower. Another was to remain as Colonel of my Regiment, 1st the Queen's Dragoon Guards, whose Colonel-in-Chief was the Prince of Wales, with whom I had had the privilege of visiting the Middle East on several occasions. I would only relinquish that role in May 2019, after eleven years in the appointment, handing over to Brigadier Alan Richmond.

My grandmother had arrived in Malta in 1916, and over three generations the Mayall family had been engaged in the Middle East, for around 100 years. My grandparents witnessed the collapse of the Ottoman Empire and the abolition of the caliphate, and then my parents saw the consolidation of the modern Middle East. Born in 1956, the year of the Suez Crisis, I would be in the Army long enough to see the rise and fall of Islamic State and the passing of another caliph. The story is by no means over.

Epilogue

Since I left the Army in 2015, there has been an important and discernible shift in global politics with a continuation of the American retrenchment already detected under President Obama. This trend has been matched by a more confident, strategically agile, *revanchist* Russia, and an increasingly bold and expansionist China. This combination has seen a fraying of 'international rules-based governance', and the comfortable status quo which largely favoured the US and the West since 1945, even through the Cold War but particularly since 1989, is being progressively challenged. In this new and volatile context it is not surprising that the Middle East has continued to throw up challenges, both for the peoples of the region and for the wider world. It is unsurprising because the 'building blocks' of friction and conflict have remained painfully persistent, and most of these continue to relate to issues of power: between states themselves, between outside 'players', between ethnicities, between religious groups, between ideologies, and between the generations and genders. Many of these interlinked struggles would have been recognizable to my father's generation.

The battle between the United States and the Soviet Union for regional influence had largely been won by America in the 1970s. However, despite Soviet collapse, and despite remaining the pre-eminent global power, the United States squandered their overwhelmingly dominant position with a series of strategic miscalculations in the wake of 9/11. While understandably scarred by the experience and cost of their intervention in Iraq, and responding to domestic demands and sentiments, the Obama administration mistakenly adopted a 'hands-off' approach to the Middle East. It made poor policy choices when confronted with the challenges of the Arab Spring, while looking hesitant about sustaining US credibility and reputation in the Middle East and then failing to act on its own 'red lines' in Syria. The Middle East is a region into which you can 'surge' military forces, but not necessarily trust or confidence. This dilution of American leadership left the field open for Vladimir Putin to gamble, successfully, on stepping into the Syrian maelstrom to join forces with the Shia IRGC of Iran and Shia Lebanese Hezbollah, thereby ensuring the survival of the Alawite Assad regime. The Western response to the conflict in Syria went through an arc from supporting any declared Syrian 'opposition' group to conducting large-scale conflict against the Sunni jihadists of IS. Pursuing such strategies always threatened to assist the Iranians and Russians in further establishing a dominant and controlling influence in Syria, and in the wider region. As a result of this success, Russia established an important presence in the Eastern Mediterranean, while the Iranians consolidated some 'strategic depth' in the Levant. In addition, Russia, newly shorn of its Communist and atheist identity, now spoke the language of regional and state 'stability', and of social and religious conservatism, that struck a chord in the region.

The election of President Trump in 2016 changed the dynamic further. In 1961 President Kennedy had said in his Inaugural Address, 'Let every nation know . . . we shall pay any price, bear any burden, meet any hardship, support any friend, oppose any foe to assure the survival and success of liberty.' Trump's own Inaugural Address, and his subsequent words and actions in the Middle East, made it very clear that there would now be a much stronger appeal to American national self-interest, and that relationships would become much more transactional, indeed confrontational. This did not bode well for those who sought principled constancy or consistency in US policy. Subsequently, President Trump's various interventions confounded and unsettled friends, allies, and opponents alike. This always threatened to lead to political miscalculation, based on a misreading or misunderstanding of US intentions. The apparent 'abandonment' of the Syrian Kurds in late 2019, close allies in the successful campaign against IS, unsettled America's Sunni Arab allies, and served only to embolden President Putin, President Erdogan of Turkey, and the Iranian ayatollahs.

A second struggle had been between the new regional states and those imperial powers that had benefited most from the collapse of the Ottoman Empire, namely Britain and France. In a time when Britain and France dominated global geopolitics, and in a region where the enfeebled Iranians, Turks, Egyptians and Arabs could not gainsay them, the British and French had planted the new entities of Iraq, Syria, Lebanon, Israel and Jordan. They had also formalized the division of North Africa, from the Atlantic to the Red Sea. This dominance was challenged from the outset in these new 'states', eroded by the Second World War, and ended by the Suez Crisis of 1956, the Algerian War, and the British withdrawal from 'East of Suez' in 1971. Despite this, both Britain and France had retained strong linkages in the region through the bonds of history, language and the military. In the face of Egyptian, Iranian and Iraqi ambition and aggression, Britain had helped contribute to the protective shield under which the Gulf ruling families developed their city-states, and helped guarantee that the oil and gas, vital to the functioning of the global economy, continued to flow freely. The re-commitment of Britain to the security architecture of the Gulf that many had hoped to see again after the 1991 Gulf War was at last formalized with the opening of the new naval base in Bahrain in 2018. France's continuing attachment to the Levant was demonstrated by her rapid and robust response to the devastating Beirut blast of August 2020.

The Arab-Israeli conflict also continued to fester, and had gone through several new phases, in the context of turmoil in the wider Middle East. None of these had satisfactorily addressed the core issues of Israel's place in the Middle East and the status of the Palestinian people. Despite the high hopes raised by the Oslo Accords of 1993, competing, and sometimes insoluble, practical and emotive challenges dogged every attempt at a comprehensive peace settlement. Whatever the rights and wrongs of their case, Israel continued to arouse religious and political animosity in the Muslim world, and the occupation of Jerusalem and the West Bank amplified tensions which were real, although often used by neighbouring Muslim states to deflect domestic attention from their own failures and inadequacies. For many years Israel had dealt wisely and pragmatically with this tension, forging an accommodation with moderate Muslim states, notably Egypt and Jordan, who shared their own fears regarding Islamist extremism and its accompanying violence. However, over time, hard-line elements of the Israeli establishment led, over the last decade, by Prime Minister Benjamin Netanyahu, and unhelpfully supported by a negligent or complicit US, drove forward with aggressive occupation and 'settlement' policies in East Jerusalem and the West Bank. These changes to 'the facts on the ground' have now made the achievement of a comprehensive 'two-state solution', trading land for security, with a shared capital in Jerusalem, and underwritten by the international community, nigh-on impossible. In doing so, Israel squandered an important degree of sympathy and support among her allies and friends, although her concerns regarding Iranian ambition and expansion are shared by many in the West, and among the Sunni Arab leadership. In August 2020, UAE became only the third Muslim country to establish full diplomatic relations with Israel and, despite predictable cries of 'betrayal' from the Palestinians, it was noticeable that the most strident protests on their behalf came from the Turks and the Iranians, while Saudi Arabia remained mute. Despite diplomatic support in the West, and from other Sunni Arab states, in Israel itself the 'right wing' and the 'settler' organisations lambasted Netanyahu for appearing to suspend his 'threat', or ambition, to annex the West Bank.

A fourth struggle, in the 1950s, had been for Arab leadership of the Arab world. In the wake of the Second World War, the three contenders, Egypt, Iraq and Syria, were all led by pan-Arab, secular nationalists. None of them would succeed in establishing a unifying dominance, and Saudi Arabia, despite its oil wealth, and the moral authority which goes with custodianship of the Two Holy Cities, did not aspire to that role. Egypt's bid died with Nasser's failures in Yemen and the Six Day War, and with Anwar Sadat's peace treaty with Israel, for which he paid with his life. President Mubarak made close ties with the United States a cornerstone of his foreign policy, which lasted until the Arab Spring, while Syria and Iraq more routinely looked to Russia for diplomatic or military support. The subsequent power struggle between the traditional Egyptian state institutions, most notably the army, and the Muslim Brotherhood, led to General Abdel Fattah el-Sisi becoming President. The violent confrontation with the Muslim Brotherhood drove a major wedge between Egypt, Saudi Arabia and the UAE, who all feared the ultimate political ambitions of the Brotherhood, and Turkey and Qatar, who had sharply different views regarding their ideology and agenda. This split in the Sunni world, continues to manifest itself in Libya, where Turkey is using Syrian Islamist 'fighters', ejected from Syria, to support the government in Tripoli. All this friction has further assisted Iranian ambitions.

In Syria, the elevation of Bashar al Assad to the Syrian Presidency in 2000 had seemed to usher in a welcome new era for that country, but 9/11 and the subsequent events in Iraq derailed those hopes. By 2011, when the Americans had managed to stabilize the security situation in Iraq, the Arab Spring was challenging the Alawite hold on power. At a time when the Arab Spring was still viewed positively, there was a feeling that 'one last heave' could lead to the overthrow of yet another Middle East dictator and 'hard man'. However, the situation in Syria was more akin to that of Iraq in 1991 than it was to Tunisia in 2011. The Assad regime and its minority Alawite power-base simply were not going to capitulate in the face of Western wishful thinking, particularly having seen the fate of the Sunni minority in

Iraq. In time, many of the increasingly desperate opposition groups began to coalesce around offshoots of Al Qa'eda, and then IS. This allowed Assad, and his Iranian and Russian allies, to portray all Sunni opposition forces as 'terrorists'. In due course, Western attention switched from confronting Assad to addressing the more toxic problem of Sunni extremist groups, and Assad and his allies proceeded to crush the opposition, triggering a huge refugee crisis within and outside that country. Of a Syrian population of around 20 million in 2001, about 400–500,000 have been killed, and another million or so wounded. Nearly six million people are now refugees across the Middle East, most notably in Turkey, Lebanon and Jordan, while a further five or six million are 'internally displaced persons' (IDPs). Perhaps three million of these IDPs are eking out a dangerous and miserable existence in Idlib. Those who left for the West joined other refugees escaping from Libya, where a similarly toxic political 'cocktail' had led to state failure and violence in the wake of Gaddafi's fall. In due course, those fleeing the region coalesced with a multitude of 'economic migrants' from sub-Saharan Africa, taking advantage of the failure of state structures to contain them. This combination constituted a 'human torrent' that surged through the Balkans and across the Mediterranean between 2015 and 2018, with significant consequences for European political solidarity and cohesion. In 2020, largely forgotten or ignored by the world, the last of the Syrian 'opposition' forces sit in the north-western Syrian province of Idlib, trapped between a vengeful Assad and a calculating Erdogan. Idlib is, de facto, a microcosm of the situation in the wider area with its: ethnic struggle between Turks, Arabs, Iranians and Kurds; the confessional confrontation between Sunni and Shia; the presence of oppressed ethnic and religious minorities; the ideological fight between secularists, *takfiris*, and a range of other Sunni Islamist groups of various persuasions and mixed allegiances; and the continuing interference of external powers.

After the fall of Mosul to IS in 2014, it was patently clear that Iraq could not deal with IS on its own, and the United States, still under Obama, reluctantly and initially unconvincingly, re-entered the fray. The combination of Americans, Shia militia, IRGC, *peshmerga*, Sunni tribesmen and newly constituted Iraqi Security Forces was not without tension, but it was ultimately successful in ridding Iraq of IS, at least as a formed entity. However, inclusive, representative politics that could bind the loyalty of all Iraqis to the central state remained elusive, while a Kurdish referendum on independence in late 2017 backfired badly. I had been in Erbil while they held it, as part of a British parliamentary delegation.

As a 'friend of the Kurds', I strongly advised them not to proceed with the referendum. I told them that all Iraq, and their Western friends, owed them a great debt of honour for their fight against IS and the generosity of their humanitarian efforts. We would act as their advocates in Baghdad. They went ahead with the poll, and the reaction from Baghdad, Ankara, Tehran and Damascus, all wrestling with the political implications of significant Kurdish minorities, was predictable. Iraq, with its fractured and corrupt politics, continued to find itself caught between the need for US military support to continue to suppress IS, and the reality of Iranian influence and pressure. In addition, by 2020, the government found itself the subject of extensive demonstrations against its social, economic and political mismanagement. These mirrored similar expressions of frustration and exasperation that manifested themselves across Iran, and in Lebanon.

Since the 1970s, oil and gas wealth has given the Gulf states, particularly the Kingdom of Saudi Arabia, huge regional and global influence. The results can be seen in the extraordinary urban centres of the Arabian Peninsula, and in the status of the pre-eminent Gulf families in some of the key economic fora and councils of the world. Critics of the Gulf states often claim that Western interest in them is 'all about oil'. Of course, in many important regards, it was, and is. The global economy requires free access, at a reasonable price, to around 100 million barrels of oil per day. Over 20 million of those barrels pass through the Straits of Hormuz, and nearly 80 per cent now turns east to fuel the economies of Asia and the Pacific. China's 'One Belt, One Road' Initiative, the establishment of naval facilities from Thailand to Djibouti, and the growth of her 'blue water' navy are clearly designed to guarantee the continued, long-term, safe flow of these vital energy resources, while reducing their vulnerability to US interdiction. Energy needs are predicted to rise by another 70 per cent in the next thirty years, as the global population rises by another 2 billion. Despite the intense drive to develop renewable, non-fossil-fuel energy, much of this increased demand will have to continue to be met by oil and gas from the Middle East. The presence of around 40–50 per cent of known global energy reserves in the Gulf, is why stability in the region remains so very important. It is also why the elevation of Mohammed bin Salman to be Crown Prince in Saudi Arabia excited such initial interest and enthusiasm. In a country with a very young population, an equally young Crown Prince wielding great power raised all manner of expectations. 'Vision 2030' set out an ambitious programme of social and economic change that acknowledged the youthful demographics of the country, and also that the Kingdom's dependence on oil, as with other Gulf states, was not sustainable in the long run.

The opportunities for those who viewed the long-term security of Saudi Arabia as vital for the stability of the whole region, and for the global economy, looked good. The influence of the religious police was curtailed, women were allowed to drive, gender 'segregation' policies were amended, the 'guardianship' rules relaxed, entertainment centres and music were encouraged, and shares in the giant Saudi Aramco oil company were sold on the global market, in the largest share 'flotation' in history. The significance or popularity of these initiatives, and the skill with which they have been introduced, should not remotely be underestimated or downplayed, given the potential centres of opposition. However, the Prince and his programme proved to be a 'curate's egg', with all his energy, drive and imagination being matched by a degree of recklessness and ruthlessness. Despite some long-needed and widely welcomed measures, there was also arbitrary imprisonment and suppression of dissent, and the creation of an atmosphere of official impunity which would undoubtedly contribute to the murder of Jamal Khashoggi. King Salman is old, and not well, and whether there will be any conservative backlash against this liberalization, or a challenge to MBS from other, disaffected branches of the Saudi royal family remains to be seen. President Trump's early foray into Middle Eastern politics also gave MBS the impression that he could have a 'free hand' in intervening in the Yemeni civil war, while taking a Gulf vendetta with Qatar to a new level. In June 2017, despite reluctance within the GCC from Oman and Kuwait, a blockade of sorts was placed on Qatar which pushed that small, gas-rich country to approach both Iran and Turkey, the traditional opponents of the Arabs, for relief. It was only at this stage that President Trump seemed to become aware that Qatar hosted the largest American airbase in the Middle East, from which the majority of missions against IS were being launched. Although a desultory campaign continued, including plans to cut a channel across the Saudi-Qatari border in order to turn Qatar into an island, the blockade was largely a failure, only serving to strengthen the Qatari economy and unhelpfully institutionalizing splits in the GCC, and between the Arab monarchies.

Qatar had been a latecomer to the age of energy, but it fast became a major player, on the basis of enormous gas reserves drawn from a field shared with Iran. From 1995, under Emir Hamad al Thani, Qatar pursued an aggressive and ambitious foreign and domestic policy, aiming to build his country into a major regional player, much to the irritation of Saudi Arabia and UAE. This included a series of 'trophy' real estate and sporting purchases. However, real antagonism grew with the launch of Al Jazeera, the television station which, in the name of 'free speech', routinely criticised Arab regimes in the region, not least the Kingdom of Saudi Arabia. This media campaign intensified at the time of the Arab Spring, when the editorial policy of Al Jazeera's Arabic programmes was very supportive of the Muslim Brotherhood in Egypt and of Mohammed Morsi, their presidential candidate. This was in very direct, and public, contrast to the political objectives of Saudi Arabia and UAE, who saw the Brotherhood as an existential threat to themselves and a challenge to the stability of Egypt, the most populous Sunni Arab country, seen as crucial to the unity of the Sunni Arab world and as a counter-balance to Shia Iran. This also coincided with Qatari support for the more Islamist elements of the opposition to Gaddafi in Libya, who won the power-struggle in Tripoli and, in due course, support to similar groups in Syria, who were rather less successful. In 2014, the new Qatari Emir, Tameem, had been invited to Riyadh for a meeting with King Abdullah, at which he reportedly gave a number of undertakings regarding Al Jazeera, Qatar's foreign policy and the relationship with the Muslim Brotherhood. It was their belief that these undertakings had been disregarded that provoked Saudi Arabia and UAE to attempt to clip Qatar's wings. Qatar continues to weather the 'blockade', but it is due to host the 2022 Football World Cup, designed to showcase the Emirate, and being surrounded by antagonistic neighbours will complicate the delivery of this global event. During this period, Qatar has also acted as the 'neutral' location for talks between the US Government and the Taliban, as America has sought to conclude its military engagement in Central Asia. Despite the US commitment to support the Afghan Government against the Taliban, the only people not formally invited to these discussions have been the Afghan Government itself.

The fifth arena of persistent contention has continued to be the long-standing struggle for regional power and influence between Iranians, Turks and Arabs, in which all three are inspired by a sense of historical entitlement, based on their imperial pasts and their religious leadership roles. In my father's day, all three were weak, but over time the dynamic has changed dramatically. Iran, under the Ayatollahs, embraced 'Islamic revolution' and championship of the Shia across the region. Always in political competition, these enhanced religious pretensions brought them into more open and visceral confrontation with the Sunni Arab monarchies of the Gulf, always conscious that the Two Holy Cities 'belonged' to all

Muslims, of whatever persuasion. Iran also continued to behave like a former empire, and a major regional power, and her support of the Houthis in Yemen, very usefully from Tehran's perspective, helped provoke Saudi Arabia into a lengthy, heavy-handed military campaign that has contributed to additional reputational damage in the West, where there is already no shortage of critics. The ultimate destination of Iran's pursuit of an atomic programme, whether civil or military, remained shrouded in political obfuscation, secrecy and deception, and this has inevitably drawn in the United States and Israel, as has Iran's development of long-range ballistic missiles, their open support for the Palestinians and other Arab groups who actively oppose the Israelis, and their sponsorship of terrorist groups, particularly Hamas and Hezbollah. The 2015 JCPOA, which seemed to mitigate concerns about Iran's nuclear programme, did not satisfactorily address the other concerning elements of Iranian activity in the region. The unravelling of Iraq and the reverberations of the Arab Spring gave Iran many unanticipated opportunities for expansion and for making mischief. Saddam Hussein's control of Iraq and, with it, the Arab Sunni caliphate capital of Baghdad, was the 'cork in the bottle' that had stopped Iran 'joining up' its Shia centres of support. With his removal, and the Coalition failure to establish a strong and resilient 'new' Iraq, Iran has come to dominate, in one form or another, Baghdad, Damascus, Beirut and Sana'a. The challenge to the Sunnis could not be starker, but the Sunni world continues to be split by its own ethnic and ideological rifts.

Unfortunately, Iran's presence, influence and activities in other Middle East countries demonstrate little or no interest in their political, social or economic development. Indeed, Iranian long-term strategic objectives rely on a parasitic use of the wealth of the region for their own advantage, while keeping the Turks and Egyptians out and the local Arabs down and weakened. This became more imperative when President Trump withdrew the US from the JCPOA in May 2018, while re-imposing stringent sanctions on Iran. The consequences of these unilateral actions led to an unhelpful divergence of foreign policy objectives between Russia and China, the European nations, and the US. In addition, the potential for maritime confrontation in the narrow waters of the Gulf increased, as did the probability of escalatory violence between the US and Iran. However, if the US are forced, or choose, to leave Iraq, and there are many 'push' and 'pull' factors that make that course of action possible, it is difficult to see how the Iranian position across that area can be successfully challenged, short of a major war, or regime change in Tehran.

Turkey's trajectory has also been dramatic. When I wrote about that country in the 1990s, Turkey had a burgeoning free-market economy, a vibrant political discourse, an encouragingly free press, close relationships with NATO, and seemed set on closer alignment with the EU. Over time, however, the AK Party gained power, and once again a combination of the invasion of Iraq and the Arab Spring changed calculations, actions and perceptions. Erdogan increasingly began to restrict freedom of the press, re-energized a campaign against the Kurds, emasculated the military and sought to amend the constitution, in order to enhance the power of the President at the expense of Parliament and the secular parties. The huge influx of refugees from the Syrian conflict put great pressure on Ankara. Turkey parlayed some of this pressure into an advantageous deal with the EU to help stop the refugee flows into Europe and, in addition, by 2020 Erdogan was using Syrians from the camps to bolster support to the Libyan government in Tripoli. However, Turkish acceptance of large numbers of Arabs, at both governmental and individual level, quickly began to wear thin. The attempted military 'coup' of July 2016 probably increased the paranoia of the powerful, albeit thin-skinned, Erdogan, but it also gave him the excuse to repress other elements of opposition. The coup plot seems to have been revealed to him by Russian intelligence, and the Turkish authorities seemed surprisingly well primed to arrest 40,000 people the day after its failure, including 10,000 soldiers and 2,700 judges, while suspending 35,000 teachers and education staff. In due course Erdogan would return the favour by purchasing S400 air-defence missiles from Russia, leading to the US annulling their own F35 deal with Turkey. This combination of events has been an unhelpful blow to NATO solidarity. In 2019, the re-run of an Istanbul mayoral election saw huge gains for the secular opposition parties. This was a major blow to both Erdogan's ego and ambitions, and was an interesting indication of struggles still to come. As if upping the stakes in this competition, Erdogan re-designated the glorious sixth century century Byzantine church of Hagia Sophia, a secular museum since 1934, as a mosque.

Modern Turkey has always thrived across the region when it sought business or commercial advantage, given its strong track record in construction and infrastructure. However, whenever it became politically active, there has always been a strong push-back from its Arab neighbours, with their memories of long Ottoman Turkish dominance. In foreign policy, Turgut Ozal and others had espoused closer links to Europe, and an agenda of pan-Turanism in other Turkic parts of the world, notably

Central Asia. However, under Erdogan, Turkey increasingly seemed to be pursuing a 'neo-Ottoman' agenda, appearing to give the impression that Turkey had a right to interfere in many of those areas of the Muslim world that had previously been within the Ottoman Empire, particularly those on her southern borders. Events in Egypt brought further splits in the Sunni world into sharp focus. Erdogan, with his roots in the Muslim Brotherhood, supported Mohammed Morsi, ably assisted by Al Jazeera, while Saudi Arabia and UAE backed the military and the secularists, with greater success. When Saudi Arabia and UAE tried to isolate Qatar, Turkey ensured the blockade could not be fully effective, stationing troops in the country at the invitation of the Emir; and the killing of Jamal Khashoggi in the Saudi consulate in Istanbul played even further into Erdogan's hands. Meanwhile, the vulnerable Turkmen populations in Syria and Iraq attracted Turkish sympathy and support, while America's Kurdish allies in the fight against IS attracted their anger and a promise of military intervention. Trump's unhelpful policy statements regarding the US presence in Syria has now left the Kurds trapped between an Assad regime intent on re-imposing control over all of Syria, and a Turkey determined to destroy any Kurdish pretensions to independent 'statehood'. As if the situation in Libya was not complicated enough, Turkey chose to join Egypt and UAE in intervening in that country, albeit on the opposing side.

The sixth ongoing struggle continues to be that between nationalists, secularists and modernizers on the one hand, and conservative Salafists, fundamentalists and *takfiri* ideologues on the other. While the latter all look back to the origins of Islam for inspiration, by no means all of them support violence as the way to achieve political goals. Many Salafists support a return to some form of caliphate that embraces the global *umma*, although others see the modern Muslim Brotherhood programme as offering a more realistic path to achieving an Islamist agenda. However, many of those who end up embracing the *takfiri* ideology have begun their journey towards Al Qa'eda and IS through earlier membership of the Muslim Brotherhood, then rejected the slower political path to an Islamist destination, and the political and social compromises along the way. These saw violence as a more effective means to halt the corruption and the corrosive impact of Western political and cultural influences. The sad reality is that very many Islamist terrorists and adherents of the 'death-cults' of Al Qa'eda and Islamic State are indeed drawn from the ranks of those attracted to a fundamentalist interpretation of Islam. To try and draw a veil over this fact is no help in any confrontation with this ideology, nor does it assist reformers, modernizers and secularists in the Muslim world and in Muslim communities. The Koran can indeed be read as embracing an uplifting philosophy of peace, but that general proposition cannot excuse the actions of those who utilize selective interpretation to justify violence. It is not alone. While the Bible, certainly the New Testament, can probably make a better claim to offer encouragement to 'turn the other cheek', Saladin's emirs and battle captains would have roared with laughter at the idea that the actions of Crusader knights were motivated by a 'religion of peace'. Religion remains a prominent, often the predominant, fact of life in much of the modern Muslim world. It is a source of deeply held common interest, and deeply divisive schisms. Where important areas of political, social and cultural behaviour are deemed to be divinely inspired or directed, compromise and consensus are difficult to reach. 'Democracy' and 'liberalism', are both concepts that are difficult to square with the rigid interpretations of Islam espoused by the Salafists, let alone by the *takfiris*, who deem violence in their defence to be acceptable, indeed religiously condoned.

While Al Qa'eda and IS may have suffered major setbacks, and the eventual killings of Osama bin Laden and Abu Bakr al Baghdadi were both very symbolic and significant losses, the influence of their core message and ideology continues to have resonance among the poor, the dispossessed, the humiliated and the impressionable. No education, no money, no home, no marriage, no children, no dignity: unsurprisingly, given this lack of prospects, many young men, and numbers of young women, in the Islamic world continue to fall under the influence of charismatic leaders who promise a more rewarding purpose in life. Harnessing an ostensibly coherent narrative, with a strong central message of religious certainty, to seductive images, poetry and music, and the prospect of money, while playing on heightened senses of grievance and inspiration, and using the power of social media to spread it, will continue to attract active supporters and widespread sympathy. The challenges of defending the Muslim religion, Sunnism, and the Arab place in the Middle East will continue to attract adherents. Although Al Qa'eda and IS have been shattered and splintered, their foot soldiers and local commanders will continue to wage small-scale, vicious and violent insurgencies and guerrilla wars, while waiting to re-group and to continue the struggle, possibly with new identities. The stark population realities of the Muslim world can only make these dangerous trends more pronounced. 'Demography is destiny', and it is difficult to see how the region can generate political, economic or social models to meet the aspirations of so many young people, and thereby command the widespread loyalty of citizens. The population in the region has grown from 100 million in 1950, to 380 million in 2000, and is now on track to increase to somewhere in the region of 600 million by 2050. It is in the face of such realities that one can see why the achievement of that balanced equilibrium between religion, politics, the individual, and the law, so vital for a shared sense of stability, security and prosperity, remains a 'work in progress'

Clausewitz famously said, 'Everything in war is simple, and the most simple things are very complicated.' The same aphorism could be applied to political, social and economic change in the Islamic Middle East. It is patently obvious that part of the solution lies in addressing the release of human potential and, with it, economic growth and aspiration. The answer to some of this equation lies in the emancipation and empowerment of women, long a sensitive issue within and outwith the Middle East. In this latter area there may be more cause for hope than in others. However, social conservatism and patriarchy continue to exert an important and undeniable hold on societies, and the atrocities of Al Qa'eda and IS demonstrate how virulently some will choose to challenge and reverse such efforts. A new generation of Muslim women, with education and with access to the internet, can now see the possibilities that exist in the personal, professional, academic and employment arenas. From Afghanistan to Morocco, governments cannot realistically continue to ignore the opinions, aspirations and economic potential of half of their populations. Achieving full emancipation may require a hard, indeed depressingly violent, struggle, given the headwinds, but change is already gathering pace, as events in Saudi Arabia have shown. This is not a genie that is going to be easily put back in the bottle.

Despite a probably justifiable charge of exhibiting elements of Edward Said's 'Orientalism', I know that I shall continue to be fascinated by the Middle East to the end of my days. I have spent too much of my personal, academic and professional time there to be indifferent to the countries and peoples of this remarkable corner of the globe. I have seen it at its glorious, happy and hospitable best, and at its murderous and sectarian worst. I have witnessed the capacity of Islam to inspire great individual and community endeavour, and to generate wonderful cultural glories. However, I have also seen religion and cultural difference used to justify the destruction of lives and livelihoods, of human hope and ambition, and of the triumphs of other cultures. Their continuing and powerful capacity to provoke conflict should not be under-estimated. In 1978 you could drive safely, road conditions notwithstanding, from London to Nepal, across the Balkans, Turkey, Syria, Iraq, Iran, Afghanistan and Pakistan. Since 1979, despite all the huge advances in 'health, wealth and happiness' across great swathes of the world, significant constituent parts of the modern Middle East continue to thwart the best hopes of political, social and economic modernizers and reformers, and that journey has become increasingly dangerous and difficult, if not impossible.

However, the words, 'Could you be in Istanbul/Beirut/Muscat for lunch tomorrow?' continue to have the capacity to make me drop whatever I am doing and head for the airport. The lure of Cairo, Istanbul and Damascus remains strong. Who is not seduced by the mosques and the minarets, the souks and the bazaars, the Turkish *hamam*, the Arabic *qahwa*, the *narghile*, the sand dunes of the Empty Quarter, the mountains of the Jebel Akhdar, sunset in the desert or over the Indian Ocean, the muezzin's call? Who can resist a ferry ride on the Bosporus, the flap of a felucca's sails on the Nile or an Arabic cry from the prow of a dhowout in the Arabian Gulf? Who cannot be heartened by the relentless humour and hospitality of the people across this remarkable, diverse, frustrating, worrying and enthralling region? Still confused? Yes. But hopefully at a higher level. *Mabsoot, seedee? Naam, mabsoot jiddan. Shukran.*

Index